C000193015

The Music Goes Round and Around

– BASIL TSCHAIKOV –

FASTPRINT PUBLISHING
PETERBOROUGH, ENGLAND

Basil Tschaikov

THE MUSIC GOES ROUND AND AROUND
Copyright © Basil Tschaikov 2009

All rights reserved.

ISBN 978-184426-590-9

First Published 2009 by
FASTPRINT PUBLISHING
Peterborough, England.

Printed on FSC approved paper by
www.printondemand-worldwide.com

Basil Tschaikov

About the Author

B asil Tschaikov's life in music has spanned more than 60 years as a performer, writer, educator and administrator. Between 1943 and 1979 he was a member of three of the world's finest orchestras - the London Philharmonic, Royal Philharmonic and Philharmonia – playing with conductors such as Sir Thomas Beecham, Bruno Walter, Victor de Sabata, Herbert von Karajan, Otto Klemperer, Carlo Maria Giulini and Sir Simon Rattle.

From 1979 until 1989 he was artistic and administrative director of the National Centre for Orchestral Studies attached to Goldsmiths' College, University of London. This was a radical innovation that allowed those leaving music college or university who wished to enter the music profession as orchestral musicians become familiar with the conditions of playing in a high quality professional orchestra. They were able to gain the necessary experience by working with outstanding international conductors and performers for a year before taking up their careers. He was also the prime force in the creation of a unique archive, the Music Performance Research Centre, now Music Preserved. This archive of non-commercial recordings of public concert and opera performances enables many thousands of valuable performances to be preserved and made available, free, for enjoyment and study.

Acknowledgements

My thanks are due to Allan Cooban for finding several references for me; to Jon Tolansky for the help and advice he has given me throughout the writing of this book; to Jo Spaul for creating the book cover; to Shaun Barns for his skill in preparing the photographs and to Mary Tyrie for creating the index. Above all I am particularly indebted to Alison Womack for her tireless work in proof reading my text and her eagle eye which found and corrected my many spelling and typing errors and who also provided such valuable editorial advice.

My thanks to EMI Classics for their courtesy in allowing me to include the following photographs:

Yehudi Menuhin and Sir Edward Elgar
Herbert von Karajan
Victor de Sabata
Gennadi Rozhdestvensky
Simon Rattle
Malcolm Arnold
Ernest Ansermet
Dennis Brain
John Barbirolli
Bruno Walter

And to Joyce Stone, Timothy and Helen Brymer, The Sir Thomas Beecham Society, Lotte Klemperer.

The author has been unable to ascertain the identities of the rights holders of a few of the other photographs that are contained in this book. If he has inadvertently transgressed any copyrights, he requests rights holders to let him know.

Basil Tschaikov

For Dorothy, with love and thanks for your patience and inspiration.

Basil Tschaikov

Contents

Basil Tschaikov

1 It must be in the Genes

Sir Thomas Beecham's return to the London Philharmonic Orchestra in 1944. The author's family roots – the Royal Concertgebouw Orchestra in the 1890s, escaping the East European Jewish pogroms, arriving as refugees in England near the turn of the century, playing in cinema orchestras and other groups in England in the first two decades of the 20th Century.

It was the 30th September 1944, and the London Philharmonic Orchestra were in Wembley Town Hall (now Brent Town Hall). A small man with a little white beard walked majestically towards the platform followed at a respectful distance by his wife, his manager, the orchestra's general manager, the concert manager, and several other members of the management staff. He came onto the platform and took his place on the podium. 'Good morning, gentlemen! It is very good to be back with you again. Let us begin with the Berlioz Overture – Carnaval Romain.' Those few words of greeting were the first I heard in Sir Thomas Beecham's rich, plummy Edwardian voice, with its inimitable inflection. He had just returned to Britain from the Americas, where he had been since 1940, to rejoin his old orchestra. This was to be our first rehearsal with him and it was also my first experience of the great man. After those few brief words of greeting and a swift glance round the orchestra, up went his baton and we were off.

The orchestra had been awaiting his arrival with some anxiety because it was still wartime and we all knew that his voyage across the Atlantic might be long and dangerous. In fact the rehearsals and the tour to follow had to be delayed because he had arrived back three weeks later than expected. Now, on the morning of his first rehearsal, scheduled for 10 o'clock, everyone had been ready and we were keen to get started. True to form, he was well-known for frequently being late, on this occasion he was over an hour late.

Though I had already played with several fine conductors I knew at once that this was something special. As soon as we started the *Carnaval Romain Overture* by Berlioz I was immediately aware that the *allegro* was so alive and vibrant and the slow section that follows, though still taut rhythmically, had the flexible lyricism that I soon came to learn was characteristic of this remarkable conductor. Then back into the *allegro* six-eight again. With mounting excitement we approached the main theme. Just when the first allegro melody returns there is a big accent. At that moment an astonishing thing happened. Beecham gave a great lunge, to emphasise the accent, and stuck the baton through the palm of his left hand. It went right through and came out the other side. He was immediately rushed off to hospital leaving a bewildered and worried orchestra wondering what would be the outcome.

In the afternoon he returned with his left hand bandaged and his arm in a sling, but in good humour and his usual ebullient self. After a short tour – Watford, Leeds, Huddersfield, Sheffield, and Peterborough we returned to London, where for so long Beecham had had an enthusiastic and adoring audience. Not to the Queen's Hall, the scene of his former triumphs before the war, as this had been destroyed by a bomb in 1941, but in the wide open spaces of the Royal Albert Hall. On the 7th October 1944 I had my first experience of a 'great occasion', the first of many wonderful concerts over the next 16 years during which I had the good fortune to play under Sir Thomas's direction.

I had joined the London Philharmonic eighteen months before Sir Thomas's return, just before my eighteenth birthday. I did not expect to be able to remain with the orchestra for very long since once I was eighteen I knew it would not be long before I would receive my call-up papers. It was unlikely that I would be considered fit for a unit that would go into action, but I thought I would be expected to undertake work of national importance instead. I had a short and slightly wasted leg, caused by an accident when I was a child. In the event I was designated unfit for military service on that account. I received this news with mixed feelings. Naturally I was delighted to be able to continue playing in the orchestra, but at the same time I felt uncomfortable at having to explain why as an apparently healthy young man I was not in the army.

Without that childhood accident, which at the time had been serious and kept me from school for the best part of a year, the rest of my life might have been very different, though it was probably destined that I would earn my living as a musician. It is rather unusual now, but in the past there were a good many musicians who belonged to 'musical families', families such as the Goossens, Drapers, Brains, Penns and the Tschaikovs in which grandfathers, father and uncles, aunts and cousins were all musicians. Most of my family had been or were musicians: two grandfathers, my father, a very successful clarinettist, and his brothers and sisters; it was likely I would follow in their footsteps as did my younger brother. Because of what I learned from them my memories of the past go back long before I started in the profession in 1942.

My maternal grandfather, David Belinfante, had been the second clarinettist and librarian in the Concertgebouw Orchestra in Amsterdam in the 1890s. Like many European musicians at that time he was attracted by the prospect of employment opportunities in London and Manchester. In 1900 he arrived with his young family – my mother, then a year old, and her elder brother, later to become a professional violinist.

The Belinfantes were an old Portuguese Jewish family living in Lisbon. When the Inquisition arrived in Portugal, around 1530, they were obliged to flee for their lives and seek refuge elsewhere. They first went to Turkey, where the family remained for several generations before finally settling in Holland in about 1660. The records show that since the 16th century there have been musicians and lawyers in the Belinfante family.

I never knew my father's father. He died long before I was born. Most of the knowledge I have of him comes filtered through the somewhat unreliable recollections of a rather eccentric aunt. It is a measure of her eccentricity that she believed that her constipation – her main topic of conversation for many years – had been cured by her spirit-guide, a holy medicine man of some long lost tribe.

Grandfather Tschaikov, as well as being a violinist, also played the clarinet and the double bass. He probably belonged to one of the families of musicians that formed the Klezmer bands that went from village to village in Russia and Poland, playing at weddings and other celebrations. By the time my father was born, grandfather had moved on and was conducting small orchestras on the pleasure boats that used to cruise from Sukhumi, Sotshi, and Botumi, on the Black Sea, where a Mediterranean climate and an abundance of vineyards and orchards made for a most enjoyable life. 'Conducting' probably meant that he stood in front of the orchestra and 'led', standing in front of the other players, playing the violin and using the bow to conduct when necessary. This was the traditional style in small orchestras playing light music until the 1940s – now only seen at concerts of Viennese waltzes. It was also the style adopted by dance and jazz bandleaders, though they would play clarinet, trumpet, trombone or piano.

Through his association with the influential people he met on these cruises he could have avoided the consequences of the pogroms that were then sweeping through Russia and bringing terror and exile. He had the opportunity to convert to Christianity, and this was the course his rich and powerful friends recommended. Had he taken their advice he could have continued to follow his profession as a musician. But he was a proud and stubborn man and preferred to retain his integrity and independence. He set off, with his large family, for what he hoped would be a more welcoming environment.

It is a long way from the warmth of those Black Sea holiday resorts to Warsaw, and the journey was to be slow and painful. One stopping place was Tiflis, now Tblisi, in Georgia, where my father was born in 1894. Tblisi is the Georgian word for hot. Legend has it that 1500 years ago King Vakhang Gorgasali went hunting in the woods near Mtskheta, the ancient capital. His falcon was chasing a pheasant when it suddenly dropped into a pool and was boiled alive. The hot springs that caused this interesting phenomenon led to the King moving his capital to Tblisi.

Soon after my father was born the *pogrom* reached Tblisi, making it impossible for the family to remain there. They were obliged to set off once again. This time they decided to make the long journey to Warsaw. Each Friday evening at dusk they would all get off the train, since travel on the Sabbath was proscribed by their religion, and wait patiently by the side of the track until dusk the following day before continuing on their journey. Once settled in Warsaw Uncle Anton, who was only about six or seven years old, was heard playing the violin by a distinguished teacher who decided to take him under his wing. He thought that the boy showed outstanding talent and that he could become a successful solo violinist. But after a year or so the pogrom caught up with them yet again. This time they decided to leave mainland Europe altogether.

The Tschaikov family in London about 1905. My father aged 8 or 9 is sitting in the middle, holding his clarinet. His elder brother, Anton, is standing behind with his violin. The other members of the group are his father and two of his sisters, one a flautist the other a cellist. Groups like this, in traditional dress, were very popular at the beginning of the 20ᵗʰ century.

By the end of the 19th century the east-end of London had already become home to many European Jewish refugees including a number of musicians. Knowing this and speaking virtually no English, the Tschaikovs quickly made their way to where at least they would find some people who would understand them. When a year or so later the father left the family the responsibility for providing for mother and eight children fell on the two eldest boys, Anton and Anissim, my father.

Even in the first years of the 20th century employment opportunities for boys aged eleven and eight were limited. However, by now my father had already acquired a good deal of skill on the clarinet and so, with Anton playing the violin, he made his début on the streets of East London. With their youth and instrumental facility they probably picked up a reasonable number of pennies, but not always enough to support a large family. My father told me how when things were really bad his mother had on one occasion been forced to break into the gas-meter so that they could buy some food.

One day as they were playing in the street Mr Mandelbaum, a wealthy antique dealer who was a great music lover, heard them. Their talent impressed him and he made arrangements for them to attend the Guildhall School of Music where they were both later awarded scholarships. It was not long before Anton was leading the student orchestra. Unfortunately the need to earn money meant he had to accept engagements, which from time to time required him to be absent from some of the orchestra's rehearsals. Excuses and guile got him through for a time until one day he was away from a performance the College considered important. When he was subjected to some searching questions and it was revealed that he had accepted a paid engagement, in place of fulfilling his obligation to the College, his Scholarship was withdrawn.

My father, then still only a boy, was extraordinarily fortunate to have the opportunity of studying with the great Charles Draper, the father of the British school of clarinet playing. His influence on clarinet playing was considerable since at one time or another he was also professor at both the Royal College of Music and the Royal Academy. His pupils included, amongst many others, Frederick Thurston and Ralph Clarke, principal and second clarinet in the BBC Symphony Orchestra, who in their turn were both professors at the Royal College of Music. Through them and subsequent generations of players Draper's influence can still be heard today.

When my father had finished his lesson and the next pupil came in Professor Draper would sometimes say 'All right young Tschai; get this chap started and see how he's doing – I'm just off to get a newspaper.' He usually did not return for an hour or so. Of course that sort of thing could not possibly happen now; nor could a boy of ten any longer be studying at one of our national music colleges. The following year, 1906, 'young Tschai' whilst still at the Guildhall started to earn his living as a professional musician. He was now eleven – a little younger than usual to be working in the profession, though it was not uncommon for children of thirteen or fourteen, whilst still at school, to be playing in music halls, and some years later for the silent cinema. He must have been exceptionally gifted as the *Musical Times* reported that in 1908 Anissim Tschaikov was the soloist at one of the Guildhall School of Music's concerts playing the Mozart Clarinet Concerto and again in 1909, this time playing the Clarinet Concerto in F minor by Weber.

If a boy or girl in a poor Jewish family showed musical talent at an early age it would be encouraged. This was true in poor immigrant Jewish families everywhere. Of all the professions music is the easiest for a foreigner to join when they have only a limited knowledge of the language of their new home. This may account for the remarkable number of famous Jewish musicians, especially solo pianists and violinists, during the first half of the 20th century.

Most professional musicians at that time, certainly those who were Jewish, came from lower middle-class or poor working-class families. For those with talent music provided an opportunity to jump their class. In more recent times the children of black families, especially in the USA from the 1920s onwards, have followed a similar escape route through jazz and the dance and swing bands. Sport rather than music seems to have become the preferred way out of poverty and social deprivation since the 1950s.

In musical families there were always parents, uncles and cousins able to provide free or inexpensive lessons. A child that showed talent would be encouraged, though encouragement could sometimes be a euphemism for being obliged to work exceedingly hard, and by no means always willingly. A number of the older musicians that I worked with in the past (mostly string players) told me how they were made to practise for many hours and of the harsh criticism with which their efforts were quite frequently rewarded. Many of these young string players gained their early professional experience in the smaller music halls and cinemas. For wind players the main route into the profession was often from army and brass bands, where they learned to play in ensemble and to sight-read.

By 1910 when a father, a skilled artisan – a tailor, shoemaker or hairdresser – might still be earning no more than thirty shillings (£1.50) a week, his violinist son, if really talented, might by the age of only sixteen or seventeen be earning five or six pounds a week leading one of the larger cinema orchestras. Some idea of the extent of the employment opportunities for musicians to work in the 'silent' cinemas can be gained from the number of cinemas in London alone: between 1909 and 1912 their number leapt from 90 to 400 and by 1927 it is estimated that over 15,000 musicians were playing in cinemas throughout the country. Then suddenly, with the arrival of sound films, the 'talkies', everything changed and by 1932 all those musicians were unemployed. A sense of insecurity is endemic in all performers; doubt about their own ability has always been compounded by the vagaries of employment opportunities. The trauma caused by the loss of employment for thousands of musicians that the coming of the 'talkies' created had a lasting influence on the psychology of musicians for a number of generations.

Though my own circumstances in the 1930s when I was still a child protected me from the harsh realities of life that afflicted so many others, I was aware of something of the hardship and humiliation that they suffered. There was a regular stream of relations, all musicians, seeking financial aid from my father, at that time the only member of the family with a steady income. They were good musicians and competent players who had devoted their lives from an early age to practising their instrumental skills to the best of their ability. Now they were unwanted. And, worse, their skills fitted them for no other trade or occupation. Their indignity affected me profoundly and at a very early age I vowed that I would never allow myself to be in that situation.

2 The BBC Symphony Orchestra

The author's father joins the new BBC Symphony Orchestra as principal clarinet. BBC Symphony Orchestra in the 1930s – conditions, players, conductors (including Sir Adrian Boult, Arturo Toscanini and Willem Mengelberg), sections A, B, C, D, E, repertoire performed, and the author's memories of Toscanini rehearsing.

In 1930 my father joined the newly formed BBC Symphony Orchestra as one of the principal clarinettists; the other was Frederick Thurston, later to be my teacher at the Royal College of Music, where he was the principal professor of clarinet. The BBC Symphony Orchestra was the first full-time contract symphony orchestra in Britain. It offered the players a degree of security and conditions undreamed of until then: a yearly contract that was likely to be renewed unless you did something really dreadful, a month's holiday on full pay, and four weeks' sick pay. With these advantages came some restrictions. Members of the orchestra were not allowed to accept engagements with any other orchestra, even if it was on a day when they were not required by the orchestra or during their holiday period. Permission was nearly always given to any player who was offered a solo or chamber music engagement.

Another condition of the contract, certainly for the principal players, was that they must have a telephone, still quite unusual in the 1930s. This was so that they could be contacted at any time if there was a change of programme or if they were required to replace a colleague at short notice. It seems that some players had developed the practice that if the phone rang on one of their free days, whoever answered would always say that the person required was out and that no one knew where they were, or when they would return.

At that time (during the 1930s) the orchestral manager was particularly disliked, probably rather unfairly, because he carried out the Corporation's policy extremely efficiently. He also had an unfortunate name and a rather forbidding appearance. Mr Pratt had eyes and ears everywhere. Should any covert date be accepted and come to his ever-watchful attention, the unfortunate musician would be called to account and threatened with instant dismissal should this offence be repeated.

In 1939, just before the war, we were in the middle of lunch one Sunday when we heard the front-door bell. A few minutes later the maid knocked at the door and said, 'Mr Pratt to see you, Sir.' Before there was time to reply the dreaded Mr Pratt was in the room. Jack Thurston had been taken ill and my father was required to take his place. Mr Pratt, experienced in the ways of his flock, had come in person; he knew that phoning might not be the best way of contacting my father.

This event has stayed in my memory because as Mr Pratt was leaving, with my father in tow, he asked me if I liked music. When I told him I had recently started to learn the clarinet, he said 'Learn the Eb clarinet, good Eb players are always in demand.' I was then thirteen, and it was not until very many years later that I learned the truth of his words. The higher pitched Eb clarinet is used infrequently, but always has an important and exposed part to play. It requires particular study, if it is to be played well. Few clarinettists, at that time, made the effort to do this.

Conditions in the BBC Symphony Orchestra were not only better than in any other British orchestra, but the salary was regular and at a high level for those days. Tutti players (often referred to as 'rank and file'), that is those string players other than the principals and sub-principals of each section, received £11.00 a week. Several woodwind and brass principals received £1000 a year. £750 was the average salary for principals, ten times the national average wage at that time, a far greater differential than any orchestral musician can achieve now. But this was nothing compared with what some of the most sought after players in the best dance bands received. A few were earning as much as £45 a week, more than double the salary of a bank manager. The security and conditions the BBC could offer and the opportunity to play great music in a fine orchestra was sufficient for my father to turn down a tempting invitation to join Jack Hylton's famous Band. The advent of the BBC and the high salaries paid to those in a number of dance bands was in stark contrast to the many musicians who were only able to find occasional employment and those forced to give up their profession altogether.

When Dr Adrian Boult (as he was then, later Sir Adrian) was appointed Director of Music and chief conductor of the BBC Symphony Orchestra he was able to attract a number of the most outstanding players to the orchestra as section principals, some of whom already had established solo careers. Distinguished artists happy to accept contracts included Lauri Kennedy, as principal cello. In the early 1950's his son, John, was principal cello with Beecham in the Royal Philharmonic Orchestra and his grandson Nigel is the splendid, if controversial, solo violinist of our own time. Aubrey Brain, the eminent horn player, father of Dennis (horn) and Leonard (oboe), Eugene Cruft, double bass, Robert Murchie, flute, Bernard Shore, viola and Arthur Catterall, as leader. They were joined by younger artists who were already forging prestigious careers – Frederick Thurston, clarinet, Ernest Hall, trumpet and Sidonie Goossens, the harpist.

These players and a number of other principals were selected on the strength of their reputations. The majority of the other players gained their places following auditions held all over the country. As a result many very talented young musicians, some straight out of music college, were also offered contracts. The BBC used this method of recruiting, unusual at that time, from the start and, with a few exceptions, auditions have always been held when players have been required for any of the BBC orchestras. Today auditions are the norm, except for players with a known reputation who will usually be given a few 'try out' dates, followed by a trial period, sometimes quite protracted, before being offered a position.

From when I was five or six, my father would occasionally take me to a rehearsal where I would meet some of these legendary players. To me they were 'uncles' and 'aunts'. It was quite common for kindly and generous 'uncles' and 'aunts' at that time to give youngsters a 'tip' – they would usually give sixpence (2½p) or a shilling (5p), the equivalent of £5 and £10 today. If one was 'nicely brought up' one had been taught to say, 'I don't take money, thank you.' But they always insisted and said 'Don't tell Dad'. And so one would take it!

Perhaps, as I have mentioned 'aunts' as well as 'uncles', it is worth noting the position of women in the profession at that time. Though there had been women in the profession for many years, except for harpists there were virtually none in the symphony orchestras until after 1945. During the time I was in the London Philharmonic and Royal Philharmonic Orchestras, from 1943 until 1960 the only women were the harpists. As late as 1948 even the harpist in the Royal Philharmonic was a man.

The BBC Symphony was the exception, as far as the major orchestras were concerned, though even in that orchestra only one wind player was a woman, the oboist Helen Gaskell. It was not until Walter Legge founded the Philharmonia in 1945 that women players started to be given an opportunity to show that they could match the men in skill and artistry – and surpass them! It was more than 30 years before equality of opportunity reigned in all the London orchestras. In those days of unabashed male chauvinism it was possible for Sir Thomas Beecham to declare, when asked why there were no women in his orchestra, 'I find that if they are attractive they distract my musicians, and if they are not they distract me.'

One of my earliest memories is of going to Broadcasting House, shortly after it was built, when I was 6 or 7 years old. My father took my mother and myself on a tour of the newly opened building in Portland Place, a few yards from Oxford Circus. When we went onto the roof of this tall building, being a curious child, I wandered off on my own and was only just rescued from going over the edge. Many years later – when I was involved as a representative of musicians and engaged in battle with the BBC about the creation of Radio 1 and 2 (in order to close down the pirate radio stations) – I mentioned this to one of the BBC Directors. I had the impression that perhaps he might have preferred that the outstretched hand had not saved me from a fatal fall.

When the BBC Symphony Orchestra was formed, and to some extent until 1945/46, there were far fewer rules and regulations than there are now. It was quite easy for my father to take me to rehearsals at the BBC Maida Vale studios where the Symphony Orchestra usually rehearsed and performed for broadcasts. It is much more difficult now that everything has become so much more bureaucratic. On the other hand standards of discipline, behaviour and speech were high. But neither Sir John Reith's highly moral regime nor Mr Pratt's strictures had much influence on the strongly entrenched drinking habits of some members of the orchestra. Sir Adrian, a most abstemious man himself, seems to have taken a fairly relaxed attitude to this sometimes damaging foible. One or two of his most outstanding principal players would appear from time to time more than a little the worse for wear. But, remarkably, these players were usually able to continue to play extremely well, even when they had become unable to perform other movements with any degree of accuracy.

One very stout member of the violin section, an excellent musician, was sometimes unable to maintain his equilibrium and would fall off his chair. I was told that on one occasion, when this happened on a broadcast, Sir Adrian whispered to Paul Beard, who was then the leader, 'Oh! Dear! I think Mr ... is not feeling very well again tonight'. Now that standards are so high and competition so great, behaviour of that kind would not be countenanced for a moment.

The full orchestra of one hundred and fourteen musicians came together only for the major concerts, usually in the Queen's Hall. For the majority of broadcasts the orchestra was divided into a number of sections, the largest of which was between 75 and 85. However, the studio required for broadcasts had to be large enough to accommodate the whole orchestra if necessary. A suitable space that size is very difficult to find.

The Queen's Hall, close to Oxford Circus in the centre of London, was much loved for its fine acoustics and an elegant appearance. When it was destroyed by a bomb during the war London was left without a really suitable concert hall. At the end of the war a fund was raised for its reconstruction, but for reasons never fully explained this money was not used for this purpose and the hall has not been rebuilt.

I never experienced them myself but the horrors of studio Number 10 were known to me from childhood. Number 10 was an old warehouse, more or less under Waterloo Bridge, on the south bank of the Thames. It was damp and somewhat smelly and quite inappropriate as the home of Britain's 'premier orchestra', (as my father always called it – especially once I had joined the London Philharmonic). But the acoustics were good and the players came to have a kind of affection for it. The main cause for alarm, especially for the ladies, was the regular appearance of rats.

These would run about on the rafters overhead and up and down the staircase at one end of the studio. I never heard that anyone was attacked by these unwelcome guests. It may be that rats are a music-loving species, or perhaps this particular colony became so as a result of their association with this fine band of musicians.

By 1931 the BBC was describing the Concert Hall that was to be created within Broadcasting House as 'Where a Thousand People will Hear Great Music'. It was designed especially to be the home of the BBC Symphony Orchestra – a very large orchestra – and it was said that it would provide Londoners with a major new concert venue.

Quite soon after the Hall was completed in 1932 it became clear that those responsible for instructing the architects were unfamiliar with musical instruments and the amount of space required in which to play them. This first became evident when the piano was to be installed. The very fine, beautifully panelled doors, even when opened to their full extent, were just not wide enough to allow the piano into the hall. This was not an insurmountable problem, and though troublesome and quite costly, it was not to be the worst of their difficulties. When all the members of the orchestra assembled on stage they found that there was insufficient room for all the players and their instruments. In fact there was not even enough room for them all without their instruments. This was more serious and though in the end the BBC did find somewhere else it took quite a while to do so.

The orchestra had to remain in the dreaded studio Number 10 until somewhere else could be found. Eventually, in 1934, a more suitable venue was found: a disused former roller-skating rink in Maida Vale, a residential area a couple of miles from the centre of London. Over the years a great deal of time and money has been spent on improving the big studio – Studio One – which has been 'home' for the BBC Symphony Orchestra for sixty years. Though devoid of rats it has never been popular with musicians, perhaps because the lighting, air conditioning, and the acoustic are 'un-loving'. That indefinable something that can make a place a delight to play in is missing.

In the *Radio Times*, which provided details of all the BBC's programmes, the orchestra was shown as The BBC Symphony Orchestra (section A), or section B, C, D, or E. Section A was the full orchestra; sections B and D, usually between 60 and 85 strong, were responsible for the 'serious' (classical) music content. Sections C and E, with 40 to 55 players, played 'lighter' music.

A great deal of the music performed by sections C and E, still at that time played with the original orchestrations, has had little place in radio or concert programmes for some years. Too often when it has been played it has been re-orchestrated for a smaller orchestra than the original. With the advent of the commercial radio station Classic FM, some of this lovely music is being heard once again as the composer intended. The programmes section C and E played included works by Delibes – the ballet music from *Coppelia, La Source* and *Sylvia;* Massenet, and Messager (a favourite was *The Two Pigeons* ballet music); Bizet's *Jeux d'Enfants,* and the orchestral suite from his opera *Carmen;* the lovely *Wand of Youth* suites by Elgar; and music by Coleridge-Taylor, Grieg, Niels Gade, Edward German, Percy Grainger ... They also played the inspired and delightful shorter compositions by Brahms, Schubert, Tchaikovsky, Sibelius, and Saint-Saëns, not to mention Beethoven, Mozart, and many others.

This music is often difficult technically and needs to be played with bravura and style. Just as much time is needed for rehearsal as for symphonies and concertos, and nowadays rather more because the repertoire is unfamiliar. Sadly, when it is performed – and even when recorded – it is too frequently under-prepared and un-stylistically performed.

It is a measure of that strange musical snobbery still endemic in Britain that in the otherwise excellent and highly informative book *The BBC Symphony Orchestra* by Nicholas Kenyon, there is virtually no mention of this music which between 1930 and 1941 made up about half the Symphony Orchestra's broadcast output. Composers such as Eric Coates, Lehar, Satie, Britten, and many others, whose music we know but would be hard put to name – Haydn Wood, Montague Phillips, and Fraser-Simson, for example, all received first performances or first broadcast performances from these two sections of the BBC Symphony Orchestra (section C or Section E) under one or other of their two principal conductors.

At the beginning and for the first eight years Joseph Lewis was their most frequent conductor. Joe Lewis, as he was affectionately known by everyone, came from Birmingham. He was not a very good conductor but was unpretentious, a really delightful man (he even welcomed me with grace and charm when I was only about eight or nine). He gave the players time to express themselves in the music without getting in the way too much – always a virtue in an indifferent conductor. In 1938 he was succeeded as staff conductor by Clarence Raybould. Though a fine musician he lacked Lewis's charm, was pretentious, and did get in the way.

But, of course, the main virtue of the BBC Symphony Orchestra was that in 1930 it set extremely high standards, which were to influence orchestral performance in the years to come. It was the first orchestra in Britain to combine first-class players throughout every section with conditions that allowed them to display their potential. It was the BBC's declared intention to match the world class orchestras in Vienna, Berlin, Amsterdam and New York, Philadelphia and Boston. The Symphony Orchestra's sheltered position within the BBC provided the opportunity for the performance of a far wider repertoire, especially of contemporary music, than any of the other British orchestras of the time. This is still true today.

Sir Adrian Boult, was often characterised as rather a 'fuddy-duddy' (he was nicknamed 'Saidie' by the orchestra), and thought conventional as a musician. In fact he was remarkably catholic in his musical sympathies and adventurous in his programme building. His choice of programme for the orchestra's first concert shows this very clearly:

The Overture *Flying Dutchman*	Richard Wagner
Cello Concerto	Camille Saint-Saëns
Symphony No.4	Johannes Brahms
Daphnis and Chloe Suite No.2	Maurice Ravel

It required considerable courage in 1930 to include *Daphnis and Chloe*, completed only 18 years previously, in the inaugural concert of a newly formed, and in some circles controversial, symphony orchestra. In their public concerts and studio broadcasts under his direction the orchestra performed a remarkable range of music. Between 1930 and 1950 the BBC and Boult continually extended the repertoire of the orchestra bringing to an ever-increasing radio audience music that until then only a very small number of music lovers had been able to enjoy.

First performances in Britain included compositions as diverse as Schoenberg's *Erwartung* (conducted by the composer) and his *Variations for Orchestra* op.31, Mossolov's *Factory* (more usually known as *Music of Machines*), a number of Alban Berg's major compositions including the *Three Orchestral Pieces* op.6, 3 pieces from the *Lyric Suite,* the Symphonic extracts from *Lulu,* the Violin Concerto and the first complete performance of *Wozzeck* – in the studio, with an all British cast – for which there were 18 rehearsals. In 1934 the orchestra, for whom this music was both strange and difficult, found this number of rehearsals somewhat of a strain on their tolerance. In the event it was a considerable success and Berg later expressed himself 'delighted'. Other major works premiered in Britain included symphonies by Bruckner (9th), Mahler (9th) – and the first London performances of symphonies by Roussel (3rd), Martinu (2nd), and Stravinsky (Symphony in C), the *Dumbarton Oaks Concerto*, also by Stravinsky. When I was 16 and was about to start at the Royal College of Music Sir Adrian allowed me to sit next to my father in the orchestra during the broadcast of the *Dumbarton Oaks Concerto* – I very much doubt if that would be allowed now. Also important compositions by Webern, Richard Strauss, Bartók, Hindemith, Kodály, Prokofiev, Shostakovich, Copland, Piston, William Schuman and Chávez.

British composers were particularly well represented with world premieres of works by Delius, Walton (1st Symphony, 2nd *Facade* suite), Bax, Ireland, Lambert, Bliss (the Colour Symphony, in its revised version), Vaughan Williams (4th and 6th Symphonies, Piano Concerto, *Serenade to Music*), and Britten (Piano Concerto).

This wide ranging repertoire that included many works that made use of harmonic and rhythmic innovations and instrumental techniques that were completely new and strange to the musicians, was broadcast before the invention of tape recording. Each programme, whether relayed from a concert hall performance or from a broadcasting studio, was played straight through. There was no possibility of 'editing' or re-playing short sections, where there may have been some false entry or poor ensemble, and then splicing it in.

Many of the most outstanding conductors were attracted by the standard and growing reputation of the orchestra. As well as the best British conductors, Sir Thomas Beecham, Sir Hamilton Harty, Sir Henry Wood, and Sir John Barbirolli, there were visits from the great names from around the world; Bruno Walter, Monteux, Koussevitsky, and what was considered the ultimate stamp of approval, Arturo Toscanini. He was given complete freedom with rehearsal time and everyone, including Boult, treated him with the greatest deference. All except Edgar Mays, officially titled Assistant (Orchestra and Artists). His job was to see that the orchestra was correctly seated, that there were the right number of chairs and stands, and that anything the conductor and soloists might need was provided. He was a large man, probably, though I am not sure, with an Army background. He certainly had the manner of an ex-Sergeant Major; jovially tyrannical, he had a loud voice and a pronounced Cockney accent. He was not at all intimidated by Toscanini and would welcome him when he arrived for rehearsal, 'Well! How's it this morning Tosci!' At the interval of rehearsals he was prone to put his arm around the diminutive conductor's shoulders and inquire if Tosci 'would care for a cuppa?'

In the first half of 1939, the BBC mounted the London Music Festival and invited Toscanini to conduct all the Beethoven symphonies and the *Mass in D*. I was starting to get really interested in music and so my father thought it would be a treat for me to attend one of Toscanini's rehearsals even though this had been strictly forbidden, since this conductor like many others and most musicians intensely disliked having anyone present at rehearsals. Because of his fame and the press interest in his every move, as well as his own volatile personality, his response to intruders could be volcanic.

The rehearsal was held in the elegant Queen's Hall, where the concert would take place the following day. Somehow my father managed to smuggle me in and I was now sitting very still, well back in the stalls, which were shrouded in darkness. The orchestra assembled, tuned up, and then fell silent at a sign from the ever present Edgar Mays. A small figure appeared at the side of the platform and as he walked towards the podium carrying a large score I got my first and only extremely brief chance to see this legendary conductor. But I was not the only one to have hidden myself in the darkened auditorium. When the Maestro was nearing the centre of the platform there was a bright flash of light from near the front of the stalls. Toscanini turned and hurled the score at the light, and with a shout of annoyance rushed off the platform. The intruder, a press photographer, made a rapid exit, Mays returned to tell the orchestra the rehearsal was cancelled, everyone quickly packed up, and before I knew it my father and I were on our way down Oxford Street heading for Speakers' Corner. Listening to the impromptu speakers and those who barracked them was to be my alternative treat.

It was only many years later that I learned why Toscanini reacted quite so violently. I am sure none of those present on that occasion will have known. It will have been assumed that this was just another example of his violent response to what displeased him. Harvey Sachs, in his remarkable book *Toscanini*, recounts how on two previous occasions Toscanini had had bad experiences with flashlights exploding right in front of his exceedingly weak eyes. Both times these should have been special and joyous celebrations.

The first time this occurred was at the farewell concert given to mark the end of his long association with the New York Philharmonic-Symphony Orchestra (later 'Symphony' was omitted. Every item in the programme received rapturous applause but no sooner had the final work ended – *The Ride of the Valkyrie* – than a reporter ran forward and snapped a picture of him. The flash temporarily blinded him and he rushed from the stage and did not return again. The next occasion was at the official first concert inaugurating the Palestine Orchestra (later to become the Israel Philharmonic Orchestra). This was an occasion of great excitement. Dr Chaim Weizmann, David Ben-Gurion and the British High Commissioner were present, and the demand for tickets was so great that those unable to obtain tickets climbed onto the roof of the hall in the hope of at least hearing something! Once more the evening ended badly. Another ardent photographer exploded his flashlight right in front of Toscanini's eyes.

The relationship between Toscanini and the BBC Orchestra was always warm and over the years they developed an extraordinary mutual regard and affection. The recordings the orchestra made with him in the 1930s bear witness to this. In some way the orchestra seems to have been able to allow Toscanini to invest his performances with them with a special kind of spontaneity and freedom.

Another conductor of renown that Boult invited to conduct the orchestra, Willem Mengelberg, created a quite different relationship with the orchestra. Mengelberg was the long-time Principal Conductor of the Concertgebouw Orchestra in Amsterdam. He had a considerable reputation and with this orchestra had given many fine performances (a few recordings made in the 1940s provide evidence) that were distinguished by extremes of tempi and dynamics and by their flexible and subtle *rubato* which was always controlled and retained impeccable ensemble. He also had a reputation for being abrasive and on occasion quite disagreeable. When the members of the BBC Symphony Orchestra learned that he was scheduled to conduct them it caused some apprehension.

In the event he made himself unpopular from the start. At the first rehearsal, after the usual introductions, he spent a good deal of time balancing the various sections and checking intonation. Then he started rehearsing the first item. After they had been playing for about 20 minutes or so he called for the orchestral manager. In his gruff voice and thick Dutch accent, loudly enough for the whole orchestra to hear, he said, 'Iss dis a professional orchestre?' It was not uncommon at that time for some conductors to adopt a rude and sometimes overbearing stance. This fine and proud orchestra did not respond well to this kind of treatment. Though the concerts went well the relationship never mended.

In its first fifteen years, the BBC's enlightened music policy profoundly affected musical life in Britain. It played an enormous part in making it possible for everyone, wherever they lived, to hear an extraordinarily eclectic repertoire, thereby creating an audience for music throughout Britain that barely existed previously.

3 The War 1939 - 1945

The Author wants to learn the Clarinet.
His father is against it – he hopes his son will be a doctor.
The author's school is evacuated and he plays in the school orchestra.
The joy of playing chamber music.
He hears a recording of Menuhin: his future is sealed.

Had I been born into a comfortable middle-class family in 1875 instead of 1925 I would probably have satisfied my father's wish and become a doctor or lawyer. To become an orchestral musician would have been out of the question. By 1940 attitudes had begun to change and children like myself were having their aspirations to become musicians satisfied. Nonetheless, my father remained opposed to me becoming a professional musician. I am sure that his opposition did not stem from any lack of respect for his own profession, but was caused by his fear of unemployment and the financial insecurity inherent in being a musician. At that time, 1936, there were still very many musicians looking for work.

When the 'talkies' replaced the 'silent' films, thousands of musicians previously employed in the 'orchestras' in every cinema to accompany the silent films were thrown into the already large army of unemployed. The relatives I referred to earlier who were sustained by my father's kindness were amongst those affected by this technological advance.

I suppose it is not surprising that having had very little formal education himself, my father was anxious to give me the opportunities he felt he had been denied. He certainly was not keen for me to develop any ideas of following him into a profession that remained extremely precarious. He resisted my desire to learn the clarinet, but in the end agreed to let me have piano lessons. It was not long before he realised that he was wasting his money. My lack of talent and interest in playing the piano was all too apparent. Being a practical man, he at last gave in to my persistence and agreed to start giving me clarinet lessons.

I was then eleven. When he was that age he was just starting out on his professional career and must already have been 'street-wise' and something of a man of the world, whereas I had only known the comfort and security of a middle-class home. I was at Colet Court, the preparatory school for St. Paul's, where he hoped I would acquire an education that would enable me to fulfil his ambition that I should become a doctor, or a barrister. In fact, that I might join any other profession than that of music. And to satisfy this ambition he was prepared to make financial sacrifices.

Probably the great differences between my father's youthful circumstances, personality and talents and mine did little to make the teacher/pupil relationship easy. In retrospect it is so obvious and understandable. At the time it was the cause of considerable impatience and disappointment to him, and distress to me.

In the early stages all went well, as is usually the case. One makes most progress in the first lesson, going rapidly from not being able to produce a note to playing three or four different notes, and, perhaps, even playing a short, simple melody. The clarinet is particularly rewarding in the early stages. It is quite easy to play in the low register – no doubt this is why it is so popular with youngsters who have already made some headway on the recorder.

Of course I had quite a lot of school homework to do each evening and, though I was keen to make progress on the clarinet, my motivation was just to enjoy myself. I had as yet no thoughts about the future, nor had I remotely considered the possibility of playing the clarinet to earn my living. In the light of my own experience of teaching the clarinet for many years at all levels, I think it fair to say that I made above average progress. But to my father I am sure it seemed that I was moving forward at a snail's pace, and with little sense of purpose. He had done very little teaching and because of his own quite remarkable gifts as a clarinettist – he was generally recognised as a technical virtuoso in his day – he had no understanding of those less gifted than himself. In addition he was one of those players who are never really happy unless they have their instrument in their hands. By contrast I am naturally indolent, and though it took many years for me to realise it, I am now aware that I was always more interested in music than actually playing an instrument. I think it is unlikely that anyone will become a really outstanding instrumental performer unless the actual act of playing the instrument continues to give a great deal of satisfaction throughout his or her life.

Doing something easily and well is a great spur to making further progress. I found playing reasonably easy, but with the sound of my father's expertise constantly in my ears I did not think very highly of my own performance and this inhibited my enthusiasm and confidence. This was compounded by the fact that there was no set day for lessons, say once a week, as is usual. If my father was at home and heard me playing, up in my room, and he heard something that was incorrect, out of rhythm, tempo, or a wrong note – as was frequently the case – he would come up and put me right. This could be a lengthy process, as he appeared to have little sense of the passing of time. At that age a half-hour, or at most a forty-minute lesson, is quite long enough. I recall times when an hour and a half or even longer passed before, mercifully, we 'packed up'.

The hardest single technical difficulty on the clarinet is 'crossing the break'. At one point, (between the notes A and B, in the middle of the treble clef) one moves from having one finger on a key to covering seven holes and pressing three keys. You may wonder how it is possible to perform ten actions with only eight fingers and a thumb (the other is used to support the instrument). In fact that is a large part of the problem. The thumb of the left hand has to do two things; cover a hole, and press a key, at the same time. Early attempts at this feat are generally unsuccessful, resulting in the dreaded 'squeaks' to which the clarinet alone is heir. This is usually the cause of merriment to others, but is humiliating to the player. It takes quite a while, and a good deal of persistence, before this move can be made with confidence. In fact passages involving crossing the break at speed, several times in succession, remain one of the most difficult things to do, however long one plays and however accomplished one becomes.

There is one particular study in Klosé's famous *Tutor for the Clarinet*, written to develop the ability to cross the break. The first note of each group is above the break and the following two are below. If the top note is emphasised, and especially when the study is played up to speed, it sounds like a tune with its own accompaniment. Even after several weeks' practice I was still stumbling and squeaking, but I was starting to hear and enjoy the faint outline of the melody. 'No! No! No!' shouted my father, 'It goes like this', and he then dashed it off at a very fast speed, so that the top notes sounded like a row of ringing bells, each with its own delicate accompaniment. I listened with delight, but wondered what hope there was for me. I felt like someone with a broken foot hobbling along as an Olympic athlete races past.

Looking back, having mastered that study, I realise that he was trying to set me an example, a target to aim for. For some, my father included, that style of teaching will provoke the right response – 'You think you're good – I'll show you!' For many others like myself it has a very different effect, inhibiting and creating doubt in one's capacity ever to reach one's goal. My own experience was to have a considerable influence on my future method of teaching.

Many years later I was talking to my father about a pupil I had who was using the same study book that had caused me to feel so inadequate, the one written by the very great French clarinettist Camille Klosé. He had developed the Boehm system clarinet in 1843 by applying Boehm's flute ring-mechanism to the clarinet. I had learned from the copy of this *Tutor* that my father had used when he was a boy at the Guildhall School of Music. I asked him why so many of the pages were separate though the volume as a whole seemed to be complete. He explained to me that he was given a halfpenny for the tram to take him to the Guildhall because as well as his clarinets he had this large and rather heavy book of studies to carry. But he had decided that the money would be better spent on buying some sweets and so he had torn out the pages he was currently studying, put them in his clarinet case and walked – no doubt happily sucking his illicit purchase.

In August 1939, a few weeks before the outbreak of war, St. Paul's School left London. Along with tens of thousands of other children we became 'evacuees'. It was an exciting experience; rather unsettling, but as it turned out, fortunate for me. Had I not left home when I was just fourteen I think it is unlikely that I would have spent most of my life as a clarinettist. The tension between my own self confidence and unwillingness to bow to authority, and my sense of inadequacy in the face of my father's overwhelming ability, would have led to my abandoning my efforts to master the technique required to become a useful player.

In contrast to the situation today, woodwind players were rather thin on the ground at a public school such as St. Paul's. In fact they could not have been thinner. Apart from one of the more elderly masters, a Mr Bartlett, who performed on the flute in a frail and indecisive manner, I was the only other woodwind player. The combination of his indecision and my inaccuracy did not make for a very strong or effective woodwind section.

There were a reasonable number of strings, but here again neither technique nor musicality were of a high order. Just the same, I enjoyed the weekly rehearsals even though the music master, Mr Wilson, often seemed to be rather bad tempered. Looking back, I suppose that he must have been quite a kindly and patient man not to have cursed us and run screaming from the noise we were making.

Sometime in the late nineteen seventies or early eighties, I was invited to adjudicate at the school's annual music competition and award the prize to the best woodwind player. There were a great many entrants and the standard was remarkably high. The best were up to music college entrance level and could tackle something as difficult as the Nielsen clarinet or flute Concerto, unthinkable in my time at school. There was no longer any difficulty in forming a full and competent woodwind section. In contrast, the number of string players had not increased to anything like the same extent, nor had the quality of the playing much improved.

The very first concert in which I took part was in the school orchestra. We played a symphony by Boyce, in an edition that would make today's 'authentic' specialists go white (I do not recall ever again playing another piece by Boyce during the rest of my life as a musician), and the *Fantasia on Christmas Carols* by Vaughan Williams. This is quite an attractive work though seldom played today. It is written to be played on the 'A' clarinet. In the orchestra clarinettists use two clarinets – not at the same time, of course! – one in 'Bb' and the other in 'A'.★

Faced with the problem of playing an 'A' clarinet part on the 'Bb', the only one I possessed, I decided to rewrite the part transposing the notes in the process. My lack of skill in playing the

clarinet was matched by my inexperience in transposition. The
next rehearsal was marred not only by my normal failings, but had
the added disadvantage of a great number of wrong notes. Whole
passages were well ahead of their time – they would be more
acceptable today, in Boulez, or Stockhausen, than they were then
in Vaughan Williams. When I wrote home and reported this
disaster, my father with remarkable generosity sent me an 'A'
clarinet. Subsequent rehearsals only suffered from my usual
inadequacies. Though I was aware that our efforts were pretty
awful, it gave me pleasure to be making music with other people,
and whetted my appetite for more.

★ *The clarinet is a transposing instrument. The note you read from the
music, and finger on the instrument, is different from the note that actually
sounds. When you read and finger the note 'C', on the 'Bb' clarinet, it will
sound one tone lower, 'Bb'. When you read and finger this same note ('C')
on the 'A' clarinet, you will hear the note 'A ', a tone and a half lower. The
instrument the composer selects to write for depends on the key he intends to
write in. If he is writing a piece in the key of D major, he will probably
write for the 'A' clarinet, so that the clarinet part will be in F major, rather
than for the 'Bb' clarinet, on which, to play **the same sounds**, the player
would have to play in E major, making the fast passages much more difficult
technically.*

In 1939, when the school left London to escape the bombing,
we were evacuated to Crowthorne, still a quiet Berkshire village.
Here I was free from discerning parental ears. Wrong notes,
inaccurate rhythms, and mistakes of every kind went by without
interference from anyone but myself. If I was away on the wings of
a melody I let them pass, and came back later to try to improve
what had been wrong. I blossomed. The occasional 'stroking' that
praise from my uncritical friends provided, rather than the
constant criticism I had experienced at home, increased my desire
to 'perform'.

For the first year that we were in Crowthorne I was billeted in
a small house with a family of rather modest means – in those days
it would be referred to as a 'working-class' family – Mr and Mrs
Benham, their two daughters, and Mrs Benham's old father. Mr
Benham drove lorries for the army, and his wife had been a nurse
at Broadmoor, the criminal asylum, just at the top of the road.

I got along with the family very well, except for Mrs Benham's father who was an evil-tempered chap. He had been in the army, and at some time played the clarinet in a part-time army band. He took an instant dislike to my middle-class style, and made it clear he considered me a 'Nancy-boy'. On one occasion he decided to search out his very ancient instrument, and insisted on displaying his ability. This had always been primitive; the passing of time and his age had reduced his performance to a ghastly series of squawks, squeaks, and gurgles. I was unable to respond with the enthusiasm that he no doubt anticipated. Naturally this did little to improve our relationship.

I suppose it was a measure of my enthusiasm for the clarinet that I got up early each morning to practise, from seven-thirty until eight o'clock – before breakfast. I used the 'front-room', normally reserved for special occasions such as christenings, deaths, and the like. In winter it was freezing cold. The only room that was warm was the kitchen, which was heated by a traditional range, on which they cooked as well. This was very different from my cosy middle-class home in Bedford Park, but the Benhams were kind, and somehow came to terms with this strange unruly lad they had had deposited on them. I was happy, and learned to know and appreciate a way of life I would otherwise never have experienced.

In the second year I had the opportunity to join two of my closest friends in what the school called a 'hostel'. This was one of the big houses in the village where the owner(s) still lived, but which was large enough to accommodate twenty or more boys, usually with some poor unfortunate master in charge. The hostel I was in had the charming name 'Pooks Hill', and an equally charming owner, Mrs Bryant, whose husband had been called up and was in the Royal Air Force. She was probably about thirty at the time, though like nearly everyone else who was not my own age, she seemed to me to be in the same age group as my parents. She was an amateur musician, played the piano, and was not too critical – she thought I played quite well.

Through her I learned the joy of playing chamber music. As well as accompanying me in some of the solo pieces I was vain enough to attempt, she invited a violinist, a violist, and a cellist to join her so that we could play the Mozart Clarinet Quintet. My own skills were limited, but compared to the string players, gentle and delightful ladies from good families around Crowthorne, I was a virtuoso. The first violin part was usually played on the piano, as the violinist had sufficient problems with the second violin part. The viola and cello parts were sketched in fairly adequately, if you were of an understanding and forgiving nature. Unfortunately the violist was inclined to be wayward – perhaps impatient – she tended to dislike staying on one note for more than a couple of beats, and would dash off on her own. We seldom played more than sixteen bars (often far fewer) without a stop, and every bar was flawed in some way or another. Yet I waited each week for Wednesday afternoon to come round again so that I could wallow in those wonderful sounds, and the thrill of making music with other people.

There were several events during this time that were of some importance for the future. From time to time the whole school was subjected to concerts of Good Music. They were not very popular, and were sometimes the occasion for fooling about – not always without good reason. I remember one time when a singer of distinction, but past her prime, came to give a song recital. The hall in which Assembly and concerts took place had rather grand doors that opened from the centre in two halves. Normally only one half of the doorway was used. The door was opened for our soloist to enter, and she made to do so. Unfortunately she was a lady of extremely ample proportions, and neither her full frontal, nor her sideways efforts to gain access to the hall were to any avail. Amidst some tittering and general merriment, and the discomfort of our visitor, the other half of the door was unlatched, and she sailed in.

Why it was thought that a song recital that would appeal to a limited and sophisticated audience should be suitable for boys aged between fourteen and eighteen, lacking any experience of classical music, remains a mystery. I do remember that I spent most of the concert with a handkerchief stuffed into my mouth, trying to suppress my giggles, and nearly bursting in the attempt. There were to be a number of occasions during my professional life when I was reduced to a similar condition.

Other concerts included the performance of a symphony by the 18th century composer William Boyce, the *Christmas Fantasia* by Vaughan Williams, referred to earlier, and my first solo effort – the slow movement from the Clarinet Concerto No.1 by Weber. The mis-fingered note I played in the middle of this attractive movement still haunts my memory. It was also at one of these concerts that I allowed myself to be persuaded to turn the pages for one of the two pianists, in a performance of *Scaramouche,* by Milhaud. This terrifying experience was so nerve-racking that I vowed – a vow I have kept – never to undertake that responsibility again.

But the most important experience for me took place one Sunday evening. The Music Society – or was it the Gramophone Society? – met at Mr Wilson's house each Sunday. There would be about fifteen or

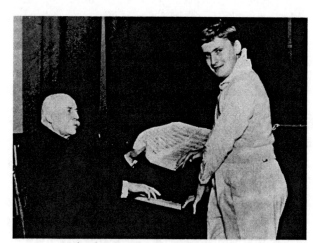

Yehudi Menuhin with Sir Edward Elgar.

twenty of us, to whom Mr Wilson would play music of his choice. This was still the era of then as now the 78 rpm. 12 inch record, requiring one to leap up and down every four minutes, to turn the record over, change the record or needle, and, on some machines, even wind it up – I think we had a radiogram, so that was not necessary. One Sunday he put on the Elgar Violin Concerto, the recording made by the fifteen-year-old Yehudi Menuhin. I was overwhelmed, as I am to this day, by this miraculous performance. Not because a performance of such remarkable dexterity was possible from a boy of that age, nor even because I was aware of the extraordinary musical maturity of someone so young. I was just captured by the sheer beauty of the music, and the feelings it aroused in me. I felt an intense desire to make music like that; to affect others, as I had been affected. At that moment my future was sealed.

4 *Starting Out*

*The BBC Symphony Orchestra in Bristol and Bedford. Small 'orchestras'
in restaurants – Lyons Corner Houses – Alfredo Campoli, Albert
Sammons, Max Jaffa. The Author at Royal College of Music.
Many musicians now in the armed forces provides author with opportunity
of professional experience that leads to full-time orchestra employment.*

In September 1941 I was standing at the top of the steps behind
the Royal Albert Hall facing the imposing but not unfriendly
facade of the Royal College of Music. I was full of hope,
confidence, and the ignorance of youth. I was to study clarinet
with Frederick Thurston, principal clarinet of the BBC Symphony
Orchestra and an established soloist. My second study was piano,
and for this Mr Harry Stubbs was to be my kindly but
unsuccessful guide. There were to be history lectures and theory
and aural training sessions, and also the opportunity to play in one
of the orchestras. As I set off down the steps and approached the
doors of the RCM I thought, 'This is it! I'm on my way.' I was
going in the direction I wanted to go, but, as always, I had no idea
of what or where it might lead.

Early that morning I had left Bedford, where the BBC
Symphony Orchestra had been moved and where my family were
now living, and travelled by train to St. Pancras station in London.
This was a journey I would do several times a week in the coming
year, an empty first-class compartment often providing an
impromptu practice studio. The LMS (as it then was) rolling stock
and uneven railway lines were no better than the current privatised
rail companies', making embouchure control (the subtle formation
of the lips and muscles around the mouthpiece) difficult. Still, it
was possible to make up for lost time, when scales or arpeggios had
received less attention than they needed.

The BBC Symphony Orchestra were now stationed in
Bedford, then a quiet and attractive county town. In 1939, very
soon after the outbreak of war, the orchestra had been evacuated to
Bristol. The BBC orchestras, resident in London before the war,

had all been relocated; the Symphony Orchestra, the Theatre Orchestra (later renamed the Opera Orchestra, and now called the Concert Orchestra), and the Variety and Revue Orchestras, (both disbanded many years ago), were all sent to Bristol. At that time, before the bombing had destroyed the oldest and loveliest part, Bristol was especially beautiful, and even now, in my view, it remains one of the most agreeable cities in Britain. Many years later it was, for a time, a very important city for me.

In their wisdom the BBC chose the CWS (Co-operative Wholesale Society) building as the headquarters for the Symphony Orchestra, and made the top floor into their studio. This had to be abandoned fairly soon as the frequent air-raid warnings required the conductor and orchestra to yo-yo up and down five or six floors, from the studio to the air-raid shelter in the basement. For the next year or so the orchestra used various churches for studio broadcasts, and the Colston Hall for their season of public concerts, before relocating to Bedford, where they remained until the end of the war. The old Hall was excellent with good acoustics. Later I played there many times with the London Philharmonic. It survived the bombing, but in February 1945 before the end of the war it was accidentally destroyed by fire, (as the original hall had been). In 1951 I played at the opening of the present Colston Hall, in a concert given by the Royal Philharmonic, conducted by Sir Thomas Beecham.

Playing in orchestral concerts in the Colston Hall, or anywhere else, still lay a few years ahead, though in fact it was to be much sooner than I could have imagined as I stood outside the Royal College of Music on that first day and daydreamed of things to come. A combination of circumstances beyond my control led to me remaining at the College for only one year. After two years of war a great many musicians had been called up and were in the Army, Navy, or Air Force. A number of them had joined or been posted to line regimental Military Bands, or the various entertainment units formed to entertain the troops. Many of the best younger wind players, had joined Guards' Bands and the RAF Central Band, all stationed in London. In fact the RAF Central Band attracted a number of outstanding string players, too. It was their absence that gave me the opportunity in 1942 to join the Wessex Philharmonic Orchestra, based in Bournemouth.

As well as the musicians in the Bournemouth Municipal Orchestra there were a number of other musicians working in Bournemouth. In most English towns of any size at that time there were still musicians playing in theatres, music halls and in restaurants. It was the custom, one that finally died out around 1950, for the larger restaurants and cafes, serving the 'carriage trade', to have a small 'orchestra'. It was also usual for most large Department Stores to have a restaurant with its own small 'orchestra'. The number of musicians would usually be between two and five, depending on the size of the restaurant.

Joseph Lyons, whose world famous Corner Houses in London were the flagships of his vast empire of Tea Shops throughout the country, employed 500 musicians on a full-time basis – as many as the BBC in its heyday employed on contract. In some of the Lyons Corner House orchestras there were as many as twelve players, and perhaps a singer as well. These orchestras played a very large and varied repertoire, ranging from Novelty numbers, such as *The Teddy Bears' Picnic*, and *The March of the Little Tin Soldiers*, to selections from popular ballets – *Coppélia, Swan Lake,* or *The Dance of the Hours*, and operas – *Pagliacci, La Bohème, Rigoletto*, and even *Rienzi*. The *Slavonic Dances* by Dvorak, *Hungarian Dances* by Brahms, and some of the shorter Classics by Haydn, Mozart, Beethoven and Schubert rubbed shoulders with selections from *The Merry Widow*, *The Student Prince,* and *Chu Chin Chow*.

When I was a child, my mother would occasionally take me on a shopping expedition to the 'West End' of London. I hated these visits. My especial hate was Oxford Street where I trudged along, down amongst a forest of legs, seeing nothing, and with no one to talk to. My mother and her friend would be chattering away and enjoying the shop windows way above my head – with only Mummy's hand to assure me that I was not totally abandoned. There was one redeeming feature to these dreadful visits: at some point we would leave the horrors of the pavement to enter what seemed like an enchanted palace. It was brightly lit and everything sparkled; there were great columns from the floor to the high ceiling, with golden decoration, and the walls and floor were richly coloured. Wherever you looked there were counters laden with foodstuffs of every kind. There were boxes of chocolate and sweets, cakes of every size and description – piles of little cakes covered in 'hundreds and thousands', or with cherries on top;

birthday cakes and wedding cakes like castles. Piles of buns, rolls, croissants, macaroons, biscuits large and small, loose or in decorated tins and packets, all inviting and tempting. There were counters with every sort of delicatessen – less inviting to me – with fancy bottles, tins, and packets of roll mops, anchovies, caviar, tongues, hams, exotic oils and sweetmeats. The display seemed never ending.

This was one of Mr Joe Lyons's famous Corner Houses. We usually went to the one in Tottenham Court Road. As in all the Corner Houses there were several restaurants of different sizes in the same building, each with its own orchestra. We went to the one that served afternoon tea because it was there that my Uncle Jimmy conducted and led one of the orchestras, as his father had done years before on the pleasure boats on the Black Sea.

A smartly dressed man or lady (one can hardly refer to someone so grand as a 'woman'), would direct us to our table. We always asked for one near the band, so that we could see and hear Uncle Jimmy – no doubt there will have been some who asked to be as far from the band as possible! – though on the whole, people went to a Lyons Corner House because it was special; not only did you get excellent food, you were waited on with style and civility, and you had musical entertainment as well, and all at a modest price.

Uncle Jimmy was considered to be good-looking, and as was the custom 'played to the ladies', directing some sweet and charming melody in their direction. The orchestra's efforts would generally be rewarded by discreet and genteel applause. On the one or two occasions when my father accompanied us, he was always determined that the band should receive greater recognition. He would clap with considerable vigour; some of those enjoying their tea and seated nearby would be startled; others, thinking something was going on that they should be part of would join in. After several items the applause had grown considerably and by the time we left it was tumultuous.

During each 'set' the conductor/leader would be expected to play a couple of solos, though each and every piece was, to all intents and purposes, a 'concerto', since the leader played the first violin part on his own a very great deal of the time. But that wasn't enough. He (it was almost always a 'he', though there were some

Ladies Orchestras), would play one of the charming pieces by Fritz Kreisler, the great violinist, or one of the popular encore pieces – *Meditation* from *Thais*, by Massenet, or perhaps *The Flight of the Bumble-Bee*. In the best groups, if he was a really good player, he might include a movement from a concerto; perhaps by Max Bruch, the Mendelssohn, or one by Wieniawski.

```
         LONDON'S NEWEST
      And, in every way, most attractive Hotel.
         HOT AND COLD WATER,
           CENTRAL HEATING,
            AND TELEPHONE
     IN EVERY ONE OF THE 150 BED ROOMS.
     FIRST-CLASS RESTAURANT AND GRILL.
         Orchestra under the direction of
              TSCHAIKOV.
     Bed rooms from 10s. 6d., with breakfast, 12s. 6d.
       Inclusive Terms from one guinea per day.
            HOWARD HOTEL,
       NORFOLK-STREET, STRAND, W.C.2.
     Telephone, Central 3242 (Extensions to all rooms).
```

Sometimes a restaurant or hotel would advertise its orchestra, as an attraction. This advert comes from the 27th April 1926 issue of the Times when my father's elder brother Anton and his orchestra were at the Howard Hotel in the centre of London.

Some outstanding violinists played in restaurants and cafes: de Groot, Albert Sandler, Alfredo Campoli (who subsequently had a long and distinguished solo career), Max Jaffa, and Albert Sammons, who was probably the best of them all. Later he was to become Beecham's first leader, before becoming a very successful and popular soloist. I remember his performance of the Elgar and Mendelssohn Concertos with particular pleasure, from my earliest days in the orchestra. He was also highly respected as a teacher, and is fondly remembered as a professor at the Royal College of Music.

In 1939, when the war started, virtually all the seaside orchestras were disbanded. Even the Bournemouth Municipal Orchestra with its long history and considerable reputation, which unlike the other seaside orchestras employed musicians throughout the year, was forced to severely reduce its numbers. The players who had been made redundant by the Municipal Orchestra quickly formed a rehearsal orchestra, so as to keep in practice. They invited some of the best musicians who were playing in the theatres and the restaurant and cafe orchestras in the town and a few of the local instrumental teachers to join them. Two ladies living in Bournemouth heard about this group and decided to provide the money for them to put on a concert and appointed a young conductor, Reginald Goodall, to be its Music Director. They named the orchestra The Wessex Philharmonic. The extra players that were required were mostly recruited from students who were in their final year at the Royal College and Royal Academy of Music.

Many years later Goodall found fame conducting at the English National Opera and the Royal Opera House. His interpretations of the Wagner operas in particular were much admired. He was knighted in 1986. In 1939, when the Wessex Philharmonic Orchestra (later called the Bournemouth Philharmonic Orchestra) was formed, he was inexperienced, profoundly musical, and technically maladroit, as far as his control of the baton was concerned. He became increasingly experienced, and developed into a remarkable musician. Only his stick technique did not improve.

Whilst still in my first year at the Royal College of Music I heard about this orchestra from one of my fellow students, a composer/pianist, who also played percussion in the College orchestra. He told me that he had been to Bournemouth to play in this orchestra, and that it rehearsed on Friday evening, had two more rehearsals on Saturday, and a rehearsal and concert on Sunday. Sometimes this concert was repeated in a nearby town on Monday. And you got paid! Not Musicians' Union rates – about which I knew nothing – but it sounded like a king's ransom to me.

Without giving any thought to my suitability, I asked my friend, 'Do you think there is any chance that I could play in this orchestra?' 'I'll ask Mr Goodall,' he said, 'he comes into College from time to time.' Some weeks later my friend told me that he had spoken to Mr Goodall who had said he would be willing to hear me play and that I should prepare some music and be ready to play for an audition in about ten days' time.

I was so keen to do this entirely on my own that I decided not to tell my father or my RCM Professor, Jack Thurston (he was always called Jack by his friends and colleagues, though his name was Frederick). The relationship between Thurston and my father – both principal clarinettists in the BBC Symphony Orchestra –

had caused some tension in my College lessons. My father's remarkable virtuosity, especially his ability to play fast staccato passages (involving the rapid tonguing of detached notes) was envied by Thurston, and Thurston's senior position as 'First' principal in the section was resented by my father. Sometimes, when I wanted help with a technical problem Thurston would say, 'ask your Dad – he's the one with the technique!' When I asked 'Dad' he'd say, 'You're having lessons with Mr Thurston, ask him.' So, though my teacher had sufficient confidence in me to allow me to teach his daughter, I never had the sort of confidential relationship with him that I tried to achieve with my own pupils.

On the day of the audition I was very nervous. I remember going into the room where Mr Goodall was sitting at the piano. I had expected a very assured and authoritarian person. In fact, he asked rather diffidently for the piano part of the music I was going to play, which gave me a bit of courage. I had decided to play the *Four Characteristic Pieces* by William Hurlstone. They are quite short attractive pieces by a gifted composer, now forgotten, who died when he was only thirty. I enjoyed playing them, and they had the added advantage of not being too difficult. I have no recollection of how well or badly I performed as I had no idea of the standard that was required. It must have been adequate because a month or so later I was asked to go to Bournemouth to play in the Wessex for one weekend. Fantastic! The second clarinettist had been called up, and Goodall, hard pressed to find anyone at short notice, thought I might get by.

Once the initial joy and surprise had evaporated, terror set in. My only experience until then had been to play in my school orchestra, plus a few rehearsals and concerts in the amateur Bedford Symphony Orchestra and two terms in the College orchestra. Awareness of my ignorance and incompetence gradually grew as the date of the first rehearsal approached. It dawned on me that though I had listened to a lot of music, I had only played a handful of works. I had no experience of even the standard repertoire, the Mozart, Beethoven, Dvorak, and Tchaikovsky symphonies were still virgin territory, and I still had no real understanding of what skills and knowledge were required if I was to become even an adequate orchestral musician.

The repertoire I had played in the College orchestra was very small, and not particularly useful. I had played the Overture *Euryanthe* by Weber, which I think I only played once or twice again during the next thirty-five years or so, and a violin concerto by Sir George Dyson, who was Director of the RCM at that time. He is now remembered for his choral work *The Canterbury Pilgrims* which is still played occasionally. Sir George seemed a rather stern man to me then. I knew he had invented some piece of equipment that improved the machine-gun of his day. But he proved to be kind. When, a couple of years later, a corrupt management tried to treat me badly he was very helpful. Willie Reed, who usually conducted the orchestra, played his violin concerto. Reed was no conductor, but he had been the leader of the London Symphony Orchestra for many years, and had a profound knowledge and experience of everything to do with the orchestra. When Sir Edward Elgar was composing his wonderful violin concerto, which had so inspired me when I was still a schoolboy, it was to Willie Reed that he had gone for advice on the technical aspects of the solo part.

The only works we played that I can recall as being useful to me in later years were the César Franck Symphony, a Piano Concerto by Mozart, and the *Water Music* by Handel, in the version re-scored by Hamilton Harty, which was always used until the 1980s. The advances of the 'authenticity' movement have, for the present, banished this version and other re-scorings to memory and older recordings. The only conductor of note for whom I had played until then, Leslie Heward, conducted the *Water Music*. He was highly respected in the music world and it was thought that he might join Beecham and Barbirolli as another British conductor with the imagination and charisma to raise an orchestra above itself. I certainly enjoyed the couple of rehearsals we had with him. Unfortunately he died too young for his promise to be realised.

At last the great day arrived when my effrontery would be put to the test. I set off by train for Bournemouth, excited and anxious, with my instruments, and a suitcase full of second-hand clothes. I had had to buy a dress suit, a 'dark' suit (for afternoon concerts), white shirts, a bow tie, and some black shoes and socks. If they had not been second-hand I would have used up the family's ration of clothing coupons for a year or so. A couple of years later, when I had become more worldly-wise, I would resort, as so many others did, to the black market, and buy additional clothing coupons.

When I arrived at the rehearsal venue I made my way to the second clarinet chair and looked at the music. I had arrived early so that I could try through some of the more difficult-looking passages in my part. If you don't know the music – whether the *Allegros* will be fast, or the *Andantes* slow, or which passages are important and which are not – you can find that you have prepared the music at the wrong speed and wasted time practising those passages that are completely covered by the brass. The trumpets and trombones will be blowing away like mad – whilst you have ignored what will prove to be exposed and unexpectedly difficult passages. It takes quite a while before one gets the 'feel' of what is really important and what is not, when looking at a piece of music for the first time.

The other members of the orchestra gradually arrived and took their places and I was comforted to see one or two faces that I recognised from College. But there was still no sign of Mr James Brown, who was to play principal clarinet. I knew his name because he had been the principal clarinet in the BBC Empire Orchestra until it was suspended (never to be revived) shortly after the outbreak of war in 1939. It was never certain whether this orchestra, which broadcast to the furthest reaches of the Empire, usually in the middle of the night (it was all 'live' broadcasting in those days), had been set up to instil a love of Western European music in the hearts and minds of our then Colonial cousins, or whether Sir John Reith, the BBC Director General and a strict disciplinarian, believed it would serve to keep some of the unruly citizens of our far-flung Empire under control.

The musicians who had been employed under contract by the BBC, but whose services were not required because of wartime circumstances, could have whatever they earned elsewhere made up to something like their previous BBC salary, as long as it was considered to be work of national importance. James Brown had found employment as a postman. Only a few minutes before the rehearsal was to begin the news filtered through to me that Mr Brown was not going to attend that evening's rehearsal. It seems that he had decided that The Royal Mail required his services more than the Wessex. Though it is so long ago, I recall that we rehearsed *Valse Triste* by Sibelius and a Beethoven Symphony.

I was therefore asked to move up to play the first clarinet part. Fear and delight struggled for supremacy in my ambitious breast. Throughout the rehearsal inexperience and incompetence vied with youthful, naive musicality. My egotism undoubtedly led me to believe that everything I had to play was as important to the performance as it was to me. It often comes as a surprise, when listening to a piece of music one has played many times, to find how little of one's efforts are actually heard. Sometimes something more important is going on! – as the double bass player in the Paris Opera Orchestra of many years ago discovered. Whilst convalescing from an illness he thought he would go to the opera, something he had not done since he was a student. The night he went they were doing Bizet's *Carmen*. After the performance he met a few of his colleagues from the bass section.

'How did you enjoy the show?' one of them asked him. 'It was terrific! Do you know,' he said, 'when we are playing tu-te-tum-te all the time, there is a marvellous tune going on, Tum-tum-ti-tum-tum- tum-ti-tum-ti-tum!' (the Toreador's song).

At that first rehearsal my efforts would not have borne close scrutiny, but I suppose the general standard was such that I got away with it. Sufficiently, anyway, to be invited back again for subsequent weekends.

I had not told either my professor or my father that I had auditioned for Reginald Goodall because, from the moment that I decided I wanted to be a professional musician, I was worried that I would never achieve anything without people saying it was because of my father's influence. I was so obsessed by this fear that I was determined to do something without any help from anyone. I was also aware that the family finances were not in too good a shape, and that keeping me at College, even though I had gained a small scholarship, was an added strain on their resources.

Having survived several weekends at Bournemouth I thought it was now time to tell them my good news. In fact neither of them was at all pleased, even though the outcome had been favourable. I was too young, not ready yet, and, anyway, why had I not consulted them? – I was only just seventeen and had no right to go off and do whatever I liked. I was self-willed, undisciplined ... and

... and ... And it was all true! But though I understood what they were saying was intended for my good, I knew that what I was doing was right for me.

The weekend concerts the Wessex gave in Bournemouth and elsewhere attracted good audiences and were well received. This encouraged the management to embark on a more ambitious project, a month's tour of some of the towns and cities of southern England. It was to start in the last week in July, during the College vacation, and I was invited to join the orchestra as second clarinet. I accepted with enthusiasm, unaware that this was to be the start of my professional life, and that I would not return to the Royal College of Music for another twenty years.

5 The Joys of Touring

The pleasure and hazards of touring with London orchestras and the pre-war BBC Symphony Orchestra. The Wessex Philharmonic Orchestra touring in war-time – its musicians, conductors (a young Reginald Goodall), soloists and repertoire. Experience in this orchestra leads to many distinguished careers. Author leaves to join London Philharmonic Orchestra.

'My boy, you've never really lived till you've been on tour.', comments a character in Smetana's lovely opera *The Bartered Bride*. Well, it can be enjoyable – in small doses! Whether it's really living is another matter. I set off for that month's tour in the summer of 1942 in high spirits. I was very young and everything was set fair for a good time; we were going to visit places which sounded interesting; there were girls in the orchestra and above all I would be playing nearly every day, and getting paid for it.

Going away on tour in wartime in the Wessex Philharmonic Orchestra under an inexperienced semi-professional management was something very special indeed. No tour I was to undertake for the rest of my life compared with this first venture into nomadic life. For one thing it lasted longer than any other tour by a British symphony orchestra that I have heard of – I left after nine months and the tour went on for quite a while after that.

Nonetheless, going on tour is always a special experience. Over the next thirty-eight years I went on a good number of tours with the London orchestras, under a variety of conditions, sometimes very good, at other times much less so. I certainly had the opportunity to visit many places that I would never have seen if I had not been a musician. But though one can hold friends and relatives entranced with tales of travel to exotic places such as Mexico, Japan, or Uruguay, and tours of the USA, Israel, and throughout Europe, the reality of these visits is frequently less exciting.

The best tours, those that I have nearly always enjoyed, involved going to only one town or city; a visit to Vienna, Lucerne, or Tokyo, when one stays for perhaps three or four days, or even for a week or two, can often be quite delightful. Then there are tours when one goes to a large city, say New York, where one plays several concerts and then the orchestra makes a few forays to nearby towns, somewhere between seventy-five and a hundred and fifty miles away, returning to base after the concert each night. These, too, can be very pleasant, if well organised.

Least agreeable, most tiring, and sometimes unbearable, are 'one-night stands' – especially if they go on for more than four or five days. Such tours involve setting out each morning and travelling by train, or, more usually during my touring days, by coach. There was more often than not an early start; sometimes as early as six-thirty or seven o'clock. The worst I can remember was leaving Barcelona at four-thirty a.m. More often one left between eight and nine-thirty. However, there were a number of hitches that often had to be overcome before a successful departure was accomplished.

There was the problem of getting the suitcases of a hundred or more musicians onto the coaches. There were two methods, neither of which was wholly satisfactory. One was to leave it to the musicians to make their own way to the coach, with their cases and instruments. The large instruments – the cellos, basses, tuba, etc., were left at the hall, and were put on the orchestra's van by the orchestral porters, along with the music stands, music, and percussion instruments. With a group of thirty-five or forty players this method can work reasonably well, but with a large orchestra it is a recipe for disaster.

In the big hotels, the bedrooms are on many floors – certainly on seven or eight, and in the USA, Japan and a good many European Hotels, possibly on as many as twenty or more. As might be expected, nearly everyone left it until the last moment to take his or her case to the coach. Sometimes one or more of the lifts would be out of order. Those whose rooms were on the upper floors got angry, because the lifts never seemed to come up to them; meanwhile those on the lower floors became increasingly indignant as they saw lifts whizzing past to the floors above. When a lift did at last stop at their landing, twenty people, all carrying large cases, tried to force their way into a lift intended for no more than fifteen – without cases. This is not conducive to goodwill, or to the harmony that will lead to a happy and contented group of musicians able to give of their best at the end of what is often a long and tiring journey. An even more serious risk was that carrying a heavy case and fighting one's way in and out of lifts could lead to injuries to arms and hands.

For some years another system was also used; more sensible on the face of it, but not by any means foolproof. This method required everyone to put their case outside their room, as a rule about an hour before departure time. The first snag was that not everyone received their 'wake-up' call – some may have omitted to ask for it; others may have fallen asleep again. So their cases will not have been collected and taken to the coaches.

The next hurdle to be negotiated was breakfast. Hotels are as a rule not geared up to deal with a large number of guests all demanding service at about the same time, especially between seven and eight-thirty a.m. There will usually be one or two sleepy waiters who, when they have been goaded into action, find that their colleagues in the kitchen go berserk if more than three or four pots of coffee are ordered at once. Even five-star hotels can fail when required to serve eighty or so croissants and coffees quickly. Indeed, they have sometimes been known to run out of croissants. For one reason or another some members of the orchestra still remain only partially served, or not served at all, by the time decreed for the coaches to leave. Not surprisingly they are unhappy; on occasion they let their feelings be known rather forcibly to the hotel staff who, already harassed and discontented by the demands being made of them, sometimes respond in kind. Not a good start to the day. A few minutes before the coaches are due to leave, the personnel manager goes to each coach (there were generally three with a large orchestra) to take a roll-call. It can be a disaster if on arrival at the next town some essential player is found to have been left behind. Tchaikovsky's Fifth Symphony minus one trombone or the *New World* Symphony without the cor anglais can sound rather bare in places.

Not infrequently one or more of the company could have enjoyed the 'strong waters' after the concert the previous evening. On tours overseas the alcoholic beverages available can be strange and quite often very agreeable. Their effect can be devastating. It can and does happen that one of the previous evening's revellers is still abed, or struggling to dress and pack, when he or she should be sitting quietly in the coach. The personnel manager goes off in search of the miscreants. When they appear, stumbling along with their suitcases and instruments, bleary and unshaven, or without make-up, or with it too hastily applied, they are greeted with mildly benevolent jeering, mixed with some obscene expletives if this is already the fifth or sixth day on the road.

I remember my father telling me about some of the incidents that occurred when the BBC Symphony Orchestra went on a grand tour of Europe in 1936. It was still a major event for a British orchestra to visit Berlin, Paris, Vienna, and Prague and the BBC had arranged everything with great care. Sir Adrian Boult and the Orchestra were received with ceremony everywhere they went. There were receptions and speeches and the players in the resident orchestra and those in the BBC Symphony would meet and exchange experiences. After the reception groups of players would go off to continue their reminiscing in the bars and taverns frequented by the local players.

In Prague, one distinguished cellist was so overcome by the hospitality offered by his companions that the following morning he had to be carried to the railway station. He arrived, still in full evening dress, laid out like a corpse on his cello case, with four of his colleagues acting as impromptu pallbearers.

On Tour in Wartime

This was a far cry from my first experience of touring with the Wessex Philharmonic Orchestra, which was a much less sophisticated affair. There were no five-star, or even one-star hotels; no reserved carriages on the trains, nor personnel managers. It was all pretty much catch-as-catch-can, relying a good deal of the time on a 'wing and a prayer'. We travelled mostly by train, quite often requiring a number of changes, with long waits on unfriendly station platforms. When the weather was warm it was not too bad, but during the winter, with the rain, snow and cold winds, it became increasingly unpleasant.

The biggest problem was finding 'digs'. In 1942 nearly every town still had its own theatre, or music hall, to which touring theatrical companies would come each week. Accommodation for the artists was provided by landladies, who ran 'theatrical digs'. Pre-1939 very few actors, or music-hall artists, including the most famous and prestigious names, would stay in hotels. The theatrical landladies understood the needs of their visitors, who would want a good meal after the show, and a late breakfast, at ten or ten-thirty in the morning. In the best digs artists were well cared for, and their particular likes and dislikes remembered; younger members of the profession would be mothered, and, if necessary, offered practical advice in times of trouble. Landladies took great pride in those who had stayed with them, and evidence of their success was displayed on their sitting room walls by signed photographs from their more famous and grateful visitors.

Of course, not all were so good, by any means. The worst could be dreadful. Dirty and unkempt, with indifferently cooked food, a lack of hot water – vital on tour with washing to be done. The very best landladies would even undertake this task for their most favoured 'gentlemen' visitors. Worst of all were those where the rooms were cold in winter. Everyone with any experience tried to avoid these torture-chambers. The best places would always be booked well ahead and landladies who knew that they were much sought after would be selective. Artists of distinction, and those with charm, would flatter their hosts, provide them with free seats at the show they were in, bring a bunch of flowers at the end of the week, and write complimentary remarks in the visitors' book. These guests would be assured of good, comfortable accommodation on their next visit to that town.

Our problem was that we stayed in each town for only one night, and all these places took weekly bookings. In addition, we didn't know where accommodation was to be found. One got off the train in a strange town with a largish case and one's instrument and just didn't know where to begin. It was especially bad at the start of the tour because we didn't know the ropes. As time went by and we returned to a town for a second or third time it became easier. One would write off beforehand, rather than look for somewhere on the day.

In Reading, where we stayed for a week giving concerts each evening in the theatre, I stayed with Mrs Perry, a tiny, elderly lady, who in her small house in Zinzan Street provided the best accommodation I can remember. There were four of us; Jack Greenstone, the leader of the orchestra, and Alfie Friedlander, a violist and one of the most amusing men I have met, had one double bedroom. I shared the other room with my friend Dennis Wood, then an oboist but later principal viola in the BBC Radio Orchestra. The four of us also had a sitting room to ourselves in which Mrs Perry served our meals. Although there was food rationing, she seemed to have a special relationship with her butcher. We had bacon and eggs each morning for breakfast, meat every day, and, on one occasion, steak – a real luxury at that time. For this she charged each of us £1.00, for the rooms, and an extra seven and sixpence each (37$^1/_2$p) for the food – she totalled up what it cost and would not allow us to pay her anything for preparing and cooking it. Of course, £1.37$^1/_2$ went a very great deal further in 1943 than it would today, but even so it was incredibly good value.

Unfortunately we never went to Reading again. We did go to Swansea, where my friend Dennis and I searched for seven hours for somewhere to rest our weary heads. In despair we were obliged to accept accommodation of a very different kind to Mrs Perry's. On the many occasions I have returned to Swansea to play in Brangwyn Hall, with its wonderfully exciting (though strangely undervalued) murals by Sir Frank Brangwyn, I have always found somewhere reasonable to stay. But never anywhere to match Mrs Perry. Sadly her like have virtually disappeared.

Playing in the Wessex Philharmonic Orchestra

When we set off in July, Jimmy Brown, (the BBC Empire Orchestra clarinettist, now Bournemouth postman) was the principal clarinet, but when, because of good audiences, the management decided to continue beyond the original month's tour, he decided not to stay on. The Post Office had already extended his holiday leave, so that he could do the month's tour. The fees the Wessex could offer did not compare with his Post Office salary, which the BBC made up so that it equalled his previous salary in the Empire Orchestra, and so he returned to Bournemouth.

No doubt working on the principle that the devil you know is better than the one you do not, the management let me take over as principal clarinet. I write 'let' rather than 'invited' as I do not recall that this decision was taken with any enthusiasm, which is hardly surprising. What I could play I think I probably played in a musical and attractive way. There was a good deal that I found technically difficult, and, of course, my inexperience was such that I made mistakes. It is too long ago to evaluate with any accuracy what it must all have sounded like.

The level of ability of the players in the orchestra varied considerably. There were some excellent players, who went on to distinguished careers: Henry Datyner, a Polish violinist and an excellent musician, came to England when the Germans advanced into Poland. The only work he could get when he arrived was playing the piano in London nightclubs. After playing in the Wessex he went on to become leader of the Liverpool Philharmonic and a few years later of the London Philharmonic Orchestra. Stuart Knussen, father of Oliver Knussen, the composer/conductor, was an outstanding double bass player and, later, principal double bass, and a feared Chairman, of the London Symphony Orchestra. For a time Alfred Barker, a former leader of the Hallé Orchestra, led the orchestra, before going on to become leader of the BBC Theatre Orchestra. A number of others, like Jack Greenstone and Alfred Friedlander, flourished in the highly paid light music session world, playing for recordings, broadcasts, TV, and films.

For many, playing in the Wessex Philharmonic Orchestra was to be the start of what would be a long and successful career in one of the BBC Orchestras or in a London or Regional symphony orchestra. For others it led to a very successful freelance career. But a number, for whom only wartime conditions had provided the opportunity to play in a symphony orchestra for a short time, drifted into teaching supplemented by the occasional semi-pro engagement. In many ways conditions for musicians are now much better than at the time about which I am writing – touring, in particular, is now usually much better organised. But the opportunities to learn one's craft in relatively less stressful conditions than in a major orchestra have gone.

In the past there were a considerable number of 'characters': colleagues in the orchestra, conductors, and solo artists. Today everyone is so serious, concerned that they may not be engaged again if they don't conform. Now that the 'music business' has replaced the music profession there is no room for the oddball who can be wonderful on Tuesday and rather less good on Friday. Recording demands consistency; neither for conductors nor members of the orchestra is there room for the improvisory freedom of expression that can make a public performance so exciting.

The bassoonist in the Wessex, Albert Entwhistle, was a marvellous 'character'. He was a decent player, in a quiet, undemonstrative way; what used to be called a 'nice little player'. Some years later, when Entwhistle was second bassoon in the Hallé Orchestra, he was required to step up to play principal in place of his colleague who had been taken ill. During the rehearsal, when there was a solo that required the bassoon to take on the role of a musical clown, Sir Malcolm Sargent, who was the orchestra's guest conductor on this occasion, said, 'Come along Mr Entwhistle. You really must make that passage sound much more amusing.' So Albert roared it out in a rather raucous style that caused some laughter. 'No. No. No. Mr Entwhistle. That will not do at all', said Sir Malcolm, with some asperity. 'Well' replies Albert, in a pronounced Lancastrian accent, 'You asked for it fooney, so I plays it fooney.'

Our repertoire was limited by the size of the orchestra. We usually had eight, sometimes ten first violins, and the appropriate number of second violins, violas, cellos, and double basses; two each of flutes, oboes, clarinets, and bassoons; four horns, though we sometimes had to manage with only two, two trumpets, three trombones, and tuba; a timpanist, and one percussionist. Very occasionally an extra percussionist would be engaged, but as a rule the one player, with a little help from the timpanist, seemed to manage what now calls for five or more players. No doubt some of the parts will have been left out, though these chaps achieved miracles with a stick in one hand and a tambourine in the other, hitting out in all directions. The percussionists of today would certainly not be willing, or be allowed by Musicians' Union (MU) rules, to do anything like that.

This was the normal practice in the theatre, music hall and many small orchestras that played on the bandstands at seaside resorts, in the parks and elsewhere, and in the large number of light orchestras and ensembles that broadcast regularly until about the 1960s. It was usual in these bands and little orchestras for there only to be one flute, two clarinets, sometimes an oboe, but very seldom a bassoon, instead of the necessary two of each. There would be one or two trumpets and a trombone when two trumpets, three trombones and tuba had been requested by the composer. The missing woodwind and brass parts would be 'cued' into other player's parts. Whenever there were bars rest or a part of more importance than in that player's part, notes from another part would be printed in smaller notation so that they could be played if required. Any other missing instrumental parts or harmonies would be played by the pianist. Nearly all the well-known orchestral repertoire – overtures, suites, symphonies, opera and ballet selections – had been 'boiled down' by Emile Tavan. Though his name is not to be found in the dictionaries and encyclopaedias of music, his arrangements were played world-wide and enabled ensembles of all sizes, from only 5 or 6 players to small orchestras of 30 or more, to bring a wide repertoire of music to the general public.

Even in the symphony orchestras it was quite common until the 50s for extra woodwind, brass or percussion parts to be omitted and for the few really important notes to be put in by one of the other players. Very frequently when three flutes were called for – two flutes and piccolo – the second flute would play whichever part, second flute or piccolo, was most important.

Sir Malcolm Sargent was a dab hand at 'boiling down'. Delius, who frequently wrote for triple wind, would appear in Sargent's version, with only two required in each woodwind section. If essential to the harmony, the missing part was inserted into one of the other player's part, perhaps a 3rd oboe part being played by one of the clarinettists. The amateur choral societies that engaged Sargent were naturally delighted by his reduced scoring; they could include items in their programme that would otherwise be too costly. Always a favourite with the ladies of the chorus, on these occasions the society's treasurer and finance committees were equally pleased with him. On occasion, when he conducted the major orchestras he would also try to get away with using his own reduced parts, but as the years went by the players objected more and more vociferously, until he reluctantly gave way and used the proper printed parts.

Although Reginald Goodall was the principal conductor we had many guest conductors. Dr Malcolm Sargent, as he was then, was one of the most celebrated. An extremely efficient conductor,

Anatole Fistoulari who conducted the major orchestras, also worked with us frequently. He had been principal conductor with the Monte Carlo Ballet for some years, before he settled in Britain. A charming, quiet man, he always succeeded in getting a good performance at the concert, though his rehearsals could be boring. He had little to say, and seemed content to play through the music, allowing the players to become familiar with it. If you already knew the music pretty well this could become tedious. He had good rhythm and a clear beat, and these qualities, combined with an innate musical feeling for a limited repertoire, produced very good results. Perhaps because he was amiable (he was always referred to as Fisti), spoke softly with a foreign accent, and used some rather idiosyncratic phrases, there was a tendency to laugh at him, and not take him seriously enough.

I enjoyed playing for Fisti, as I have for all conductors who gave me the space to play with some freedom of expression. He indulged my liking, especially when I was young, for making *ritardandos* at the end of phrases, even when the composer did not indicate one. One piece we frequently played with him was the Overture *The Italian Girl in Algiers* by Rossini. In the slow introduction there is a short solo for the clarinet, at the end of which I always made a *ritardando*. A few months later on one of my visits home I was talking to my father about some of the conductors that I had played for and mentioned Fistoulari. 'Oh, Yes!', said my father, 'He conducted us recently. He's quite good. But, do you know, in *The Italian Girl in Algiers* – in the slow introduction, at the end of that little solo – he made me make the most dreadful *ritardando*. Goodness knows where he got that idea from.' I felt it best to leave my father in ignorance of from whom, or where, he had picked up this bad habit.

Charles Hambourg was a very different sort of conductor. He made up for not being very good by being extremely pleasant to work with – sadly, lack of ability is not always accompanied by an agreeable personality. He was quite wealthy (the source was believed to come from manufacturing shoes) and had a passion for music, but little talent for conducting. Later, when I was in the LPO, colleagues told me that the orchestra had done a four or five day tour with him. Each concert had commenced with the Overture to *The Bartered Bride* by Smetana. This is a well-known disaster area for conductors. The Overture, which is in a fast tempo, starts with a silent beat: the conductor has to bring the baton down in silence in the tempo at which the piece is to continue, the first notes sounding a moment or to two later. Poor Charles just couldn't manage this at all, and his efforts became less successful at each succeeding concert. At the last concert of the tour he made such a determined and violent attempt to get it right that he fell off the rostrum into the viola section. In the interval, I was told, he went round to all the members of the orchestra, apologising and distributing £1 notes (a reasonable amount in those days).

Even some of the very finest conductors find the 'silent beat' difficult. George Alexandra, who was for many years principal bassoon in the London Philharmonic Orchestra (LPO), told me of an experience he had had shortly after joining the LPO as second bassoon. The orchestra was giving a concert in Bristol Cathedral, a lovely building, but disadvantaged, as far as concert giving is concerned, by being extremely resonant. Sir Thomas Beecham was conducting a programme that commenced with one of these problematic works. Fairly near the beginning there were a number of loud chords interspersed with 'silent' bars, which are marked by the conductor bringing the baton down gently in rhythm. On this occasion Sir Thomas brought the stick down in one of the silent bars with one of his extremely vigorous downbeats. George, being young and inexperienced, followed Sir Thomas's beat, and played the low note in his part *fortissimo* – and all on his own. The rest of the orchestra had realised that Tommy had made a mistake and remained silent. The loud, low bassoon note rang out and reverberated round and round the Cathedral, much to George's consternation and distress. In the interval he went to see Beecham to apologise. 'Don't worry, my boy. Thank God you came in – I might have broken my arm if you hadn't.'

The most devastating chaos resulting from an unsatisfactory silent beat that I can recall occurred in the Royal Albert Hall. The conductor, a charming and refined musician, who broadcast from time to time with a chamber orchestra he had formed, engaging some of the best players in London. The then first flute of the Royal Philharmonic Orchestra (RPO), Gerald Jackson, was one of them. After having undertaken a number of broadcasts under this conductor's direction, and since he was Chairman of the RPO's orchestral committee at the time, he recommended to the management that Mr B ... might perhaps be given the opportunity to conduct the RPO.

At the first rehearsal Mr B. was introduced as 'An Artist and a Gentleman'. No doubt this was true. What was not announced was the fact that he was also a rather poor conductor. This became evident very soon. In fact almost immediately he started to rehearse *Manfred* Overture by Schumann. The overture begins with a bar requiring four quick beats in a fast tempo. The first beat is silent. Several attempts at starting the overture did not inspire confidence that the concert was likely to begin well.

At the concert Mr B. came onto the platform, took his bow, turned to the orchestra, looked round, giving everyone the benefit of his tremendously toothy smile, and swiftly brought the baton down. There was no upbeat and the movement of the baton then or subsequently gave no indication of the tempo. The sound of 85 musicians playing very loudly at 85 different speeds, even for a short time, is to be avoided. Fortunately, after the first bar there is a pause, when it was possible for the orchestra to regroup itself, before proceeding into calmer waters at a slower and more dignified pace. For some years to come the phrase 'An Artist and a Gentleman' was a Royal Philharmonic Orchestra euphemism for someone seriously lacking in ability.

Reginald Goodall continued to be the Wessex orchestra's most frequent conductor. He had joined Oswald Mosley's Fascist party before the war and he and his wife had made themselves unpopular by distributing pamphlets for their chosen cause. He had intense admiration for German culture in general and German music in particular. He had studied in Germany, and been very influenced by Wilhelm Furtwängler, whose readings of Beethoven and Wagner he greatly admired. He was a very serious musician of considerable integrity, and I learned a lot from him, especially in the classical repertoire. But at that time he was not a very agreeable man. He never appeared satisfied with anything he conducted, quite often returning only once to take a bow, even when the audience showed evident approval and continued to applaud. He also seemed unable to show any pleasure or positive response however hard the orchestra tried to satisfy his wishes.

It must have been about thirty years later that I played for him again. One of the clarinettists in the Royal Opera House Orchestra had fallen ill and I had been called in at the last moment to replace him in a performance of *Die Meistersinger* by Wagner. Goodall had established a considerable reputation as a conductor of Wagner's operas and was enjoying some celebrity, after many years of obscurity. As a result he had become far more benign. *Die Meistersinger* is a very long opera; with Goodall's propensity for slow tempi it became a very long opera indeed.

Composers have written some of their most inspired works for solo piano, solo violin, and solo cello, with orchestral accompaniment. I soon realised that one of the pleasures of playing in an orchestra is the opportunity of performing with outstanding instrumental soloists, and comparing, and enjoying, each artist's interpretation. In general the standard of the soloists and singers who came to play or sing with the Wessex was well above that of the conductors. This continued to be the case all through my professional life. I suppose there are many more good instrumentalists and singers than conductors.

Two fine violinists, Albert Sammons and Eda Kersey, were outstanding; I particularly remember performances of the Mendelssohn and Max Bruch Concertos. Later, in the LPO, I enjoyed playing a number of other concertos with them.

Then, as now, piano concertos were the most frequent solo items in our programmes. The Tchaikovsky First Piano Concerto, the Beethoven Concertos Nos. 3, 4, and 5 – No.5 especially – Rakhmaninov's Second Piano Concerto, the Grieg Concerto, and the *Warsaw Concerto* were the most popular. The last of these has virtually disappeared, though during the war and for a the next few years it was immensely popular. Every orchestra included it in their programmes – it was a 'must' on Saturday nights – and it could also be heard in a variety of arrangements. Written by Richard Addinsell for the film *Dangerous Moonlight* in 1941, he expanded it later into a very short, romantic, one movement concerto, in a style sometimes called 'film-Rakhmaninov'. It was most often played by Eileen Joyce. I wonder how many times she must have played it? I recall a great many performances, first with the Wessex, and then with the LPO and she will also have played it many more times elsewhere. She was a good pianist, very popular, and marketed extremely well, something practically unheard of then. She usually played one piece in the first half of the programme, the Grieg, or Rach. 2 (the musicians' abbreviation), and the *Warsaw Concerto* in the second half. She always wore a different coloured dress in each half. They were usually frilly and had an inviting décolletage. They gave her a film-starry glamour and that somehow spurious sexiness that seemed to be the style of the 'forties'.

Cyril Smith dazzled us with his virtuosity – our own British Horowitz, we thought then – though it was rather brittle and lacking in warmth. Moura Lympany delighted us with her brilliance and charm, and Moiseiwitsch, though no longer in his prime technically, brought musical insight and beauty of tone to everything he played. Here was an artist one never tired of hearing.

Music and playing the clarinet remained my overriding preoccupation though I was not unaware of members of the opposite sex. During the nine months I was on tour with the Wessex I had formed an attachment with the young lady who was the principal oboist. She had also been at the Royal College of Music, but as she was several years older than I was, and in her final year when I arrived at College, we had only met once or twice at College orchestra rehearsals. Amongst many other attractive qualities she had red hair, and wore a vivid green fake-fur coat, a combination that I found both dramatic and irresistible. Later she became my wife, and together we produced two splendid daughters.

She was far more worldly-wise and informed than I was. Indeed, I hardly knew what day of the week it was, being preoccupied with playing the clarinet. I knew nothing of the Musicians' Union; indeed, I had only a vague idea of its existence. I certainly did not know that if I wanted to be a professional musician I needed to join, because members of the Union – and all professional musicians were members – were not allowed to play with non-members. She took me up to the London Branch Office, nominated me, and saw to it that I paid my first year's subscription.

Having made sure that I was now persona grata as far as the profession was concerned, she suggested that I should try for another, better job. After nearly nine months 'on the road' I had become rather dissatisfied with the continual touring, and some of the less satisfactory performances we gave. But I had no idea of what else might be available, and I didn't think I was really good enough for anything much better. On my own initiative I would not have considered taking the step she now initiated. She said I must write to the London Philharmonic Orchestra. She dictated what I should write, and she saw that I sent it off. In due course I received a reply asking me to arrange an appointment to meet Mr Haines, the Assistant Secretary, at the LPO offices in Welbeck Street. When I met him, to my great surprise, he asked if I would be free to play with the LPO for three weeks as second clarinet, starting on the 9th of May. Of course, I did make myself available, and thereby took another step forward; a step that was to shape the rest of my life.

6 The London Philharmonic Orchestra

History from 1932 until 1939 when it was obliged to go into voluntary liquidation. The orchestra reforms and is administered by the players themselves. J. B. Priestley, Jack Hylton, Sir Henry Wood.
Life in a self-managed orchestra. 1944, Sir Thomas returns to his old orchestra. He leaves and in 1946 forms the Royal Philharmonic Orchestra. 1947 the author follows.

When the war started, in 1939, everyone in the London Philharmonic Orchestra felt very insecure; would the concerts and recordings already booked, or planned, take place? Some of the players were already expressing doubts as to whether the shaky financial basis upon which the orchestra was founded could possibly survive. In fact it was not long before London Philharmonic Ltd. was obliged to call the creditors to a Liquidation meeting.

The Company had been founded by Sir Thomas Beecham in 1932, with himself as Artistic Director, and with a number of well-born and wealthy music lovers as co-directors. At the meeting it was left to Sir Thomas to explain that there was no money at all, and therefore no one would get any. He used his famed eloquence and charm to impart this disagreeable information, and somehow succeeded in soothing and placating his audience. The players in the orchestra, all of whom were owed money for unpaid fees, made no opposition to the voluntary liquidation of the company; their main concern was to keep the orchestra in being.

Almost at once the musicians decided to form a new company, with themselves as shareholders. Sir Thomas gave his blessing, the company was created and named Musical Culture Limited. A Board of Directors was elected and staff engaged to administer the affairs of the orchestra. Charles Gregory, a very fine player who had been Beecham's principal horn for some years, was elected Chairman of the Board. He was held in considerable respect, and, as I was to learn for myself a few years later, he was a man of imagination and integrity. Thomas Russell, one of the viola players, also elected to the Board, became their Secretary and

Business Manager. The orchestra then set about looking for engagements.

In 1940, after undertaking a few concerts, Sir Thomas left for the USA, leaving the members of the orchestra to take full responsibility for the administration and artistic control of the newly re-formed London Philharmonic Orchestra. The full story of this remarkable achievement is contained in two books by Thomas Russell, *Philharmonic* and *Philharmonic Decade,* essential reading for anyone interested in the development of orchestral music in Britain.

Because of his stirring wartime broadcasts J.B.Priestley, the famous author of *The Good Companions* and of many successful novels and plays, had become a household name. After a chance meeting with Tom Russell he became concerned about the difficulties the orchestra was facing and decided that something needed to be done to rally support for it. He suggested that a concert be put on that would attract a prestigious audience, and which could be used to generate funds from the general public. It should be called 'A Musical Manifesto'. Sir Adrian Boult, Basil Cameron and Dr Malcolm Sargent (he did not become Sir Malcolm until 1947) readily agreed to conduct one item each, and Eileen Joyce was willing to play the Grieg Piano Concerto.

On the night of 8th July 1940, the Queen's Hall was full, which was unusual at that early stage of the war, before everyone had become accustomed to the blackout. The programme for this auspicious occasion was: Elgar's *Cockaigne Overture,* conducted by Sir Adrian Boult, Eileen Joyce played the Grieg Piano Concerto, with Basil Cameron conducting and, after the interval, Dr Sargent conducted the Second Symphony by Sibelius. The concert started with Priestley making one of his most effective speeches, a mixture of homespun philosophy and good Yorkshire hard-nosed practicality; this was his Musical Manifesto. It was well received by the capacity audience, and widely reported by the press. In the next few weeks thousands of donations were received, ranging from postal orders for a few shillings to very substantial cheques. This was the turning point for the orchestra, putting it (for the time being) in a relatively strong financial position.

Priestley's speech and part of the performance of *Cockaigne* Overture are re-enacted in a film the orchestra made in 1941, called *Battle for Music*. It was quite widely shown at the time and is still occasionally shown on TV. The film tells of the trials and tribulations the LPO and the members of the orchestra experienced in the early years of the war and how they triumphed in the face of adversity. Some of the musicians, in particular members of the Board, 'act' their role in this story with varying degrees of success. As well as Priestley, Dr Malcolm Sargent, Sir Adrian Boult and Jack Hylton also have 'acting' roles.

QUEEN'S HALL - LANGHAM PLACE
(Sole Lessees - Messrs. Chappell & Co., Ltd.)

Thursday, July 18th, 1940, at 8.15 p.m.

MUSICAL CULTURE LIMITED
presents

A
MUSICAL MANIFESTO
Speaker:
J. B. PRIESTLEY

THE LONDON PHILHARMONIC ORCHESTRA

Conductors:
SIR ADRIAN BOULT
BASIL CAMERON
DR. MALCOLM SARGENT

Solo Pianoforte:
EILEEN JOYCE

Programme and Notes price 6d.

Programme cover for the concert suggested by J. B. Priestley.

Battle for Music is not up to Hollywood standards, but it fulfilled its purpose at the time and remains an interesting and entertaining historical document. Such shortcomings as it has are outweighed by the honesty of its intent and the excellence of the performances of the music, conducted by Dr Sargent, Constant Lambert, and Warwick Braithwaite, with Eileen Joyce and Moiseiwitsch as soloists.

The film ends on a high note. Superimposed over newsreel footage of Sir Winston Churchill inspecting the troops, to the accompaniment of *Land of Hope and Glory*, are the following words:

An Orchestra is like a country. It has its triumphs, its disasters and despairs. Only with unity and faith can it become great.

The London Philharmonic Orchestra has these qualities. These musicians played on during the darkest days and blazed the trail for other fine orchestras.

They showed how musicians themselves can organise their own lives and their own art. This spirit, which inspired this orchestra to struggle against adversity, to adapt their lives courageously to changing conditions, cannot be defeated.

The London Philharmonic becomes the treasured possession of the British people.

Further support for the orchestra came from a most surprising quarter. Jack Hylton, formerly a famous dance-band leader, was now an impresario, with interests in the theatre world. He undertook to present the LPO for a week at a time in a number of large theatres all over the country. These theatres usually presented either Music Hall (later to be known as Variety), or companies touring successful musical comedies, following their West End run.

Hylton saw to it that the concerts were well advertised, and took especial care over the presentation of the orchestra. He had a rostrum built, that could be assembled in every theatre the orchestra visited, with sides and a ceiling, so that all the sound did not get lost up in the 'flies', making it much better acoustically than orchestral performances on theatre stages usually are. The whole presentation was rather more attractive than in many of the conventional venues in which concerts were given.

Each week there was a concert every evening and one on Wednesday and Saturday afternoons as well. These concerts were extremely successful, playing to full houses virtually the whole time. A great many of those attending the concerts had never seen or heard a full symphony orchestra before. Their enthusiasm for this new experience was heart-warming.

When I had accepted Mr Haines's offer of a three weeks' engagement with the LPO I had no idea of what I was letting myself in for. Perhaps this was fortunate; fools rush in where angels fear to tread.

My first engagement with the LPO was at the Royal Albert Hall on Sunday, the 9th of May 1943. There was a rehearsal at 10.00, and a concert at 2.30. George Weldon (I had played for him before in the Wessex) conducted a mainly Tchaikovsky programme that included the ever popular 1st Piano Concerto, and the *Theme and Variations* from the Suite in G.

Within the first few minutes I realised that this was something very different to anything I had experienced before. The quality of the string tone was much better, and the range of dynamics throughout the orchestra far greater – *ppp* really did mean very softly, and because of the number of string players and the volume of tone they produced, *fff* was very, very loud. To be playing in the Royal Albert Hall! I had only been there previously to attend Prom concerts when I was still a student, and now to be in this exalted company! The few important solo passages went reasonably well, so I left at the end of the concert on quite a 'high'.

Early on Monday morning we set off for what for me was to be the first of three of these 'Hylton' weeks. We travelled to Norwich by train; in the afternoon there was a rehearsal and at 7.30 a concert. This was followed by seven more concerts that week, each with a different programme. With that number of concerts there was no time for even one rehearsal for each performance, but as the orchestra had played the works many times, in most cases with these same conductors, and as they were very good players anyway, the results were quite satisfactory. For me the situation was rather different; all but a handful of the pieces we played were unknown to me.

Those pieces that were rehearsed were usually just 'topped and tailed', and only the tricky passages played through, giving a novice, such as I was, only a rough idea of the whole work. If one does not know the music and the conductor's beat is at all unclear (by no means an infrequent event), it can be difficult to know whether they are beating two or four beats to the bar; or know what they are doing at the end of a pause, or at a 'cut-off', when there is a sudden silence in the music. It is all too easy to find that you are the only one left playing when everyone else has stopped, or, worse still, you have come in loudly all on your own – that, for some strange reason, is called a 'domino'. This can be amusing to one's colleagues, especially if it is a particularly high or low note, or results in a terrible strangulated sound, as the player seeks to suppress the unwanted intrusion. It is never anything but the source of acute embarrassment to the player. The pieces that went unrehearsed I had to sight-read at the concert. Skating on thin ice is a less hazardous undertaking! Dazed and exhausted I got to the end of the week, the adrenaline pumping hard.

On Saturday evening, after the second concert that day, we returned to London, arriving back in the early hours of the morning. Sunday morning dawned much too early for me; at 10.00 we were rehearsing again in the Royal Albert Hall (RAH) for the concert that afternoon.

Monday morning found us on the train again, this time bound for Northampton, where we had another week with eight concerts. I found the second week a little easier; I had played a good deal of the music once. But occasionally overconfidence and tiredness led to mistakes; I also had more time to contemplate how much I needed to learn, if I was to match the accomplishment of my colleagues. At the end of the week, back to London again arriving late on Saturday night with only a few hours before another rehearsal and concert in the RAH – and more new music to learn. The next morning we were off again, this time to Newcastle for a repeat of the previous two weeks. I now started to worry whether I would be offered any more work with the orchestra, or if this would prove to be just a

NEW THEATRE

NORTHAMPTON

Week commencing MONDAY, MAY 17th, 1943.

MUSICAL CULTURE LIMITED

presents

THE

LONDON PHILHARMONIC ORCHESTRA

(Leader: JEAN POUGNET)

Conducted by

WARWICK BRAITHWAITE
(Monday)

DR. HEATHCOTE STATHAM   **EDRIC CUNDELL**
(Tuesday)   (Wednesday and Thursday)

CONSTANT LAMBERT
(Friday and Saturday)

Solo Pianoforte:

SIDNEY HARRISON   **REIZENSTEIN**
(Monday)   (Tuesday)

MARGARET MADDISON   **IRENE KOHLER**
(Thursday)   (Friday and Saturday)

Solo Violin: **JEAN POUGNET**

NIGHTLY at 6.30 p.m.
MATINEES—THURS. & SAT. at 2.30 p.m.

Vail & Co., London, E.C.1   For Programmes see over

Northampton leaflet.

flash in the pan. I didn't feel too confident about what I was doing, but at least I now knew what page I was on – most of the time.

REPERTOIRE

(subject to alteration).

MONDAY EVENING.

Overture : Carneval	*Dvorak*
Elegiac Melodies	*Grieg*
Boabdil	*Moskowski*
Hungarian Rhapsody No. 2	*Liszt*
Piano Concerto	*Grieg*
Capriccio Italien	*Tchaikovsky*

TUESDAY EVENING.

Grand March from " Aida "	*Verdi*
Haffner Symphony	*Mozart*
Chant sans paroles	*Tchaikovsky*
Gopak	*Moussorgsky*
Dance of the Tumblers	*Rimsky-Korsakov*
Emperor Concerto (No. 5, in E flat)	*Beethoven*
Hungarian March	*Berlioz*

WEDNESDAY MATINEE.

Overture : Beatrice and Benedict	*Berlioz*
Suite : Jeux d'Enfants (Children's Games)	*Bizet*
Walk to the Paradise Garden	*Delius*
Finale from Symphony No. 2	*Tchaikovsky*
Piano Solos	*Chopin*
Trumpet Voluntary	*Purcell-Clarke-Wood*
Enigma Variations	*Elgar*

WEDNESDAY EVENING.

Overture : Russlan and Ludmilla	*Glinka*
Symphony No. 7 in A	*Beethoven*
Piano Concerto No. 2 in C minor	*Rachmaninoff*
La Calinda	*Delius*
Habanera	*Chabrier*
Capriccio Espagnol	*Rimsky-Korsakov*

THURSDAY EVENING.

Overture : Egmont	*Beethoven*
Symphony No. 5 in E minor	*Tchaikovsky*
Violin Concerto in G minor	*Bruch*
Irmelin	*Delius*
Overture : Tannhauser	*Wagner*

FRIDAY EVENING.

Slavonic March	*Tchaikovsky*
Ballet : Swan Lake	*Tchaikovsky*
Piano Concerto No. 1 in B flat minor	*Tchaikovsky*
Symphony No. 4 in F minor	*Tchaikovsky*

SATURDAY MATINEE.

Overture : The Mastersingers	*Wagner*
Symphony No. 6 in B minor (" Pathetic ")	*Tchaikovsky*
Waltz from " The Sleeping Beauty "	*Tchaikovsky*
Warsaw Concerto	*Addinsell*
Romeo and Juliet	*Tchaikovsky*

SATURDAY EVENING.

Overture : Merry Wives of Windsor	*Nicolai*
Andante Cantabile	*Tchaikovsky*
Hungarian Fantasia for Piano and Orchestra	*Liszt*
Vitava (Moldau)	*Smetana*
Piano Solos	
Suite : Carmen	*Bizet*
L'Apres Midi d'un Faune	*Debussy*
Overture : 1812	*Tchaikovsky*

Our repertoire, popular with audiences in 1943, remains popular more than 60 years later (see chapter 25. 'The concerts promoted by Raymond Gubbay).

On Friday, as I was leaving the stage at the end of the concert, Charlie Gregory, the Chairman of the Orchestra, stopped me, and said, 'Can you spare a moment? I'd like to have a word with you.' My heart sank and, as usual, I feared the worst. 'They've had enough', I thought. When I heard Gregory say 'How would you like to join the orchestra, as our second clarinet?' the gates of Heaven opened, and I heard the sound of the Great Trumpets! 'Oh! Yes, that would be wonderful! Thank you.' That was one of the best moments of my life. I could hardly believe my ears, or really take in the tremendous opportunity I was being given.

Sir Henry Wood (a photograph he signed for me in 1943).

As usual we returned to London on Saturday evening. On Sunday, 30th May 1943, we had another concert in the RAH. It was also my eighteenth birthday, and I was in luck – it was a very special concert – Sir Henry Wood conducted, and the soloist was the very fine pianist, Solomon, a truly great artist. This was the first time I played for Sir Henry, though I had heard my father speak about him many times. In fact I always felt that my father was rather pleased with his impersonation he liked to give of Sir Henry. Since my father retained his Russian accent all his life even though he came to Britain as a young boy, and Sir Henry spoke with a slightly Edwardian/Cockney accent, the impression he gave of Sir Henry was none too accurate.

Sir Henry belonged to the 'no-nonsense' school of conducting. There was nothing flamboyant, or showy, about his style. He used a longish, rather thick baton, and gave a good clear beat. He concentrated on getting a precise performance with firm rhythm, clean attack and ensemble, and good orchestral discipline. His performances did not enthral you, but pleased with their honesty and straightforward musicality. 'Timber', as he was known affectionately in the profession, had a passion for establishing good habits. He used to stand at the entrance to the platform at the Queen's Hall, with a tuning fork, which he struck as each player went past him. The musician would then play his 'A' (the note the whole orchestra tunes to, usually sounded by the oboe). I am told that he was never heard to say 'flat', but that quite frequently he would say, in his rather nasal voice, 'shaaarp!'

He believed that a three-hour rehearsal should last three hours – there was no attempt to get the goodwill of the orchestra by finishing early, a device employed by some conductors. He had a very large watch, which he used to put on his music stand. If he had completed the music to be rehearsed by ten minutes to one, he would start at a place that allowed him to continue until one o'clock. Keeping a careful eye on his watch, he would stop exactly at one o'clock, whether this made good sense musically or not.

He also liked his musicians to mark in their music any instructions he gave them. My father had a congenital dislike for writing anything in the part that would remind him, or anyone else using that part in the future, of any changes, additions or corrections that had been made, preferring to rely on his memory. Noting a lack of activity, when my father should have been busily inserting some instruction, Sir Henry said, 'Mr Tschaikov! Remember! – a bad pencil is better than a good memory'.

That concert on my 18th birthday, conducted by Sir Henry Wood, was the beginning of the most exciting and important period of my life. At that age with my background I might have expected to go to university, except that I had not acquired the academic qualifications required, nor the desire to acquire them. Instead, between 1943 and 1947 the LPO served as my university. Here I not only received a wonderful musical education playing for some of the finest conductors from the pre-1939 war years, alongside first-class musicians, but also a schooling that provided a unique foundation course in living, for which I have been grateful all my life.

In May 1945, at the cessation of hostilities in Europe, there were still only three London orchestras: the London Symphony, the London Philharmonic, and the BBC Symphony Orchestras. The BBC Symphony Orchestra did not return to London until September 1945 and the London Symphony Orchestra was at a rather low ebb, financially and artistically. The LPO with its dynamic and imaginative management was able to take the lead in bringing back to London's musical life the international element that had been missing during the war years. Tom Russell, with admirable foresight, had already booked some outstanding conductors and soloists prior to the end of the war. We were off to a flying start and for the next few years a number of very fine artists who had not played in Britain since before the war were engaged by the LPO.

For a very young musician, such as I was then, the opportunity to work and associate with musicians like Sir Thomas Beecham, Bruno Walter, Eduard van Beinum, Victor de Sabata, Jaques Thibaud, Heifetz, Francescatti, Fournier, Gendron – the list is endless – was incredible.

Playing in the LPO as well as being extremely enjoyable and rewarding musically was for me a profoundly enriching learning experience. The structure of the LPO at that time led to everyone being involved to a far greater extent than is normal. Nearly everyone took part in the quite frequent orchestral meetings at which important decisions on what course of action the orchestra should take were discussed. Naturally, the members of an orchestra will come from a great variety of backgrounds, educationally, socially and economically and hold very different political views.

Age plays little part in the position that a musician may hold within his section so that an outstanding and exciting young violinist may become the leader of the orchestra when he or she is still only in their early or mid-twenties, whilst players sitting at the rear of the section may have had thirty or more years experience. The principal flautist, who has played with the finest conductors for a lifetime, may be sitting next to a brilliant young principal oboist just out of conservatoire. While this is always accepted as far as musical ability is concerned, when it came to the discussions at meetings the 'young' and the 'old' – roughly those over and under forty – opposed each other fairly regularly. It was rather more serious when there was a difference of opinion between those with very strongly held but opposing political points of view. On these occasions age would play no part. The older and younger players would join together in line with their political convictions.

This greater involvement in the affairs and running of the orchestra revealed all these differences of background, age and opinion quite starkly and increased the stress, frustration and the highs and lows that are a normal part of a musician's life. As a result the virtues and failings in one's own character, and those of one's colleagues, could be on display for all to see. The pull of personal ambition versus responsibility to the group, the courage to take an unpopular stand, and not run for cover when a decision one had supported turned out to have been mistaken, had to be faced.

I saw all those qualities and faults of character that I was to meet throughout my life, and see at first hand the effect virtues and vices had on our communal life. One witnessed courage and determination contrasted with cowardice, duplicity and betrayal; tolerance, kindness and sensitivity, as well as bigotry and a brutal disregard for the feelings of others. Sometimes hard decisions had to be made. Loyalty and friendship were tested. One did not always come up to the mark in one's own estimation, and, worse still, one failed the test of the good opinion of one's fellows.

Feelings can run pretty high in an orchestra and sometimes lead to bitter disputes between colleagues so that players obliged to sit next to one another within a section may not be on speaking terms for a while – possibly for years. Yet, even when dislike is so great that messages or instructions have to be passed through a third party, musicians will play together with a sweetness and unanimity that suggests that they are lovers.

For most of the 1940s the LPO was generally thought of as a 'left-wing' orchestra, largely because its members had elected Thomas Russell and Charles Gregory, both Communists, to the Board of Directors. With Tom Russell as the Business Manager (later General Manager) and Charlie Gregory as Chairman of the Board of Directors, their influence was indeed considerable.

As a very young man I was attracted by the idealism and intellectual vigour of both these men, especially Gregory, and also by other Communists in the orchestra, who were fine players and set an example I wanted to emulate.

In view of the immense changes that have taken place in Eastern Europe it is worth recalling that this was wartime, and that the Soviet Union was our ally. Uncle Joe, the now despised and rejected Joseph Stalin, was a popular figure. Throughout the world, and especially in Europe and the USA, a considerable number of the most outstanding creative and performing artists had joined the Communist Party. In 1944 I did so too. But following a 'party line' of any kind is not something for which I think I am suited and I proved to be a difficult, recalcitrant and rather short-lived member.

It is not surprising that the LPO was not too popular with the old-guard arts hierarchy. Perhaps, even more than the spectre of a 'red' orchestra in its midst, the knowledge that the members of the orchestra alone were responsible for its management decisions and successful artistic policy sent shivers down the spine of those who felt that musicians who play instruments should stick to doing just that, and leave management and artistic decisions to their betters (who don't dirty their hands with violas, trumpets, or the like). Sadly, this same attitude can still be heard today from some of the backwoodsmen amongst our critics and administrators.

Tom Russell had both flair and insight; and he had the energy and drive to achieve his objectives. As an administrator he lacked the patience for the humdrum chores of everyday office routine; he was more concerned with ideas, and when those around him in the office did not check carefully there could be quite serious mistakes. I have always found it ironic that the LPO dismissed Russell, many years later, not for any mistakes he had made or any lack of ability, but because he went to China for his holiday! But this did not stop the Orchestra from taking advantage of Russell's visit, and the contacts he had made. They were the first British orchestra to tour China.

Towards the end of 1944, several weeks before the Annual General Meeting I received the notice and the audited accounts. It was the first time I had ever seen accounts and so they were a complete mystery to me. I assumed that everyone else would understand them, so I decided to take professional advice. I phoned the chap who looked after my income tax returns (my only contact with the world of finance) and he agreed to have a look at the accounts with me. Like many accountants he was a serious man, and as he examined the LPO accounts his face assumed an even more serious expression. It seems that there were a number of entries that in his view required questioning. His advice was that I should not under any circumstances agree to the accounts before I had received satisfactory answers to the questions he told me I should ask.

I expected that at the AGM the older and more experienced members of the orchestra would be leaping to their feet and peppering Tom Russell with questions about the balance sheet. But there wasn't a murmur from anyone. Always willing to rush in when caution might be wiser, I thought I might as well put in my pennyworth. I stood up and asked a couple of questions. Consternation! Mr Haines, the Assistant Secretary, was dispatched to seek further information. On his return one or two more searching questions caused increasing discomposure, until, after his third attempt to find evidence to silence this unwanted flow of questions, Tom Russell decided to throw himself on the mercy of the meeting. It seems there was really nothing to worry about; the cause of the apparent inconsistencies was a move by the accounts department from the basement to the second floor. In the process one or two of the books had been mislaid, nonetheless he could assure the meeting there was absolutely nothing to worry about. After a short discussion he asked for a vote of confidence, which he received, though not without some dissent. The democratic process has always appealed to me as the cut and thrust of debate is natural to my temperament. The LPO provided the ideal environment in which it could flourish.

Though the orchestra's artistic policy was splendid, inattention to detail had led to a decline in our financial position. On a previous occasion, before I joined the orchestra, the players had had to make sacrifices to keep the orchestra afloat. It looked as if this might occur again. At one meeting this question was the subject of considerable concern. Various solutions were put forward: we should play programmes that did not require the engagement of costly extra players, especially when we played in smaller halls on tour; we should engage conductors whose fees were relatively modest. These suggestions so infuriated one of the members that he stood up and declaimed in a very loud voice, his face red with indignation, 'We must never make artistic concessions. We should take Maestro de Sabata to every fishing village in Britain.' This piece of high-flown rhetoric referred to the remarkable Italian conductor, Victor de Sabata, who conducted the orchestra frequently at that time. Unfortunately Maestro de Sabata liked programmes that included works for a large orchestra, requiring additional wind and percussion players and extra rehearsals, making his visits extremely costly.

This suggestion seemed so absurd to me that I felt it was time to put forward a solution. Tom Russell had a fairly large staff, some thought too large, and had attracted a number of interesting, valuable and worthy people around him. Each time I went to the LPO offices in Welbeck Street it seemed that their number had grown. With tongue firmly in cheek I said, 'I think I have the answer to our difficulties.' All heads turned towards me. 'Why don't we increase the office staff to forty, and send a trio on tour? That way we could balance the books!' My suggestion met with a variety of responses. Some of my colleagues smiled, a few laughed; others looked incredulous; several appeared to be about to have an apoplectic fit. I learned that it is dangerous, when one is young, to address one's elders and betters in this way. My performance in the orchestra was listened to with increasingly critical ears. And fault was found – because, of course, fault there was. But I weathered the storm, and remained unrepentant.

When in 1944 Sir Thomas Beecham returned to his old orchestra he found that it was now managing itself very successfully. After a year or so his need to be able to be in charge of everything to do with the orchestra made it increasingly difficult for him to work together with the orchestra's elected management. Reluctantly the orchestra and Sir Thomas parted company. By 1946 he had formed the Royal Philharmonic Orchestra (RPO) and in 1947 I left the LPO and started playing in his new orchestra.

This was a step into a very different environment. Now I was not one of a group of musicians making decisions about their own future. In the RPO I no longer had any part in the management. However, there were benefits: I was paid considerably more, I was playing in an even better orchestra with some of the most outstanding woodwind players at that time. And above all I would be playing a great deal of the time with one of the greatest conductors. The following years were to be probably the happiest of my musical life.

7 *Sir Thomas Beecham*

The Beecham Wind Orchestra – a unique wind ensemble. Memories and anecdotes from musicians who played for him, including my father (from 1912 onwards) and myself (from 1944 until his last concert in 1960). His rehearsal methods, repertoire and influence on all who played for him. Playing for him at concerts, on recordings, film and TV. His last concert.

The first really great musician that I worked with was Sir Thomas Beecham. This was a quite wonderful experience and a source of great pleasure that I was to enjoy for the following sixteen years – for a year or so in the LPO and then, from 1947, in the Royal Philharmonic Orchestra.

Those of us who made music under Sir Thomas's direction were extremely fortunate, because he was a conductor of a particularly unusual, indeed unique, kind. There have, of course, been a number of outstanding and a few 'great' conductors – artists who inspired performances that reached the heart of the music, bringing it to life and inspiring players and audiences alike. But, having played for nearly all the most renowned conductors between 1943 and 1980 and worked with many, in a different capacity, for a further ten years, no one else has seemed to me to have had the remarkable qualities Beecham possessed.

Though I did not play for Beecham until 1944,

Sir Thomas Beecham (a photograph he signed for me in 1945).

the wonderful records he made with the London Philharmonic Orchestra, between 1932 and 1939, were known to me. His leading players – Reginald Kell, Leon Goosens, Anthony Pini and David McCallum, had become my boyhood heroes. One always heard the solos so clearly and the players seemed to have such freedom of expression and an opportunity to be creative. I was to learn later, from personal experience, that when playing for Sir Thomas one never had to fight one's way through a barrage of strings 'scraping away regardless', as Sir Henry Wood used to call it, when playing a soft, delicate solo passage.

Beecham formed the LPO in 1932 and from the start he and the orchestra were a great success. The audience at the first concert was stunned and excited by the verve and virtuosity of the performance of the very first item *Carnaval Romain Overture* by Berlioz. It was also the first piece Beecham conducted when he returned to the LPO exactly 12 years later. It was to remain one of Beecham's favourite works.

I first heard about Sir Thomas from my father. He had played for Beecham in the short-lived, but adventurous Beecham Wind Orchestra in 1912. Later he played for Sir Thomas, several times, in various orchestras. As a child I remember him speaking of these occasions with enthusiasm.

The Beecham Wind Orchestra, in contrast to a military band, is of historical interest in that it predated the rise of the wind bands of the 1950s by some 40 years. The Wind Orchestra's first concert (I believe the Orchestra only gave three concerts) took place in St. Helens, Thomas Beecham's (as he then was) home

Programme cover for the first concert of the short-lived Beecham Wind orchestra.

town. It was billed as 'The Mayor's Invitation Concert', and was probably funded by Beecham's wealthy father.

The programme notes for this occasion, first printed in the *Daily Telegraph,* included the following information: *Mr Thomas Beecham, convinced that wind-instrument playing in this country is – and has for some time past been – steadily deteriorating, has founded a new wind orchestra, primarily with the view of raising the standard of wind playing and opening a new field to composers and executants. The formation of the orchestra is the practical outcome of several years study of (i) the possibilities generally of wind-instrument music; and (ii) the condition of wind-instrument playing in the British Isles.*

Mr Beecham maintains that with the improvement of the manufacture of most wind instruments and the invention of several others of great beauty, which are still unfamiliar to the average player, there is a field for new development both in the practical reorganisation and theoretical treatment of wind combinations. It must, therefore, be made quite clear that this body of players is not in the least what is generally known as a brass or military band; it is essentially a wind orchestra. Whereas in the brass or military bands of the Grenadier Guards, the Coldstream Guards, etc., the proportion of brass to woodwind is in the approximate ratio of two to one, in the Beecham Wind Orchestra the proportion is reversed to one to two. It is hardly necessary to point out that this preponderance of a woodwind quality of sound alters the entire nature of the combination, and justifies the description of it as a 'wind orchestra'.

There were 52 musicians and as on the orchestra list it included a number of instruments not usually found in a military band: cor anglais, heckelphone (or bass oboe), 2 corni di bassetto (or basset horns), contra bassoons (the 2 bassoons have been omitted from the list, though they are mentioned elsewhere), bass trumpet, and, rather surprisingly, celeste.

The programme has the mixture of classical and entertainment music one would expect to find in a programme of that date. H.F. Willemson, who had worked as a copyist and also scored for Brahms, specially arranged the Wagner overture. I think he did a number of other arrangements for the band and these, plus a great deal more music and a wonderful collection of Beecham's personal belongings, are housed in the Sir Thomas Beecham Archive.

Listening to some of the Music Preserved Oral History recordings that have been made since 1987, it has been interesting to hear the views of some of the players who had played with Beecham during the 1930s, when he was much younger than I ever knew him.

Richard Walton, his principal trumpet, in both the LPO and RPO, recalled that 'he had authority – and he used that authority. He could be quite a tartar. It had to be really good.' 'He always implied a lyrical line – I'm sure both the orchestras, the LPO and the RPO, had this from Beecham – the importance of a beautiful, lyrical line.' Leo Birnbaum, one of the violas, remembers the excitement of working with Tommy, 'He was one of those few rare conductors who could really get better playing out of us than other conductors. At the first rehearsal Tommy would conduct the whole work, straight through. He'd get excited and we'd get excited, too. At the end we'd all cheer. I think that sometimes these rehearsals were even more exciting to us than the actual performance. Even after the last rehearsal he'd use a blue pencil to put in what we call *hairpins* – crescendos and diminuendos – he was always marking and re-marking nuances.'

Playing for Tommy that 'beautiful lyrical line' gave me continual pleasure and the changed 'blue pencil marks' always gave one new insight into the music.

In 1946 Sir Thomas formed The Royal Philharmonic Orchestra and in 1947 I joined that orchestra, at the same time as Jack Brymer, Terence MacDonagh and Gwydion Brooke. When I was reviving old memories with Jack and remembering some of the works we had played many times with Tommy, I recalled how different his rehearsal methods were from other conductors. Jack Brymer responded with his own recollections, 'His rehearsals were more a matter of familiarisation than anything else – you hadn't the faintest idea what the old man wanted, really, because he didn't put it into words. But when you got to the performance you looked at him, you looked at those eyes and the whole body, and the gestures, and you knew what he wanted, because this was real conducting, the art of gesture. I remember one day, Beecham had just returned from America, and he said, "Let's see what we can do with this little bit of music" and we played the First Cuckoo [*On Hearing the First Cuckoo in Spring*], by Delius. If you listen to that recording – fantastic – it is affection in music.' And indeed it was. He had such a great influence on all those who had the privilege of making music with him that it has always seemed to me that I could tell, from their playing, those musicians who had played for Tommy. Whatever their own individual ability, their playing was infused with some special element of imagination, whomever they were playing for.

However many times you played a piece – perhaps Mozart Symphony No. 39, which I must have played dozens of times with him – he always rehearsed it again. His method of rehearsal was to say, 'Oh! Gentlemen, I think we'll have a look at Mozart 39.' After we had played right through to the end, without any stops, he would say, 'Yes, that was very nice, gentlemen.' and I would say to my friend Jack Brymer, 'That means we're going through it again.' Then Tommy would say, 'Just one or two points – it's going extremely well' – and we'd play straight through the symphony again.

But, of course, you didn't just play through it again, because he would do different things with the baton, he would look in a different way, his gestures would change. He knew what he wanted to hear, he knew what had not gone the way he wished and he would do what was needed, in some subtle extraordinary way, that enabled the players to produce the sounds he heard in his head and wanted to hear again. He didn't tell you what to do, or explain it. It was at his eightieth birthday party that he said, 'You don't have to teach musicians – they're good musicians – they probably know more about the music than you do. All that you can do is help them play that music together, come together to make a performance. As I get older I've learned to do less and less.' Some people might think that he didn't really mean it, but it was absolutely true. He did do less and less, that is he got in the way less and less. He conducted like a man bowling a hoop along. He tapped the hoop only when it was necessary. When he came to a corner he tapped it so that it started to go round and left it alone until it had gone round. Then he tapped it again. Others tap it all the way round the corner, and as likely as not it goes into the wall.

No other conductor that I have known was able to get an orchestra to play with such a degree of *rubato* and yet at the same time, achieve outstanding precision of attack and ensemble. There was something so inevitable in his rhythm, that however wayward his beat might appear you always knew what was happening. In the 1947 recording of *Ein Heldenleben* by Richard Strauss, there are some wonderful examples of this talent. In particular towards the end of that work where there is a lovely duet between the violin and the horn that is of breath-taking loveliness. On this first recording (we recorded it again with him in 1958) this passage is played with great sensitivity by the then leader, Oscar Lampe, and the late, great Dennis Brain. It was taking part in performances like that, when Beecham combined masculine tenderness, subtle *rubato*, sensitive phrasing and dynamic outbursts of energy, that made working with him something very special indeed.

Sir Thomas was a man of many sides and moods. Not withstanding his autocratic style, more usually with managements, the press and those he wanted to impress, Beecham was always popular with musicians who felt considerable affection for him and always referred to him as 'Tommy' when they spoke of him. Although he had a reputation for being a martinet – perhaps this was true when he was younger – he was always extremely pleasant and courteous to the orchestra during the time I played for him. However, he did not respond well if players, especially those he held in high regard and who he wanted always to be available to him, decided to follow their own interests and not his. I remember that on one occasion Dennis Brain had told the orchestral manager he would not be available for a concert when *Ein Heldenleben* (which has a very important part for the principal horn) was on the programme because he had already accepted an engagement to play one of the Mozart Horn Concertos with another orchestra. When Beecham was informed he said, 'Please tell Mr Brain that he either makes himself available for our concert, or he will not play with the orchestra again.' Dennis Brain did not do the concert and though Brain was one of Sir Thomas's favourite players he did not play in the orchestra again for about a year. Beecham would rather let him go than have his authority challenged.

Of course, Beecham provided a great deal of employment, paid well and from time to time put his own money, as well as other people's, into his musical enterprises. But that was not the main thing – it was, as always, the pleasure everyone got from taking part in magical performances that made the difficult and often unrewarding life of an orchestral musician really worthwhile.

Rehearsals could also be enjoyable because he was usually in a good humour when making music. His reputation for off-the-cuff ripostes and asides is not something I experienced very often. It was more his timing, his tone of voice, and his manner of speaking that led to quite ordinary remarks being greeted with howls of laughter. He could make 'pass the salt' sound amusing. There are two anecdotes that I can vouch for and one must have been spontaneous. It was when my father played for Sir Thomas for the first time, about 1910 or 1911. He had been engaged as deputy principal clarinet in one of the orchestras Sir Thomas was conducting. During the rehearsal Beecham wanted to make a musical point to my father. Not knowing his name he turned to the principal second violinist and asked him, 'Who is playing principal clarinet today?' Unfortunately this player suffered with a quite dreadful stammer. 'It's Mr ch – ch – ch – chhh… ' 'Oh! dear!' said Sir Thomas, 'I didn't know we had a train with us today.'

The other time was when we were doing a TV programme that Sir Thomas was presenting as well as conducting. We had already rehearsed everything that morning and had reassembled for a short rehearsal before the actual telecast – this was still in the 1950s when TV broadcasts went out 'live'. As usual Beecham was very late arriving and as we neared the time of the transmission the studio manager was becoming more and more agitated. When Tommy eventually arrived the studio manager by then extremely flustered rushed up to him and said 'Oh! Sir Thomas it's so terribly late we really must have some voice levels.' 'There's nothing to worry about my boy' said Tommy as he went towards the microphone and in his most serious voice started to recite:

> Mary had a little watch,
> She swallowed it one day.
> She took a box of Beecham's Pills,
> To pass the time away.

Beecham was able to rescue music that had been neglected, often because it required someone with his special kind of imagination to bring it to life. One such work that I enjoyed very much, to which Tommy brought his magic, was *Fifine at the Fair* by Granville Bantock. This employs a very large orchestra, in the Strauss/Mahler tradition. Though rather too long, it has some fine dramatic moments and lyrical interludes, which Beecham realised to their full potential.

Goldmark's *Rustic Wedding* Symphony, surely deserving of more performances, was another of Tommy's favourites. In the recording he made with the RPO, the slow movement is played with particular sensitivity and beauty of tonal colouring. One hears the lyrical, firm yet infinitely flexible rhythm Beecham brought to everything he conducted. The music moves forward, never dragging, always unhurried and timeless. *The Last Sleep of the Virgin,* by Massenet, usually consigned to the 'lollipop' category, is a small gem. It was intensely moving when the recording he had made with the RPO was played at his reburial in St. Peter's Churchyard, Limpsfield, close to his beloved Delius, on the 29th April 1991.

His championship of Delius is well-known and his recordings of the very large works, *The Mass of Life, A Village Romeo and Juliet,* and many smaller works remain a touchstone for performance of these great compositions. The sounds he drew from the orchestra were transparent and airy, supported by an extraordinary rhythmic spine that moves the music along, never letting it become shapeless, as it can become in other hands. I remember very clearly the week of performances of *Irmelin* in Oxford. The cast, the scenery and the production were not of the highest standard. Indeed, it was even rumoured that the scenery for the previous year's pantomime, *Cinderella*, had been called into service. The opera was unknown and with the poor notices the first performance received the audiences were very thin. Box office takings were nowhere near sufficient to cover the costs incurred and it took a long time for the deficit to be paid off. There is so much lovely music in this opera, though no doubt it would benefit from some cuts (it is said that the best operas are known by their cuts), that it is a shame it is not heard more often. Beecham's love and understanding of the music shone through every performance. Without his magic could it ever be the same?

Though Beecham had been an innovator for the first thirty or more years of his career, he showed little sympathy for music written after 1940. Nonetheless his programmes were extremely varied. He loved French music – especially Berlioz and Bizet, César Franck, Saint-Saëns, Massenet, Debussy and occasionally Ravel.

The performance of Ravel's *Daphnis and Chloe* Suite No 2 at a Royal Festival Hall concert remains as a memory of what, in other hands, would have been a major catastrophe. Not withstanding his wonderful sense of rhythm Tommy had no liking for 5/4 or 7/8 time signatures. He was frightened of the 5/4 section towards the end of *Daphnis and Chloe* and therefore barely rehearsed it. At the concert one player, with an important solo entry, came in a bar early. Some sections of the orchestra followed him, some did not. Beecham bellowed and wagged the baton frenetically under the conductor's stand. Gradually the music fell apart. At one point I think only the two flutes were still 'wiffling' away. But the orchestra rallied and we finished together, always an asset. 'How about that for a near disaster' I said to Norman Del Mar, when I met him after the concert. 'Well,' he replied, 'it was a bit untidy in one place, but, my goodness, what an exciting and splendid performance!'

As well as Richard Strauss, Sibelius, Tchaikovsky and regular performances of his beloved Mozart, and to a lesser extent Haydn, we played a good deal of Brahms and Beethoven. Beecham is sometimes thought to have ignored the German masterpieces. This was not so. Brahms's Second Symphony and the *St. Anthony Variations* were regularly in his programmes and the other symphonies rather less frequently. We often played Beethoven's Second, Fourth and Sixth symphonies. The Pastoral was rather slower than usual, but the Second and Fourth were the best renditions of these works that I can recall. He also liked the Seventh Symphony, which we played quite frequently. The Ninth Symphony was scheduled several times, but for some reason Beecham seemed to be heir to ill-health on most of these occasions and his place was taken by someone else.

Beecham was a conductor who always needed to be musically 'in charge'. He was a wonderful accompanist, within the framework of his own conception. For players and singers who shared his view of a work he was a delightful collaborator: with those soloists who did not, the collaboration could be less happy. His recordings of *Magic Flute, Carmen,* and *La Boheme* are ample evidence of his powers as an opera conductor and the rapport he had with singers. For his concert performances he used soloists rather infrequently. I recall an outstanding performance with Clifford Curzon, who put his subtle artistry at Beecham's disposal in a magnificent reading of Brahms's Second Piano Concerto. There were a number of performances of the Sibelius Violin Concerto with Isaac Stern, who also made a splendid recording of this work with him. The recording of the Mendelssohn Violin Concerto with Jascha Heifetz was a less happy occasion. At one point it seemed unlikely that the recording would ever be completed satisfactorily. Heifetz had decided that he wanted to play the last movement extremely quickly. Certainly much faster than Sir Thomas was inclined to think correct. Heifetz played at one tempo, Beecham conducted at another. The rest of us, in particular the woodwind, had to do the best we could. The result was interesting, if not quite orthodox.

Sir Thomas in a very good mood.

When we travelled to Portsmouth in May 1960, none of us thought for a moment that this would be the last concert that Sir Thomas would conduct. He was in good shape and it seemed he would go on for ever. We all hoped he would. As on the occasion that I first encountered Sir Thomas, when he put the baton through his hand, this concert had strange and unusual events connected with it. For some reason he decided to invite the whole orchestra to luncheon when we arrived in Portsmouth. This was extremely unusual, indeed unique in my experience. Though always polite and courteous, Beecham never became familiar with members of his orchestras. He neither travelled with the players nor indulged in any kind of social relationship with them. However, this was a very pleasant occasion and he was at his most benign. After lunch we went to the concert hall and rehearsed for about twenty minutes. Then, another surprise. A large television set was brought on to the platform and Sir Thomas invited the orchestra to join him in watching the cup final. Liverpool, the football team closest to St. Helens where he was born, was playing that year. There was no more rehearsal and after the match we went our separate ways.

It was a splendid concert and it was received with enthusiasm. The concert ended with a characteristically ebullient performance of the *Bacchanale,* from *Samson and Delilah* by Saint-Saëns. Tommy was loved by audiences and he in his turn loved them and was generous with his encores. He loved music and enjoyed it more than any other conductor I have played for. It was this enjoyment that was so infectious, affecting audiences and players alike. Shirley, Lady Beecham, told me that Tommy had related to her how on an occasion, when he was very, very young, there was a little concert in his home town. He was terrified of the audience. His nurse led him to the curtain and let him peep through. 'Now, Master Thomas, you mustn't be nervous' she said 'out there are all your little friends.' On this occasion, in Portsmouth, a great many of his friends, in the audience and all of us in the orchestra, were treated to an encore, *Sleigh Ride* by one of his favourite composers, Frederick Delius. It was the last piece he was to conduct.

Beecham has left a treasury of incomparable recordings to enrich the listening hours of all music lovers. For those of us who were fortunate enough to make music with him, he has left a gap that remains unfilled. Though I was fortunate enough to play under the direction of a number of other outstanding conductors, none gave me the continuous musical satisfaction I enjoyed when working with Beecham. Even when he conducted music that he was not suited for temperamentally the spontaneity and the feeling that the music was being recreated in performance was exhilarating.

8 The Royal Philharmonic Orchestra's 1950 American Tour

Beecham's intention, from 1944, to take an orchestra to the USA. 64 day tour from New England, New York, down the East Coast to New Orleans – experience of hearing genuine trad jazz – segregation in the South (and in the North) – up through the mid-west to Chicago and back to New York.

In March 1944 it was reported in *London Philharmonic Post*, the Journal the LPO published from time to time, that Sir Thomas (who was then still in America) was sending letters and cables to the management with the news that he was making arrangements for the orchestra to tour Canada and America as soon as this became possible. When he returned to London in September of that year he began talking seriously to the orchestra about his intention of taking the orchestra to America, something he had wanted to do for many years. The last British orchestra to visit America had been the London Symphony Orchestra in 1912. The orchestra had been booked to travel on the ill-fated *Titanic,* but fortunately, because some of the arrangements for the tour had not been finalised by the American agents, their departure was delayed and the orchestra travelled safely a few days later on the *Baltic.*

Beecham insisted that the LPO contracts in 1945 and 1946 included a clause stipulating that we agree to go on a tour of America if it could be arranged. In 1947, when I joined the Royal Philharmonic Orchestra and for each of the following three years I signed a similar agreement. At last in 1950 the tour was organised. On the 6th October we left from Waterloo on the special train arranged for Cunard Line passengers that took us to Southampton where we boarded the *Queen Mary*. The following morning at 8.15 we left Southampton for the short journey to Cherbourg to pick up passengers before setting sail across the Atlantic.

We had all become accustomed to war-time rationing, to the shortage and limited choice of food and clothing, and much else that was still rationed in 1950 Britain. As soon as we were aboard the *Queen Mary* everything changed. Wonderful menus were presented at every meal and alcoholic beverages were available all day – and night! With five days at sea, many of the instruments safely stored in the hold and no opportunity for practising in the small cabins, the orchestra enjoyed a complete holiday away from work and family life.

I see from the ship's log that I still have that most of the time the weather was reported as 'moderate gale, rough sea, heavy swell'. I did not require this information as along with a few of my colleagues, also bad sailors, I spent a great deal of time up on deck, away from the sight of food and the stifling heat in the cabins.

On the 12th October we arrived at New York in the middle of the night and missed the welcoming sight of the Statue of Liberty. At that time entry into America still required everyone to go through immigration on Ellis Island. Somehow, Beecham had arranged for the members of the orchestra to avoid this trauma. We had our passports examined rather quickly while still on board – in the First Class Stateroom. How had he managed to arrange this, at the same time that the celebrated conductor Victor de Sabata with an Italian ensemble that had landed from another ship were all held on Ellis Island for several days? In those days it was easier to get round regulations if you had influence, or what the Americans called 'drag'.

We were taken to the Great Northern Hotel where we stayed each time we returned to New York. Once settled in our first thought was to have a look round and find something to eat. The first place we found was something we had not seen before and that I think never came over to Britain: the Automat. It is probably best remembered now from the song, memorably sung by Marilyn Monroe in the film *Some like it Hot*,

> A kiss on the hand may be quite continental
> But diamonds are a girl's best friend
> A kiss may be grand but it won't pay the rent
> on your humble flat, or help you at the automat …

At the Automat there was a wall of small, glass-fronted cubicles just large enough to hold a plateful of food. By the side of each cubicle was a slot for the appropriate coin that would allow you to withdraw your choice. The quality was good and the prices very reasonable, so we made use of their service quite often.

The shops were full of so many things we had not seen in England for a long time and, of course, everything was available without the necessary coupons that so restricted what we could buy at home. In particular I remember buying a nylon shirt. At that time they were much thicker than they are now and had the disadvantage that they did not 'breathe' so that one became extremely hot at times. Their great advantage on a tour such as we were undertaking was that they were easily washed and they dried quickly. Ladies' nylon stockings, so scarce, expensive and mostly 'under the counter' at home, were in all the shops. I sent a pair home to my wife every day. One put 'Present' on the form that was attached to each parcel. If you were lucky it got through without custom duty. On average about 50% did.

Later, at about 9.00 p.m, my friend Steve Trier our bass clarinettist and I decided we would take a stroll and find somewhere for a quiet drink. After a short walk we suddenly found ourselves in Times Square. By now it was dark so we were astonished to find that all the shops were open, a great number of people were shopping and that large illuminated signs were flashing on and off all round the Square. Neither of us, still in our 20s, had ever experienced anything like this at home where since 1939 shops had closed at 5.00 p.m. and there had been no illuminations. But that was not all. We could hear the most amazing singing; strange music sung by a voice that ranged from high soprano to deep bass. It was lovely, but quite eerie. I found out later that it was a recording of Yma Sumac being played from one of the shops. Yma Sumac was a remarkable Peruvian singer with a range of four and a half octaves who at that time had only recorded Indian folk music in Argentina. After 1950, when she married and went to live in the USA she, like so many other fine folk musicians, made many recordings of much more commercial versions of her native folk music and other commercial music.

The crowds, lights, music and the vast array of goods of every kind on sale came as a real shock and a wonderful introduction to a way of life we had not experienced before. In 1950 the difference between life in America and Britain was much greater than it is today; quite suddenly we did really find ourselves in a New World.

The following morning we set off for Hartford, the state capital of Connecticut, where our lengthy and tiring tour started; between October and December, we were to give fifty-two concerts. We had been told that this concert in Hartford would be our 'blooding'. If this concert was well received by the critics, who would travel up from New York to vet us, the concerts we were to give in New York a couple of weeks later would be well received. If the concert did not go well we could expect a hostile reception.

The first rehearsal in the afternoon in Hartford preceding the evening concert got off to a bad start. Quite a few of the principals arrived late for the rehearsal. Unused to American restaurants they had not yet learned that where there were tablecloths diners were expected to be taking a leisurely lunch. As a consequence service was exceedingly slow and lunch had taken much longer than expected. Sir Thomas, habitually late himself, was on this occasion ready and anxious to start on time, quickly became angry.

When the orchestra was eventually assembled it sounded extremely rough, out of tune, lacking in dynamics and finesse, and with poor ensemble. Life on the luxury liner, with its abundance of good food and alcohol and no opportunity for practice had done little for playing standards. Added to this the orchestra had taken on a number of extra players, some of whom were unfamiliar with the repertoire.

It did not bode well for a successful concert. Many of us arrived for the concert with a good deal of apprehension. There was the usual buzz of expectancy as the audience waited for us to take our place on the platform and for the arrival of this very popular conductor. Sir Thomas walked on in his usual slow, stately way and acknowledged the applause with a dignified bow. Then, with a mighty swipe he brought the baton down to start the National Anthem. He was famous for his rendition of the Anthem, but on this occasion it was done with such courage and passion that he inspired and enthused the whole orchestra. The concert went extremely well, there were excellent notices and the tour started on a high.

Leaving Hartford we toured New England by coach and could enjoy the scenery, especially the trees in their wonderful rich autumn colouring. We gave concerts in Washington D.C., in Boston, in its splendid Symphony Hall, in Connecticut, New

Jersey, Pennsylvania, Maryland, Massachusetts and Rhode Island, before returning to New York for two concerts in Carnegie Hall. All this was very exciting but increasingly tiring, as we travelled by coach each day. When we arrived in each town we had to check into a hotel, unpack and then and go to the Hall for a rehearsal before returning to the hotel again to change into evening dress for the concert. To begin with the newness of everything and the excitement of visiting interesting cities kept us going, but after a couple of weeks, when the novelty had worn off, it became increasingly hard.

From New York we travelled down the East Coast giving concerts every day with the journeys often becoming very long, anything from two to six hours. Then a major shock: we crossed the Mason-Dixon Line. We were now in the South where segregation was in force. Suddenly we were made aware of the black/white divide. No black people were allowed in the hotels, restaurants or concert halls. On buses and trams black people were only allowed to sit in the rear seats: everywhere the races were separated. This was, in effect, apartheid. Less overtly brutal than apartheid, as practised in South Africa, it denied most employment opportunities to Negroes (the term African-American had not even been thought of at that time), except of a menial kind. Even in the North, when we were in Evanston, near Chicago, when it was late November and extremely cold, a black woman who collapsed in the street died from exposure in the cold because no white doctor could be found willing to attend to her. For many of us in the orchestra this deliberate demeaning of other people, only because of their race and colour, was sickening. After the terrible 1939-45 war that had revealed the horror of the Nazi regime's racial policy and the deliberate slaughter of millions in the concentration camps, to find this policy still in operation in 'the land of the free' was very hard to take.

When we arrived in New Orleans we were surprised to find that it was very different from any of the other towns we had been to so far. It was much more European, with fine houses dating back to the 18th century redolent with Creole, French, Spanish and Portuguese influences. The metal tracery of the ironwork on the balconies of many of the old buildings was a delight. We gave two concerts in New Orleans so we had the opportunity to enjoy another delight. This was the time when the revival of traditional jazz was in full flood. Black musicians, some of whom had not played for many years, were sought out. Some had only been able to find work as janitors or night watchmen, and a few had even been forced to return to the country areas to find work in the fields.

After the first concert, six or seven of us who were keen on jazz decided to see if we could find where these chaps were playing. As we walked around we found ourselves in streets with names made famous by their use in the title of jazz standards: Basin Street, South Rampart, Canal and Bourbon Streets. At many of the bars we found that there was a jazz group on a little stage behind the bar. The traditional line up of clarinet, trumpet and trombone with guitar or banjo, bass and drums was the norm, though sometimes there would be a piano. We heard some terrific jazz that night, uninhibited and genuine; in one place Bunk Johnson's old band, in another Papa Celestin's in which the legendary clarinettist Alphonse Picou, remembered especially for his famous 'break' in *High Society*, based on the piccolo variation in the Sousa march *Stars and Stripes,* was playing. He was still playing on his old and unique clarinet with its little turned up wooden bell. It was here that my friend Jack Brymer, our principal clarinettist, not only a great orchestral musician and soloist, but also an experienced jazz musician, was persuaded to join the group for a couple of numbers. It was wonderful to see Jack, still in full evening dress, white tie and tails, alongside the five black musicians. In the deep South this was indeed a unique occasion. Though, since those times, mixed groups of musicians are not at all unusual, it would be unlikely that one would even now find one white musician with five that were black.

Jack Brymer

As the tour proceeded and we wilted, Beecham seemed to go from strength to strength – one Southern critic called him 'The Great Little Metrognome!' He was not pleased, preferring to jest at the expense of others rather than being on the receiving end.

Leaving New Orleans we continued to make our way north through Tennessee and Kentucky and up through the mid-west on towards Chicago, but never crossing the Mississippi. The journeys had now become even longer, several of seven and eight hours. When a journey like that was followed by a concert at 8.30 p.m., as happened on a few occasions, one was quite exhausted. By now it was nearly the end of November, we had been on the road for eight weeks and when we arrived in Chicago it was very cold. Walking towards our hotel, which was right by Lake Michigan, with the wind blowing straight at one off the lake, it was like swallowing carving knives. It is not called 'The Windy City' for nothing.

One of the many concerts we gave on the way back towards New York was in Buffalo. When the concert ended at about 11.00 p.m. the orchestra was taken by coach to Niagara Falls, about 25 miles from Buffalo. In 1950 it was still possible for someone with the prestige that Beecham enjoyed to make special arrangements so that when we arrived at the Falls, even though it was near midnight and the viewing platform was closed it was opened up and the lights turned on especially for us. It was a quite magical experience. I wonder if it would be possible to arrange for this today, just for a visiting orchestra?

The following day we made the five-hour coach journey to Syracuse, for what proved to be perhaps the hardest part of the tour. After the concert, which ended at 10.45 p.m., we were taken by coach to the railway station to catch the 11.55 p.m. night train to New York. When we arrived there we had to leave the train at 7.00 a.m., go to our hotel to check in and then make our way to Carnegie Hall in time for a short rehearsal at 11.00 a.m. As it was a Sunday the concert was in the afternoon at 3.00 p.m. The next day we rehearsed in New York in preparation for an evening concert the following day in Philadelphia at 8.30 p.m., after which we returned to New York once again. The next day we gave our final concert in Carnegie Hall. With only two more days to go we were given one of our merciful free days. We had all thought that the concert in Carnegie Hall would be the last one, before going home. But no! They managed to squeeze in one more, in the small town of Bethlehem.

It had been a great experience and in a way a nodal point in our lives. Just as there was for my generation always to be 'before and after the war', for those on that tour there would always be 'before and after we went to America'. Looking through the schedule for the tour I see that there were only three days on which we did not do a concert, have a rehearsal or travel. In all we did 52 concerts in 64 days. It was very tiring but never boring: with Beecham no two concerts of the same programme were ever quite the same. However, on this tour we had an exceptionally large repertoire, playing 50 different compositions in all.

9 The Orchestra Conductor: a Unique Phenomenon

The conductor's authority, control and power. Orchestra/Conductor relationship changes over the past 60 years. Wagner, Stokowski, Beecham and others. Schwarzkopf recalls singing for Karajan. International questionnaire produces surprising results.

The orchestra conductor is a unique phenomenon. He alone of those who have to direct large forces has to control them from instant to instant. Until quite recently it was nearly always a 'he' as there were very few women conductors. Now there are an increasing number and a few who are very good indeed. In considering the orchestra conductor it is important to appreciate that his/her instrument is the orchestra. They need to have the same degree of control over their instrument that all fine musicians require if they are to realise their musical intentions. Every performance is an act of re-creation and must have spontaneity, an element of improvisation that will provide the vitality and excitement so essential if it is to be a unique experience. No two performances can ever be exactly the same. It is only on recordings that we hear exactly the same performance each time. But an orchestra is far more complex than any other musical instrument. It is made up of 75/100 musicians playing a variety of instruments and in opera and choral works there may be a chorus of as many as 250 or more, as well as soloists. And each of them is highly skilled, individualistic and will have his or her own idea of how the music should be played.

Once audiences at concerts and those buying recordings, CDs, videos or DVDs of orchestral music have decided what piece of music they want to listen to it is very often who is conducting that is of most concern. In fact it is not unusual that the choice of what to buy is determined by who is conducting. Who is conducting is also of paramount concern to the orchestra.

During an interview on television in 1958, before a concert at Lincoln's Inn Fields with the Royal Philharmonic Orchestra, Sir Thomas Beecham said 'When you come to face the orchestra signs are not very much. Facial expression is immense – the face and the eyes are everything …but more than that there is a link between an intelligent player in a fine orchestra … now these people notice my expression and also there is the link between us by which what I am thinking, with fierce concentration – everything – is communicated to them – they know.' He was then asked 'What do you do?' 'I let them play. That's what all the orchestral players say when asked what does this man do – and the answer is, he lets us play. He doesn't stop us every 5 bars; he doesn't agitate us every 10 bars with some idiotic movement. I let them go on playing!'

His conducting, like that of all the great conductors, had little to do with beating time. As he said he 'did let the orchestra play'. But his direction involved far more than just his face and eyes, important though they were. No! Beecham was also the master of the art of gesture. He had that mysterious gift of being able to convey by his body language his most subtle intentions, held, as he said, 'with fierce concentration'. Musicians loved to play for him because he shared his delight and love of music with them. There are very fine musicians who give immense pleasure to audiences but who do not love music as much as they love playing their instrument or conducting.

If a conductor is to have the absolute control required that will give him and the artists he is directing the freedom and flexibility to create a great performance, he must have authority. Everyone, whether they are soloists, opera singers, chorus singers, principal musicians in the orchestra who have solo parts to play and all the section players, must follow his every move. Conductors, good or bad, take that for granted. Whether useless or great, by virtue of their role as conductor they exert, for good or ill, the same effect over everyone involved in the performance: instant response to their every move, moment to moment. Very few people are born with a natural authority as well as the ability to allow others to have freedom within that authority. These attributes are essential in a great conductor. For others it will take time before they can acquire the necessary confidence and humility. Many more never succeed in this respect, even if they have the necessary musical ability.

The necessary gestures and body language have nothing to do with 'beating time'. Conducting is a mystery. The essentials cannot be taught. Each and every movement, however slight, affects the orchestra, and the chorus and soloists if they are involved. It is this combination of authority and allowing freedom, or at least the impression of freedom, that is the essential gift a conductor requires.

Felix Weingartner, an outstanding conductor of his day, and successor to Gustav Mahler with the Vienna Court Orchestra, relates how Fürstenau, the second flute in the Dresden orchestras, told him 'When Wagner conducted the players had no sense of being led. Each believed himself to be following freely his own feeling, yet they all worked together wonderfully. It was Wagner's mighty will that powerfully but unperceived had overborne their single wills, so that each thought himself free while in reality he only followed the leader, whose artistic force lived and worked in him. Everything went so easily and beautifully that it was the height of enjoyment.' Weingartner adds that as he spoke of this experience Fürstenau's 'eyes gleamed with joyful enthusiasm'.

It is wonderful experiences like that, all too rare, that every orchestral musician treasures. Wagner displayed the overwhelming self-confidence that all the greatest conductors have. They can embrace an orchestra, chorus and soloists within their musical concept while at the same time interacting with and responding to them, allowing everyone to make their contribution to the performance. My experience during the years I played for Beecham was similar to that described by Fürstenau. I remember that time with the same joyful enthusiasm.

Another conductor with this ability was Leopold Stokowski. He was one of the very few conductors who could get the sound he wanted from any orchestra within a very short time, without any talking. By some extraordinary magic he enabled every orchestra he conducted to sound very like the Philadelphia Orchestra of which he had been the principal conductor for many years. I experienced this remarkable talent playing for him in three orchestras, the Royal Philharmonic, the London Symphony and the Philharmonia.

In order to obtain the sonority he wanted, depending on the concert hall or studio he was performing in, he would change the way the orchestra was seated. He was always trying to find a way to get the richest, most resonant sound from his orchestra. Sometimes he would have the first violins to his left and the seconds to his right, at other times both sections to his left; he would place the cellos and violas so

Leopold Stokowski in the 1960s.

that the violas sat on his right and the cellos in the middle; instead of the basses being in a group on one side or other of the orchestra he would have them strung out along the back of the orchestra. This was one way in which he exercised his authority. Of course some members of the orchestra may be unhappy when their seating position is altered and the aural environment is changed.

Stokowski's authority was challenged when he asked the woodwind section in the Philharmonia to sit to his right where the cello section is normally seated. The woodwind section, composed of some very fine players confident in their own power, refused. Even though Stokowski asked again the following day and on a third occasion really pleaded with them to 'let us just try' they still held out against his wishes. This loss of authority had a profound effect on him and for a time he lost some of his confidence and a certain amount of his charisma with the Philharmonia. On another occasion when I was playing with the London Symphony Orchestra not long after this confrontation I witnessed a very different response. When he asked their excellent young woodwind section to change position with the cellos they immediately complied. He was clearly much happier and I am sure this played a part in his working much more with the LSO from then onwards.

In addition to his outstanding qualities as a conductor, Stokowski was probably the first to appreciate just what could be achieved in the recording studio. In the early recordings he made with the Philadelphia Orchestra, when recording was still in mono, he somehow managed to achieve results that sounded like stereo. This was particularly the case with the wonderful virtuoso recording he made of the Bach *Toccata and Fugue* that he had arranged for orchestra.

Though Stokowski is nearly always referred to as a showman, his platform manner and conducting style was not at all showy. When he came onto the platform and when he took a bow at the end of any item he was very restrained and never 'milked' the applause as quite a few artists do. His appearance in *Fantasia* shaking hands with Mickey Mouse and his relationship with Greta Garbo attracted a lot of publicity and his bogus foreign accent led to a good deal of speculation about whether his name was Stokes or Stokowski. His name was Stokowski and he was born in London and went to school in Marylebone – there is a plaque on the wall of the school just round the corner from where I lived for many years. He then went to the Royal College of Music, where he studied the organ.

There are a lot of stories about this colourful character, as indeed there are about quite a few conductors. The anecdotes here come directly from the musicians involved and are not, as so often these tales are, apocryphal. Stokowski, who conducted the LSO quite frequently, had been rehearsing with them in the Royal Festival Hall (RFH). At the end of the morning rehearsal the taxi that had been ordered to take him back to a hotel failed to arrive, so one of the musicians, the bass trombonist, Tony Thorp, was asked if he would take the conductor in his car. This trombone player happened to be a renowned fantasist who because he was for ever telling everyone about his prowess as a medical doctor was generally referred to ironically as Dr Thorp. As he was driving over Westminster Bridge and just passing Big Ben, Stokowski turned to him and said, ' What that big clock?' Thorp replied immediately, 'I don't know – I'm a stranger here, too.'

When my old friend Stuart Knussen, an outstanding double bass player and father of the composer Oliver Knussen, was principal double bass and the chairman of the LSO Board, Stokowski used to stay with him in his nice house on the outskirts of London. Stuart had driven Stokowski home after the rehearsal that morning in the RFH, they had had lunch and were sitting resting when Stuart told Stokey, as musicians tended to call him, that he had devised a method of producing the tone one achieves when using a mute, but without the need for a mute. 'Play to me' said the *Maestro*. Double bass players have little opportunity to display their solo talents and so Stuart dashed off a couple of movements of the Bottesini and Dragonetti concertos. 'Very good! Now, I hear without mute playing.' Stuart plays and Stokowski tells him 'Good – very good.'

They had something to eat and then returned to the RFH for the evening rehearsal. After they had been playing for about 20 minutes they came to a passage where the basses were required to be muted. After only a few bars Stokowski stops the orchestra. 'Principal bass – why you play without mute? Is written for mute – no?' In some confusion Stuart tries to explain that he had shown him he didn't need a mute and did not have one with him. 'No mute. Please leave orchestra.' And poor Stuart, principal and chairman was obliged to leave the platform. On the way back in the car, after the rehearsal, Stuart asked Stokowski 'Why did you humiliate me like that in front of the whole orchestra? I had played to you and you said, "That's very good."' 'Yes, my boy.' replies Stokey, 'Today you learn lesson. Never trust anyone.'

In a lighter vein: it is reported that when Ernest Fleischman, then manager of the LSO, introduced Georg Solti to him, 'May I introduce *Maestro* Solti?' Stokowski gave a slight bow to Solti and said 'And what is a *Maestro*?', leaving both Solti and Fleischman discomforted and at a loss for a reply. Something very unusual for Solti, a master at always having the last word.

The authority and control conductors require and their desire to have everything just as they are hearing it in their 'mind's ear' does sometimes lead them to be inconsiderate to artists. Elizabeth Schwarzkopf was not only a great soprano but also a favourite of Herbert von Karajan. In an interview she relates how she had to respond to his unreasonable demands. She was singing on the recording of Beethoven's *Missa Solemnis* in Vienna with Karajan and the Philharmonia Orchestra. 'I did a performance of *Don Giovanni* with Karl Böhm on the 10th, *Così* on the 12th and *Falstaff* on Sunday the 14th. Now, these alone would have been quite sufficient for me, I think. But in addition to that we were recording the *Missa Solemnis* between the 12th and 15th. On the 13th we had a rehearsal for *Falstaff* with Mr von Karajan in the morning, when he

Herbert von Karajan.

had laughingly said to me "You, my dear, of course need not sing out because after all you have to record in the afternoon of that Saturday at 3 o'clock, so be silent." So that is what I started out to be. But when, of course, it came to me singing on the stage and he downstairs in the pit, hardly had a second passed when he put his left hand to his left ear and he said, "I can't hear you. Please sing out. How shall I put a balance if you don't sing? Come out! Sing out!" – Well!'

It is at rehearsals that the relationship between conductor and orchestra is established. Can he get what he wants by his conducting gestures, or does he have to talk a great deal, trying to explain what he wants but fails to indicate? Is the orchestra spending more time listening to him than playing the music? Are they becoming increasingly bored? Nothing destroys a performer's ability to act, dance or play their instrument well than just sitting not 'doing'.

Some conductors are much better at the rehearsals than at the performance. For some reason they become nervous or more inhibited at the concert. A few of them are able to achieve much better results in the recording studio. On the other hand there are one or two who are boring at rehearsal doing nothing more than constantly repeating the same passage over and over again without giving any reason why they are doing so, yet at the concert they can be inspiring. With a very good orchestra this can work.

Age can be very important for a conductor. Whereas instrumentalists can practise for many hours a day, a conductor cannot. His only opportunity to practise on his instrument is at rehearsals and concerts. Orchestras do not like being practised on. They resent being told what to do by someone who clearly knows less than they do. Curiously, the very best orchestras, with the best and most experienced musicians tend to be the most patient. They probably have sufficient understanding and self-confidence to deal with the incompetence and absence of tact that sometimes go with a lack of experience in a young conductor. If they recognise real talent, they will tolerate it and perhaps the leader and one or two of the senior principals may have a quiet word with him.

There are some conductors, now held in high esteem by musicians and the public, for whom I played many years ago when they were young. At that time they had not yet learned 'people skills' and were still awkward in their gestures. They often upset orchestras and were sometimes heartily disliked. Of course this resulted in the performances they achieved being less good than perhaps they deserved. Over the years, having had the opportunity to practise at many rehearsals, they have gained in confidence, learned to respect the musicians they depend on and found a way to make the gestures necessary to produce the performance they hear in their head. Now, 35/40 years later a few have developed into outstanding artists.

Unfortunately, there are quite a few conductors who do not learn with age, just as many instrumentalists and singers do not improve however long they are in the profession. But when a conductor continues to make unreasonable demands on players and remains unable to indicate his intentions by his gestures, his own shortcomings quite often cause him to be less than agreeable to the orchestra as a whole and sometimes unpleasant to individual players. With an orchestra that may have some weaknesses or, young, inexperienced players, conductors can be quite ruthless when pointing out faults. Too often this further destroys an already poor relationship, reduces confidence and does nothing to improve the performance. If a conductor of this kind does get the opportunity to conduct a very good, experienced orchestra the players will extremely quickly recognise his shortcomings. If he tries to 'teach' them how to play their parts and does not 'let them play', to quote Sir Thomas, they may find they have a rather hard time. When the final performance is unsatisfactory and unrewarding everyone is unhappy and frustrated.

Those fortunate enough to play in the major orchestras suffer less because they generally get the best conductors. But now there are a lot more good orchestras than good conductors. There are quite a number of musicians who only rarely experience the joy of taking part in a really rewarding performance. For them frustration and unhappiness can turn to anger and bitterness. In the mid-1980s Dr Ian James and a group of doctors, some of who were amateur musicians, established the Elmdon Trust, which became the British Performing Arts Medicine Trust (BPAMT). They were concerned at the increasing prevalence of physical and mental problems within the music profession. There are a number of doctors specialising in these problems and now nearly all the full-time orchestras in Britain have a doctor available for consultation. Another organisation, the International Society for the Study of Tension in Performance (ISSTIP) decided that an international survey was required. A questionnaire was planned and distributed to orchestras in Britain and one or two other countries in Europe.

In the section of the questionnaire in which players were invited to comment on what caused them the most distress, by far the most frequent response was relevant to the problem of working with conductors deemed to be less than satisfactory. At that time I was Director of the National Centre for Orchestral Studies and involved with the investigation into the problems besetting musicians. I was astonished to see that when players expressed their feelings about conductors even their handwriting displayed real signs of agitation. The importance of having a good conductor and the harm caused by a bad one was referred to by 57% of those in the regional orchestras. When I said that I did not share these feelings I was told that I had been fortunate to spend my life in the best orchestras working mainly with the very best conductors.

Is there any other occupation or circumstance where the person in charge has such moment to moment control over a large number of people? No one else, employer, general in the army, even a dictator, has this power, and especially when those to be commanded are highly skilled and have themselves to be making decisions all the time in the performance of their own actions. In orchestras with a permanent conductor or music director that person will probably also have the power to determine whether one remains in the orchestra. The four London orchestras have overcome this by becoming self-managed; in most countries the musicians will be protected, when necessary, by the collective power of either their trade union or an association to which they belong. This was not so in the past and a good many conductors were referred to as tyrants. Changed attitudes to authority have also played a large part in curbing any tendency in that direction.

The relationship between conductors and orchestras has changed a great deal since I joined the profession in 1942. It is a very complex relationship and difficult to appreciate for anyone who has not had a good deal of experience in a professional orchestra. Sometimes those who write about the orchestra and orchestral musicians do not realise that the conductor/orchestra relationship with a very experienced orchestra is very different from that in a school, college, amateur or semi-professional orchestra. The majority of the members of a major symphony orchestra will have had far more experience of the repertoire than even the oldest and most experienced conductor because they will have played whatever is to be rehearsed with many conductors, good and bad. Marie Wilson, who was one of the leaders of the BBC Symphony Orchestra for many years from the early 1930s, put it very well in an interview I recorded with her in 1987, when she was still playing in the LPO. She had played with all the great conductors from Toscanini, Wilhelm Furtwängler to Karajan and Giulini. She said 'We should have conductors who know so much more than we do. We are at the top of our profession: we should be looking up to somebody at least better than us. Someone who can inspire you.'

Since I became a member of the London Philharmonic Orchestra in 1942 the general standard of technical skill on all instruments has increased tremendously. Music that even the two or three most outstanding players would consider taxing is now playable by everyone hoping to join the profession. It is not too much to say that virtuosity is relatively commonplace. The 'teaching' element at rehearsal that was required in all but the finest orchestras is no longer needed. The ability to obtain the right balance of the various sections and inspiring the orchestra are now what every orchestra is looking for.

The skill conductors now have has also developed so that they can mostly deal with the demands composers have made since the beginning of the 20th century. Many have employed far more complex rhythms and changing time signatures. Instead of writing whole movements in 4/4, 3/4 or 6/8, each bar may have a different time signature, 3/8 then 5/4 followed by 2/4 and so on. Instead of melodic lines, sections of the orchestra and individual instruments have been used in a way similar to how Seurat and the other pointillist artists applied spots of paint. The separate dots of paint only make sense when one stands away from the painting and one can see what the artist intended, or, in the case of music, hear what the composer envisaged. Then again, to continue the analogy with painting, some composers became interested in creating 'sound experiences', new and original aural worlds in the way artists have used pure colour or changed perspectives.

The development of these new compositional techniques, serial or twelve-tone music and other compositional techniques drew further and further away from the idea of 'tunes' as normally considered. For this music the musicians in the orchestra now often only needed someone just to indicate the beats accurately. A conductor needing a good 'stick technique', rather than the ability to inspire was required, so that conductors attracted to this new music were often those for whom representing in sound, as accurately as possible, the notes just as they see them written in the score was most important.

The coming of the long-playing 33 rpm record in the early 1950s required conductors to share their authority with the recording producer and technicians to an extent conductors in the past would not have allowed. New techniques, in particular the use of tape for recording that allowed the extensive use of editing made this possible. With the additional use of many more microphones individual sections could now be balanced separately, finally putting the control over the finished recording in the hands of the producer. This has affected conductors and those playing in symphony orchestras to a greater extent than those playing in smaller groups of musicians. The essential element in jazz of improvisation would be removed if the recordings were edited. Recordings of pop music rely to a considerable extent on the use of the most sophisticated recording techniques, some of which are now used when recording symphony orchestras. Other popular compositions are usually not so long as the overtures, concertos and symphonies that are the core repertoire of the symphony orchestra and so they can frequently be recorded without the need for so much editing. In the case of chamber music the ensemble will have rehearsed the music extensively before coming to the studio. Again, there will be much less need for editing.

In spite of all the changes that have taken place over the years the conductor remains the cross that orchestral musicians still have to bear because too often he does not know more than the players do and is unable to inspire them. Yet, it is only with a very good or great conductor that it is possible for those playing in an orchestra to fully express themselves musically. That paradox remains whatever else changes.

Famous conductors bring in audiences and sell recordings and so managements, recording companies and virtually everyone they have contact with respond to their every wish. For several years whilst I was Chairman of the Philharmonia Orchestra's Council of Management (its board of Directors), as well as playing in the orchestra, I had quite a lot to do with conductors. I quickly learned that it was necessary to think of the very good, sometimes great artists we were privileged to work with as extremely intelligent, highly gifted and wayward children. I also found that some of these wonderful artists had become so used to their slightest whim being complied with that they had become prone to change their mind from one moment to another. The qualities that enabled them to get outstanding results when they were on the podium had led some of them to be rather autocratic and dictatorial in their relationships when they were not conducting. It was necessary to be absolutely firm and establish that 'yes' really meant 'yes' and 'no' meant 'no', today, tomorrow, and next week, otherwise it was possible to find oneself running around in circles all the time. It was not always easy. We wanted them to be happy, not only with how the orchestra played, but to feel that the orchestra respected them. If they were outstanding, perhaps great conductors, we wanted to work with them again. They could make playing in the orchestra a really enjoyable and enriching experience.

10 The Great and the Good

*Playing for great, good, very good and outstanding conductors – in the
London Philharmonic, Royal Philharmonic and Philharmonia and
elsewhere – Victor de Sabata, Bruno Walter, Charles Munch,
Thomas Beecham, Herbert von Karajan, Otto Klemperer, Lorin Maazel,
Colin Davis, Simon Rattle and many more.*

What is it that makes us consider some conductors 'great'? What qualities do they possess that distinguishes them from those we assess as good, very good or outstanding? Are those we think of as great always dead? It seems to me that I remember artists, composers and politicians being referred to as 'great' during their lifetime. Perhaps because we now see them so often on TV and no longer treated with the deference accorded them in the past we only think of them as personalities or celebrities.

It is difficult to describe what it is that a very few conductors have that makes us believe they are great, yet we always recognise it when we are in its presence. We sense that they are beyond the ordinary, have remarkable ability, are in some way unique and have something extraordinary that separates them from most of the rest of us. In some way they command our respect and inspire us.

All the very best conductors, those that my colleagues and I would consider great, combine the authority and control I referred to in a previous chapter with the self-confidence that allows them to respond to musicians in the orchestra who have solo passages to play. This interplay between conductor and members of the orchestra is one of the elements that leads to an orchestra playing 'better than it can'. The whole orchestra is inspired by the conductor and by the playing of individual musicians in the orchestra. Together, they combine to produce a great performance.

Because there are so many less good than good conductors, orchestral musicians quite often feel that the conductor stands in the way of them playing as well as they can. Every musician who has taken part in a great performance will tell you that this is only possible with a great conductor. However demanding he may have been, and however extreme the demands one has to make on oneself, the reward of taking part in a great performance is what makes playing in an orchestra worthwhile. It is something very special. One is enlarged by being part of something much bigger than oneself.

When one takes part in a performance of a great piece of music with a great conductor in a fine orchestra it is like being an eagle flying over Everest. At other times one may only fly over Mount Blanc and that is very pleasant, too. However, a lot of the time one is coasting along just above a range of hills. Unfortunately, there are quite a number of occasions when one is at ground level and, on the darkest days, even down in a valley.

From 1943 until 1979 it was my good fortune to play with many of the very best conductors who came to London: in 1943 in the London Philharmonic Orchestra (LPO), from 1947 until 1960 in the Royal Philharmonic Orchestra (RPO) and finally in the Philharmonia, from 1955 (while still playing in the RPO) until 1979. Over these years I also played with nearly all the other orchestras in London, either as a deputy or an extra, in particular with the London Symphony Orchestra (LSO).

I worked with several of the conductors that I refer to in more than one of these orchestras. The very best of them obtained excellent performances from whichever orchestra they were directing; other conductors, though very good, would get much better results with one orchestra than another.

The London Philharmonic Orchestra (LPO)

Towards the end of the 2nd World War, from 1944, many conductors who had not been to Britain for a number of years came to conduct the London Philharmonic Orchestra. Some were probably at the height of their powers and came with the advantage of an established reputation. The first to arrive was Sir Thomas Beecham, about whom I have written earlier.

No one I can recall had a greater or more instantaneous effect on an orchestra than Victor de Sabata. We knew very little about him other than that he was the Musical Director at La Scala in Milan. On his arrival for his first rehearsal with us he presented a rather romantic figure. He was quite tall, walked with a limp and had the face of a Roman emperor. He wore a wide brimmed black hat and wore his overcoat over his shoulders like a cape. Quickly removing his hat and coat he stepped on to the podium. 'Good morning, Gentlemen. We start with Dvorak Symphony.' We played through the whole of the *New World* Symphony, from beginning to end as if it had been a performance. It was tremendous. Incredibly volatile,

Victor de Sabata.

his unique conducting style at once electrified the orchestra. We had all played this symphony many times before, but never quite like this. In fact, I have never taken part in any performance of this work as rewarding as those we did with him.

During the next few years de Sabata conducted a wide-ranging repertoire with us and though he never used a score, at rehearsals or concerts, his ear was so discerning that I felt that even in the loudest orchestral passages he could hear every note I played. At times he asked for such extremes of dynamic, from the quietest *pianissimo* to the loudest *fortissimo* that he quite frightened us. On one occasion, when we were recording the Third Symphony by Beethoven with him, he demanded that the strings play the *spiccato* passage in the third movement very quietly indeed. When playing *spiccato* the violinist uses a bouncing stroke of the bow to detach each note. Especially to do this very quickly and very softly is extremely difficult. After several attempts that did not satisfy him, one of the first violinists said, '*Maestro*, it is getting worse – you are frightening us.' de Sabata, eyes flashing replied, 'You are frightened, I am frightened – we must do it.' He remained a legend for all of us who played for him at that time and one of a handful of truly great conductors.

Bruno Walter.

Bruno Walter was a man with a very different personality. He was charming, courteous and urbane. His approach to music was essentially lyrical. To play Mozart and Schubert with him was a delight. I still have a programme for the concert he conducted with us in January 1947 at the Royal Albert Hall – the Overture *Leonora No.3* by Beethoven, Mozart Symphony in G minor No.40, and the Symphony No.9, the great C major, by Schubert. Now, nearly sixty years later I remember it as one of the great concerts I was fortunate to take part in. His tempi might be thought rather slow by today's standards but for me the 'heavenly length' of this beautiful symphony by Schubert, though even longer than usual in this performance, was quite wonderful.

It was with Bruno Walter that I first played a Mahler symphony. At that time, in the 1940s, Mahler's music was practically unknown in Britain and was considered long and boring. In the 1939 edition of *The Oxford Companion to Music*, in the article on German and Austrian music, Mahler is only mentioned in a paragraph about the ban the Nazi regime imposed on the performance of music by Jewish composers. In the very short article under his name it states, 'He left nine symphonies which have been taken very seriously in Germany and Holland but have never had much hearing elsewhere'. His 4th Symphony was the first one we played, perhaps because being the shortest and least complicated it was felt it would be the easiest one for the audience to accept. Later we also played the 1st Symphony. It is now difficult to understand the opposition there was to his music, not only from the public but also from the musicians in the orchestras.

In many of his compositions Mahler makes use of techniques that in the late 1940s and early 1950s were resented by musicians in Britain and elsewhere. They resisted playing in ways that they felt went against not only good taste but also against some of the techniques they had practised so long and hard to perfect. String players were instructed, at times, to *glissando*, slide from one note to another. At its best this style can be heard in the recordings made by the great violinists Fritz Kreisler and Jascha Heifetz and other outstanding string instrument players in the first part of the 20th century. The leaders of the many small light orchestras playing in cafes, restaurants and holiday resorts were still playing in this way in the 1940s. Increasingly, conservatoire trained musicians had come to see this way of playing as vulgar and old fashioned and to be avoided. Wind players were instructed by Mahler, at certain points in the music, to raise their instruments so that they pointed straight forward, rather than at an angle to the ground. Clarinettists and oboists in particular were unhappy because it affected their embouchure and to begin with many refused to follow this instruction. After the mid-1960s, as performances of the Mahler symphonies became increasingly popular, the complaints disappeared.

Charles Munch was another conductor the LPO played under many times. He had immense charm (and the most beautiful smile I've ever seen) as well as the ability to inspire. Before he became a conductor he had been a fine violinist and was the leader of the famous Leipzig Gewandhaus Orchestra when Wilhelm Furtwangler was their conductor. He could on occasion be rather wayward. I remember when we were to play a Brahms symphony, which for some reason it seemed he did not want to conduct, he barely rehearsed it at all. But to play the French repertoire, Debussy, Ravel, Berlioz and Rameau with him was really a great joy. In particular I remember wonderful performances of *Daphnis and Chloe, L'Apres Midi d'un faune , La Valse* and in particular *La Mer*. Years later I remember playing it again with him with the Philharmonia in Vienna in the wonderful *Musikvereinsaal*.

The Philharmonia playing in the beautiful Musikvereinsaal with Ricardo Muti conducting.

Someone, not really a conductor, with whom the orchestra always enjoyed playing was Richard Tauber, generally remembered as one of the great tenors of his time, equally at home in the Mozart operas as in operettas and musicals. He proved, if proof is needed, that formal lessons in conducting and conventional technique are not required in order to obtain wonderful performances. Danny Kaye, years later, displayed this same talent. Tauber brought a Viennese charm to his Mozart and Schubert and an innate musical understanding to everything he conducted. Unfortunately his vanity did not allow him to wear glasses in public and this limited his repertoire as it meant he had to conduct everything from memory.

Eduard van Beinum, then principal conductor with the Concertgebouw Orchestra in Amsterdam, worked a great deal with the LPO. A very fine musician, he was a restrained, undemonstrative conductor who obtained very fine results in a wide repertoire. He was greatly respected by the orchestra who really enjoyed working with him. He was also a kind and remarkably tolerant man. When we were recording *The Songs of a*

Wayfarer by Mahler with him in 1946 or 1947, our regular bass clarinettist was absent for some reason and his replacement on that day was less than up to the standard required. In one very quiet passage for the three clarinets this player just could not play as softly as necessary. He was either too loud, or came in too early, or did not come in at all. Finally, after a number of unsuccessful attempts he became so nervous that he produced the dreaded 'squeak'. Rather than being cross and humiliating the player in front of the whole orchestra, as many other conductors might have done, he let it pass and left recording that section until another day when another player had been engaged. It is a great pity that he died before he had made as great an international reputation as surely he would have done.

The Swiss conductor Ernest Ansermet, famous for his performances of the music of Stravinsky, was engaged by Decca to record the music Stravinsky had composed for the ballet *Petrushka*. Today this is accepted as a regular work in the concert repertoire. In 1946 it was still a very exciting and difficult composition for the orchestra. At that time we were still making records in the 78 rpm format. Each side of a record lasted about four minutes without any facility for editing. If there was anything unsatisfactory – a wrong note, poor intonation or ensemble, or a cracked note in the brass, the whole side had to be recorded again. Decca allowed 10 three-hour sessions to record this 40-minute work, more sessions than would normally be allocated for recording a piece of this length even in 1946. But it was worthwhile; this recording, the first major recording to make use of Decca's new full frequency recording technique, FFRR (Full Frequency Range Recording), was a great success and won an award. Years later I remember recording *Petrushka* again with the Royal Philharmonic Orchestra, in the 'long play' 33 rpm format, when we were only allowed two sessions. On that occasion quite a few of the musicians in the orchestra had never played *Petrushka* before and so it required rather more retakes than usual to splice the performance together to produce an acceptable recording.

In 1946 when Leonard Bernstein came to conduct the LPO he was still very young and full of New York ebullience and *chutzpah*. He had recently had a great success with the New York Philharmonic and did not seem to be at all impressed by the LPO, no doubt finding it lacking in the kind of 'attack' he was used to with American orchestras, and nothing like as virtuoso as the New York Phil. For their part the orchestra did not like him because he was young, brash and far too sure of himself. Nonetheless, I recall the performances were good, even if performed through gritted teeth. He survived this brief encounter to become one of the most outstanding conductors of his time and a remarkable many-faceted musician: a virtuoso pianist – his recording of the Ravel Piano Concerto in G major remains one of the best still available – and a fine composer. As a composer he is probably most widely remembered for *West Side Story* and *Candide*. But his symphonies and much orchestral, choral and chamber music still remain in the repertoire, though not performed so frequently. Later, after a similarly false start to that he had had with the LPO, he established a very good relationship with the LSO. In time they came to like him very much and they did many splendid concerts and recordings together. He was less successful when working with the BBC Symphony Orchestra where on one occasion there was an unfortunate confrontation between him and some of the brass section on a 'live' TV broadcast.

The LPO engaged a number of conductors who came to Britain for the first time in the early post-war years. One of them, Sergiu Celibidache, at that time a very young man, made a considerable impression and showed great promise. He had at one time been a footballer and was still rather wild. Later he made a considerable reputation as a conductor of great integrity, though rather eccentric. He was one of the only conductors with an international reputation who came to dislike commercial recording to such an extent that after a few years he refused to do any further recording.

As well as Charles Munch two other very good French conductors were engaged by the orchestra: Paul Paray, and Jean Martinon. Like Munch they conducted a lot of French music, a great joy to me – the repertoire is so dominated by the Austro-German composers. The orchestra liked Paul Paray very much. He got very good, exciting performances and we were sorry he did not return. He had been a fighter in the French Résistance and was extremely tough. On one occasion he refused to come onto the platform at the beginning of a concert until he received his fee – in cash! He was the Principal Conductor of the Colonne Orchestra in Paris from 1945 until he went to Detroit in 1952 where he had a very successful career with the Detroit Symphony Orchestra before returning to Paris again in 1963. Though he continued to conduct in France until his death in 1979 he never returned to Britain. Jean Martinon was also admired by the orchestra. He was a fine musician and a very good conductor and the orchestra did a number of very good concerts with him. He had a considerable success but, perhaps because of his easy personality and the fact that when he first conducted us in 1945 he brought Ginette Neveu with him, who was so charismatic and such a wonderful violinist, I remember her more than him.

Three more conductors who had some success with the orchestra were Albert Coates, Erich Leinsdorf and Nicolai Malko. They could not have been more different from each other, though each succeeded in getting good results. Albert Coates was already elderly at the time and went out of his way to be pleasant to the orchestra. He had made his reputation in Britain before the war and, later, also in Russia and by the time he conducted us was rather too easy going and laid back to get outstanding results. In contrast Erich Leinsdorf was fairly young, not particularly agreeable, but showed that he had real ability. Many years later I took part in a number of recording sessions with him when he conducted some extracts from the Wagner operas with the LSO. By then he had established himself as an outstanding concert and opera conductor. Though he was able to get first-class results he did not inspire orchestras sufficiently to receive the accolade 'great'. Nicolai Malko was a good conductor of the old school; authoritarian, efficient but not inspiring.

Of course we played frequently for British conductors, most notably Sir Henry Wood, Sir Adrian Boult, Dr Malcolm Sargent (still to be knighted) and John Barbirolli (also to be knighted) and then Beecham, when he returned from the USA. Sir Henry will always be remembered for his part in creating the Promenade Concert season, the ever-popular 'Proms'. He was also the first truly English conductor to make a great reputation. I only played for him a few times after I joined the LPO in 1943 before the Prom season that summer when the orchestra was to do all the concerts in the first two weeks of the season. I was looking forward to this and the opportunity to play a large repertoire with him but, sadly, he was taken ill and was able to conduct only the first two concerts before he became too unwell to continue.

Now, in 2008, as I listen to a newly released CD of the 1943 First Night of the Proms which had been privately recorded off-air on acetate discs (illegal, at that time), I am transported back 65 years to when I took part in that concert as a very young man of 18. Is it just my imagination or are these performances more 'loving'? The tempi are generally slightly slower than is usual now and the soloists, the tenor Heddle Nash, the pianist Moura Lympany and the orchestra, all seem to me more involved emotionally. Was this, perhaps, because of the occasion – there was an audience of 9000, even larger than now, as the top gallery was still in use for a standing audience? Or was it because there were fewer performances and recordings then, so that audiences and musicians alike came with less sophisticated responses than is possible today?

I don't feel that Boult's talents were sufficiently recognised at the time by those who worked with him. It is true that even those who played for him for many years in the BBC Symphony Orchestra were often unable to tell what he was doing with the very long baton that he favoured and though he could be dull there was some music he did extremely well. I remember several performances of the 'Great' C major Symphony by Schubert that were very fine. The part he played in the formation of the BBC Symphony Orchestra in 1930, his selection of the players that would make it, at that time, the best orchestra in the country, and his subsequent role in bringing a very great deal of new music to the public's attention was a very considerable achievement.

Sargent was unique in my experience in that he was greatly admired by audiences and choruses, especially by the ladies, and universally disliked, both as a man and a musician, by orchestras. Only in the last years of his life, when he had somewhat mellowed and his past was largely forgotten by a new, younger generation of musicians, did orchestras come to have a better relationship with him. His vanity and obvious contempt for orchestral musicians was such that he would try to teach even the most distinguished and experienced players how to play their part. His publicly expressed opinion that a musician 'ought to give of his life-blood with every bar he plays' and that 'the feeling of instability about where next year's bread and butter was to come from had made many an artist give continuously of his best', did nothing to create good feeling between him and the orchestras. These remarks were particularly resented because in 1933 the orchestral musicians in London had made a substantial collection for him when he was seriously ill. The great violinist Fritz Kreisler said 'I am sure that musicians the world over play better for feeling secure. The more secure a musician feels the happier he is and the better he plays'. Years later Sargent was involved in constant quarrels with several leading principals in one of the orchestras. On at least one occasion this led to him becoming so distraught that he started to cry when outspoken criticisms about his ability were openly expressed by some of the musicians in the orchestra. This did nothing to raise his reputation as a man: orchestral musicians are only too accustomed to very direct and sometimes wounding criticism.

The conductor that we admired the most after Beecham was John Barbirolli, later Sir John, known by his many admirers as 'Glorious John'. In the LPO, when Beecham left to form the RPO, the orchestra would have liked Barbirolli to have become their Principal Conductor, but he had already taken up that position with the Hallé Orchestra in Manchester when he returned to Britain in 1943, after being with the New York Philharmonic, and was not willing to leave Manchester. I also worked with him in the RPO and the Philharmonia, always with pleasure. He did inspire both the orchestra and the audience and must join the 'great' category. When the Philharmonia toured South America in the 1960s Barbirolli conducted most of the concerts. He created such enthusiasm from the audience that on several occasions at the end of a concert, during tumultuous applause, women bearing young infants would approach the stage apparently seeking to have their children blessed by the *Maestro*. The last time he conducted was at a rehearsal with the Philharmonia, in preparation for a visit to Japan we were about to undertake in 1970. During a rehearsal he suddenly became unwell and was unable to do the tour. It was only a short while later that he died. His place for the tour was very ably taken at extremely short notice by John Pritchard (later Sir John), an extremely talented conductor.

The Royal Philharmonic Orchestra (RPO)

The Royal Philharmonic was really the only one of the four London orchestras to have a Musical Director, Sir Thomas Beecham. It could be said, indeed it was, that it was his orchestra. He not only conducted the orchestra a great deal but he also influenced the management of the orchestra in every way. In most British orchestras the Principal Conductor usually does no more than about 12 concerts a year, a number of recordings and perhaps a tour. Quite often, especially in the past when there was a great deal more recording, the choice of a Principal Conductor was often determined by the number of recording sessions he brought with him. The only other conductors of a British orchestra that I can recall who performed a similar role to Beecham were Sir John Barbirolli with the Hallé and Simon Rattle (later Sir Simon) with the City of Birmingham Symphony Orchestra.

Though Beecham gave me more pleasure whilst I was playing in the orchestra than anyone else and has continued to do so whenever I listen to the recordings he made, I can also recall that at times he could behave very badly and very autocratically, especially if one of his favourite players was not available. On one occasion we were rehearsing with him in St. Pancras Town Hall when, just before the tea break, the personnel manager came to announce that an additional concert had been arranged several weeks hence. The principal cello, Raymond Clarke, a magnificent player whom Beecham admired and who greatly admired him in return, said, 'I'm extremely sorry Sir Thomas, I afraid I am not free on that date. I have already accepted another engagement on that day'. Beecham went mad, shouting and raving and being very rude and disagreeable to poor Clarke. He worked himself into such a state that he came off the podium and went storming through the orchestra, kicking chairs and music stands in all directions, finally leaving the Hall and the rehearsal. With anyone else the players would have found it difficult to forgive this kind of behaviour. However, most of us recognised that at times he could behave like a spoilt child, but forgave him because making music with him was so rewarding.

When for some strange reason it had been decided to present a series of concerts at the Earls Court ice rink, Beecham displayed the autocratic side of his nature. A quite low platform for the orchestra had been built on top of the ice. As we waited for Sir Thomas to arrive for the first rehearsal, not surprisingly, we found that we were getting very cold. Of course, as usual Tommy was late. Someone must have told him about the prevailing conditions, so that when he did arrive he came storming onto the ice, shouting at the top of his voice, 'I have been deceived – I have been

deceived! It's a disgrace. Cancel the concert. Everyone go home.'
And with that he went off again. It always seemed to me he walked
with one leg in 2/4 and the other in 6/8 – I used to refer to him to
my friends as 'goody two-shoes' – on this occasion it was a miracle
he did not tumble over on the slippery ice.

A few minutes later the personnel manager came on to the
stand and announced that the concert was cancelled and that we
could all leave. At about half-past four that afternoon I received a
telegram, as did all the members of the orchestra, instructing us to
return to Earls Court for a short rehearsal at six-thirty to be
followed by the concert at eight o'clock. It was quite remarkable
that everyone was still at home and able to respond to his call to
return. When we arrived back nothing had changed except that
Beecham now seemed to be in his normal good humour. The
concert went quite well, even though we were all frozen and it was
very difficult to keep one's instrument up to pitch if one had more
than a few bars rest.

With Beecham conducting the orchestra a great deal of the time
the RPO did not have so many guest conductors as the other
orchestras in London. However, we did have some very fine
conductors, including Stokowski, about whom I wrote earlier. We
did a great deal of recording with Artur Rodzinski who was an
excellent conductor though he was not a pleasant man to work
with; a martinet and, possibly because at the time he was elderly
and in poor health, short-tempered and inclined to be rude. In
1956 when Gennadi Rozhdestvensky came to London with the
Bolshoi Ballet it seems that Beecham was impressed by him
because it was not long before he was engaged by the RPO. He at
once made a great impression on the orchestra. His conducting
style was absolutely idiosyncratic and his gestures, though
frequently unconnected to beating time in the generally accepted
manner, were extremely effective. I played with him in three
orchestras, the RPO, LSO and the Philharmonia and with all of
them he obtained splendid performances. Subsequently he was
appointed Principal Conductor of the BBC Symphony Orchestra.
This relationship was finally unsuccessful, largely because he
disliked rehearsing, a rare failing in a conductor. Though
orchestras often feel that conductors go on rehearsing far too long,
Rozhdestvensky would at times not rehearse a work that was

unfamiliar to the orchestra sufficiently for them to feel confident that they understood his very unusual gestures.

Gennadi Rozhdestvensky.

Nonetheless, as I was to learn years later when I invited him a number of times to conduct the orchestra at the National Centre for Orchestral Studies for concerts and broadcasts, he got the most remarkable performances from an inexperienced young orchestra with the minimum of rehearsal time. On one occasion I decided that we should create the tension of the recording studio for the young musicians by asking Rozhdestvensky to record the suite from the ballet *The Miraculous Mandarin* by Béla Bartók. This is an extremely difficult piece for every section of the orchestra, technically and rhythmically, so it was arranged that there should be two extra rehearsals with another conductor before Rozhdestvensky joined us. Rozhdestvensky was booked for two sessions, 10.00 a.m. until 1.00 p.m. in the morning and 2.00 p.m. until 5.00 p.m. in the afternoon. In the morning he arrived somewhat later than ten o'clock, rehearsed for just over two hours and decided it was time for lunch. As he wanted to get back home to central London (we were working in Greenwich) he asked if we could restart at 1.30 instead of 2.00. He rehearsed a few of the tricky places for about twenty minutes and decided to record straight away. He recorded the whole work without any re-takes or edits, said ' Thank you. Goodbye' and at about three o'clock went home. I have played this work a number of times, with

Rozhdestvensky and with other conductors, and always found it difficult. Listening to this recording I find it hard to believe it was done in one 'take', with so little preparation and with young inexperienced players.

The Philharmonia Orchestra

When Walter Legge formed the Philharmonia Orchestra in 1945, his position at EMI and the acclaim his new orchestra quickly achieved enabled him to attract the most celebrated and sought after conductors. Arturo Toscanini, Wilhelm Furtwängler, George Szell and Karl Böhm delighted the orchestra, audiences and critics alike. Perhaps Legge's greatest coup was to capture Herbert von Karajan for the Philharmonia in the years before he replaced Furtwängler as Principal Conductor of the Berlin Philharmonic Orchestra. I have already written about Karajan, probably the most successful conductor of the second half of the 20th century. At one time he dominated Europe and had more power than any conductor before or since. His style was to influence many younger conductors.

I was still in the RPO when Toscanini, Furtwängler and Böhm conducted the Philharmonia, but I did play for Karajan and always found it a rewarding experience. I also played for George Szell. Though he was an outstanding musician and conductor I did not enjoy the experience. I do not think it unfair to say that most musicians around the world disliked him.

Karajan conducted the Philharmonia frequently before he took over the Berlin Philharmonic after Furtwangler died in 1954. When I was still in the RPO the Philharmonia asked me to do a concert with them in the Royal Albert Hall. This was the first time I had played for Karajan and I remember how disconcerting it was that he kept his eyes closed all the time (so different from Beecham for whom the eyes were so important). He was a remarkable conductor who combined nearly all the qualities required by a great conductor. The wonderful sinuous musical line he obtained and the subtle gradation of dynamic from the quietest pianissimo to the loudest, powerful fortissimo was unsurpassed. A good example of this ability can be heard in the fourth movement of Respighi's *The Pines of Rome* on the recording he made in 1958 with the Philharmonia. His many recordings with the Berlin

Philharmonic are evidence of the breadth of his repertoire and his ability to create a truly magnificent virtuoso orchestra.

I had the opportunity of witnessing his astonishing gifts when we were in Vienna for several days recording the Beethoven's *Missa Solemnis*. I was delighted to be able to get a ticket for a performance of Verdi's *Falstaff* at the famous Vienna Opera House. My seat was in a box that gave me a good view of the pit. It was a wonderful cast: Elisabeth Schwarzkopf, Giulietta Simionato, Tito Gobbi and with Karajan conducting. After recording the *Missa Solemnis* during the day Karajan came into the pit that evening and conducted, without a score, an immaculate performance of this difficult opera. He demonstrated some of the essential qualities a great conductor must have: a fantastic memory, energy and stamina and a powerful musical intention with the skill to convey that intention.

Another quality nearly all great conductors share is their ability to conduct 'light' music, now seldom played by symphony orchestras in the concert hall other than at the famous Vienna Philharmonic's New Year's Day concerts, or Johann Strauss evenings that have become so popular. Barbirolli, Beecham, Charles Munch and Karajan immediately come to mind. A recording of *The Skater's Waltz* by Waldteufel conducted by Karajan with the Philharmonia is a very good example. In the introduction to the waltz there is a lovely horn solo. On this occasion it was played by Alan Civil, a fine artist in his own right. Like all great conductors Karajan lets Civil play expressively and freely. The player feels he is playing just as he wants to, but in fact it is within the context of the conductor's conception.

Carlo Maria Giulini, extraordinarily elegant and refined in both appearance and in his conducting, was very fine in a wide-ranging repertoire, above all in his reading of the Verdi *Requiem*. He did it a number of times in London with the Philharmonia, each time better than the last, culminating in 1964 with what may well be the definitive performance of this wonderful work. A video of that performance can be seen and heard at the Music Preserved's archives in its Listening Studio in the Barbican library within the Barbican Centre, in the Jerwood Library of the Performing Arts at Trinity College of Music and in the Borthwick Institute at York University. Though he was not actually a pupil of de Sabata, he was much influenced by him and shared some of his charisma and intensity.

The last of the giants (and not only musically) was, in my experience, Otto Klemperer. He was a big man and extremely tall. Even towards the end of his life, when he was in ill health, he stood so erect that as he came in through a doorway his fine head of silver hair brushed against the top lintel. I probably worked with him more often than any

Otto Klemperer
(a photograph he signed for me in 1967).

other conductor except Beecham. No two conductors could have been more dissimilar. Beecham had a rapier-like wit and a sparkling temperament, whilst Klemperer was rock-like with a caustic and devastating humour.

On one of the Philharmonia's trips to Paris, Klemperer was to conduct Mahler's 9th Symphony which we had played several times at concerts and also recorded with him. Towards the end of his life Klemperer never rehearsed on the day of the concert so it had been arranged for him to rehearse in Paris on the evening before the concert. I had already accepted an engagement with another orchestra for that evening so I told the management I was sorry but I was not able go to Paris for the rehearsal. Gerald McDonald, the General Manager, agreed that I could come over on the day of the concert and they would get a player in Paris to take my place for the rehearsal. When I arrived the following day Hugh Bean, then the leader of the orchestra, told me that at the end of the rehearsal the previous evening Klemperer, perhaps wishing to thank my deputy, had called out, 'Eb clarinet!' As there was no response, and his sight was not good, he called out again, 'Eb clarinet'; still no reply. Turning to Hugh he asked, 'where is the Eb player?'. Hugh, seeing that the player had already left the platform, no doubt thinking the rehearsal was over, replied, 'Oh dear! He seems to have gone home'. 'And I don't blame him' said Klemperer.

As a young man he must have been quite frightening, a big man, very tall, with a stern and fierce expression. I have been told that he had a habit, when he wanted to tell a player something at rehearsal, of rushing across the platform and towering over the player. At one rehearsal he suddenly rushed towards the 4th horn player, a small, nervous man. 'Do not be afraid! I am your friend. I have come to tell you, you are no good.' As always he was being himself, direct and honest. It was this quality that he brought to his performances of Beethoven's and Mahler's 9th symphonies. No one else in my experience gave these works the epic quality he did. They had the structure and vastness of a great cathedral – quite overwhelming.

When in 1964 Legge decided to abandon the Philharmonia, he also took its name away. This was a great surprise and devastating for the players. But, in the same way and with the same spirit that the players in the London Philharmonic Orchestra had shown 25 years earlier, they decided to carry on. They re-formed the orchestra, elected their own board of management and asked Otto Klemperer, who had been the Philharmonia's Principal Conductor, if he would continue in that position. He agreed to remain with the orchestra, when it became the New Philharmonia. At that time the future for the orchestra did not look at all certain, so his loyalty was of tremendous importance in the eyes of the public and of immense value to the orchestra. He was a man of great integrity and strength of character, unwilling at any time to bow to expediency.

Throughout this book I have referred to the Philharmonia Orchestra though for a period from 1964, after Legge had gone the orchestra was obliged to call itself the New Philharmonia for about 10 years. I believe that most people thinking of this orchestra think of it as the Philharmonia, certainly musicians do.

As well as capturing a number of the already established 'greats' Legge also had a fine discerning ear and quickly recognised emerging talent. He introduced some remarkable young conductors of outstanding ability to London audiences, including Guido Cantelli, Lorin Maazel and Colin Davis.

Cantelli was thought by quite a few of the critics to be the conductor who would take on the mantle of Toscanini, who in 1950 had said, 'This is the first time in my long career that I have met a young man so gifted. He will go far, very far'. He achieved some very good concert performances and made some fine recordings with the Philharmonia, but unfortunately he was killed in a plane crash when he was only 36 before he was able to fulfil the very high expectations Toscanini had forecast. He was exceptionally demanding, both on and off the platform, even insisting that all the toilets back stage at the Royal Festival Hall be kept locked during all his rehearsals and concerts.

Lorin Maazel immediately astonished everyone with his incredible memory and conducting technique – especially his memory, which was truly remarkable. He never used a score, at rehearsals or concerts, even when there was a soloist. Not only did he know every note of the score, but all the rehearsal numbers or letters. He was still young at that time and though the performances were excellent he was inclined to be extremely cerebral in his interpretations. He was also a fine violinist and had some success as a soloist. When we recorded the opera *Thais* by Massenet he insisted on playing the *Meditation,* the famous violin solo, himself and brought in someone else to conduct that section of the opera. He worked a great deal with the Philharmonia conducting a large repertoire with them and for a time was their Principal Guest Conductor.

I first met Colin Davis a very long time ago when we were both clarinettists. In the early 1950s he came down to Glyndebourne a few times to deputise as second clarinet when I was in the RPO and we were doing the opera season there. He was a very good player but, though at that time I don't think he had done any conducting at all, it was obvious that he had other intentions than playing the clarinet for the rest of his life. We were doing one of the Mozart operas, I think it was *The Marriage of Figaro*, and he had brought the full score of the opera with him. During the arias in which the clarinets do not have a part to play Colin was so intent on studying the score that he was not always ready for his next entry without being prompted.

His big chance came when he took over from Otto Klemperer at the last minute to conduct a concert performance of Mozart's *Don Giovanni* with the Philharmonia at a concert in the Royal Festival Hall. He was an immediate success and his career took off at once. Perhaps it was because he was young and his manner was inclined to be abrasive, plus the very proud attitude of several of the Philharmonia principals, that he only conducted the orchestra very occasionally. At that time his communication and people skills were not yet well developed. Many years later, when I had become Chairman, I felt it was quite unjustified that Colin Davis who had by then achieved a considerable reputation should not be conducting our orchestra. I suggested that we should engage him, but I still met resistance from a number of players and the orchestra lost the opportunity of creating a relationship with a musician who I had believed for a long time was the only young British conductor with the potential to become outstanding and possibly a 'great' conductor. It is not often that one makes a correct forecast but this time there is no doubt that I was right: his collaboration with the LSO as the years went by developed into perhaps the best relationship a London Orchestra has had with a British conductor since that which Beecham had with his orchestras, especially the Royal Philharmonic.

During the years that I played in the Philharmonia we worked with many of the conductors on the international circuit. All of them, in my opinion, were good or very good in the repertoire that suited their temperament: Claudio Abbado, Vladimir Ashkenazy, Rafael Frubeck de Burgos, Andrew Davis, Edward Downes, Bernard Haitink, Norman Del Mar, Igor Markevitch, Kurt Masur, Eduardo Mata, Riccardo Muti, Seiji Ozawa, Mstislav Rostropovich, Kurt Sanderling, Wolfgang Sawallisch, Georg Solti and Yevgeni Svetlanov.

Riccardo Muti was Principal Conductor with the Philharmonia for some years. He took over this position at about the same time that I was elected Chairman of the Council. The orchestra's fortunes and reputation were at a low ebb at that time and we needed someone to instil some discipline into our performances.

Muti was still relatively young and this was his first major appointment. He was respected but made life difficult for himself in that he was very critical and even when everyone was trying as hard as they could to please him he never seemed to be satisfied. Musicians do not need to be

The author with Riccardo Muti.

praised but some kind of response showing that their efforts have not been in vain is necessary if they are not to become discouraged. I had the task of trying to help him understand this. Like many perfectionists he found it very difficult, and often impossible to accept anything but his ideal. He did improve the orchestra to a considerable extent before he took the position of Musical Director of the Philadelphia Orchestra. Now, 30 years later, I have heard several broadcasts, radio and TV, with him conducting, one in particular conducting the Vienna Philharmonic Orchestra at one of their New Year's Day concerts when they play Strauss overtures, waltzes and polkas. This is not the kind of music we associated him with, so that it was a surprise how really good it was, beautifully elegant and charming. Once again showing how dangerous it is to decide about a conductor's talent when he or she is under 40.

Simon Rattle, when he first conducted the Philharmonia.

In 1974 I was tipped off that there was an extremely talented conducting student at the Royal Academy of Music and that I should go to see and hear him that afternoon. When we finished rehearsing I went home to my flat in Welbeck Street, which is only three minutes walk from the Academy. When I arrived at the Royal Academy I found this young conductor, Simon Rattle, rehearsing the student orchestra in preparation for a concert performance of *L'enfant et les Sortileges* by Ravel. After quite a short while I thought, 'this is the real thing.' After consulting with two of my colleagues we decided that although he was then still only 19, the Philharmonia should offer him the opportunity of making his debut with the orchestra at the Royal Festival Hall in 1976, when he would be 21. When he arrived to conduct us he impressed the orchestra from the first rehearsal with his technique, knowledge of the music and his light-handed authority. His ability as a very young man to take charge of a famous orchestra with such ease and charm was remarkable – I have never seen it matched.

His first concert with us was on the 15th of February 1976 when he conducted a splendid programme that included Shostakovich's 10th symphony, which he conducted from memory. At one point our very distinguished principal bassoonist made a false entry and started to play a couple of bars too early. Without any fuss or disturbing his control over the rest of the orchestra

Rattle stopped him after only a note or two and then brought him in again at the correct place in the music.

I have written elsewhere about the qualities a conductor requires but I left out one quality that few have and that Rattle has in abundance – the ability to keep an orchestra happy, even when playing music it does not enjoy playing or that makes demands of an unusual kind. There was one particular composition that I remember him coping with that with anyone else might well have created open hostility from the players. The orchestra had commissioned Peter Maxwell Davies to compose a symphony and undertaken to give the first and some subsequent performances. Maxwell Davies had asked particularly that Simon Rattle should conduct it. The symphony was not difficult technically but it was rhythmically complex and however many times one played it one could never feel sure one was in the right place; so many contrary rhythms were going on at the same time and there seemed to be no melodic pattern to hold on to. At the first performance, as I recall, Rattle conducted it from memory. If I am right, it was an astonishing achievement. We also played *The Song of the Earth* by Mahler and again he conducted from memory. This was a rather ordinary performance that seemed uninspired by sufficient sensitivity, but perhaps this was because he had not allowed enough time for the rehearsal of this wonderful, evocative music, which is difficult in a quite different way to the Maxwell Davies symphony. Learning how to use the available rehearsal time, in Britain usually insufficient, is a skill that comes with experience. Many conductors never learn to organise their time well, and others ask for more time than is needed and alienate the orchestra by boring them. Simon Rattle learned amazingly quickly and therefore soon became welcomed by major orchestras everywhere.

His decision, when he was the conductor and Music Director of the City of Birmingham Orchestra, to remain there for so many years enabled him to create a very fine orchestra from what had previously been a rather ordinary regional orchestra. He also built a regular audience that was prepared to come to concerts and take on trust programmes that in London would have played to a half empty hall. It is not surprising that the Berlin Philharmonic Orchestra decided to appoint him as their Principal Conductor before he was 50.

The conductors I have written about with enthusiasm were respected for their knowledge, ability and musical integrity. But above all it was those who created performances that inspired orchestras to extend themselves to the limit, so that they played better than they thought they could, that were most welcome. Whenever I have heard a relay of a concert or a recording broadcast, when I did not know who the artists involved were, within a few bars I have thought 'this is really good – something special'. When the performers are announced I have nearly always found that it was a performance I had enjoyed in the past, sometimes many years previously. However, I have to admit there have also been other occasions when I have thought 'this is a very good orchestra and an outstanding conductor', only to learn later that it had been an orchestra and conductor for whom I had little regard.

11 The Composer as Conductor

Playing for Benjamin Britten, Malcolm Arnold, Pierre Boulez,
Aaron Copland, Michael Tippett, William Walton,
Ralph Vaughan Williams, John Cage, Igor Stravinsky.

Malcolm Arnold.

During the 19th century, as orchestras became much larger and the music more complex, it was necessary for someone to direct this larger body of musicians. A number of the finest composers, Spohr, Weber, Mendelssohn, Berlioz and, in particular Wagner, whose treatise *On Conducting* had such an influence on the conductor's role, were all also renowned in their lifetime as conductors, as well as composers. Richard Strauss and Mahler were also famous as conductors. Mahler, in particular, was so busy as a conductor that he had difficulty in finding time to compose between engagements. There have also been a number of outstanding conductors who would in fact have preferred to be remembered as composers. Furtwängler, Weingartner, Koussevitsky, de Sabata and Klemperer were all composers whose compositions were published and received a number of performances.

I played for quite a few composers who when conducting their own music did so extremely well. There were some others who were excellent conductors of whatever music they directed: Constant Lambert, who had a successful career as a conductor, mainly with the Sadler's Wells Ballet and the Royal Ballet; Benjamin Britten, a wonderful musician who was also a fine pianist and an outstanding conductor. The best performance I have ever heard of the *German Requiem* by Brahms was conducted by him, as well as some very fine readings of Mozart and Schubert symphonies. He could be a hard taskmaster and could be caustic in his criticism. I played under his direction a number of times in the orchestra and on one occasion, the most frightening, I took part in a performance of the Janacek *Concertino* for piano and sextet at the Aldeburgh Festival, with Britten playing the piano. Oliver Knussen (the son of my old friend Stuart, from my Wessex Orchestra touring days) is another composer who has done a good deal of conducting mainly concentrating on his own music and the music from the second half of the 20th century, always obtaining very good results.

Pierre Boulez has an international reputation as a conductor – he was chief conductor of the BBC Symphony Orchestra from 1971 until 1975 and the New York Philharmonic from 1971 till 1978 – and is probably better known in this capacity than as a composer. His compositions are yet to join the mainstream orchestral repertoire – will he be remembered as a composer or a conductor? There can be no doubt that since 1960 Boulez has brought his composer's insight, sensitive ear and analytical mind to his interpretation of 'modern' music from Schoenberg and Webern to the present day and in the process demanded from orchestras a degree of accuracy that had frequently been absent. In my own experience it was his conducting of the *Rite of Spring* by Stravinsky that was particularly impressive. The part he played in establishing a standard of accuracy in the performance of the *Rite of Spring* cannot be exaggerated. It was with him when he came to conduct the Philharmonia, sometime in the 1960s, that for the first time that I can recall, we actually played what Stravinsky had written, rhythmically, in regard to note values and the correct balance of the parts. Over the years we played a wide-ranging repertoire with him including Debussy, Stravinsky, Webern and Messiaen, Haydn and Beethoven. He always brought clarity and balance to everything he conducted, but was most admirably suited to contemporary music.

Malcolm Arnold was for some years principal trumpet in the LPO. He was a very good player and brought that particular insight composers have to everything he played in the orchestra. There were some passages that, for me at least, when he played them (he frequently sat just behind me in the orchestra) made more musical sense than when played by anyone else. He was a natural conductor and not only of his own music. While he was still in the LPO we did a public rehearsal of *Larch Trees,* the first orchestral composition of his to be performed in public. It was also the first orchestral work to be given this opportunity with funds from the Society for the Promotion of New Music (SPNM). Later I played for him many times on film sessions when we recorded the music he had written. Some 40 years later I was able to arrange for Sir Charles Groves and the National Centre for Orchestral Studies Orchestra to give the first performance of his 9th Symphony, now a well-respected work, commissioned by the BBC but which they refused to broadcast until a good many years later.

Aaron Copland, Michael Tippett, William Walton and Vaughan Williams immediately come to mind as composers who, though they lacked technical expertise to a varying extent as conductors, brought a special musical insight to performances of their own music. There were some composers, of course, who were hopeless as conductors, having neither the temperament nor the necessary skill. When Sir Thomas Beecham, a friend of Frederick Delius and a champion of his music, was asked in a broadcast interview, 'Did Delius conduct his own music?' 'Well', he said, 'I have seen in my time good conductors, not so good, competent conductors, indifferent conductors – but I have never come across such an abysmal depth of ineptitude as revealed by poor old Frederick. It was quite a common thing for him to beat five in the bar when it should be four. He beat 1,2,3,4 and, which turned it into five. Well, of course, the orchestra became almost distracted. The public became restless, "What's going on? – what's going on?" Something always went on when Delius conducted a work of his own. But there was a time when he used to practise many hours a day – for weeks at a time in front of a mirror, endeavouring to understand this mysterious craft, but to no purpose at all.'

Working for John Cage was a very different experience from playing for anyone else. I played for him for a week when he was conducting the small group of musicians providing the music for the Merce Cunningham Dance Company. The music Cage had written for this avant-garde dance company and the music that had been commissioned from other composers did not use music notation in the conventional way, nor were any two performances alike.

In one piece we were instructed to play as many notes as possible in the top register of our instrument in the length of time of each note value in the part, perhaps a crotchet or minim (1/4 or 1/2 note). How many notes each of us could play depended on the tempo that Cage selected. In another composition the players had to decide how much time to allow for each line of music in their part. Cage conducted this piece by holding up his arm as if it was the hand of a clock. He then moved his arm round the imaginary clock face, but at varying speeds. He might on one occasion go from 12 to 1 o'clock very slowly, when one had allowed a long time for that section, and then move from 1 to 3 very much more quickly. Depending on the section of music, one might have to play a section with long notes extremely slowly and the next section, which already had a good many fast notes, even faster, perhaps faster than one could manage. At the next performance it might be the reverse.

There was one composition with the instruction that when another player played a certain phrase one had to go immediately to another place in one's part or perform some particular action. At one point in the trumpet part the player was instructed to make the loudest sound he could. The player on this occasion had an intense dislike for this kind of music and resented having to do things he considered inappropriate. We were playing in the large orchestra pit at Sadler's Wells Theatre, which has a concrete floor and walls, and, as always, the normal heavy iron fire doors. At the appointed point in his part the trumpeter got up from his seat, walked slowly and deliberately across the pit to one of the fire doors and slammed it shut as hard as he could. The bang this made was like a bomb exploding. His intention was that Cage should be displeased, perhaps upset. Instead, Cage was delighted and said 'Thank you. That is the best I have ever heard it!

Igor Stravinsky was an undoubted genius and to have the opportunity to work with him even once was good fortune; I had this opportunity three times. That was indeed to have been smiled on by the gods. In 1936 in his book *Chronicle of my Life,* Stravinsky writes very outspokenly about the way conductors 'interpreted' his music. 'With regard to the *Sacre,* which I was tackling for the first time, I was particularly anxious in some of the parts *(Glorification of the Elect, Evocation of Ancestors, Dance of Consecration)* to give the bars their true metric value, and to have them played exactly as they were written. I lay stress on this point, which may seem to the reader to be a purely professional detail. But with a few exceptions, such as Monteux and Ansermet, for example, most conductors are inclined to cope with the metric difficulties of these passages in such a cavalier fashion as to distort alike my music and my intentions. This is what happens. Fearing to make a mistake in a sequence of bars of varying values, some conductors do not hesitate to ease their task by treating them as of equal length. By such methods the strong and weak tempi are obviously displaced, and it is left to the musicians to perform the onerous task of readjusting the accents in the new bars as improvised by the conductors, a task so difficult that even if there is no catastrophe the listener expects one at any moment and is immersed in an atmosphere of intolerable strain.'

The first time I played for Stravinsky was in 1954, when I was in the Royal Philharmonic Orchestra. He had come to London to conduct a programme of his own works at a Royal Philharmonic Society concert. He was already 72 and one might have expected that he would no longer be at his most vigorous, but though he appeared physically quite frail his mind was as agile and incisive as any I have experienced. His clarity of thought and certainty of intention was exciting in itself and he had the ability to make his wishes as a conductor clear, both in words and by his gestures.

A feature of much of Stravinsky's music is his use of small note values: sixteenth, thirty-second and sixty-fourth notes. When combined with the many changes of time signature, varying through 3/4, 2/8, 7/16, the very small note values call for great accuracy of performance. I had already worked with Ernest

Ansermet, praised by Stravinsky, when we recorded the original version of *Petrushka* with the London Philharmonic in 1946. (I also took part in the recording of the complete ballet music for *The Firebird* when Ansermet conducted the Philharmonia many years later in 1968, a year before he died). But working with Ansermet had not prepared me for the extreme precision that Stravinsky demanded when he rehearsed his *Orpheus*. One felt his intelligence was like a razor-sharp blade, stripping away everything that was inessential and dross.

Ernest Ansermet.

In the interval of that concert he was presented with the Gold Medal of the Royal Philharmonic Society. Perhaps because only that which is true and without blemish was acceptable to him, he pursued this ideal with his usual concentration of purpose. When he was presented with the medal by Sir Arthur Bliss, he put it between his teeth and gave it an examining bite. Fortunately for the honour of the Society and the composure of Sir Arthur, the medal passed this rigorous test and received Stravinsky's approbation.

On the 29th May 1963 Pierre Monteux's long association with Stravinsky was celebrated at a concert given by the London Symphony Orchestra at the Royal Albert Hall. On that date, exactly 50 years previously, Monteux had conducted the first performance of the *Rite of Spring*. In 1913 the work created a *scandale*; the audience were so inflamed and noisy that Nijinsky had been obliged to stand on a chair at the side of the stage and shout out the numbers to the dancers. On this occasion Stravinsky, who earlier that evening had attended a gala performance of *The Marriage of Figaro* by Mozart at the Royal Opera House, Covent Garden, only arrived in time to hear the second half of this work, which even in 1963 was not often performed and one that orchestras still found difficult, and to witness the tremendous ovation this previously controversial music received.

The orchestra was unaware of his presence and it came as a surprise to them to see the very elderly Pierre Monteux leave the platform to make his way through the audience to greet Stravinsky who was sitting in one of the boxes. I have been told that the sight of these two veterans of 20th century music embracing with such affection was a very moving and unforgettable sight.

However, despite what Stravinsky had written in 1936 in his book *Chronicle of my Life,* it seems that Monteux was indeed one of the conductors who later in life decided to cope with the metric difficulties of bars of varying values by changing the way they were written and therefore conducted. Though Stravinsky did not show his displeasure, it is reported that he was rather unhappy with the performance.

The next time I played for Stravinsky was in the summer of 1963 when the Philharmonia was on an extensive tour of South America. To our surprise, in the middle of the tour, we suddenly found we were scheduled to do a concert in Rio de Janeiro with Stravinsky and his close associate Robert Craft. The programme consisted of *Fireworks,* the Symphony in C, and the ballet music for *Le Baiser de la Fée,* which Stravinsky conducted. In the years since 1954 he had become even more frail, but his mind was as clear and precise as before, and the performance was exact and memorable.

The third and last occasion when Stravinsky enriched my experience was in September 1965. He was now a mere wisp of a man, ill, and it seemed somewhat dejected, or perhaps just tired. He had flown to London from Hamburg to appear at the Royal Festival Hall for the European premiere of his *Variations in Memory of Aldous Huxley.* The other works in the programme were, *Fireworks, The Rite of Spring* and *The Firebird Suite,* in the infrequently performed 1945 version. Stravinsky conducted *Fireworks* and *The Firebird Suite* and Robert Craft, his associate conductor again, the rest of the programme.

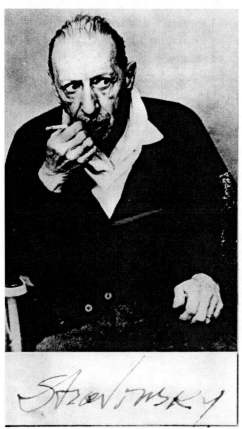

Igor Stravinsky signed this for me when he was unwell, during the rehearsals in 1965 for the wonderful concert he gave with the Philharmonia in the Royal Festival Hall.

Though he was unwell, during the interval of the rehearsal, as he sat, cosseted by his wife and wrapped in towels and blankets, he was kind enough to inscribe a copy of his *Conversations with Robert Craft* for me. A copy of that signature is testimony to the energy that still propelled this remarkable man, now 83, through a creative life spanning over 60 years, during which he had startled, affronted, and delighted generations of audiences.

I remember that it was a wonderful performance. The orchestra played at its very best; in fact above its best, as can happen on very special occasions when in the presence of someone inspirational, someone for whom everyone has respect. Every member of the orchestra took risks: played softer and louder than was safe, attacked entries with abandon.

Now, nearly forty years later it is no longer necessary just to rely on the ageing memories of elderly musicians or members of the audience who were present on that historic evening. The second half of the programme was televised by the BBC who several years ago made a video copy of this wonderful performance available to Music Preserved, on Licence, for its archives (at the

Barbican library within the Barbican Centre, the Jerwood Library of the Performing Arts at Trinity College of Music and now also in the Borthwick Institute at York University). Now a commercial video has been issued of Stravinsky conducting this performance of *The Firebird*. On the video in the Music Preserved Archives the whole of the BBC programme is available: Robert Craft conducts the *Variations in Memory of Aldous Huxley*, twice, with Stravinsky in the audience, and the concert ends with Stravinsky conducting his *Firebird Suite*. It is really moving to see how the performance and the audience's standing ovation reanimated and delighted him. The audience demanded so many bows, obviously hoping for an encore, that in the end they would only let him go when he returned with his overcoat on, making it clear he was leaving.

12 The London Orchestras

The London Philharmonic, Royal Philharmonic, Philharmonia – between 1904 and 1963 – all become self-managed. Despite financial problems – lack of subsidy and patronage – the orchestras survive. The Goodman Committee. Comparison with orchestras in Europe and USA – their financial support and conditions.

All four of the 'London Orchestras', the usual description that includes the London Symphony Orchestra (LSO), the London Philharmonic Orchestra (LPO), the Royal Philharmonic Orchestra (RPO) and the Philharmonia (sometimes, on tour abroad, called the Philharmonia of London) are self-administered. Their Boards of Directors are wholly, or to a considerable extent, elected members of the orchestra. They employ a General Manager (or Managing Director) and the necessary staff. The members of the other orchestras based in London, the BBC Orchestras, the Royal Opera House and the English National Opera Orchestra are employed on contract in the usual way.

While I was a professional musician, from 1943 until 1979, I was in turn a member of three of the London orchestras, the LPO, the RPO and finally the Philharmonia – the last two when they were Sir Thomas's and Walter Legge's, and then when they were self-administered. Some years later, from 1974-79 I was Chairman of the Council of the Philharmonia (as its Board of Directors is called because it is a Company Limited by Guarantee). Although I was never a member of the LSO I was engaged by them on a good many occasions during the 1960s as an extra or deputy. Between 1964 and 1979 I was also very involved as an elected member of the Executive Committee of the Musicians' Union that from time to time played a considerable part in coming to the rescue of several of the London orchestras.

There are not many other self-administered orchestras in the world; the Vienna Philharmonic is an outstanding exception; all the other orchestras in Britain are managed. Self-management has over the years been the cause of considerable opposition from those who believe that musicians, like other groups of workers, whether in industry, commerce or the arts are unsuited to manage their own affairs. In particular, in the case of musicians, there have always been those who feel that they should not be given the responsibility for managing their financial affairs.

Before going into why the musicians in three of the London orchestras were obliged to take over the management of their orchestras between 1939 and 1964, in order to maintain their existence, it is necessary to understand the economics of the symphony orchestra. An orchestra is labour intensive requiring a large number of performers to rehearse and then perform in concert halls that will hold an audience of from 1200/1500 to 3000. The same is true for opera houses.

Symphony orchestras everywhere have always been dependent on patronage. It is impossible for any concert hall or opera house to take sufficient money at the box office even with a full house when every seat is taken, to pay for the number of musicians, singers, the conductor and soloist, that a concert or opera performance requires. Patronage for the groups of musicians that developed into orchestras was first provided by the church and then by kings and the many princes and counts of the principalities all over Europe. Later, with the growth of the bourgeoisie in the 19th century, many city authorities took on this responsibility. In America, from the beginning of the 20th century, men who had arrived penniless from Europe and made their fortunes in the USA, endowed orchestras in the major cities as a way of establishing themselves, and particularly their wives, as members of local society.

It was only in 1940, when the Council for the Encouragement of Music and the Arts (CEMA) was established with funding from the Treasury, that for the first time a state subsidy for the arts became available in Britain. CEMA, which was set up to provide entertainment and to raise morale for both the armed forces and the civilian population was a quite revolutionary step and was taken with barely any resistance and, in fact, with hardly anyone noticing. It at once gave artists, actors and musicians the opportunity to play an important part in the war effort. Then, after the end of the war in 1945, CEMA, once again without any protest, was quietly transformed into the Arts Council of Great Britain.

The establishment of the Arts Council with funding from the Government allowed public money to be allocated to arts organisations of all kinds, especially those that had in the past had to rely entirely on private financial aid. Unlike the situation in most other European countries where during the 19th century a tradition had developed all over Europe of supporting orchestras, for historical and social reasons this did not happen in Britain until 1946, very much later than elsewhere. However, the Government in Britain, in contrast to the policy in most other countries, has operated a 'hands off' policy, leaving the Arts Council free to designate where funding should be provided.

The first full-time symphony orchestra was not established in Britain until the formation of the BBC Symphony Orchestra in 1930. An orchestra, the Bournemouth Municipal, was formed in 1893 by Dan Godfrey and funded by the local authority and, though not a symphony orchestra it did provide regular employment throughout the year. It is interesting to see what that orchestra played at their first performance.

March	The Standard Bearer	Fahrbach
Overture	Raymond	Thomas
Valse	Je t'aime	Waldteufel
Ballet Music	Rosamunde	Schubert
Russian Masurka	La Czarine	Ganne
Entr'acte	La Colombe	Gounod
Selection	The Gondoliers	Sullivan

During the 19th century a number of orchestras were created: the Hallé in Manchester, the Liverpool Philharmonic and several elsewhere, but none gave concerts throughout the year, usually only having at most a six-month season.

In 1895 Henry Wood, later Sir Henry, was engaged by Robert Newman to conduct a season of Promenade Concerts at the Queen's Hall in London. His first Promenade season programme was of a similar character to that played by the Bournemouth Orchestra. It consisted of overtures including *Rienzi* by Wagner and *Mignon* by Ambroise Thomas, a number of songs such as Leoncavallo's *The Prologue to Pagliacci* and *Loch Lomond* and popular instrumental solos like that for the bassoon, *Lucy Long,* and flute and cornet solos.

Henry Wood conducted his Queen's Hall Orchestra in a series of concerts each year as well as for the Promenade season. The orchestra still retained the deputy system that had operated throughout the music profession in Britain for many years. It was because of the lack of regular employment that musicians felt it was necessary to maintain as many of their connections as possible. However, Henry Wood was determined to create a really good orchestra so that it would not be possible for anyone in future to say that England was 'das Land ohne Musik'. To this end he needed to weld a group of musicians, playing together on a fairly regular basis under his direction, into an ensemble that could compare with the finest orchestras in Europe and America. He was frustrated by the deputy system which resulted in the constant absence of some of his key players from rehearsals, and sometimes even from performances. As time went by Henry Wood became increasingly exasperated by the constant appearance of deputies until one day the matter came to a head. In his autobiography *My Life of Music* he recalls how he arrived for rehearsal and 'found an orchestra with seventy or eighty unknown faces in it. Even my leader was missing'.

He had to contend with this until in 1904, by which time his reputation and authority had grown sufficiently for him to instruct his manager to inform the orchestra 'In future there will be no deputies'. The next day 40 members of the orchestra resigned. Those 40 musicians were to form the nucleus of the London Symphony Orchestra, a co-operative organisation in which the players accepted the financial responsibility, controlled the orchestra's artistic policy, and engaged conductors and soloists. From being employees they became the employers. As there was no contract the musicians were paid at the end of each engagement, and always in cash. I remember being paid in this way whenever I played with them well into the 1960s. It was the only major orchestra in my experience to do this.

In 1905 three outstanding players formed the New Symphony Orchestra, another self-administered orchestra, which in 1920 became the Royal Albert Hall Orchestra and in 1909 Sir Thomas Beecham founded the Beecham Symphony Orchestra but, unlike the LSO, neither lasted for many years. The next major orchestra to be formed was the BBC Symphony Orchestra, in 1930, the first orchestra to offer the players a full-time contract. The Corporation went even further than Sir Henry Wood: not only were deputies absolutely forbidden, members of the orchestra were not allowed to do any other orchestral work

The London Philharmonic Orchestra Limited was formed in 1932, with Sir Thomas Beecham as Founder and Artistic Director. His co-directors were distinguished and wealthy patrons of the arts: Viscount Esher, Robert Mayer, Samuel Courtauld and Baron Frederick Alfred d'Erlanger. Though the others joined him in providing the initial funding to establish the London Philharmonic Orchestra, it was in reality Beecham's orchestra. His intention was to have an orchestra that would, like the BBC Symphony, have no deputies and be as full-time as possible. He put together a schedule that included the Beecham Sunday Concerts, the Courtauld-Sargent Concerts and providing the orchestra for the Royal Philharmonic Society and the Royal Choral Society concerts. He also accepted engagements from organisations around the country, and arranged to do a number of gramophone recordings. Longer periods of employment for the orchestra were provided by the International Opera Season and the Russian Ballet season both at the Royal Opera House, Covent Garden. Even so, this did not create enough work for the orchestra to be engaged on a full-time basis so that the players did still have to maintain their other professional connections.

In 1940, at the beginning of, Beecham went to America, leaving his orchestra without any work or financial support. To keep the orchestra going the players decided to form a co-operative company, which they named Musical Culture Limited. The first thing the new board of management had to do was to find engagements for the orchestra, not an easy task for those more used to playing their instruments than managing an orchestra and with the country at war. The members of the orchestra did the first concerts on a truly co-operative basis: they shared out what little was left after all expenses had been paid. I was told that for the first concert this amounted to 5 shillings (25p), the equivalent of about £12/15 today.

It was not long before a number of the players were being called up to join one or other of the armed services. The task of replacing them and getting deputies of the required standard was becoming increasingly difficult. In addition, the orchestra was obliged to do many more engagements away from London, which many of the best players were not too keen on. The orchestra decided that the best thing would be for everyone to receive a regular weekly salary. By the time I joined the orchestra in 1943 as second clarinet, my salary was £10.50 a week with a small amount extra to help with the cost of over-night accommodation, depending on how many 'out-of-town' dates there were in the week. When I left to join the Royal Philharmonic in 1947 I was receiving around £12/13 a week.

Until I joined the RPO I had always been on a weekly salary. Suddenly I found I was paid for each engagement I played. The fee would depend on whether it was for a concert in London, an out of town concert or for an extra rehearsal, a children's concert, broadcast, recording or film session. I see from my old diaries that in 1947 there were weeks when I earned as much as £45, followed by a week when I only earned as little as £10 or £15. After a time, when I had made some freelance connections, I found, as I had been told I would, that I was earning a great deal more than I had in the LPO. Beecham paid his musicians well. As second clarinet I was paid £4.20 for a concert instead of the Musicians' Union rate which was £2.75. Principal players received £5.25 instead of £3.00.

Walter Legge, who was employed by the major recording company, at that time EMI, created the Philharmonia in 1945 mainly for making what were then called gramophone records. They were those large, black, double-sided discs that played for about four and a half minutes on each side, and can still sometimes be found lurking at the back of the second-hand section of record shops. For some years the Philharmonia was fully occupied making records and gave very few concerts.

Then, in 1946 Sir Thomas founded the Royal Philharmonic Orchestra. He established an exclusive contract with EMI for his orchestra to make a considerable number of records each year for five years and an agreement with Glyndebourne Opera for the orchestra to play for their season each year. He also persuaded the Royal Philharmonic Society, with which he had been associated for so many years, that the orchestra could use the title 'Royal Philharmonic' and undertake the Society's concerts.

There was a good deal of competition for players between the RPO and the Philharmonia and one or two players like Dennis Brain managed to play in both for a time. In the early years both orchestras were very busy making recordings. The conditions were very similar in both orchestras, though the Philharmonia probably had rather more recording sessions, much sought after as one was paid the same for a session of three hours as for a concert with a three-hour rehearsal in the morning.

Dennis Brain.

Everything went very well until Sir Thomas ceased conducting in 1960. When he died in 1961 Rudolf Kempe became the Principal Conductor but, of course, he had other commitments and was not involved in such a personal way as Beecham had been. The management gradually found the task of finding work for the orchestra more and more difficult, their problems being made very much worse, first by the loss of the Glyndebourne season and then by the decision of the Royal Philharmonic Society to terminate their agreement with the Orchestra whereby it would lose the use of the title 'Royal'. In 1963, The Anglo-American Music Association Ltd., the company Beecham had established, gave up control of the Orchestra and the players decided to emulate the course taken by the musicians in the LPO in 1939, when they had found themselves in a similar unhappy situation. They formed a new company, Rophora Ltd., elected a board of Directors from the members of the orchestra, managed to retain their name intact, and became another self-administered orchestra.

I had been playing in the Philharmonia from the late 1950s and was a member of the orchestra in 1964 when Walter Legge decided he no longer wanted the responsibility of owning an orchestra. He not only disbanded the orchestra; he took its name away as well. Again the players had to take the only course open to them if they wished to survive; they too became a self-administered orchestra and were obliged to rename themselves The New Philharmonia Orchestra. It was to be more than 10 years before they were able to obtain their original name again and once more become the Philharmonia.

Notwithstanding adversity the four London orchestras survived. None of them had either an outstanding conductor like Beecham, or a man with a personality like Legge, with his involvement in the recording industry at EMI as well as his many close associates in the world of music. More serious was the decline in the volume of recording. This particularly affected the two orchestras that had been created in the aftermath of the war in 1945/6, the Philharmonia and the RPO, which depended to a considerable extent on their recording work.

There was a body of opinion that felt there were too many orchestras in London and not a large enough audience to sustain four orchestras. It was said that two was ample and that, perhaps, one large orchestra assembled from the best players from the current four orchestras might enable Britain to have an orchestra to match those in Berlin, Amsterdam, New York and Chicago. On the other hand, there were others who believed that the current number should not be changed.

In December 1964 the Arts Council and the London County Council, which in 1965 became the Greater London Council (GLC), appointed the Committee on the London Orchestras under the Chairmanship of Arnold Goodman, who shortly after the Report was issued in 1965 became Lord Goodman. The Committee's terms of reference were: to examine the organisation of the four orchestras; decide whether their number should be maintained, increased, reduced or regrouped and what steps should be taken to improve the stability and working conditions of the musicians. The Committee was told that it should consider the desirability of a co-ordinated orchestral concert policy, so as to ensure that programmes and performances were of the highest standard.

In 1965 the then Labour government held the view that the Performing Arts – music, opera, ballet and theatre – which had been the preserve of the upper and middle-classes, should also be available to what was still referred to as the Working-class. It was also determined, if possible, to maintain employment wherever it could. I was elected by the Executive Committee of the Musicians' Union to represent the Union, alongside the General Secretary Hardie Ratcliffe. The other interests represented were the Arts Council, the London County Council and the Orchestral Employers' Association, now the Association of British Orchestras (ABO).

The Report, usually referred to as the Goodman Report, was accepted by Lord Cottesloe with the commendation to Miss Jennie Lee, the Parliamentary Under-Secretary of State at the Department of Education and Science, expressing the hope that the necessary financial resources to implement the Report would be made available. It is not too much to say that Jennie Lee and Lord Goodman, both Labour supporters (today they would certainly be considered on the left of the Party though at that time they were much more mainstream) were responsible for the four orchestras remaining, and continuing to do so until the present time.

I had already been involved in negotiations with quite a few employers in several areas of musical employment, but this was my first experience of taking part in preparing a report that was likely to have a profound effect on the future of my colleagues alongside people representing such conflicting interests. Only Arnold Goodman's legendary skills as a diplomat enabled us to complete our task.

There were some members of the Committee who wanted to reduce the number of orchestras in London, opposed by those of us representing the welfare of the musicians currently working in the four orchestras. Other members of the Committee were concerned that in looking after the London orchestras it might be at the expense of the Regional orchestras. The most important group, those with the responsibility for providing the funding for all the orchestras, were ever watchful that no decisions were arrived at that would be too costly.

There was unanimous agreement on the Committee and among those from whom they took evidence that if first class playing standards were to be maintained a musician should not be required to work more than 10 sessions a week or 35/36 in any four-week period. That would mean approximately 27/30 hours a week, still more hours than nearly all orchestras around the world, especially for the woodwind and brass principals. Most orchestras in Europe and America, even those in the smaller cities, had four of each woodwind instrument with co-principals in the woodwind and brass who would share the work between themselves, so that each of them usually did no more than about 18/20 hours a week as part of their contract.

The Committee then considered the amount of work there was likely to be for the orchestras. It came to the conclusion that with the agreed work schedule there was enough for more than three but less than four. The fact that we were shown the plans for building the Barbican Centre with a large new concert hall (it was some years before this was finally built) played a part in the final decision that the four orchestras should continue as before. Now, 40 years later, we still have four orchestras.

The Committee made a number of other recommendations: some were implemented, others were not. The London Orchestral Concert Board was created and was given the task of overseeing the administration of the orchestras, the distribution of subsidies, organising the concert dates at the Royal Festival Hall, and the co-ordination of programme planning. This last had been a big problem for some time; popular works such as the Tchaikovsky Piano Concerto No.1, or Beethoven's 5th Symphony might feature in several programmes within a matter of weeks.

A major recommendation was that a standard contract be established that would guarantee a basic salary, and include provision for holiday and sick pay and some sort of pension scheme. This has not come to pass for a number of reasons. First and foremost there has never been the possibility of sufficient funds being made available, by either Local or National Government, to pay for the administration of the orchestras and the salaries of the musicians, if they were only to work the recommended number of hours and have a paid holiday.

The members of the orchestras were not keen on the idea of a contract unless their salaries were to match what they could earn from their current orchestral employment plus what they could earn from their freelance work. It was clear from the start that this would never happen. But there were two other reasons why the players were not enthusiastic: they did not trust those who would be in charge of the 'money bags' and they feared that a full-time contract would incur a change in their taxation status.

They knew how managed orchestras in London had collapsed in the past and how each time it had required the musicians to take responsibility for the survival of their orchestra. This had made them suspicious of putting their future in anyone else's hands again. They were also concerned that as full-time employees they would have to give up the advantages of being on Schedule D. When registered on Schedule D their home was considered their 'work base', so that they could (and still can) claim expenses for all travelling, by car or public transport, repairs to their instrument, dress clothes for concert wear and so on; even the cost of a room in which to practise and give lessons. I enjoyed these benefits throughout my performing career until I became Director of the National Centre for Orchestral Studies and was paid a regular salary. Fortunately my salary was sufficient for the loss of my Schedule D benefits to no longer be of concern. However, like most musicians, who Lord Goodman noted, 'are as conversant with Schedule D as with D major', I continued to remain on 'D' for my private teaching, examining and other odds and ends.

Throughout the time I have been involved with what we used to refer to as the 'music profession' that then became the 'music business', and is now the 'music industry' (Oh! Dear!), London has had a much envied music scene: four orchestras, employing the finest conductors and soloists from all over the world, providing at least one symphony concert every evening throughout the year, and two full-time opera houses. The amount of financial support received from Local and National Government to pay for the salaries of the musicians in all the orchestras in London has been about a quarter of what has been given practically anywhere else in Europe. In the USA the orchestras in Cleveland, New York, Chicago and other cities with major orchestras have had the benefit of an income derived from the interest from the donations they had received in the past from those wishing to gain entry into 'society', in addition to a continuing tradition of private patronage to the arts.

How has London achieved this? With financial assistance from the Arts Council and the hard work of the musicians in the symphony orchestras themselves. Without the input from the Arts Council it is unlikely it would have been possible. However, from the start in 1946 the funding they have provided has been inadequate, at times better than at others, but never sufficient to support a year round concert season bringing in the finest and most expensive conductors and soloists. These star artists were essential if audiences were to be attracted in sufficient numbers though they soaked up virtually the whole subsidy, leaving nothing over to pay for the cost of the orchestras and their administration. For 60 years it has been a bumpy ride with everyone just managing to stay on board.

But, in the end, it has only really been possible because the musicians themselves have continued to subsidise the concerts in London by doing recordings and film sessions, overseas tours, and working nearly twice as many hours and earning much less than their colleagues in Europe and America. The recommendation of the Goodman Committee in 1964 that the orchestras should work 27/30 hours a week still remains unfulfilled. However, musicians in Britain continue to enable Londoners and the many music lovers who visit London from all over the world to enjoy an envied musical experience that has continued to flourish for over half a century.

13 Keep Music Live

Musicians playing in theatres – incidental music, opera, musicals; in Music Halls – conditions – playing for jugglers, trapeze artists and the Diaghilev Ballet Company and Sir Harry Lauder; for the 'silent cinema'; for dancing.

Since men and women first started to make noises that through time developed into music, those who made the sounds and those who have heard them had to be in the same place at the same time. The Musicians' Union's long-time clarion call 'Keep Music Live' represents how musicians responded to the erosion of the relationship music makers and their audience had always had until the invention of moving pictures, sound recording and broadcasting changed this relationship for ever.

When my father became a professional musician in 1906, aged 12, there were more musicians playing in theatres of one kind or another than anywhere else. There was also a great deal of employment in hotels, restaurants and cafes, and on bandstands in the parks. During the summer months most seaside resorts had Pierrot shows and a band on the pier or on the municipal bandstand and a few of the larger resorts had orchestras with as many as 40 or 50 players. Musicians, as in nearly all cultures, were required whenever and wherever there was dancing.

Gradually from 1927 onwards, when the 'talkies' supplanted silent films and more and more people had wireless sets and gramophones, the number of musicians employed for outdoor entertainment reduced. There were still a considerable number of musicians employed playing in hotels, restaurants and cafes until the start of the war in 1939, but the call-up of musicians to the armed forces and rationing reduced their number considerably and within a few years this field of employment had virtually disappeared. In 1942, when I joined the profession, there was still a good deal of employment in theatres and Music Halls, though nothing like as much as in my father's day. Dancing continued to be extremely popular, providing one of the main opportunities for men and women to meet each other outside the workplace.

Musicians playing in the Theatres

At the beginning of the 20th century many musicians were employed playing for a variety of theatrical entertainment in the London theatres. There were musical comedies and operettas, such as *The Arcadians, The Chocolate Soldier* and *Naughty Marietta,* the Gilbert and Sullivan operas, and seasons of opera and ballet at the Royal Opera House, Covent Garden and Drury Lane Theatre. After a successful London run productions would usually go on tour to the larger towns all over the country.

Many theatres employed a trio or quartet to play 'Incidental Music' before the performance of plays, between the acts, during the intervals and at the end as the audience was leaving. Some productions had music especially written for them when there might be a small orchestra of as many as twenty players to play background music in appropriate places and, as in a number of the Shakespeare plays, to accompany songs, as well as play incidental music. Some of this music, such as Roger Quilter's incidental music for *As You Like It,* the music Delius wrote for *Hassan* and, most famous of all, the beautiful music Mendelssohn wrote for *A Midsummer Night's Dream,* have become part of the concert repertoire.

An essential talent required by all theatre musicians is the ability to sight-read quickly and accurately. Wherever musicians were employed there was usually less time allowed for rehearsals in my father's day than there is now. When a show was on tour there would seldom be more than one rehearsal for the local musicians to run through all the music and, of course, for a deputy there was none. When one goes as a deputy one will not have seen the music before and will often find that the manuscript, from which one has to read the music, is in poor condition because during the rehearsals and on the tour, which nearly always precedes the London opening, a good many changes to the original production and music may have been made. Some sections may have been cut and then, possibly, reinstated; some of the notes may have been altered and in places additional music may have been inserted – and then taken out again. More often than not these alterations will have been made by each player in their own part at the time. All these amendments will have been recognisable to the player, but for anyone seeing the music for the first time and not being accustomed to the writer's possibly rough and ready music penmanship, they can be very difficult, sometimes even impossible, to decipher.

These hazards are often multiplied by poor lighting (far worse in the early years of the last century), difficulty in seeing the conductor because of the cramped conditions in the pit and the fact that if the show has been running for a while the conductor will frequently take it for granted that everyone understands his beat. He is unlikely to be in the class of conductor I have written about with enthusiasm and, if the show has been on for a while, he may be rather bored. There will be places when, because the singer holds a note for longer than the written notation indicates, or the action on stage needs more time than the composed music allows for, the music has had to be stretched out. Some beats will have had to be subdivided so that the conductor has to give some more beats. In another place he will suddenly, without warning, start beating very much faster to deal with a hastening of the action on stage. If, as is quite common, there is nothing in the part to alert the deputy that one of these surprising events is to occur, the result can be a minor disaster. My own experience, when deputising at one show, was that it took me several visits before I could make sense of what the conductor was doing. One or two passages remained un-played. Fortunately for me they were well covered by what others were playing. Once again the famous caution that has saved me on a number of occasions – 'if in doubt, leave it out' – came to my rescue.

The few occasions when I have taken on the hazardous task of being a deputy I have found it quite terrifying. One feels under additional pressure because, generally, managements have an understandable dislike of deputies and would prefer that they could disallow them. You know that if you make a mistake, that in itself might be quite small, it could have a devastating effect. If it happens that someone on stage relies on a note or a passage of music to make their entry and it is missing, or in the wrong place, it can have serious consequences and if you were the deputy responsible it is unlikely you will be engaged for that show again. If you were the player who sent the deputy you will be in trouble and may lose your right to be away again.

When I was engaged to play at the Royal Opera House, Covent Garden in the quite large stage band required in Richard Strauss's *Der Rosenkavalier* there were only going to be two performances each week for four or five weeks. After several performances I was offered several lucrative engagements elsewhere, one of which coincided with a performance of *Der Rosenkavalier*. I decided to send a deputy, a player of some standing, to take my place. Unfortunately my deputy made one entry a bar earlier than the composer had intended and it happened to be in one of those places that was important for someone on stage. A day or two later, before the next performance of that opera, I received a less than pleasant letter from the orchestral manager at the Opera House telling me that my services were no longer required. Fortunately, as I only intended to do one of the three remaining performances I was not too concerned.

Many years ago, at a time when there was a great deal of theatre work, my father, who liked to show off his technical skill by improvising around the music actually written in the part, came a cropper when he sent a deputy who played exactly what was written. In the interval the artists on stage came to complain to the conductor, who was already on his way to the deputy at whom he had been scowling at each clarinet solo entry, to find out why the music sounded so different from what he was accustomed to. The conductor was starting to give him a hard time when the player showed him his part. On my father's return the following day there was a stormy scene and for the rest of the run he had to be there putting in all his additional improvisations.

My own experience of playing for musicals is very limited. The only one that I remember enjoying after the first week or so was *West Side Story,* with Leonard Bernstein's wonderful music and an outstanding production. The American cast, directed by Jerome Robbins, was tremendous and hyped up every night at a short stage rehearsal before each show so that when it came to the *Rumble* the Sharks and the Jets were appropriately violent in their fight. On several occasions actors were injured.

The orchestra was made up of very good players from both the 'straight' and 'jazz' side of the profession. There were four of us in the woodwind section, all doubling, that is required to play more than one instrument. Both the alto sax players doubled on clarinet, flute and piccolo, another played tenor sax, clarinet, oboe and cor anglais and I, as the 'straight' man, played clarinet, Eb clarinet and bass clarinet. The string section was outstanding, most playing or having played in one of the major symphony or chamber orchestras in contrast to the brass which was made up of very good jazz musicians. Above all we had a great jazz drummer, Phil Seaman, who drove the music forward when needed.

Leonard Bernstein.

At the same time as being the resident player for this show I was also playing in the Philharmonia so it was necessary for me to be away quite a lot. I was determined to make sure that my deputies never put a foot wrong. I went to a lot of trouble to see that none of the problems I have written about assailed them. I did it for them and also to make sure I had no difficulties with the management as it was rather a well-paid job. I rewrote, in very clear manuscript, the pages where there had been changes, and also prepared instructions telling whoever took my place where there was anything not clear. At that time in the late 1950s there were not many clarinettists who could play all three clarinets demanded by the score; now there are very many.

Musicians in the Music Halls

The Music Halls were the most popular form of entertainment for at least 30 years or more before 1900 by when there were music halls in even quite small towns. Conditions and pay for the musicians were poor and for the mainly working-class audience the seating arrangements varied but were generally lacking in quality and comfort. Some music halls were in pretty rough areas where, if you were sitting in the stalls, you might be unfortunate enough to receive a piece of orange peel (or worse) on your lap or head. In the large towns, on the No.1 circuit, they were quite grand, with red plush, comfortable seats (and no orange peel), serving a more discerning and affluent clientele.

In London the best music halls were very fine indeed and attracted a high-class clientele, which used to be called the 'carriage trade'. My father played at one when he was a young man, the Palace Theatre in Shaftesbury Avenue. Here the conductor was the renowned Herman Finck; his composition *In the Shadows* was for many years very popular and to be heard in restaurants, on bandstands and, until the 1950s, it was often in the programmes of the many light orchestras broadcasting at that time. He was a good theatre conductor and something of a disciplinarian. It seems that my father frequently got the sack because he sent deputies without first getting permission, but as he was such a good player Finck would give him back his job each time. It was a job worth having and very well paid. It was truly a Palace of Varieties with artists of many kinds and it was chosen as the venue for the first Royal Command Performance in 1912. The programme would usually consist of 10 or 12 acts, or 'turns', and would include at least one comedian or a double act, a song and dance group , a singer or group of singers, a comedy or dramatic sketch, tap dancers or adagio dancers, who would sometimes do the Apache Dance. An updated version of this dance was used very effectively many years later in *On Your Toes,* the Rogers and Hart musical in which the jazz ballet, *Slaughter on 10th Avenue,* with choreography by George Balanchine, was a 'show stopper'. The rest of the programme would be made up of perhaps, jugglers, magicians doing card tricks or other sleight of hand deceptions, animal acts, a hypnotist, a contortionist, balancing acts that had tumblers and trapeze artists. Musical groups, often dressed as Gypsies or Russians and playing appropriate music, were very popular. Some of the musicians might be genuine Gypsies or Russians, though a good many had never been further east than Whitechapel in the east-end of London.

The Palace Theatre was so highly thought of that the Diàghilev Ballet Company and on one occasion Anna Pavlova, were willing to appear there. Pavlova, after her career as the most celebrated ballerina of her time, continued to dance as a soloist; her *pièce de résistance* was *Le Sygne (The Swan),* to a movement from *Le Carnival des Animaux* by Saint-Saëns. It was assumed that with a name like Tschaikov, and a noticeable foreign accent, my father would speak Russian, and that he would be able to interpret for her, but as he had come to England when he was only five or six years old he remembered only a very few words of Russian and was of no help.

The conditions for those working in the music halls in the London suburbs and around the country were quite different to those my father enjoyed at the Palace Theatre. The expected standard of performance and quality of the music was usually not very high. There would be new artists each week, bringing their own set of parts for the orchestra. The parts were often in a very poor condition, well worn and covered in the markings of the many musicians who had attempted to play from them over the years. There would always be a rehearsal on Monday morning when the parts were handed out along with arcane instructions from the conductor, perhaps '2,2,1 and coda', or 2,3,2, and coda or whatever was required. 2,2,1 and coda meant that you were to play the first section of music twice, the second section twice, the third section once and then, at a sign, go to the section marked coda, bringing the music to an end. There would probably be brief instructions about getting faster and slower to match whatever was required on stage. The drummer had a particularly difficult job. He had to play the necessary 'effects' for the comedians and clowns when they fell over or hit each other. For them he might have to bang the bass drum or cymbal, hit the wood-block or blow a whistle; for jugglers, tight-rope and trapeze artists a side-drum role would usually be required before an especially difficult or hazardous trick. He had to be very wide-awake as no two performances would ever be just the same. With 10 to 12 turns to rehearse there was no time for much refinement. I am thankful I never had to do work of that kind, and particularly that I didn't have to go as a deputy.

By the 1930s there were fewer music halls though some of those that remained had quite good orchestras. I remember going to see pantomimes at Christmas time at the Shepherd's Bush Empire and Chiswick Empire. The orchestras at both were considered good enough to make regular broadcasts. The popularity of the cinema and television gradually killed off most of the few remaining Variety Theatres, as Music Halls came to be called. The last one to close was the Metropolitan Edgware Road, in London, finally bringing to an end a tradition of remarkable popular entertainment where there was a real interaction between the performers on stage and the audience.

Not long before it was to be demolished I did a couple of recording sessions in the old 'Met', when we recorded some of the old music hall tunes made famous by artists like Sir Harry Lauder and the Chocolate Coloured Coon. It was sad to see its former glory, now faded and in such poor condition and know that it was soon to be pulled down.

Playing for the 'Silent' Cinema

The arrival of the cinema was the first of the early 20th century inventions to have a profound effect on the lives and employment of musicians. It was welcomed by them because it brought an ever increasing amount of employment. There were musicians in every 'silent' cinema in the country and by 1914 it was estimated that there were more than 3500 halls throughout the country showing films. Quite a number of them had been theatres and music halls and though a few of them did for a time also have some stage performances it was not long before these ceased. Villages, not large enough to support a theatre, could afford to have a cinema, with seating for as few as 80 or 100 because cinemas required so much less labour and were therefore much cheaper to run. But, it seems silence was not golden and every cinema had to have music to accompany the films. In the small cinemas there were usually less than four players and in many of the smallest only a pianist or piano and violin, but in the large cities – London, Manchester, Glasgow and a few other large towns – there were orchestras of anything from thirty to sixty musicians.

While it lasted the 'silent' cinema provided an enormous amount of employment, in some cases to players of a standard not much higher than an average amateur though in the best cinema orchestras there were many fine players. In 1927 when *The Jazz Singer,* the first sound film, was released, ironically a 'musical', it was estimated that the majority of musicians were working in cinemas. Over the next five years the number of 'talkies' increased until by 1932 they had completely taken over. As a result more than 15,000 musicians were thrown onto the labour market, at a time when there was already considerable national unemployment.

Some of the musicians outside London and one or two other places were able to return to the jobs they had given up for the more financially and personally rewarding career as a musician. Some of the best players continued to have successful careers once the 'talkies' arrived, but there were far too many excellent players for the amount of employment available and a good many were reduced to playing in the streets in an endeavour to stave off complete ruin. It did at least give them the opportunity to keep playing, in the hope that they might at some time find employment again. If musicians are to maintain their playing ability they need to play their instrument regularly, every day if possible.

Alberto Lombardo, who sheltered in the porch of our house, had been the leader of a cinema orchestra. The film director Cavalcanti saw him playing in the street and chose him to play a part in his film Nicholas Nickleby.

In the 1930s when I was a child, I remember an elderly man who used to walk round our neighbourhood playing the violin. As he walked down our road people would throw pennies out of their windows to him. One day when it was raining he sheltered in the porch of our house. Seeing him my mother invited him in for a cup of tea and as they talked it turned out that my father had known him many years previously. After that, every time he came round our way he would come in for a cup of tea and a piece of my mother's celebrated Dundee cake.

When a new film arrived it was the job of the leader of the group or the 'Musical Director' in each cinema to select the music he or she thought most suitable to accompany it. The cinema would own a library of music similar to that played in the restaurants and on bandstands in the parks and sea-fronts. Once again the arrangements made by Emile Tavan came in useful as they could be used by whatever size band the cinema could afford. If there was a chase, 'hurry music' would be chosen; for the love scenes, sentimental themes; for fights, loud music with plenty of bass drum and the clashing of cymbals (or in their absence loud thumping on the lowest notes of the piano) was essential.

'Trade shows' were held, usually in the morning in one of the large London cinemas, to provide the opportunity for cinema owners from all over the country to see new films and decide if they wished to show them. After a while some of the major films from Hollywood arrived with their own especially composed music for performance in the big cinemas where there would be a large orchestra. With especially composed music it was quite straightforward, except that it must be remembered that as there were no rehearsals everything had to be sight-read. But when there was no music composed especially for the film and instead sections of music had been selected from overtures, symphonies, selections from operettas, musical comedies and novelty numbers it was more difficult. On those occasions there would be a great pile of music on the stand and when a light flashed one had to go immediately to the next selected piece. For those who had the necessary technique and quick responses to do this these engagements were some of the most financially rewarding for the orchestral or 'band' musician.

Playing for Dancing

The traditional area of employment for musicians has always been to provide music for dancing. The coming of the gramophone and the increasing availability of recordings made from about 1901 onwards were by 1920 to bring about some big changes and the need for another kind of musician.

At the beginning of the 20th century the music for dancing was provided for the upper classes by groups of musicians very similar to those who played in the restaurants and on the bandstands, anything from a trio to a group of five or six players, violin, piano and drums with a flute, clarinet or trumpet added depending on the money available. At a grand ball there would probably be two or three violins, perhaps a viola, a cello and a double bass (nowadays often called a 'string bass' to distinguish it from the 'electric bass' now dominant outside orchestral circles), a flute, clarinet, trumpet, piano and drums. If it was a very grand occasion a trombone and a second clarinet and second trumpet might be added.

For most working people, in town or country, dancing would probably be inside or outside a pub, depending on the weather. On Saturday night it could be at the farm, Village Hall or Town Hall. Often a single fiddler, pianist or accordionist would be the only musician employed, possibly a member of the community with some natural talent. At a wedding or some other special occasion they might be able to afford a violin, double bass, and drums plus a flute or clarinet or trumpet if there were local players available.

Whether grand or not, the dances would be sequence dances such as the waltz, perhaps the St. George's Waltz, the Valeta or the Eva Three-step. There were also the one-step, two-step, tangos and foxtrots (still called saunters in Britain at that time). There were also the 'turning couple' dances, the Waltz, Polka and Schottische and the set dances such as the quadrilles, contra or country dances, and some of the older dancers still enjoyed the Lancers. At the same time as sequence dancing, the younger members of the upper classes had come to prefer free style though the less well-off remained keen on the sequence dances.

From about 1910, when the first ragtime records began to be issued in Britain, followed by more jazz type music, keen dancers in Britain started to hear about dances that were already becoming popular in the USA, and the music to which they were being danced. The new dances often had rather amusing names such as The Turkey Trot, Bunny Hug, and the Lindy Hop. At the end of the war in 1918, many women, who had been increasingly employed in the factories producing armaments and uniforms, as well as the men weary from life in the services, were ready for something new and exciting.

In Europe, from the beginning of the 20th century, the Military bands had started to give the saxophone a more prominent role; then, in America, the Gilmore and Sousa Show bands started to feature the instrument. Just as recordings were becoming more available, Rudy Wiedoft began recording saxophone solos, many written by himself. He was a virtuoso and a charismatic performer whose most well-known composition, *Waltz Vanite,* was tuneful and difficult, and it inspired many young players to follow his example. In the 1920s there were more and more young musicians who wanted to play the saxophone. In fact it became a craze that, with the influence of recordings from America, was to change the personnel in the bands that played for dancing and lead to what came to be called dance bands. They were to provide the music for dancing until the end of the 1950s, when the advent of new forms of popular music once again changed the music and the bands young dancers preferred.

Between 1910 and 1920 the new dances were played by the same kind of bands as before except that the wind instruments, in particular the cornet or trumpet, were given the melody more frequently. If you are willing to accept the sound quality you can hear what these bands sounded like on a number of recordings made at that time. To those brought up listening to CDs it may come as a shock to hear what delighted even the most discerning music lovers well into the 1930s.

After 1920 the old style dance orchestra now rapidly became the dance band with the saxophones replacing the violins and cello and the brass instruments playing a bigger part in carrying the melody. Naturally, it was where the Upper Class danced (yes, class was still very important then), that the new style music was played and the bands were first heard. This was to be the Jazz Age, the era of the 'flapper', with much shorter skirts, the Charleston and High

Jinx. Older folk saw this as the road to ruin and the loosening of moral restraint. Thirty or so years later quite a few of those who had danced to the 'sinful' saxophone could be heard saying the same thing about Rock and Roll and jitterbugging. Dancing and the music for dancing have a lot to answer for and no doubt will continue to do so. For some strange reason the saxophone continued to be associated with sin even as late as 1945. At the Three Choirs Festival held in Worcester that year, it is reported that in a part of Vaughan Williams's *Job,* where there is a solo for the saxophone, the ecclesiastical authorities demanded that the movement in which the saxophone was heard be omitted. They did not want the profane sound of the saxophone to be heard within the Cathedral.

As always the size of the band would depend on the venue and the clientele. Most bands had 7 or 8 players; a big band in the 1940s might have as many as five saxes, four trumpets, three trombones, guitar, bass and drums. In the night clubs and hotels, where the Jack Hylton, Roy Fox, Jack Payne, Lew Stone, Ambrose, Billy Cotton and many other bands played in the 1920s and 1930s, the players were paid by the week, in what might be called a 'full-time' engagement. In time the top bands would become Show Bands often being top of the bill at music halls and in due course broadcasting regularly. The BBC was to have its own resident band, Henry Hall's BBC Dance Band.

Many of the best players were in the big name bands, though some of the very best actually wanted to play jazz. There has never been enough work in Britain for a musician to earn his living entirely by playing jazz so those musicians with families settled for the next best thing, playing commercial dance music. However, the vast majority of musicians playing for dances were not in the name bands. They were predominantly freelance musicians. Some were full-time musicians, but many more were part-time, more usually known as semi-pros. The latter earned their living in many different ways: as clerks, manual workers, professional men, including quite a few school teachers.

I first met Jack Brymer, the doyen of clarinettists until his death in 2003, when we both joined the Royal Philharmonic Orchestra in 1947. Previously he had been a schoolmaster who also played five or six nights a week in 'gig' bands. He told me that quite frequently he earned more from playing in the bands than he did as a schoolmaster. But being a schoolmaster was regular employment he could rely on, and there would be a pension when he retired.

There were as many gig bands as years later there were to be pop groups, but there were also a lot of freelance 'pick-up' bands, groups of musicians that were engaged for 'hops' in the local Town Hall, Dance Halls, Working Men's Clubs and anywhere else large enough. The new bands varied just as much as the old-style bands had always done. Now a trio would be piano, bass and drums, or the same group with a front man playing clarinet, saxophone or trumpet, depending on the funds available. Larger bands with 2 altos and a tenor sax, two trumpets and trombone and a rhythm section, and the 'big' bands and swing bands of the 30s and later might have two altos, two tenors and a baritone sax, three trumpets and two or three trombones, guitar, piano, bass and drums, and often one or two vocalists. There was a vast amount of employment for freelance full and part-time dance musicians. The best paid work, Hunt Balls, Debutante Balls, Marriage Receptions, University celebrations and Barmitzvahs, was mainly done by the considerable number of freelance musicians based in London.

From 1920 onwards the separation of those musicians playing 'straight' music – orchestral musicians – and those playing 'dance' or jazz orientated music increased. For some years this led to them joining separate organisations that would look after their employment protection. I will return to this topic in a later chapter.

14 Illusion and Reality

Recordings – from wax cylinders to the most recent innovations. Early recordings – folk music, Caruso, Chaliapin, Joachim. 78s, LPs, tape, stereo. The dominance of the producer and engineer – the manipulation of performances. Most music now heard on recordings.

We are now so used to our senses being manipulated that we are no longer aware that so much of what we see, hear and taste is not actually the 'real thing'. Photographs are 'doctored', sometimes to flatter, or to distort a scene for political reasons, or to create a vision of something not possible in nature. From the beginning film has used illusion as a major technique for creating excitement and amazement by cutting and mixing so that we see events juxtaposed in a way quite impossible in reality. So much of what we eat and drink is now adulterated to induce us to eat and drink more – even its aroma is increased to stimulate our desire – to the advantage of the manufacturers rather than ourselves. Can we any longer be sure when listening to music whether what we are hearing is what the artists actually played or if their performance has been manipulated or 'enhanced'?

In the last chapter I wrote about a time when most music was still being played in the presence of those listening to it. From about 1900 onwards everything began to change. First to arrive were gramophone recordings, though to begin with they were not yet generally of a quality to replace the real thing. Then, with the invention of electric recording and better play-back equipment, the quality of what could be listened to on a wind-up gramophone improved considerably. In 1927 the BBC (the British Broadcasting Corporation) was established (though from 1922 the British Broadcasting Company had been broadcasting a limited amount of music). At about the same time, with the coming of the talkies it became impossible to tell if the music one was hearing was actually being played by the musicians one saw on the screen or if the music had been recorded by other musicians and those you saw had only taken part in what used to be called 'dummy sessions' (this work was mainly undertaken by those musicians who had become redundant because of the demise of the silent films).

In the 1890s recordings had already become available – there is now a digitally restored wax cylinder recording of Brahms playing his Hungarian Dance No.1, made in 1889. It is only a faint reproduction of that performance, but it does allow us to make contact with the great man across the years. If one had a phonograph it was as easy to make one's own recordings as many years later everyone was able to do on their cassette recorders. A good many private recordings from that time still exist including recordings of Florence Nightingale, Gladstone, Bismarck and, much more widely known since they have now been issued commercially, the recordings Lionel Mapleson made clandestinely on wax cylinders at the New York Metropolitan Opera House in the first years of the 20th century. We can hear Nellie Melba, Jean de Reszke and Emma Calve and other legendary artists actually singing to an audience at that time.

Though the sound quality is not up to present day standards we can listen and enjoy these artists un-edited or interfered with by a record producer or engineer. No recording, however accurate, coming out of one or many loudspeakers, however refined they or the play-back equipment may be, can reproduce what is heard in the presence of the artists as they perform. We are frequently told that the recording and the equipment it is played on is so true that 'it is like being in the concert hall or opera house'. This disregards an integral element of a performance: the actual presence of the performer. All of us know how very different it is being with the person you are conversing with rather than speaking to that person on the telephone. But, if we cannot be together, hearing our friend's voice on the telephone is very much better than not hearing them at all. This is the wonderful benefit that recordings and broadcasts now provide. And not only can we listen to those who are still alive: we can listen to artists sadly no longer with us.

Thanks to Thomas Edison and Emile Berliner, it was possible for Béla Bartók, Cecil Sharp, Vaughan Williams and many others to record folk music, sung and played by those still part of an aural tradition that was about to die out. Without recording we would not be able to listen to Enrico Caruso, Fyodor Shalyapin (Chaliapin), Adelina Patti, or Joseph Joachim, Pablo Sarasate,

Eugene Ysaye and many other artists who recorded during the first decade of the 20th century. They were all playing and singing the music of their own time, often having studied with or been directed by the composers themselves - Verdi, Puccini, Leoncavallo, Tchaikovsky, Mendelssohn and Brahms.

It is difficult now, a century later, when far more music is listened to by radio, the Internet and recordings, to understand the extent of the opposition to recordings from composers, critics and 'serious music lovers' that continued to some extent until World War II. The belief that it is only when the performers and audience are in each others' presence that real communication and artistic pleasure can take place and that recordings and broadcasts can never achieve this was still the view of the eminent critic Frank Howes in the 1920s.

But this was not the main objection that those imbued with the tradition that had developed during the 19th century when composers and their audiences, especially in Germany and those countries most influenced by its culture, put their art on a pedestal of idealism. Composers were then addressing a small, leisured, educated middle and upper-middle-class European audience and it was this tradition that it was felt would be destroyed by radio and recordings making music too easily available. They had forgotten that the truly classical composers such as Mozart had had no problem in composing serenades, dances and marches as well as symphonies and masses; nor had Schubert and many others.

I think they would be surprised to find that in 2006, a generation that were downloading pop music from the Internet, those they might well have thought of as shallow, apathetic listeners, the opposite of the 'serious music lover', were still flocking to concerts given by the group Arctic Monkeys, though this group's success – they had the fastest-selling debut album ever – was to a large extent the result of it being first available by downloading from the Internet.

From 1900 until 1923 all recordings were made acoustically. This involved the artists playing into a large horn whereby the sounds they made were recorded straight onto a wax disc. This worked very well for singers and fairly well for instrumental soloists but was far less good when it came to recording orchestras. The first problem when recording an orchestra was that only a limited number of players could get near enough to the recording 'horn' to make any impression. The acoustic method was unable to capture very high or low notes and made little difference between loud and soft sounds. In fact often in the early days woodwind and brass instruments had to be used to replace the strings. The double basses in particular were so unsatisfactory that they were frequently replaced by a tuba. Each side of a record only played for about four to four and a half minutes. For longer compositions suitable breaks had to be found to allow the record to be turned over so that the music could continue.

Recording standards gradually improved until in 1923, following the use of microphones in broadcasting, microphones began to be used in the recording industry. After 1925 it became the accepted method. This was a great improvement and enabled the successful recording of orchestral and choral works, though each side of a gramophone record still remained about four minutes. When making recordings, whether acoustically or electronically, each four-minute 'take' was a 'one-off'. There was no editing possible as the wax still used for recording would be destroyed in the process. If there was any fault the whole side had to be recorded again. In fact, playing for every 'take' was just like playing at a concert, with the added strain that you were aware that if you made a mistake of any kind you would ruin whatever had been played up to that point and that it would all have to be done again.

In 1945, when I was in the LPO and first took part in some recording sessions with Sir Thomas Beecham, we recorded the *Royal Hunt and Storm* from *The Trojans* by Berlioz. Sir Thomas and the orchestra tried to recapture the sound of the performance we would give at a concert when an audience was present. Whether it was a distinguished conductor such as Beecham, Bruno Walter, de Sabata, Munch or any other conductor, they would make all the decisions regarding balance and the overall style of the recording by going into the recording suite to listen to each test recording. Their intention was to hear on the recording a reproduction of the performance they were obtaining in the studio. If they thought the balance they heard in the recording suite did not accurately reproduce what they heard in the studio they would have the position of the microphones (at that time there would be only a few) adjusted until they achieved the balance they required. This is how we recorded *Petrushka* with Ansermet, about which I wrote in chapter 10.

For many years there had been experiments in an attempt to use tape in place of wax so that more than four minutes music could be recorded in a single 'take'. In 1936 when the London Philharmonic Orchestra was on tour in Germany they did a concert in Ludwigshafen. Unbeknown to the orchestra, BASF recorded the concert as an experiment in the use of tape. It was not known to more than a very few people until many years later, when in 1979 Shirley, Lady Beecham agreed that two of the items from that concert could be issued, Mozart's Symphony No. 39 and the Suite from *Le Coq D'Or* by Rimsky-Korsakov.

Though EMI were experimenting using tape to record the Royal Philharmonic Orchestra from 1948 their records were still being sold in the 78 rpm format with four minutes music on each side. *Fifine at the Fair,* by Granville Bantock, which the RPO recorded with Beecham on tape in 1949, was first issued in the old 78 rpm format and only became available on LP (Long Play) a few years later. In *Fifine* there is a very long and demanding cadenza for the clarinet, which my colleague Jack Brymer played brilliantly. For some reason it was decided to re-record this section at a separate session without the rest of the orchestra present and then edit it in. Listening to the finished recording I cannot tell whether what I am hearing is the occasion Jack played this demanding cadenza when I was sitting next to him, or when he recorded it on his own.

In the previous chapter, in the section *Music for Dancing,* I referred to the effect that the first ragtime recordings had on dancers from around 1912. Recordings of many forms of popular music had been made since the beginning of the century, many more than of 'serious' music. Light music, often played by brass bands or military bands, music hall songs, and, in America in particular, banjo solos with early examples of ragtime were all very popular. Soon military bands playing arrangements of ragtime were being recorded. From 1917 onwards more and more recordings of jazz became available and from the 1920s were selling in very large numbers. When recording jazz, the time limitation of only being able to record for four minutes imposed by the 78 rpm format does not seem to have been a problem. Nor, when recording jazz and dance bands, largely made up of wind instruments, were there the dynamic problems that arose when recording orchestral music, with dynamics ranging from a mere whisper to the loudest fortissimo.

When in the 1930s I first started to listen to music, what I most enjoyed were the dance bands broadcast by the BBC, such as Henry Hall and Jack Payne, and the broadcasts from Radio Luxembourg that we used to listen to at breakfast time. While I was at school, though I had started learning the clarinet and had begun listening to orchestral and chamber music, it was the recordings of Duke Ellington, Count Basie, Louis Armstrong, and especially the two wonderful clarinettists Benny Goodman and Artie Shaw that excited me most. It was these recordings and the recordings made by Fritz Kreisler playing his own compositions, Stokowski and the Philadelphia Orchestra and the London Philharmonic conducted by Beecham, and finally the experience of hearing Menuhin playing the Elgar Violin Concerto, that convinced me that I had to try to become a musician. Now, 60 years later, I am still inspired by these marvellous performances captured on record.

In Britain, from about 1918, when 78 rpm started to become the standard format, until 1950, whether in fact recorded acoustically or electrically, on wax or tape, all commercial records continued to be issued on 78s. When the much lighter vinyl 33 and 45 rpm format arrived so that up to about 25 minutes music could be held on each side, 78s were abandoned. This changed everything for everyone who had been involved in making recordings, especially those of us in the symphony orchestras. The whole way we approached the performance of music in the recording studio changed. No longer did we make short, one-off four minute performances, with all the nervous tension that involved. No performer, whether a conductor, solo artist or orchestral musician any longer had the freedom to be spontaneous in the same way as at a concert. Now we were making a 'take', then listening to the playback, doing short sections to edit anything the producer thought should be done again, not usually in regard to the interpretation of the music, but because he didn't like the balance or the tuning, the ensemble or some other technical fault he had noticed. As a result performers also became increasingly concerned about these aspects of their performance.

When making the edits it was essential that everyone played as nearly as possible as they had done before (without the faults), but now no longer in the one-off performance style that had been possible previously. We became increasingly 'note-getters', and more self-conscious. After a while I felt that perhaps if we each came in and played some scales and arpeggios the producer could put a record together without us (some years later 'sampling' was used to create some records in just this way). One also lost the sense of being in charge of one's own performance because one had no idea which bits the producer had chosen to use in the compilation of everything that had been recorded and then included on the final record. In fact, no one, conductor, soloist or anyone taking part could be absolutely certain how the final performance had been achieved. Only the producer and the engineers could be certain. Performers were no longer in control of the finished product.

Indeed the producer now took on a responsibility and a role that previously had been enjoyed by conductors and soloists. In Elisabeth Schwarzkopf's compilation of the writings of Walter Legge and conversations with him *On and Off the Record* she quotes him as writing *I was the first of what are called 'Producers' of records. Before I established myself and my ideas, the attitude of recording managers of all companies was 'we are here in the studio to record as well as we can on wax what the artists habitually do in the opera house or on the concert platform'. My predecessor, Fred Gaisberg, told me, 'We are out to make sound photographs of as many sides as we can get during each session'. My ideas were different. It was my aim to make records that would set the standards by which public performances and the artist of the future would be judged – to leave behind a large series of examples of the best performances of my epoch.* In fact he wanted to assume responsibility for every aspect of the recording.

The producer and engineers became more and more in control of the performance that music lovers could purchase. Equally important, music lovers themselves were now in charge of when and where they wished to listen to their chosen music. It was no longer necessary to make the commitment of being where, when and at what time the artists were performing; they also had the power to change the dynamic, making the loudest fortissimo as soft as a whisper and the quietest murmur loud enough to bring the house down.

Later, with the arrival of the inexpensive tape player and later the tape recorder, the listeners' control was extended. Having selected the music they wanted to record, either off-air or from a commercial recording, it became easy to cut out any sections found tedious or less enjoyable, just by fast forwarding or editing out. On the other hand, if a particularly lovely few bars found favour they could be replayed as often as was desired. With the tape recorder it became possible for anyone to compile their own selection of music by re-recording just those passages they wished to hear. The commercial broadcasting and recording companies then decided to save each listener from having to do this themselves by producing compilations that did it far better than any individual could. Now, over 50 years after the introduction of tape, everyone can make their own CDs and DVDs of music of their choice from any source – radio, TV, the Internet, commercial CDs or any other format.

However, all that still lay in the future. To return to the 1950s, the era of Walter Legge at EMI and John Culshaw at Decca, when the ability to edit soon led to this facility being used to remedy the shortcomings in a performer's ability or flaws in a performance. The recording was no longer a memento of a concert. It had established an independent life of its own. When I was first involved in playing for recording, from 1944, we tried to recreate in the studio as nearly as possible what took place at a concert performance. As record sales increased it was not long before the concert performance began to try to recreate what could be heard on recordings. A far more powerful tyrant than any conductor had now arisen – the record producer and his accomplices the engineers.

In 1952, only a couple of years after the introduction of recording on tape, Kirsten Flagstad was taking part in a recording of *Tristan und Isolde* by Richard Wagner, with the Philharmonia conducted by Wilhelm Furtwängler. The ageing Flagstad was having difficulty with a couple of top Cs. It was agreed, with Flagstad's consent, that Elisabeth Schwarzkopf, then a young woman, should sing these two high notes and that they be edited into the master tape. Later, knowledge of this device leaked out. Naturally Flagstad was furious, and though the recording was very successful she refused to record again for that company.

There have been a good many occasions when for various reasons similar editing devices have been used. I have taken part in a number of recordings where a singer or instrumentalist has been 'helped out' with the use of editing. When the great Russian ballerina Galina Ulanova was dancing in *Giselle* at the Royal Opera House with the Bolshoi Company the performance was filmed. At one place in the film the camera moves in to a close up of Ulanova and as it does it was felt that the clarinet solo at that point, as played in the orchestra pit, sounded too distant. There was no fault in the way the ROH orchestra clarinettist had played, but it was decided to re-record about eight or twelve bars in the studio. I went into the studio with a few string players and played the solo. It was then edited onto the sound track and a patina of sound, similar to that on the rest of the performance was added to disguise the clinical studio sound. This was not the only time I took part in additions of this kind.

Recordings of public performances of concerts and opera have routinely been the product of what was decided were the 'best' parts of the several performances by the same artists, and on occasion short sections have been added later in the studio when it has not been possible to find a patch from any of the 'live' performances. While the performance is being recorded 'on-site', during the concert, the producer is able to manipulate the microphones so as to achieve the instrumental balance he thinks best. What those listening at home on their record players will hear may be different to what the audience at the concert heard.

There have been occasions when snippets from another recording of the same work, recorded by other artists, have been inserted in an effort to achieve the 'perfect' recording. A known occasion was when this was done to a recording Sergiu Celibidache had made. It was only after the recording had been issued that his keen ear detected something not quite as he had heard it at the time he had made the recording. There have been other occasions, known only to a few insiders.

With the coming of the long playing record music lovers at last had the great advantage of being able to listen to a whole concerto or symphony without having to get up every four minutes to turn the record over or put another one on. I have quite recently tried to listen to some old 78s that I have of Casals playing the Bach unaccompanied cello sonatas. I found it impossible to tolerate the constant interruptions to the music and having to change the record so often. It was difficult to understand how we had found this perfectly acceptable years ago.

As time went by increasingly sophisticated techniques were employed. Multi-tracking allowed the use of separate microphones for each section of the orchestra and even for each instrument. One might have played one's part *forte* and yet find on playback, because another part of the score has been made more audible, one might as well have not played at all. Multi-tracking enabled us to record an opera at a time when because of other engagements one of the singers was not available. We would complete the recording with that part missing. At a later date the missing artist would record the part on their own and it would be edited in. On occasion this might even be done in another country.

Performances could now be enhanced by the use of echo chambers and added ambience. As the engineers and producers gained more and more control acoustic screens were placed between sections of the orchestra thereby enabling the balance between them to be 'managed', not in the studio but in the control room. With smaller groups of musicians, especially when providing backing to pop groups and individual artists, the musicians would often be so separated that they were unable to hear each other except by using headphones.

The next development was the introduction of stereo recordings in 1958. We had been recording in stereo from 1954 though the recordings had still been issued in mono. Later they were re-issued in stereo. In fact Alan Blumlein, a remarkable British inventor, also responsible for developing radar, had already demonstrated the possibilities of stereo many years previously. In 1935, as a test, Sir Thomas Beecham was recorded in stereo rehearsing Mozart's *Jupiter* Symphony. It was not until years later with the advent of tape recording that the use of stereo became practical.

The coming of stereo was good news for musicians as it meant the repertoire had to be recorded again in this new format creating a great deal more employment. After a time quadraphonic and then 'all-round' sound was introduced. The record companies and the manufacturers of play-back equipment have constantly made attempts to convince us that listening in the comfort of our own home to recordings can be 'as if you are in the concert hall'. These devices and the Compact Disc, which arrived in the 1990s, are really only the sonic equivalents of The Emperor's New Clothes. A visit to any concert hall immediately makes it clear that however improved the sound coming out of one or many loudspeakers may be, it can never be 'the real thing'.

However, this is how most music is now heard. A very large number of music lovers do not live near enough to a concert hall and for a great many more the cost for a husband and wife to attend a public performance is too costly. A survey, in which I was involved some years ago, showed that even those fortunate enough to be able to afford frequent visits to the Royal Opera House were still listening to far more music on recordings and broadcasts than in the opera house or concert hall.

From 1930 onwards the broadcasting of music by the BBC – not just symphony orchestras, but opera, chamber music, solo instrumental and vocal music and a great deal of so-called light music – brought music into the lives of far more people than ever before. The broadcasts by the BBC's own orchestras as well as relays from public concerts, opera performances and studio broadcasts by the London and Regional Orchestras, the LPO, LSO, the Hallé and other orchestras and groups from around the country had created a large audience for this music. Commercial recordings made by artists and orchestras from all over the world were also broadcast. I believe it was this new audience, created by broadcasting, that during and after World War Two (WW2) filled so many concert halls to capacity.

My family only had a handful of records which we played very occasionally – we still had to re-wind the gramophone after each record was played. Listening to the radio, the 'wireless' as we called it then, to the studio broadcasts from the BBC and the commercial records they and Radio Luxembourg broadcast was how I heard most music when I was still at school and music college.

It was not only in the commercial recording studios that it became necessary for musicians to adapt to new technologies. From 1927, when my father broadcast regularly in the famous Wireless Military Band, now completely forgotten, and for all the years he was in the BBC Symphony Orchestra, taking part in studio performances that were to be broadcast was similar to playing at a performance in a concert hall, what is now usually called a 'live' performance. When in 1943 I began playing for broadcast performances, whether in the BBC studios at Maida Vale, or when public concerts I was taking part in were transmitted as relays, nothing had changed. Whenever and whatever you played, when the red light was on in the studio, was broadcast, faults and all. It was impossible to stop, replay, or edit anything.

There was one occasion when the BBC were attempting to broadcast a simulation of a Victorian soirée, with a tenor singing some ballads and a small section of the BBC Symphony Orchestra impersonating a Salon Orchestra accompanying him. At the rehearsal the orchestra was asked by the producer to applaud discreetly after each item. Unfortunately, my father, though an outstanding player and a charming and amusing man, was not always as attentive as might be desired. He had not heard this request from the producer during the rehearsal so that when he heard the applause at the broadcast he responded, without thinking, by making one of those exceedingly loud 'wolf-whistles' made by putting two fingers in one's mouth and blowing very hard. Being a 'live' broadcast it just went out over the air, no doubt giving a number of middle-class music lovers something of a surprise. It was still possible in the 1930s, when very good players were much thinner on the ground than they are now, for him to get away with it. A musician today would not risk anything like that. There are far too many very good players waiting to take his or her place.

On another broadcast, a piece was being played that starts with the main tune played by an unaccompanied clarinet. This piece had been written for the A clarinet. Unfortunately the clarinettist on this occasion played it on his Bb clarinet. When the rest of the orchestra came in it was quite impossible to continue. The conductor had to stop the orchestra, the embarrassed clarinettist had to quickly change to his A clarinet and start again. Ever since it became possible to record everything before it is broadcast, musicians and listeners have been spared these catastrophes.

Until the ability to record on tape arrived, relays of public concerts had to be broadcast as they occurred. There were no deferred relays nor was it possible to replay broadcasts weeks, months or even, as frequently occurs now, years later. In the case of performances that are thought to have been particularly fine or of historical interest, the BBC can, and now does, issue them as recordings on CD.

We had been recording on tape since 1948, though we, the musicians in the recording studio were not aware of this until the recordings made at that time were re-issued on long-play 33 rpm records after 1950. However, we were not the first. In 1947 in America, Bing Crosby had already started to record his popular programmes on tape.

Since the 1950s the BBC has routinely pre-recorded broadcasts of music so that for many years it has only been occasionally that studio broadcasts of music have not been pre-recorded. To begin with it was agreed that each piece would be played without a break and, if possible, the whole programme would be recorded in this way, unless there was a technical failure in the recording equipment or events such as I have written about above were to occur. Then, wanting to broadcast the best performance, items were more and more being recorded again and again until the producer felt he had a performance that satisfied him. By about 1958 playing for broadcasting had become increasingly like doing a commercial recording session. The major drawback, as far as musicians were concerned, was that the fee for a broadcast was considerably less than for a recording session. The musicians involved in broadcasting became increasingly unhappy and insisted that the Musicians' Union inform the BBC that a larger fee was required. After protracted negotiations it was agreed that there should be what were called 'rehearse/record sessions' with an increased fee.

The next request from the BBC was that they should be allowed to put together a few items from a number of programmes, recorded for broadcasting by several different bands and orchestras, and thereby create a single composite much more varied programme. Items recorded by the BBC Concert Orchestra might be interspersed with items recorded by some of the many small orchestras then broadcasting regularly: Sid Bowman and the Promenade Players, Philip Green and his Concert Orchestra, Monia Liter and the 20th Century Serenaders, The Studio Players, Troise and his Continental Orchestra, The Bob Farnon Orchestra,

Louis Voss and the Kursall Orchestra. Three or four of these groups would be selected, or one of the many other groups broadcasting at that time, and they would be made up into a half-hour programme. Each of these groups would have recorded a half-hour programme so that the BBC would be able to mix and match them into a great many programmes.

Programmes that had previously been recorded by individual groups were now being made into something much more like the programmes of commercial recordings that had become popular. It was natural that the BBC should then want to include commercial recordings in with all the orchestras the BBC had recorded themselves. Unfortunately, the commercial recording had been recorded with superior equipment and only 15 or 20 minutes music will have been recorded in a three-hour session, whilst the BBC will have recorded double that amount of music in the same length of time. The difference in quality showed rather too clearly and it was not too long before the pattern of broadcast music changed. Strange as it may seem now, listeners had in the past made a point of listening to their chosen light orchestras. Now all these groups had become much more anonymous. What had been, even though only at a distance, an audience listening to an identifiable group of performers had turned into *muzak*.

Now the majority of music of every kind is heard either on recordings, broadcasts, the Internet or some other format. In whatever format illusion often replaces reality.

15 The Orchestral Musician

Changing attitude to the status of musicians. In the early 20th century two
strands of employment start to emerge.
Playing in an orchestra – satisfaction and frustration – how different sections
of the orchestra are affected. Ever higher standards of technique.

In 1900 the majority of professional musicians were working in theatres, restaurants or for dancing. It was only with the formation of the BBC Symphony Orchestra in 1930 and then in 1946 with the re-opening of the Royal Opera House that Britain had its first full-time symphony orchestra and opera house. Until then very few musicians earned their living wholly as 'orchestral musicians'.

The problems Sir Henry Wood was still experiencing in 1904 were caused to a considerable extent by the fact that nearly all of the musicians in the Queen's Hall Orchestra were playing in the many London theatres, where they could put in deputies. It was largely from this considerable number of musicians that the Royal Philharmonic Society recruited the musicians for its orchestra (not to be confused with the Royal Philharmonic Orchestra that Sir Thomas created in 1946). The musicians in the orchestra Sir Henry put together for the first series of Proms in 1895 which became the Queen's Hall Orchestra, were mainly theatre musicians who expected to treat their relationship with that orchestra as they did their theatre contracts.

At the beginning of the 20th century two strands of musical employment begin to emerge. Until then there had just been music. The same composer might well write sacred music, 'art-music' and 'popular music'. Art-music more precisely describes what is now always referred to as classical, or sometimes as serious music. Neither of these terms is really accurate: art-music does not have to be Classical (as distinct from Romantic or Contemporary) nor does it need to be 'serious'.

From about 1910, when a new style of dance music started to be favoured by dancers, a new and different style of playing was also required and by around 1920, when a large number of what came to be called dance bands had been formed, those who played that music began to be referred to as 'dance' musicians (and, by some of the older musicians like my father, as 'Jazzers). In the latter half of the 1950s these musicians were increasingly replaced by the arrival of the pop and rock groups. For the past 80 years, with only a very few exceptions, musicians who have provided music for dancing have not played in orchestras. However, for those orchestral musicians who have been employed in providing 'backing' for the myriad forms of contemporary popular music on recordings and TV, it has usually been extremely rewarding financially. On TV the producers of programmes featuring a pop singer or group have increasingly favoured young and attractive women musicians when a small string section is on view.

Increasingly, since about 1955, when 'popular music' in its very many forms replaced jazz orientated dance music as the music enjoyed by the majority of young people, jazz has become more and more respectable until, since the 1990s, it has been regularly played on BBC Radio 3 alongside symphonic music, while pop music has its own channel, Radio 1. Students at the music colleges and conservatoires in Britain and the USA can take Jazz as their main study and many of the leading jazz musicians are now extremely musically educated. The extent to which attitudes to popular culture have changed since the 1960s can be gauged by the fact that at that time, when a number of distinguished jazz musicians and I met representatives of the BBC on behalf of the musicians broadcasting jazz and improvised music, jazz was still classed as 'entertainment' and not 'music'.

In contrast to a good many other countries where permanent symphony orchestras had already been established during the 19th century, it was not until well into the 20th that one was created in Britain. A musician's casual and insecure way of life and income continued to make this seem an unsuitable career for the children of most middle-class families. Perhaps, if they had a very great talent as a pianist or violinist and a solo career was possible, or they wished to become music teachers, it might be considered. Most fathers would definitely not have thought that an orchestral musician would make a suitable husband for one of their daughters. One of my colleagues told me, many years after the event, that even in 1947 when he went to ask his prospective father-in-law for his daughter's hand in marriage this gentleman, who I believe was a bank manager, said, 'My daughter tells me you are a musician. Where do you play?' 'I am the principal trumpet in the Royal Opera House Orchestra', my friend replied. 'What do you do during the day-time?' he was then asked. The prospective father-in-law clearly did not think of music as a full-time occupation and thought that symphony concerts and performances of opera arrived from out of thin air without any preparation. Another colleague, a distinguished principal wind player in the RPO in 1955, formerly a principal in the BBC Symphony Orchestra since the 1930s, told me that even while he was in the BBC Orchestra if he was asked what his occupation was he would claim to be 'in insurance', rather than admit that he played in an orchestra.

With the formation in 1930 of the BBC Symphony Orchestra and the creation in 1932 of the London Philharmonic Orchestra by Sir Thomas Beecham, a number of musicians could then really be said to be orchestral musicians, in that they earned the whole or the bulk of their income from playing in an orchestra. They no longer needed to play in theatres, restaurants, or do summer seasons playing on municipal bandstands. In addition to the BBC Symphony Orchestra, during the 1930s the BBC created several other orchestras: the BBC Northern (now BBC Philharmonic), the BBC Scottish and Welsh Orchestras and the BBC Theatre Orchestra (now the BBC Concert Orchestra). The increased demand for art-music from 1940, led by 1946 to the formation of two more orchestras in London, the Philharmonia and the Royal Philharmonic Orchestra, and together with the members of the London Symphony Orchestra and London Philharmonic Orchestra being fully engaged. It was not only in London that there were many more orchestral musicians. Bournemouth, Birmingham, Liverpool, Manchester and Glasgow all by then had full-time orchestras, each employing at least 70 musicians. There were also full-time orchestras at the Royal Opera House and Sadler's Wells, later to become the English National Opera, as well as a far greater amount of employment for freelance orchestral musicians in recording, broadcasting, playing for films and in the smaller part-time orchestras that had been formed in London and around the country.

Attitudes had also changed. A number of musicians of my generation, coming into the profession around the end of the war in 1945, had been to Public Schools (for my American readers that means Private Schools). Previously very few of those who had been to a public school or university had entered the profession as orchestral musicians. Musicians in the major orchestras in London, by working very hard, could earn enough to satisfy the most hard-hearted of prospective fathers-in-law, though those in the Regional orchestras were still comparatively poorly paid. To say that you were in one of these orchestras or even a member of the London Philharmonic or the Philharmonia meant nothing to the general public in Britain. I was struck when I went with the Philharmonia to Vienna in the 1960s how, when I was on a tram and other passengers saw the name Philharmonia on my instrument case, they looked at me with interest. In shop windows photographs of the Vienna Philharmonic Orchestra and their conductors were used to advertise various goods. It seemed that in Vienna musicians were regarded with as much respect as footballers were in Britain.

Playing in an Orchestra

Symphony and opera orchestras, the true homes of the orchestral musician, are highly complex hierarchical organisations, and to a greater or lesser extent this is true in all orchestras, large or small.

In 1900, musicians, like nearly everyone else, 'knew their place', accepted their position in society, and though they might be ambitious to better themselves the idea that every one was equal had not yet generally taken root. Accepting being told what to do and doing it without questioning was for most employees still the order of the day. Rules were obeyed, children did not 'answer back', those in authority were called Sir.

In an orchestra authority stems, as elsewhere, from the management, but is wielded by the conductor, who through the power invested in him by the management had the ability to hire and fire musicians. There is no doubt that in the past some conductors did behave like tyrants, as the bandmaster of an army band might. Although they could not send a player to the guardroom or confine him to barracks, they could terrorise and humiliate him, make his life a misery, destroy his ability to play and, ultimately, sack him, with or without good reason. Happily this state of affairs is no longer tolerated but, as I wrote in a previous chapter, many musicians still feel oppressed by conductors, especially when it is one for whom they have little or no respect.

Remnants of the old style of tyranny were still in evidence when I joined the profession in 1942. Individual members of the string sections, usually someone towards the back of the section, would be singled out to play a particularly difficult passage on their own, in front of the whole orchestra. Though an adequate member of the section, he would be unused to playing alone like a soloist and now, extremely nervous, he makes a poor showing and is humiliated in front of his colleagues. After WW2 changes in society and the education system greatly changed attitudes toward authority and this form of oppression is now extremely rare. But a conductor can still pursue and distress a player by constant criticism until he is no longer able to play adequately. It is now unlikely that individual members of a string section will be affected by a conductor in this way, though I have seen a whole violin section brought to the point of desperation at being unable to satisfy a conductor's unreasonable demands. The best conductors have no need to behave like this, because they are able to indicate what they want by their gestures and are experienced enough to know what an individual player or section is capable of. It is members of the woodwind, brass and percussion sections who are obviously the most vulnerable to criticism when they have solo or exposed music to play.

Every member of an orchestra, whether the leader (or concertmaster in the USA), principal horn, or the violinist at the back of the second violin section has to give up some of her or his individuality, but some have to do so much more than others. String players have to give up most: they are always playing the same notes as a number of other players. From time to time I believe every one of them will experience a real feeling of frustration. Nearly all of them at some time will have had dreams of becoming a soloist or of playing in a string quartet, or at least in a chamber orchestra.

As a clarinettist I never had to experience the frustration of playing the same notes as a number of other players while playing in an orchestra, but I think I can understand how they must feel. Gilbert Vinter, a bassoonist (I remember that when I was a child he came to our house to rehearse a Mozart trio for two clarinets and bassoon with Pauline Juler and my father), and later a successful composer and conductor, persuaded the BBC to form a very large wind band for a series of broadcasts. It was quite a remarkable band in that it was made up of many of the woodwind and brass players from all the orchestras in London – the symphony and opera orchestras, the BBC orchestras, plus the best freelance players.

There were about 14 or 16 clarinets (in a wind band the clarinet takes on a similar role to the violins in an orchestra). At one time or another I played in every position in the clarinet section in that band, from principal (leader) to the player on the last stand. Even though the standard of all the players was so good, having to play the same notes as a lot of other people was a new experience for me. Everyone else seemed to be playing all the notes in the difficult passages except me and however loudly I played I could not really hear myself. I would not want that experience every day all through my life. The violin is a softer sounding and more subtle instrument than the clarinet, but even so I think I would find it difficult to bear.

Players, other than some of the string principals who are seated very near the conductor, start with a major disadvantage: the majority of conductors never seem able to hear or understand whatever is said to them. Conversation with the conductor from one's seat in the orchestra always seems to be what an exasperated colleague called 'one-way traffic'. Conductors expect everyone, however far away from them, to hear and understand what they say, quite often fairly quietly and with a foreign accent, though the players on the back desks of the strings and the percussion, and even the woodwind and brass in a large orchestra, can be a considerable distance from them. When a member of the orchestra asks a question many conductors either don't hear them or understand what is being asked. I learned that to get their attention it was necessary to wait until there was absolute silence, speak very loudly (with some it helped to stand up) and very clearly. It takes a fair amount of self-confidence, some might say 'hard-neck', to do that.

The phrase 'hard-boiled musicians', so beloved by critics, could not be further from the truth. Musicians, like all performers, however distinguished or famous, are extremely sensitive and aware of their own weaknesses and shortcomings as artists. Their confidence can be easily shaken. Actors, dancers and musicians have to take a great deal of criticism from directors and conductors as well as the self-criticism they constantly have to apply if they are to be any good. Quite a number of those going to music college, when faced with the demands of their teachers, who will often be a soloist or a professional orchestral player, and especially when they start doing a few orchestral engagements, find that they are temperamentally unsuited to the harsh reality of professional life. They give up and go into teaching or some other less demanding occupation.

It not easy, when one is trying one's utmost to respond to the demands being made on one, to be told one is too loud or too soft, too sharp or too flat, too early or too late, not making enough crescendo or too much, too much attack or not enough – the list is endless. All these comments come most often from the least able conductors, those who cannot achieve what they want by their gestures. Something that, after working with so many conductors, I still cannot explain is why it is that even good intonation is achieved by the very finest conductors without any obvious action or comment on their part. Perhaps the sense of security they engender by the certainty of rhythm, tempo and the balance they achieve just makes it easier to hear and play more accurately.

Attitudes within the orchestra itself have also changed a great deal over the last 30 or 40 years. Older players used to take a very decided 'who do you think you are, young man' attitude to young players. Joseph Casteldini, a fine bassoon player, told me how when he was a young man he went to deputise at a show at one of the West End theatres. He found that he was sitting next to the famous clarinettist Charles Draper, then quite elderly and at the end of his career. At the interval, intending to be friendly, Joe said 'Can I get you a cup of tea, Charlie? Draper responded with some asperity, 'Mr Draper', and did not speak to him again. I found when I joined the LPO in 1943 as a very callow youth that a few of the older players behaved in this way to me. When I complained to my colleague, the bass-clarinettist Richard Temple-Savage, by then one of the middle-aged members of the orchestra, he recounted his own experience when he had joined the orchestra in 1934. He said that for the first six months he was in the orchestra Reginald Kell, the then principal clarinet, did not speak to him at all. Nowadays, if an older player were to say 'I've had 40 years experience', as I remember being told a number of times when I was young and had only been in the profession for a couple of years, a young player would think (and might even say) 'isn't it time you made way for someone younger?'.

As well as accepting the authority of the conductor, members of all the string sections also have to accept decisions made by the principal of their own section often directed by the leader. Many conductors will leave bowing decisions to the leader who will usually consult with the principals of the other sections. Decisions about bowing, which part of the bow, whether a passage should start with an up-bow or a down-bow, whether a series of detached notes should be played 'on the string' or 'off' and many other sophisticated questions have to be decided. There can be very decided opinions on these questions and doing something one way or another can make some passages much more difficult for some players. The leader may be a very fine player but have idiosyncratic ideas regarding bowing. Paul Beard, a very fine violinist and a fine leader highly respected by conductors (he was also Beecham's leader of the LPO for a time), upset some of his section when he was leader of the BBC Symphony Orchestra because of his unusual views on bowing. It seems he was unwilling to listen to the complaints of a number of members of the first violin section, causing a degree of discontent. In contrast, when David McCallum was leader of the RPO, not all the violinists in his section were of the highest calibre, but because of his easy authority and understanding of each player's capacity he got the very best out of them and created a first-class section.

In the same way that musicians will accept a conductor's wishes, even when their own feelings about the music differ from his, especially if there is finally a rewarding performance, so the members of every section, strings, woodwind, brass and percussion must at times accept the decisions of their principal. When appointing players, regard to their temperament and ability to co-operate in the position to which they are to be appointed is extremely important. Two players, perhaps equally good oboists, may have very different personalities. One might make an excellent principal oboe but be quite unsuited to being a second oboe, being unable to subordinate his own style and musical feelings sufficiently. The other player, equally good, might find the responsibility of being principal and 'in the firing line' all the time too demanding. He might be more suited to the less demanding principal position as the cor anglais player. In that position he will have important solos to play but they occur much less frequently. Or he or she might be ideal as a second oboist, delighting in supporting their principal when there are duets or unison passages, adapting to and matching his principal's style and tone. The worst situation is when a second player believes he should be occupying the position of his principal, or if a string player feels dissatisfied, believing he should be sitting further forward in the section, perhaps right at the front. A player like that can be extremely harmful to the whole section.

Even the relationship between principals can sometimes be difficult. As Chairman of the Philharmonia I sometimes had to deal with this problem. Perhaps the principal double bass and principal cello may have very different ideas as to how some passages the cellos and basses have to play together in octaves should be bowed. After a time, the relationship between the two of them gradually becomes strained and the whole of each section gets involved. Or, perhaps the trumpets feel that the trombones always interpret the dynamic marking, whether piano or forte, too loudly, forcing them to play louder than they want to. Sometimes a very good woodwind or brass player can irritate some of his colleagues, who admire him, but find he is inclined to be rather over-assertive, perhaps because he has a strong soloistic temperament. In solo passages his playing is very personal and exciting and at times an inspiration to others in the orchestra, but whenever others have to play in unison with him or when he doesn't have the most important part in ensemble passages he always seems to dominate. The test for a really fine orchestral woodwind and brass player is whether he or she has the ability to switch from being a soloist one moment to a chamber music player the next, and then a moment or two later, when there is a melodic line in their part that they would like to play out, play as quietly as possible so that more important parts can be heard.

When I meet ex-colleagues of my own generation or older who in their day were considered very good players, there is general agreement that we would be lucky to get into the profession now with the skills we had when we started many years ago. Improved teaching methods and the many improvements that have been made in the manufacture of woodwind and brass instruments in the last 30 years or so have been important elements in making technical virtuosity relatively commonplace. But most important has been the example set by the extraordinary level of technical performance young aspiring musicians have come to accept as normal. The recordings made over many years, using the techniques I described earlier and that includes piecing together a number of 'takes' to create a performance without any blemish, have been an inspiration and the spur to achieve a similar or even a better performance.

Each year, starting in 1979, the National Centre for Orchestral Studies (NCOS) formed a symphony orchestra following the audition of students who had been at music college or university and now wished to become orchestral musicians. As the Director I sat in on the auditions for every instrument and was impressed by the generally high standard of technical skill. The oboe auditions are a good example. Before attending the audition every applicant was required to prepare a number of extracts from the orchestral repertoire that we had selected for their instrument. One of the extracts the oboists were sent was from the Overture to *La scala di seta (The Silken Ladder)* by Rossini. This overture contains a famous solo for the oboe that in my experience even the best players considered difficult. I remember that Terence MacDonagh, Leon Goossens and Evelyn Rothwell, three of the most outstanding players of their generation, would do some extra practice if they knew it was going to be on the programme. I had heard it imperfectly played by lesser players on a number of occasions. At the auditions for the NCOS from 1979 until 1989 I must have listened to about 300 young oboists. Though the technical performance of this difficult passage was generally very good only a handful played it with any real musical understanding.

Not surprisingly, the number of players able to respond to and interpret the content of the music and express it in their playing had not increased at the same time as their instrumental dexterity. In fact, musicians of my generation and those even older feel that a considerable number of concert performances have for some time lacked the expressive qualities we had heard in the past from the best principal players when they had solo and ensemble passages. In the last chapter I have written: *When I was first involved in playing for recording, from 1944, we tried to recreate in the studio as nearly as possible what took place at a concert performance.* As record sales increased it was not long before the concert performance began to try to recreate what could be heard on recordings. Inevitably, listening to playbacks, editing short sections, when the primary concern of record producers had become whether the balance, tuning, ensemble or any other technical element was as near perfect as possible, resulted in performers becoming increasingly concerned about these aspects of their performance as well. Musicians brought up on a diet of recordings have naturally been as influenced by the interpretative elements they have heard as by the technical.

Now that there are so many accomplished players there are a very large number of applicants whenever auditions are held for one of the orchestras. It is likely that 40 or more players will apply if the position of second clarinet in one of the BBC Orchestras becomes available. There may be two or three who the orchestra think might be suitable. As a rule each of them will then be given a trial period in the orchestra. As well as being a good player there are other qualities that are extremely important. How will they fit into the section musically and personally? How will they respond to conductors, and they to him? As well as being a good player, getting on well with colleagues and satisfying conductors, how consistent a player will they prove to be? Sadly, if there is only one job, two very good players are going to be disappointed

It is generally known that symphony orchestras everywhere have for some time been experiencing increasing financial problems and that the amount of employment for musicians has reduced, especially the number of recording sessions that the major orchestras in Britain had come to rely on to a considerable extent. Yet the number of young musicians seeking entry to the specialist music schools and the music colleges has not decreased. A good many of them will be hoping for a solo or chamber music career and though there are now many more opportunities for a local career in those fields, the majority of students leaving the music colleges wishing to follow a career as a performer will find they will be playing in an orchestra of some kind. The popularity of musicals, many of which have very long runs in London, a few for as long as 20 years, now provide employment for quite a few musicians. A few may be fortunate enough to obtain a position in one of the symphony orchestras. Many more will freelance, a field of employment now sadly much reduced, and make up their income by teaching. It is vitally important that anyone contemplating a career as a professional musician should remember that many of those setting out with this intention are disappointed with the type of employment they find they are obliged to undertake for a good deal of their lives. This is true for all performers, actors, dancers, singers and musicians. There are just too few opportunities available for all those who wish to spend their lives doing what they enjoy most.

When talking to other orchestral musicians, including some who also had solo and chamber music careers and were fortunate enough, as I was, to have experienced the enormous satisfaction of taking part in a wonderful performance in a very good orchestra conducted by a great conductor, they have all agreed that notwithstanding the fact that one has to give up one's freedom of expression and accept the discipline of being part of a large ensemble, nothing surpasses the satisfaction of taking part in a performance of this kind. It is an extraordinary paradox.

Over and above everything else the fact is that as an orchestral musician one spends one's whole working life in the company of men of genius who one is very rarely, indeed ever, going to meet in person. One is constantly refreshed and enriched by the thoughts, feelings and imagination of the great composers of the past and present as expressed in their music. Because over the years one takes part in a good many different interpretations of the compositions of Mozart, Beethoven, Berlioz, Brahms, Tchaikovsky, Mahler, Debussy, Stravinsky, Britten, Shostakovich and other composers, one is privileged to gain an understanding and insight that is extremely rewarding.

For me there was another continuing pleasure, that of working with outstanding solo artists. Whether the orchestra is good or not so good, or the conductor is great, good or just so-so, to accompany a great artist is always a delight. I was fortunate to take part in performances of a great deal of the piano, violin and cello repertoire with many of them. As well as that pleasure there was always the enjoyment of working with colleagues whose playing delighted and sometimes inspired. This element of the life of an orchestral musician deserves a chapter of its own.

16 The Pleasure of Taking Part

The delight of playing with great artists. Wonderful solo violinists, cellists, pianists – Heifetz, Oistrakh, Menuhin, Perlman ... Fournier, Tortelier, du Pré, Rostropovich ... Rubinstein, Solomon, Curzon, Barenboim ...

However enjoyable going to a concert may be, or listening to music on the radio, TV or a recording, there is nothing to beat actually taking part in a performance. I have tried to express how wonderful it is if one is privileged to be part of a performance of one of the masterpieces of the orchestral or opera repertoire in a very good orchestra with an inspiring conductor. In a similar way, to be in the orchestra accompanying a great artist is immensely satisfying. In addition, if one is lucky enough to play alongside musicians one admires, whether it is in a symphony orchestra, the pit in an opera house or at a film session, broadcasting or recording light or commercial music, it can be equally enjoyable to make music with congenial spirits. These are the delights I was able to enjoy a good deal of the time during my 38 years as an orchestral musician.

In writing about the artists whose performances gave me so much pleasure when taking part in concerts with them and whom I recall as one does old friends, in many cases now departed, there is no attempt to suggest these are the 'best' artists, only that in memory they are those for whom I feel great affection. Someone once asked Sir Thomas Beecham 'what is good music?' and he had to invent an answer on the spur of the moment. 'Good music', he said, 'is that which penetrates the ear with facility and quits the memory with difficulty'. This is equally true for a 'good performance'.

My very first experience of accompanying a soloist was while I was still at the Royal College of Music. Sir George Dyson, then the Director, conducted a rehearsal of his very pleasant Violin Concerto, with W. H. Reed as soloist. Willy Reed, as we called him (though Vaughan Williams calls him Billy, in his Introduction to *London Symphony, Portrait of an Orchestra*) was for many years the leader of the LSO and it was to him that Elgar turned when seeking advice at the time he was composing his violin concerto. As well as being a most distinguished violinist Reed was also a composer. He composed a violin concerto and a viola rhapsody among many other works for orchestra that were all performed between 1910 and 1930. The music by Dyson and Reed like the compositions of so many English composers of that period is now largely forgotten.

Once I had joined the Wessex Orchestra I took part in a good many concerts with a soloist. In fact, it was rare for us to do a concert without a soloist. I referred in chapter 5 to a number of the artists who played with us, but omitted to mention Mark Hambourg. He was the most internationally famous artist we worked with apart from Benno Moiseiwitsch. By 1942 when he played with us he was in his 60s and past his best, but still a formidable player and very popular with the public. He was always called upon to play an encore and most times would play the *Minute Waltz* by Chopin. He always turned to the audience and with his still fairly thick Russian accent said, 'Now, I play *Minute Waltz* – in half-minute!' And he would then proceed to do so including a fair sprinkling of wrong notes. His book *From Piano to Forte* is interesting, amusing and extraordinarily well written in marked contrast to his spoken English. This book, published in 1931, is worth reading for the last chapter alone, in which he writes so perceptively about the effect of recording (then still on 78s) and broadcasting on artists of his time and reflects on the changes in attitude this was already having on performers and audiences.

Mark Hambourg, like nearly all the soloists I shall write about, was a child prodigy who first played in public when he was seven years old. In 1895, when he was 16, he played Liszt's *Hungarian Fantasie* in the beautiful Musikvereinsaal in Vienna with the Berlin Philharmonic Orchestra, conducted by Felix Weingartner. It is usually apparent from a fairly early age, often by the time they are four or five years old, whether a young instrumentalist has a talent that may lead to a great solo career.

Violin and cello soloists

It was in 1943, the year I joined the LPO, that I first played in an orchestra accompanying Ida Haendel. She was the soloist on two occasions during the Prom season that year; on 11th July she played the Tchaikovsky Violin Concerto and only four days later on the 15th she played the *Symphonie Espagnole* by Édouard Lalo. She was then 15. This astonishing musician was truly a child prodigy. When she was only 7 years old in 1935 she was the 7th prize winner in the Wieniawski Competition. One gains some idea of the standard from the fact that Ginette Neveu, then aged 16, and David Oistrakh, aged 27, came 1st and 2nd that year. Haendel made her debut in London at the Queens Hall in 1937 playing the Beethoven Violin Concerto with Sir Henry Wood conducting. I remember the occasion very clearly because my father insisted that we listen to the broadcast of this concert. I was then 12 and he had about a year previously started giving me clarinet lessons and he wanted me to hear this incredible girl, then still only 9. Having been an outstandingly gifted boy himself, earning his living as a clarinettist when he was 11, I felt this was intended to inspire me and, perhaps, induce me to practise more. Needless to say, though I was amazed by her playing I recognised a talent so far beyond my own that it did not have the desired effect. As the years went by Ida Haendel continued to be an artist who gave me pleasure whenever she played with any orchestra I was in.

From the time when I was at school in 1940 and was bowled over listening to the young Yehudi Menuhin playing the Elgar Violin Concerto, until the end of his life in 1999 his wonderfully musical insights were always rewarding and from the mid 80s he was most helpful to me personally. He gave his support and came and worked with the orchestra at the National Centre for Orchestral Studies and when we were establishing the Music Performance Research Centre, now Music Preserved, he was also very helpful and supportive. Later, in 1990, he agreed to be the President of the Orchestra for Europe which, unfortunately, finally had to be abandoned for lack of sufficient finance.

He was an absolutely natural player and musician who perhaps to a greater extent than anyone else in my lifetime demonstrated how dangerous interfering with such a talent can be. He said that he wanted 'Kreisler's elegance, Elman's sonority and Heifetz's technique' though nature had to a considerable extent already granted that wish. 'I played more or less as a bird sings, instinctively, uncalculatingly, unthinkingly,' Menuhin was to write in his memoir *Unfinished Journey*. But this was not enough and in his forties he suddenly decided that intuition was not sufficient and could not be relied on; he needed to think about how he should play, in fact to re-teach himself.

Though for the rest of his life his musical instincts never deserted him he had ever increasing technical problems that at times seriously marred his performances. He was a perfect example of the warning exemplified in the story of the two golfers, Charles and James, one very much better than the other. Charles, the much less good player, decided that if he could not win by his golfing prowess he must use guile. Just as the other player raised his club to drive off, he went 'Um! yes.' James, stopping in mid-stroke, 'What's that? What do you mean?' 'It was just that I was interested to see what you did to get such a good swing and strike the ball so well.' This started James thinking about what he was doing so that he became increasingly introverted and inhibited until he found it harder and harder to play with his former skill.

Perhaps, because Menuhin's violin playing was causing him problems he began conducting. Again his instinctive musicality was always present but, as has been the case with so many other instrumentalists and singers who have wanted to conduct, the particular magic required had not been granted to him. When he came to conduct the Philharmonia he was quite unable to cope with the problems involved in accompanying one of the Bartók Piano Concertos. He became rather disagreeable and as a result his relationship with the orchestra deteriorated. At the time I was Chairman of the orchestra and found it extremely saddening to hear someone I so much admired spoken of by my colleagues in such an unfavourable way.

Once the war ended in 1945 a great many of the finest soloists began visiting Britain again. One of the first to arrive was the French violinist Jacques Thibaud. In 1896 when he was 16 he was joint winner of the Paris Conservatoire Violin Prize with Pierre Monteux, who went on to be a viola player (he led the violas at the Opéra-Comique for the first performance of Debussy's *Pelléas and Mélisande*) before becoming a celebrated conductor. Thibaud is best remembered now for the trio recordings he made with the cellist Pablo Casals and pianist Alfred Cortot. It is a pity that there is no recording of his performance of *The Introduction and Rondo Capriccioso* by Camille Saint-Saëns. I remember it still, though it is so many years ago, because I have never heard the Introduction played so sensitively since then. The way in which the beautiful *Introduction* is nearly always played is far too *schmaltzy* and 'romantic' for this quintessential French music. Thibaud played it delicately and tenderly and with true feeling, in the same way that a great actor can underplay a love scene making it all the more affecting, rather than sentimentalising it.

Thibaud was followed by two more superb violinists, Zino Francescatti and the incomparable Ginette Neveu who immediately made a tremendous impression on the orchestra – as well as the audience. There was something so ferociously passionate about her playing that overwhelmed one. At times she seemed to attack the violin like a gladiator and at others to draw out the most sensuous and captivating tone. Her performances of the Beethoven and Brahms Concertos were outstanding, but it was her performance of Ravel's *Tzigane* that for me was probably the most memorable. Her personality was just right for portraying the wild gypsy element in the music. This wonderfully vibrant musician was still only 26 when she played with us in 1945, four years before her tragically early death.

Around the same time two more very fine string soloists came to work with us, making the very hard schedule we undertook worthwhile. They were the two cellists, Maurice Gendron and Pierre Fournier, both French with that particular elegance that French artists of that generation still seemed to have. After Casals left the famous Thibaud-Casals-Cortot trio Fournier took his place. He had that refinement, purity of tone and musicianship similar to Thibaud that is extremely rare. I remember a lovely recording of the Dvorak Cello Concerto he did with us that was quite different from the much more 'virtuoso' readings of that beautiful composition we generally hear today.

From 1947 onwards, during the years I spent in the Royal Philharmonic and the Philharmonia, I have always enjoyed it more when the soloist has been a string player and was fortunate to have the opportunity to play in the orchestra with many wonderful violinists and cellists. It is a mystery to me why pianists and the piano repertoire appear to have been, and continue to be preferred by the public.

There have been far too many violinists to write about them all but I have very happy recollections of performances with Nathan

Milstein, Joseph Szigeti, Alfredo Campoli (who, notwithstanding his name was British and one of our leading violin soloists for many years), Henryk Szerying, Anne-Sophie Mutter (when she was only 13 Herbert von Karajan said she was 'the greatest music prodigy since the young Menuhin') and Joshua Bell. Four very special artists that made a tremendous impression on me were Jascha Heifetz, David Oistrakh, Isaac Stern and Itzhak Perlman.

Jascha Heifetz.

Jascha Heifetz has been called the greatest violinist of the 20th century and certainly in my experience his virtuosity was supreme, to such an extent that a youngster who was outstanding on his instrument whether flute, tuba or any other used to be called 'a little Heifetz'. Already at the age of six he had performed the Mendelssohn Violin Concerto in public and from when he was twelve he was touring Europe. Ever since his debut at Carnegie Hall in 1917, throughout his exceedingly long career and as a result of having recorded a vast amount of the violin repertoire, he has set the benchmark by which violinists have been judged, and his recordings still continue to delight music lovers everywhere.

In writing about Beecham I referred to the less than happy relationship he had with Heifetz when he recorded the Mendelssohn Violin Concerto with the RPO. In fact the first time I played with Heifetz was in 1945 or 1946 soon after the end of the war when he came to play with the LPO. He had not played in Britain for some years so that when this concert was announced it was the cause of considerable excitement. On the night of the concert the Royal Albert Hall was packed and many celebrated violinists were in the audience. When Heifetz came onto the platform to play the Beethoven Violin Concerto he was greeted with rapturous applause. During the orchestral introduction Heifetz stood absolutely still and looked impassive as usual. The soloist's entry, a series of octaves was played with his accustomed brilliance, but as he started on the downward melodic *legato* passage his finger slipped off the fingerboard and as it landed on the resonant belly of the violin the impact was like someone striking a snare-drum. He continued, apparently unperturbed, but for me the shock of hearing and seeing the acme of perfection falter, if only for a moment, reminded me of the shock I experienced when Beecham put the baton through his hand at his first rehearsal with us.

My memory of hearing Heifetz goes back even earlier, to the time when I was evacuated with my school to Crowthorne to escape the bombing of London. There was a small cinema in the village of a kind that in those days might have been referred to as a 'flea-pit', but the price for admission was suitably low, three pence in old money (pronounced *thripence,* about half my pocket money, and equivalent to just over 1p in today's coinage). It was there that I saw a wonderfully sentimental film, *They Shall Have Music,* about a charity that ran a music school for very poor children that was going to have to close for lack of money. By some miracle Jascha Heifetz agrees to come and play at a fund-raising concert at which he plays the slow movement of the Mendelssohn Violin Concerto. There is general rejoicing and the school is saved. I was then 14 and the effect of the story and Heifetz's beautiful playing is something I have never forgotten. Perhaps because of that experience I have rarely been affected to the same extent by any other performance of that concerto. The mood one is in and an association with a previous experience can have a profound effect on how one responds to a performance.

Heifetz was not a very sociable man and inclined to be rather formal and unfriendly. When I was in San Francisco in the 1980s I had the opportunity of spending an evening with his daughter, who had been a pianist and composer. She told me that her father would not allow her to use the family name because he did not think her work was of a high enough standard. His need to preserve the image of perfection was very strong. The leader of one of the orchestras in the USA who as a young man had attended the master classes that Heifetz gave at Berkeley told me how he had been assigned the task of driving Heifetz from his home to the University. Each time he arrived with his car to collect him Heifetz insisted on testing the tyre pressure of each tyre and if he found that the pressure in all of them was not absolutely equal he would send him to a garage to get them adjusted.

There are a few performances that remain in one's memory as fresh as the day they took place. It is over fifty years since Isaac Stern joined the RPO under Sir Thomas Beecham to perform the Sibelius Violin Concerto at the Royal Festival Hall and record it at the Abbey Road Studios a few days later. He was then in his early thirties and not yet the world renowned figure he became later as a result of his work in rescuing the Carnegie Hall from destruction, his crusading visits to Russia, Israel and, perhaps the most remarkable, to China. It was clear from the first rehearsal that Stern responded to Beecham in a way that would lead to a very satisfying musical collaboration for all concerned. Stern brought a youthful strength and passion to his performance that together with Beecham became, especially in the slow movement something quite beautifully expressive. The recording sessions were particularly enjoyable; Beecham was in his most jovial and expansive mood and Stern seemed to be influenced by him. The occasion was made even more pleasant because at one of the sessions Beecham presented a silver Loving Cup to Jack Brymer to celebrate the birth of his son.

Thirty years later in 1986 I was to participate in a Conference, rather grandly entitled *The Evolution of the Symphony Orchestra - History, Problems and Agendas,* at which Stern was the Chairman. It was sponsored by the Foundation, funded by the composer Gordon Getty, son of Jean Paul Getty the oil billionaire, who shared in the Trust, set up by his father, with his brother, Sir J. Paul Getty Jr. The Conference, attended by about thirty musicians and others concerned for the future of the symphony orchestra, including Pierre Boulez, Alfred Brendel, Alexander Goehr and Sir Isaiah Berlin, was held in Jerusalem in suitably comfortable conditions. The papers and discussions were later published by Weidenfeld and Nicolson.

When he came to play with the RPO another great violinist, David Oistrakh (also often spelled Oistrach) immediately excited the whole orchestra, especially all the violinists. It was at a BBC transmission to play the Tchaikovsky Violin Concerto with Sir Malcolm Sargent conducting. As soon as he started playing everyone was amazed by the beauty and breadth of his tone. Warm and vibrant with a lovely unobtrusive vibrato that has reminded some, including myself, of Fritz Kreisler. Kreisler was born in 1875 and was another artist who showed great promise when extremely young and continued, from the age of eleven for the next sixty-one years until 1947 to delight audiences not only with his playing but also with the many compositions he wrote for the violin which so many other violinists played, on bandstands, in restaurants and on the concert platform. I never had the opportunity of hearing him at a public performance, but he was, from when I was about sixteen, the artist I most wished to emulate. The first recording he made with the Berlin State Opera Orchestra of the Brahms Violin Concerto was ravishing; there were some passages that even on the 78 rpm records I played over and over again – not nearly so easily as one can now on a tape or CD. The small charming melodic pieces he composed for himself and recorded, some several times, and each a fresh-minted one-off performance – *Schon Rosmarin, Liebesfreud* (Love's Joy), *Liebesleid* (Love's Sorrow), *Tambourin chinois* were my favourites. Some years later I bought the violin parts so that I could adapt them and play them on the clarinet.

To return to David Oistrakh. On that occasion when he played the Tchaikovsky Concerto with the RPO I remember that in the interval of the rehearsal a lot of the string players crowded round him and one or two of the Jewish violinists in the orchestra asked him in Yiddish – he as yet spoke no English – to play to them on his own so that they could hear his wonderful tone. He started to play one of the Bach Unaccompanied Violin Sonatas, but after a few minutes begged to be excused as it was making him nervous. The sound he drew from his violin was so big – it sounded to me like a whole violin section. He played with the Philharmonia a number of times, several times with the conductor Gennadi Rozhdestvensky, and I always enjoyed his performances, whether of the standard concerto repertoire – Beethoven, Brahms, Tchaikovsky or the fiendishly difficult Shostakovich No.1.

Itzhak Perlman who was born in Israel in 1945 lost the use of his legs as a result of contracting polio when he was only four years old and as a result he has always had to play sitting in a wheelchair. He had already made a number of broadcasts in Israel before he was 13 when his family emigrated in 1958 to America. In 1959, when he was fourteen he was featured in 'Ed Sullivan's Caravan of Stars', a showcase for gifted young artists, when he played *'The Flight of the Bumble Bee'* as well as the last movement of the Mendelssohn Violin Concerto. After further study at the Juilliard School, he made his professional debut in 1963, at Carnegie Hall, playing the Wieniawski Violin Concerto. A year later he won the prestigious Leventritt Competition and began his international career.

To take part in a performance, or even a rehearsal with Perlman is always a mood raising experience. The combination of his irrepressible joy when making music, boundless energy and infectious charm are irresistible. Every time he played with the orchestra it was sheer delight. Whether it is Klezmer, Scott Joplin and the cowboy music that he has recorded with Andre Previn, the film music for *Schindler's List,* Tan Dun's music for the film *Hero* he recorded when he was in China, or the Beethoven and Tchaikovsky Concertos, he brings the same warmth and understanding to everything he plays, by turns lyrical, dramatic and effortlessly virtuoso.

The cellist Paul Tortelier was an artist who affected me in a similar way to Perlman, though he had a quite different personality. Whenever I had the pleasure of playing in an orchestra and he was the soloist it always felt to me that I had received an injection of sunshine. Yet when he was playing with the Philharmonia and we were talking about his future schedule he spoke in a very dispirited and sad way about how difficult he found it going from one engagement to another, always travelling carrying his luggage and his cello, away from his family and having to spend such a lot of time alone in unfriendly hotel bedrooms. When I suggested that perhaps he might undertake fewer engagements he said that his agent would not like that and other artists would take his place.

Unlike nearly all other soloists I have been writing about, Tortelier was working as an orchestral musician for some years before his solo career took off. He was playing in cafes and restaurants before he was sixteen and later he was sub-principal cello in the Paris Radio Orchestra and then in the Monte Carlo Philharmonic Orchestra, where he played the solo part in *Don Quixote* with the composer Richard Strauss conducting, before finally being appointed principal cello in the Boston Symphony. In 1947 he made his British debut with the RPO playing *Don Quixote* with Sir Thomas Beecham conducting. This concert was one of a series of Strauss concerts and at the rehearsal Richard Strauss was also present. At one point he came up to the clarinet section and told Jack Brymer that the little clarinet solo near the end of the piece should be played very quietly, like a memory.

As well as *Don Quixote*, which Tortelier played many times, I remember enjoying his splendid performances of the Saint-Saëns, Schumann and Dvorak Concertos and *Schelomo* by Ernest Bloch. The last time I heard him play was at a concert after I had left the orchestra and was on holiday in the Dordogne in France. I went to a concert where he was playing in what had been a fine Chateau but which was then in a state of some decay. It was a fine summer evening and as it gradually got darker a number of small bats started to fly in through the broken roof and swoop around overhead. At the end of the concert Tortelier spoke to the audience very eloquently about peace and goodwill amongst mankind and then played the lovely haunting folk song Casals had arranged for unaccompanied cello, *The Song of the Birds*. While he played a bat sat absolutely motionless on the toe of his shoe.

Jacqueline du Pré was a wonderful charismatic artist, a superb cellist and a joy to work with because of the intensity of her approach to performing. It is a tragedy that her life was cut short when she was only 42 and had been unable to play for some years before her death. Though she had lessons with William Pleeth, her main teacher, and then for a short time with both Tortelier and Rostropovich and no doubt she was influenced by each of them to some extent, she was a very individual artist. Her most famous performance is the recording of the Elgar Concerto she made with Sir John Barbirolli, but when she played it with the Philharmonia it was with her husband Daniel Barenboim. This, too, was a great performance, exciting and gloriously youthful and wildly exuberant. I am glad I was able to take part in a couple of performances with her.

Mstislav Rostropovich.

Even at the age of seventy-seven Mstislav Rostropovich remained the most outstanding and remarkable cellist of our time. He was only four when he composed a Polka and at the advanced age of eight undertaken his first major concert appearance as a solo cellist. When he arrived in Britain after leaving the Soviet Union in 1974 his first concert was with the Philharmonia and it was my privilege to introduce him to the orchestra. Of course he had visited Britain a good many times before as a cello soloist, but this was the occasion when he and his wife the soprano Galina Vishnevskaya had at last been obliged to leave the Soviet Union following their support for the dissident writer, the banned novelist Alexander Solzhenitsyn. However, this time he came to conduct the orchestra for what was in fact the beginning of an extremely distinguished international conducting career. He conducted Tchaikovsky's Symphony No.6 in a very dramatic and extrovert interpretation, which I enjoyed though a good many in the orchestra thought it rather 'over the top'.

His performances of the cello concerto repertoire are legendary and his friendships with Shostakovich (in whose composition class he had been), Prokofiev and Britten, who all wrote works especially for him, gave particular authority to his performances of their compositions. The combination of his incredible virtuosity and charismatic personality made taking part in performances of these works an extremely exciting experience. From a technical standpoint his performance of the Dvorak was probably more accurate than any other I have heard, (it has possibly been equalled by Yo-Yo Ma, but I never took part in a performance with him), but for me it was less satisfying than those with the artists I have written about earlier. I mention this because it shows how very personal and subjective any judgement or criticism is. Indeed, all the soloists I have chosen to write about are those that gave me personally the most pleasure and satisfaction and were in one way or another part of my continuing musical education.

For some a less than perfect playing of a technical passage or moments of doubtful intonation will render a performance unsatisfactory. Others, and I include myself, are more concerned with the content of the music and can allow relatively small technical faults to pass. It is, of course, the repetition of identically the same performance that one hears on a recording, that has passed in a moment at a concert, that makes even a small imperfection so difficult to accept. Now that everyone has become accustomed to technical perfection on recordings, artists have had to concentrate to an ever increasing degree on the technical aspect of their performance. There are artists whose temperament does not let them perform in this way, who vary from performance to performance (as I remember some of the finest soloists and orchestral players did before the dominance of recordings) and who therefore do not get engaged to record. Without recordings it is now virtually impossible to achieve international recognition.

Piano soloists

I have chosen to write only about those pianists whose performances gave me so much pleasure at the time they took place and which still do so now when I recall them. To write something about every celebrated pianist who was the soloist when I had the good fortune to be playing in the orchestra would require another book. In addition to the pianists I have already either mentioned this list of superb artists gives some idea of just how fortunate my colleagues and I were: Martha Argerich, Claudio Arrau, Vladimir Ashkenazy, Daniel Barenboim, Alfred Brendel, Julius Katchen, Louis Kentner, Stephen Kovacevich, John Ogdon, Murray Perahia, Sviatoslav Richter, Artur Schnabel, Mitsuko Uchida.

An artist who gave me immense pleasure was Myra Hess. Unlike the majority of solo artists Myra Hess was quite a late starter. She did not make her debut until she was seventeen when in 1907 she was invited by Sir Thomas Beecham to play Beethoven's Concerto No.4 with his orchestra. Even so it was to be some years, during which she taught and accompanied a number of artists including Nellie Melba and Lotte Lehmann, before her career took off. From 1912 her reputation rapidly increased until 1922 when she made her debut in New York. She is probably best remembered by the general public for her inauguration of the series of Lunch Time concerts at the National Gallery in London during WW2. She, and the many artists she encouraged to perform at these concerts, continued to do so during the heaviest bombing of London and was an emblem of courage in the face of adversity.

She was a wonderfully sensitive artist of a kind we so seldom hear now with a beautiful *pianissimo* legato and loving phrasing. There was nothing percussive or flaunting in her playing. Her Mozart, Beethoven and Schumann Concertos were a delight but, above all else, it was her magical performance of the César Frank *Symphonic Variations* that gave me the most pleasure. It has remained, in the same way that Thibaud's playing of Saint-Saën's *Introduction and Rondo Capriccioso* has, a very special memory, unmatched by any performance I have heard since.

Solomon, he was never known by his full name Solomon Cutner, was 12 years Myra Hess's junior. He was another astonishing prodigy, playing the Tchaikovsky and Brahms D minor when he was only 12 years old. He was a most self-effacing performer, always subordinating himself and putting his prodigious talent totally at the service of the composer. His performance of the Mozart, Beethoven and Schumann Concertos were quite different from Myra Hess's, but equally sensitive and insightful. When he played the *Emperor* Concerto by Beethoven it was majestic and not, as so often in other hands, reduced to yet another 'war-horse'. His performances were never showy whether playing Mozart, Liszt, Tchaikovsky or Brahms. Tragically, his career was cut short as the result of a stroke when he was only 54.

Another artist, in many ways similar to Hess and Solomon, was Clifford Curzon (later Sir Clifford). He was a perfectionist, never satisfied with his performance, extremely serious and sensitive in his approach and always gave the impression (to me) of being rather nervous. He was a sore trial to the gramophone companies because he was always reluctant to let any of the recordings he made be published before he was absolutely satisfied with them – and he seldom was. The performance I remember most vividly was the one I wrote about in the chapter about Beecham when Curzon played Brahms's Second Piano Concerto. The contrast between their two personalities was so great – Beecham extrovert and ebullient and Curzon withdrawn and silent – yet their collaboration was such a success. But it was Curzon's playing of Mozart and Schubert that was most magical. I was lucky enough to take part in a number of his performances of several of the Mozart piano concertos and each time it was a real treat. It was the same with the Beethoven Concertos, especially the Third and Fourth, to which he brought a wonderful lyricism.

I think Benno Moiseiwitsch was the first great pianist I saw performing in person, or as we now say 'live'. It was in Bedford, to where the BBC had been evacuated during the war, at a studio broadcast. The BBC often used the main assembly hall in Bedford School as a studio for broadcasting and on this occasion, as I was on holiday and had come home from Crowthorne where I had been evacuated, my father had taken me there to see and hear the orchestra. Moiseiwitsch was the soloist in the Rakhmaninov Second Piano Concerto. The first thing I noticed about him when he was playing was his undemonstrative and reserved manner – in this respect, as I remember, very similar to Heifetz. Years later I saw this characteristic, even more pronounced, when he was playing the Third Concerto by Rakhmaninov. When he played the soloist's opening phrase, a haunting melody in octaves, he did so hardly moving and with an absolute 'poker face'. He was in fact a keen poker player and I was not surprised when my Professor at the Royal College of Music, Frederick Thurston, at that time principal clarinet in the BBC Symphony Orchestra, who had played poker with Moiseiwitsch several times, told me that he was an extremely good player.

Moiseiwitsch was also the first major piano soloist I worked with when I was still in the Wessex Orchestra. I was to take part in many concerts with him over the years and it would nearly always be one or other of the Rakhmaninov Piano Concertos or the Rakhmaninov-Paganini Variations. He was a magnificent player and it is reported that Rakhmaninov thought he played his music better than he did himself.

There were three artists who always raised my spirits however depressed I might be at the time – the cellist Paul Tortelier, the violinist Itzhak Perlman and the pianist Artur Rubinstein. Rubinstein lived to the ripe old age of 95 and to the end of his playing days brought an infectious, youthful *joie de vivre* to everything he performed. He was the most spontaneous of artists and said that he avoided practising whatever he was going to be playing at a concert immediately beforehand so as to retain his freshness. And over seventy years as a major concert artist he succeeded. Saint-Saëns, Schumann, Mozart and Beethoven were all in their different ways equally delightful. I never had the opportunity of taking part in any performance of a Chopin concerto with him, but have heard him on broadcasts and recordings playing a good deal of the Chopin repertoire and have always been entranced.

There are two more pianists who remain very clearly in my memory, not for any particular performance, though both were very fine players and, as it happens as different from each other as they could be. I only played with Glenn Gould once, but as I remember he had a very austere personality. It was a warm day, but he came to rehearsal wearing an overcoat and scarf and wore mittens, that is gloves with the ends of all the fingers cut off (he wore these at the concert as well but discarded the coat and scarf). He had a unique posture at the piano, sitting on an extremely low stool so that his elbows were below the level of the piano keyboard. It looked very strange but seemed to suit him as it was an excellent performance.

The other pianist was Shura Cherkassky, a brilliant virtuoso and very extrovert in an unusual way. He seemed to have a piano stool fetish because on every occasion before we actually started rehearsing he would spend some time complaining about the piano stool so that a number of different stools and chairs would be tried out before he was satisfied. His personality was a mixture of cheeky, difficult and extremely 'camp', though I have read that he was married and had a family. He made a point of never playing the same work twice in the same way so that he was something of a trial to conductors trying to follow him. I had the impression that he enjoyed being difficult and having read an interview he gave, it was clear he was enjoying 'sending up' the interviewer by never answering his questions and talking about the weather instead. Nonetheless he was a remarkably exciting player with an astonishing technique.

For nearly 40 years the opportunity to play alongside all these superb artists has been both immensely enjoyable and a continuing enrichment of my music experience.

17 Woodwind and Brass Soloists and My Colleagues in the Orchestra

So many fine soloists have come out of the orchestra – Galway, Goossens, Brymer, Camden, Brooke, Brain, Bean, Parikian, Pini, and many more.

As well as the soloists I have written about there was always the pleasure of playing in the orchestra with colleagues one respected and admired, especially the woodwind and brass players. The woodwind and brass soloists when I was young and for a large part of the time I was in the profession, were all members of one of the London orchestras or freelance musicians in London so that at one time or another I played alongside all the artists I shall refer to. It is only in the last 25 or 30 years that it has been possible in Britain for a woodwind or brass player to consider a career entirely as a soloist.

Two very fine flautists Geoffrey Gilbert and Gareth Morris both had successful solo careers at the same time as being members of one or other of the London symphony orchestras. James Galway was the first flautist to leave orchestral playing altogether and make a highly successful career as a soloist, but only after he had been principal flute in the Royal Philharmonic Orchestra and then, later, of the Berlin Philharmonic Orchestra for some years. The great oboist Leon Goossens, who maintained his international solo reputation from the 1930s for the following 30 years, still continued to play in orchestras throughout his life. The same was true for the clarinettists Frederick Thurston and Reginald Kell, and later Jack Brymer and Gervase de Peyer. From when I began to be really interested in playing the clarinet in 1939 and for many years afterwards the only opportunity to hear the Mozart Clarinet Concerto was when Frederick Thurston played it each year at the Proms with the BBC Symphony Orchestra, of which he was principal clarinet.

It was not until Kell went to live in the USA in 1949 that he was able to give up orchestral playing. Previously he had at one time or another been principal clarinet in the LSO, the LPO, the RPO and Philharmonia. He had been my hero in my teens and the first time I sat alongside him remains one of the most thrilling moments of my life. He had not been able to attend the rehearsal in the morning so I had had to move up to play first clarinet – that was still in the days when a star player could get away with something like that. When he came onto the platform at the concert in the evening he introduced himself, 'My name is Reg Kell' – as if I would not know who he was! He was a big man with large hands and when he took the clarinet out of its case to assemble it, it was as if it were a piccolo. Just the way he did that was a thrill.

Many years later Gervase de Peyer, who had been principal in the LSO, followed Kell to the USA where he has had a very successful solo career for many years. He is one year younger than I am and we often played together in several orchestras. From the start it was clear he was more suited to being a soloist than an orchestral player, even though he was a fine player in the orchestra. He had a natural tendency to play as a soloist, whatever position he was in, as I found when he played second to me. I have written about Jack Brymer several times already but must refer to him again here because he was one of the great wind players of the second half of the 20th century, as Beecham said once at a rehearsal after Jack had played particularly beautifully. For me all his finest qualities, his soft, clean articulation and silken, seamless *legato* combined with a wonderful lyricism are to be heard in the stunning recording of the Mozart Clarinet Concerto he made with the RPO and Beecham. This is a rare example of conductor, soloist and orchestra coming together as if they were one. A recording to treasure.

Archie Camden and Gwydion Brooke were both outstanding bassoonists each with a very personal way of playing and totally different from each other. Camden, who was in the Hallé Orchestra before he came to the BBC Symphony Orchestra when it was formed in 1930, was the first British bassoonist to change from the French bassoon to the German or Heckel Bassoon. Adam Heckel assisted in redesigning the bassoon keywork in 1820 and soon started manufacturing instruments. Traditionally the German bassoon has a much more 'woody' tone and is rather less flexible than the French and it was in this way that Camden played. He was for many years the most outstanding player in Britain. Not long after Camden started playing the German basoon Gwydion Brooke who was still at the Royal Academy of Music heard about this new instrument and went to see Camden in Manchester and at once got himself a similar instrument. It was not long before he had persuaded his fellow bassoon students and their professor to change too. Brooke joined the RPO at the same time that I did and he was also in the Philharmonia whilst I was so I had many opportunities to witness his incredible virtuosity. He had a very idiosyncratic style and was the first to play the German bassoon with vibrato making his playing much more flexible. His performances of the Weber Concerto were dazzling.

Even the great Dennis Brain, for me the finest wind player of all, played the horn in orchestras until the end of his all too short life. It was after a concert with the Philharmonia at the Edinburgh Festival in 1957 after a performance of Tchaikovsky's 6th Symphony. He was driving back to London in the early hours of the morning when he must have dozed off for a moment, crashed his car and been killed instantly. He had been sitting just behind me on the platform of the Usher Hall and I remember thinking at the time how extraordinary it was that when, near the beginning of the symphony, the horn has just a single held note, by some magic Brain made it sound like a melody. This event remains vividly in my memory, not only because apart from Ginette Neveu I have never felt the loss of any other musician quite so powerfully, but because through chance my own life was spared on that occasion.

I had to get back to London that night as I had an unusually attractive TV engagement the following morning, one of a series of Sunday afternoon half-hour programmes, playing on screen in a quintet: two violins, cello, piano and clarinet. We played special arrangements of light music and accompanied a very popular singer in the 1950s, Elizabeth Welch. I had considered returning with Dennis by car, but as he was not feeling too well he decided to stay for a while with his friend the flautist Gareth Morris before setting off. Not wishing to risk being late I decided to take the night train instead. As it happened the train was very late and when I eventually arrived at the BBC White City TV studios I was told there was a telephone message from my wife. She had been told by a neighbour of a news item on the radio reporting the death of

Dennis Brain in a car accident and was concerned that I might have been involved.

Sixteen years later, when the Philharmonia was on the way to give a concert in Warsaw, one of several we were to give with Norman Del Mar conducting, on a tour of Poland and Romania, I was sitting chatting with him on one of the interminable coach journeys we had to undertake. We were remembering various artists we had both worked with and he mentioned Dennis Brain, with whom he had been second horn in the RAF Central Band and then in the Philharmonia. I told him about an extraordinary dream I had had about Dennis, and that it had been so vivid that when I awoke it took me a while to realise it had been a dream. I was astonished when Norman told me he had had a similar dream at about the same time. It seems that Dennis's spirit had lived on. I wonder if there were other musicians who may have had a similar experience?

Inspired by Dennis Brain there has been a succession of superb British horn soloists, Alan Civil and Barry Tuckwell, and now David Pyatt. There have also been some very fine trumpet players in a particularly English tradition. The first I remember hearing was Ernest Hall whose noble tone dominated the BBC Symphony Orchestra's brass section. Richard (Bob) Walton, his pupil, followed in the same style and was Beecham's principal trumpet in the LPO and RPO. Two more players in the same tradition were David Mason and Philip Jones who went on to form the celebrated and much recorded Philip Jones Brass Ensemble. Another very fine player in quite a different style was George Eskdale, for many years principal in the LSO and a distinguished soloist. In contrast to the Ernest Hall school of playing this was more akin to the brass band cornet sound and style, very lyrical and suited for playing melodies.

In general the difference in sheer technical ability of the woodwind and brass instrument soloists and their colleagues in the orchestras is not very great. There are a good many wind players in the orchestras with enough technical skill to perform the solo repertoire. It is usually a matter of temperament, personality and musical imagination that holds them back.

In the previous chapter I suggested that many orchestral string players at some time, probably when they were quite young, will have dreamt that perhaps they might one day have the opportunity to become a soloist or a member of a string quartet. Whereas for woodwind and brass players the possibility of a solo career was extremely unlikely, there have always been opportunities for violinists, cellists and pianists to become soloists. As a rule it has usually been clear from a fairly early age, often by the age of four or five, whether there is the outstanding talent required for a successful solo career.

Of those who show obvious natural ability only a very few will go on to have an international solo career. There will be some others who start off quite well, perhaps winning some competitions but just not having what it takes to break into the 'big time'. A number of very fine string players decide that the satisfaction of a life playing chamber music will be far more rewarding than the solitary glory of being a soloist. Nearly all the other string instrumentalists wanting to follow a career as a professional musician will play in an orchestra of some kind, most as what used always to be called 'rank and file' players, though now, in these days of political correctness, they are referred to as 'tutti' players. From amongst them will arise those with outstanding technical and musical qualities who in addition have the qualities of leadership needed to lead a section. Not all very good players have this gift so that in a very good orchestra there may be quite a few exceedingly good players within the string sections.

In chapter 4 I wrote about the small orchestras there were in the cafes, restaurants and at seaside resorts at the beginning of the last century. Until the 1940s these little orchestras provided the opportunity for violinists with sufficient technique and musical qualities to lead a small group and express themselves musically in an individual way. Now there are far more orchestras requiring good violinists, but there they have to be part of a section, playing the same notes as everyone else in the section, whether they are the leader or sitting at the back. The many opportunities for personal self-expression available in the past have gone. Now they only really exist for the soloist or chamber musician.

As well as the pleasure when sitting in an orchestra of listening to my woodwind and brass colleagues, there was also the enjoyment of hearing the violin and cello solos, the much less frequent viola solos and the extremely rare solos for the double bass. The leader (Concert Master) of an orchestra has some wonderful solos in the orchestral, opera and ballet repertoires, such as those in *Scheherazade* by Rimsky-Korsakov, the *Missa Solemnis* by Beethoven, Tchaikosky's Suite in G, in the opera from *Thais* by Massenet and the well-known violin solos in the ballet music for *Swan Lake* and *Sleeping Beauty* by Tchaikovsky.

The solo violin part in *Ein Heldenleben* by Richard Strauss is particularly demanding and calls for considerable virtuosity. Michel Schwalbé, for more than 30 years Karajan's leader of the Berlin Philharmonic, was famous for his performances and recording of the solo part in this work. He had a fantastic technique, comparable with any of the great international soloists and used to dazzle the National Centre for Orchestral Studies Orchestra each year when he came to coach them for me. Though Oscar Lampe who was leader of the RPO for some time had no pretension to be a soloist and had neither the technique nor the brilliance of Schwalbé I particularly remember him playing the big solos in *Heldenleben* with great sensitivity when we recorded it with Beecham.

Over the years I have listened to many fine leaders – outstanding players such as Rodney Friend, who was leader of the LPO and then the New York Philharmonic before returning to lead the BBC Symphony Orchestra, Hugh Bean, Carl Pini, Erich Gruenberg and Manoug Parikian, all leaders of the Philharmonia at one time. Manoug Parikian was (for me) the ideal leader. As well as being a very fine violinist, he had a bearing and authority that commanded respect from everyone, the members of his section, the whole orchestra and conductors. All of them had solo careers though they were never really able to establish themselves as full-time soloists. Not even Schwalbé with his virtuosity managed to do that. Is it, perhaps, a question of personality? Or because they had the qualities a good leader requires: a concern for their section and, at times, for the whole orchestra, rather than the over-riding ambition needed by a soloist?

The principal of the cello section also has many big solos to play. Some of the best known in the concert repertoire are those that come from operas and ballets such as the cello solos in the suites from *Swan Lake* and *Sleeping Beauty,* the Overture to *William*

Tell by Rossini, the Overtures *Morning Noon and Night in Vienna* and *Poet and Peasant* by Suppé, the solos in the slow movements of the Tchaikovsky Piano Concerto No.1 and Brahms's Second Piano Concerto. In *Jeux d'enfants* by Bizet, in the movement *Little Husband, Little Wife*, there is a lovely duet for violin and cello (sometimes now played by the whole of the violin and cello sections). One of my earliest music memories is hearing this played by Marie Wilson and Raymond Clark, when they were both in the BBC Symphony Orchestra at a broadcast from the BBC Maida Vale studios, where I had been taken by my father. Many years later I played in the RPO and the Philharmonia with Raymond when he was their principal cello. He was a beautiful player and had the musicianship and skill to have been a distinguished soloist, but always remained in the orchestra, perhaps lacking the necessary ambition.

Anthony Pini, who was principal cello with the LPO and RPO for Beecham and later of the Royal Opera House Orchestra, was a very fine orchestral cellist as well as a distinguished soloist, particularly well-known for his performances of the Elgar Cello Concerto. It is not often that the clarinet section sit near to the front desk of the cellos, but on one occasion when the RPO were playing for the opera at Glyndebourne I found that was I sitting a few feet away from Pini. We were doing *Ariadne auf Naxos* by Richard Strauss in the original version, in which the first act is a play with incidental music, often performed separately at concerts as the suite *Le Bourgeois Gentilhomme.* I was enormously impressed with the way he played every note with such immaculate accuracy. Only one other player had this same effect on me, the clarinettist Bernard Walton. During the Philharmonia tour in South America I sat next to him whenever we played the Brahms Symphonies Nos. 2 and 4. His absolute accuracy of intonation, note values, dynamics and rhythm were a model of orchestra playing. It takes great discipline to play like that and if not allied to a response to the music itself can lead to a sterile performance. Pini and Walton were both artists as well as remarkable craftsmen.

There was one other cellist who unfortunately had a rather short career. John Kennedy, the father of Nigel Kennedy the violinist, was a wonderful player. He had a most beautiful tone and a gift for playing a melody with tremendous charm and grace. Shirley, Lady Beecham showed me a video of a rehearsal for a concert at Lincoln Inn Fields, with Beecham conducting the RPO when Kennedy was playing the cello solo in the Overture *Morning, Noon and Night* by *Suppé*. Beecham hardly conducts at all and his face expresses sheer delight as he looks and listens to Kennedy. Part of this concert was televised, though unfortunately not the overture. Kennedy was a lovely man, high spirited and amusing, but sadly too fond of the strong waters. After a while he left the orchestra and went back to Australia where he died a few years later.

Even though there are so many 'viola jokes', probably the result of having been played in the past by indifferent violinists, the viola when played really well has a wonderfully rich tone. In the hands of an excellent player the viola solos in Strauss's *Don Quixote* and *Harold in Italy* by Berlioz and the ballet *Giselle* by Adolphe Adam can be very beautiful.

So far I have only written about the enjoyment of listening to the individual musicians in the orchestra who have solos to play, but anyone who has played in an orchestra, even a not very good one, will tell you that there is a special thrill when sitting in the middle of the orchestra when it is going full blast in a big tutti passage. There are places, particularly in the compositions by Wagner, Strauss, Tchaikovsky and Sibelius, when the whole of the violin or cello section have a big tune fortissimo that I found tremendously exciting.

18 Singers: Glyndebourne and Edinburgh

*The voice – the most beautiful instrument of all – heard to perfection in a
delightful opera house in the country and at the Edinburgh Festival.
An incredible catalogue of artists singing Rossini, Mozart and Strauss.*

I have left until last the most wonderful instrument of all, the
most beautiful, expressive and thrilling – the human voice.
Every instrumentalist, whether playing the tuba or piccolo, the
violin or the bassoon, the piano or bass drum, attempts to emulate
the singing quality and ability to express the whole range of
emotions with the subtlety of nuance that great singers can
achieve.

There is nothing more musically enjoyable than taking part in
performances in the company of singers who have beautiful voices
and are fine artists, whether it is in the opera house, when
recording, broadcasting, making films or in the concert hall. And
nowhere was it more enjoyable than at Glyndebourne. To begin
with, to make music in such a beautiful setting is something very
special. I was extremely fortunate to play for the Glyndebourne
opera seasons at Glyndebourne itself and when the company took
part in the Edinburgh Festival each year from 1948 until 1954
whilst I was in the Royal Philharmonic Orchestra.

There have been a number of attempts to emulate the example
set by Glyndebourne, but none have been able to match the
unique near perfection that was achieved there in the first years
after the end of WW2.

In 1920 John Christie inherited Glyndebourne, a fine country
house with beautiful gardens and several long ponds surrounded
with weeping willows. The house and gardens are part of a large
estate in the midst of the woods and downs of one of the loveliest
parts of East Sussex. When Christie inherited the estate he was
already forty and a science master at Eton, where he been for many
years and where he himself had been a schoolboy. Some years later
he married Audrey Mildmay, a young singer who at that time was
in the Carl Rosa Opera Company. Inspired by her and his own

love of music he decided to build a small opera house onto the side of the house.

It was here, in this delightful miniature opera house, later enlarged and now replaced by a splendid new Theatre, but then still seating only about 300, that I spent many very happy hours playing Mozart, Rossini and Verdi operas and hearing them sung by a wonderful cast of singers. The orchestra at that time was, in my opinion, playing as well as it ever has. All of us in the RPO felt that we were there because Beecham wanted us to be. We were full of enthusiasm and doing Glyndebourne was so enjoyable, even though nearly all the members of the orchestra had to travel back and forth from London each day so that sometimes there was a fair amount of moaning, especially as the seasons became longer. At that time I had two small children and I took advantage of the opportunity for the family to be in the country for several weeks.

Audrey and John Christie created a wonderful atmosphere at Glyndebourne. When we had the interval during rehearsals the principal singers, chorus and orchestra would have coffee outside under the covered way adjoining the opera house. There was a quality of friendliness and the feeling that one was at a country house party, making music for the sheer pleasure of doing so. It was quite unlike anything I have experienced anywhere else.

One year I had a caravan in the field about 100 yards from the stage door. It was under a great oak tree and we were awakened every morning by sheep bumping against the side of the van. Unfortunately the tree is no longer there, having had to make way for the ever-expanding car park. The administrators of the Estate Trust told me that it would be impossible for me to have a caravan anywhere on the estate as it was strictly forbidden. I thought it might be worthwhile asking Mr Christie himself. Though in books about Glyndebourne he is portrayed as being rather difficult at times, I found him very pleasant. When I told him that the estate office had refused permission he said, 'Go ahead and bring your caravan. We won't tell anyone – it will be quite all right.'

In 1948 and 1949, for various reasons, the main one being insufficient money, it was not possible to have a season at Glyndebourne before appearing at the Edinburgh Festival. Many of us used to drive up to Edinburgh for the three weeks of the Festival. Unlike today, when the journey by road from London to

Edinburgh takes about 5 hours, throughout the years I drove up it was dangerous to attempt to do it in one day. We always stopped the night at Boroughbridge and arrived in Edinburgh the following day at lunchtime.

In both the 1948 and '49 seasons and for all the years I was at Glyndebourne we did *Così fan tutte* by Mozart. From start to finish the music Mozart composed for this opera is sublime. Arias, duets, trios and ensemble follow each other, each a miracle whether expressing tenderness, subterfuge, deceit or humour. The cast was always outstanding and never better than in those first years. After several rehearsals for the orchestra alone the singers would join us, sitting in a semi-circle round the orchestra. This was always a delight because as each soloist stood up to sing their first aria one was astonished that it was possible that this one could be as good as the last.

The only performance of *Così*, from 1948 until 1954, in which Sena Jurinac did not take part was in 1948. Another very fine singer Suzanne Danco sang the part of Fiordiligi and Dorabella was sung by Eugenia Zareska, who a couple of years previously, when I was still in the LPO, had sung *The Songs of a Wayfarer* by Mahler so well when we recorded it with Eduard van Beinum. She was a fine artist. Their lovers, Ferrando and Guglielmo, were played by Petre Munteanu and Erich Kunz. Mariano Stabile played the old schemer Don Alfonso and his accomplice, the maid Despina, was Hilda Gueden. As well as being such fine singers, Stabile, Kunz and Gueden were able to bring out the sly humour that in no way distracted from the music. In Carl Ebert's magical production, conducted by Vittorio Gui and with this superb cast, it was without doubt very, very special. It remains for me the touchstone by which every opera production is judged.

What made it so delightful was the combination of beautiful music superbly sung and played and the humour and pathos enacted on stage. Mozart's insight into the human condition, conveyed so subtly in his music, was not distorted by over emphasis of the director's point of view, as so often is the case now. This was at the time when the balance of power between the music and the production was roughly 60% to 40%. Carl Ebert who was one of the finest producers (he would now be called a director) of his day was regarded as something of a tyrant by those who worked with him. He was so intent on getting his production as he wished it that it was not at all unusual for him to scrap all the scenery that had been specially built for a scene half way through rehearsals. But he always recognised that the music came first. It is so easy for the words to be flagrantly in opposition to the action the characters on stage are forced to impersonate by a wilful director and thereby distort the *mores* of the period that the librettist and composer lived in and which are an integral part of their conception.

That year we also did *Don Giovanni* with Rafael Kubelik conducting. As well as being a charming man Kubelik was certainly in the class of the 'Great and the Good'. In fact he was very good indeed. Again there was a very fine cast: Ljuba Welitsch was an impressive and dramatic Donna Anna and Richard Lewis played Don Ottavio. Lewis, a most sensitive artist with a lovely voice, was to be one of the mainstays of the Glyndebourne company for some years. The part of Zerlina was shared by Ann Ayars and Hilda Gueden. Both were good, but Gueden, who was so attractive and had such a happy knack of bringing gaiety and a sense of fun to her performances, brought an extra something special to the role. Many years later I was in an orchestra when she recorded a number of arias. Now a much more mature artist, she had retained those qualities. Paolo Silveri was the suitably macho seducing Don Giovanni and David Franklin an imposing Commendatore. Franklin probably had the longest career at Glyndebourne of anyone, appearing in numerous roles from 1936 until 1959.

At the 1949 Edinburgh Festival, we did *Così* again and *Un Ballo In Maschera (A Masked Ball)* by Verdi, with Gui conducting both operas. For *Così* Sena Jurinac joined the company and sang the mezzo soprano role, Dorabella. As in the 1948 production Suzanne Danco was a very fine Fiordiligi. From the start Jurinac won the hearts of the all-male RPO. A wonderful artist with a personality to match, she was naturally friendly and charming and totally without any affectation. This time Marko Rothmuller was our Guglielmo; very good, but without Erich Kunz's infectious sense of fun. The Australian John Brownlee, who had played Don Giovanni with such success in 1936, was Don Alfonso.

Un Ballo In Maschera by Verdi was the first of two Verdi operas Gui conducted during my time in the orchestra. Here again there was a splendid cast with Paolo Silveri as Riccardo and Margherita Grandi and Ljuba Welitsch alternating as Amelia. Oscar was played by Alda Noni who was to be another artist to appear regularly in the Glyndebourne company. In 1952 Gui conducted *Macbeth*. Marko Rothmuller played Macbeth and Dorothy Dow was an excellent Lady Macbeth.

Vittorio Gui was an extremely good opera conductor who knew the operas in that special way that Italian opera conductors all seemed to have, whether they were very good or only mediocre. One felt they knew the operas in their sleep and if woken suddenly would give the right beat and the next entry to the singer on stage without hesitation. Gui never looked very happy and often conducted while holding one hand against his face as if he was in despair, which he clearly was not as he conducted Rossini's opera buffa with such a light but disciplined hand. In this he was like all the best conductors of 'light music' I have worked with. They seemed to lack humour and were strict disciplinarians. On one occasion, I think it was when we were rehearsing *Un Ballo In Maschera*, Silveri took what Gui considered to be a liberty with the music, perhaps extending the length of a note for longer than the composer intended. When Silveri attempted to defend himself Gui would have none of it and dismissed him from the stage as if he was just a student rather than a baritone with an international reputation.

For the 1950 and 1951 seasons Fritz Busch returned to Glyndebourne where in 1934 he had conducted the first season of opera to be staged there. It was for two weeks, during which he conducted and Carl Ebert, whom he had recommended should be engaged as producer, were responsible for the performances of *Così fan tutte* and *The Marriage of Figaro* that were greeted with such enthusiasm by both the audiences and critics. Each year until 1939 when the war started, short seasons of opera were mounted at Glyndebourne.

In 1950 Busch conducted *Così* and *Die Entführung aus dem Serail* (*The Abduction from the Seraglio*) at Glyndebourne and in 1951 four Mozart operas, *Idomeneo, The Marriage of Figaro, Don Giovanni* and *Così fan tutte* at Glyndebourne and Verdi's *The Force of Destiny* and *Don Giovanni* in Edinburgh. I think there was some disappointment when he returned that his performances did not quite match the reputation that had preceded him. Only a couple of weeks after that season ended in September 1951 Busch died at the early age of 61.

Sena Jurinac was wonderful when she sang the role of Fiordiligi for the first time in 1950 and continued to enchant us each year. The role of Dorabella, which she sang the previous year, was taken by another very fine artist Blanche Thebom, who was one of the leading dramatic mezzos at the Metropolitan Opera House in New York for many years. Richard Lewis was excellent as Ferrando and the Welsh baritone Geraint Evans made the first of many subsequent appearances, sharing the role of Guglielmo with Erich Kunz. Evans was then still only 28 and quite inexperienced. He did not yet have the well-honed skill Kunz had acquired, but he brought a freshness and warm humour that immediately endeared him to the audience and the orchestra.

From the beginning in 1934, with John Christie's enthusiastic support, Busch and Ebert had demanded a good many more rehearsals than were normal elsewhere in order to attain the standard of ensemble and staging they wished to achieve. Indeed this did have the desired effect, but for the clarinet section in particular this could sometimes be burdensome. In 1951 when we did four Mozart operas – could one ask for anything better? – rehearsals at times became difficult. There is nothing more wearing for a performer – actor, dancer or musician – than sitting (or standing) around doing nothing at the same time as trying to remain alert for the next time he or she is called upon to do something.

The clarinet, the 'nouveau riche of the orchestra' as the superb oboist Terence MacDonagh always called us, was still a relative newcomer to the orchestra's woodwind section at the time Mozart was writing his operas. Though no one has written more beautifully or with greater understanding of the clarinet's potential than Mozart, he did not use it all the time. There are a number of places in the operas when the clarinets have nothing to play at all for 15 or 20 minutes. When these sections are being rehearsed one can be inactive for half an hour or more. When Gluck wrote *Alceste* in 1767, more than 20 years before *Così fan tutte*, the clarinet was still in its infancy and in that opera he uses it very sparingly, mainly to play in unison with the brass. In one act there is nothing for the clarinets to play for about 20 minutes, then four bars of long notes, quite inaudible to anyone bar the players themselves, and then another 20 minutes in which they are not required. In 1953 it was decided to mount this opera at Glyndebourne. Jack Brymer and I felt that our presence would not be missed for those four bars so we marked them TACET (remain silent). As Maestro Gui appeared to be quite happy, we went out into the garden, at both the rehearsals and the performances, to have a quiet smoke (we still smoked in those far off days and survived to tell the tale). The following year *Alceste* was to be performed again. Nothing had been said but when we looked at our parts we saw that TACET had been removed and in its place in large red letters was written PLEASE PLAY.

When we went to Edinburgh in 1950 we were in for a very special treat. As well as doing *The Marriage of Figaro* with the very fine conductor Ferenc Fricsay, we were joined by Sir Thomas Beecham. It was quite usual with Beecham, if he was not included in some event like the Edinburgh Festival or when a new hall such as the Royal Festival Hall was opened, to condemn and abuse it. He had been noticeably absent from the Festivals in 1947, '48 and '49 and had not been silent in letting the world know that he did not think much of what had taken place in those years. This led, as it usually did, to him taking the lion's share soon after. Edinburgh rewarded him for his forthrightness by allowing him to direct the original version of Strauss's *Ariadne auf Naxos* as well as conduct concerts in the Usher hall with his own orchestra on two of the three Sundays during the Festival.

Originally the one act opera *Ariadne* is preceded by a prologue, a shortened version of Moliere's *Le Bourgeois Gentilhomme,* for which Strauss wrote the delightful incidental music, now most often heard as an orchestral suite. A few years later Strauss was obliged to compose a new first act to replace the acted prologue because of the problems involved in engaging a cast of actors as well as singers. It is this second version that it usually performed. Beecham had decided to do it in the original, and very expensive version (especially as the Festival organisers would be paying), that requires 21 actors for the prologue and ten singers for the opera itself.

The casts for the prologue and the opera were both excellent. The actors were led by Miles Malleson, a wonderfully droll actor, as Monsieur Jourdain. In *Ariadne* there are two quite different sets of characters: Ariadne and Bacchus are dramatic and very serious and the *commedia dell'arte characters,* Harlequin, Brighella, Truffaldo and Scaramuccio, are led by Zerbinetta. Ariadne and her lover Bacchus were sung by Hilde Zadek and Peter Anders and the extraordinarily difficult coloratura part Strauss wrote for *Zerbinetta* by Ilse Hollweg.

In 1953 and '54 we did *Ariadne* again, but this time in Strauss's all sung version, and conducted by John Pritchard. Though Pritchard was so talented and was conducting at his very best, he did not have that inimitable something that Beecham brought to everything he conducted. Some of the parts originally spoken are sung in the later version and in particular the role of the Composer is enlarged and considerably altered. However, it was now a part in which Sena Jurinac could excel. It is a 'trouser' role, a part written to be played by a woman impersonating a young man. The part of Cherubino in *The Marriage of Figaro* is a similar role and another that Jurinac did so well. The part of Zerbinetta was now taken by an astonishing black soprano, Mattiwilda Dobbs. Her remarkable vocal virtuosity was matched by her sparkling quicksilver vivacity as an actress.

In the spoken prologue, when the Composer complains that some of his music will be lost because of the absurd arrangement Monsieur Jourdain has made that his opera and the *commedia dell'arte* ballet are to be performed at the same time, he is told 'some of the best operas are known by their cuts'. The four Mozart operas that Busch conducted in 1951 are 'some of the best operas' from which I would not wish any cuts to be made, especially when sung by casts that included Lisa Della Casa, Owen Brannigan, Murray Dickie, Sesto Bruscantini, Richard Lewis, Suzanne Danco, Leopold Simoneau, Alois Pernerstorfer and with the smaller roles performed extremely well by less well-known artists.

An especial delight from 1952 onwards was the inclusion of operas by Rossini in productions with marvellous singing and deft comic acting. As every actor will tell you it is much harder to play comedy than tragedy. When it has to be sung perhaps it is even harder. Under Ebert's and Gui's strict control there was never a moment when the comedy was overplayed or the music became coarsened.

The three I was privileged to take part in were *La Cenerentola,* in 1952 at Glyndebourne and in 1953 at Glyndebourne and Edinburgh, *The Barber of Serville* at Glyndebourne and *Le Comte Ory* in Edinburgh. The cast for *Cenerentola* was the same for all three performances. Marina De Gabarain, who sang the role of Cenerentola, was not really the coloratura mezzo-soprano the part requires, but she was more than adequate and had the sweet-natured simplicity and musicality that made her successful. Juan Oncina was her dulcet-voiced Don Ramiro. The ugly sisters were amusingly horrid but very well sung by Alda Noni and Fernanda Cadoni. But the best of all were the roles taken by Sesto Bruscantini as Dandini and our own Ian Wallace as Don Magnifico. They were truly ridiculously hilarious, never going 'over the top', and always remaining vocally secure and musically appropriate.

In 1954 there was *The Barber of Seville* at Glyndebourne and *Le Comte Ory* at Edinburgh. Some of those who had been in *Cenerentola* were also in these operas. They were joined in *Barber* by Graziella Sciutti as a splendid Rosina and in *Comte Ory* by Sari Barabas who as well as singing beautifully looked so attractive that she stole the heart of our then principal cello. Sadly his affection remained unrequited.

In 1954 it was decided to perform Ferruuccio Busoni's little known one act opera *Arlecchino* before the performance of *Ariadne*. John Pritchard conducted and Ian Wallace, Geraint Evans and Murray Dickie played the principal roles. The opera did not make a great impression and as far as I know it has not been done again at Glyndebourne.

Finally, a very different opera from those I have written about so far. In 1953 Glyndebourne gave the first performances in Britain of *The Rake's Progress* by Stravinsky. The conductor was Alfred Wallenstein. He was soon christened Mr Idris by the orchestra because his habitual expression was similar to a lemon with a very sour face as featured in an advertisement for a fruit drink of that name. This was another of Ebert's splendid productions, with a cast to match. The American Jerome Hines was outstanding as a saturnine Nick Shadow with Elsie Morison,

Richard Lewis, Nan Merriman, Mary Jarred and Murray Dickie all excellent. The whole performance was a joy and with the witty set and costumes designed by Osbert Lancaster as well this was one of the highlights of my years at Glyndebourne.

19 More Singers: Recordings, Films and Concerts

The privilege of taking part in performances in the opera house, recording and film studio and at concerts with superb artists – legendary singers from 1943 until 1979.

In previous chapters I have described the pleasure we had when playing in orchestras with wonderful solo violinists, cellists, pianists, other instrumental soloists and with our colleagues in the orchestra. It was not until I came to write about singers that I realised just how many wonderful artists I had been privileged to take part in performances with between 1943 and 1979. Before that time I had to rely like everyone else on the recordings made in the first half of the 20th century. It is fortunate that though recording techniques were primitive by today's standards the legacy of recordings made by many legendary singers at that time is still available. In contrast to the instrumental and orchestral recordings made during the same period the voices remain uncorrupted even by the crackle and hiss that even the most sophisticated techniques cannot entirely remove.

Unless one is in a full-time opera orchestra the number of opportunities one gets to play opera will usually be quite limited. I was fortunate that the standard of the performances at Glyndebourne during the years about which I have written was so extraordinarily high. In fact I have never really enjoyed playing in the orchestra pit, with the exception of my time at Glyndebourne where other factors outweighed my prejudice. However some musicians prefer to play for opera and I know that a number of my colleagues in the Royal Opera House Orchestra would not exchange their job for one in a symphony orchestra.

Though we only played two operas in the theatre with Beecham, *Ariadne auf Naxos* at the Edinburgh Festival and *Irmelin* in Oxford, about which I have already written, we broadcast and recorded *A Village Romeo and Juliet* by Delius, broadcast Richard

Strauss's *Elektra* and *The Trojans* by Berlioz, recorded Gounod's *Faust* and played for the filmed version of *The Tales of Hoffman* by Offenbach, under Sir Thomas's direction.

When we broadcast *Elektra* from the BBC studios at Maida Vale with a very large orchestra plus chorus and soloists it felt very cramped acoustically and though there was an excellent cast that included Erna Schlüter, Ljuba Welitsch and Paul Schoeffler, there was not really enough time allowed for rehearsal. On the other hand *Faust* and *The Tales of Hoffman* were both wonderful. We recorded *Faust* at the EMI Abbey Road studios with an all-French cast. I remember a most terrific Mephistopheles, Roger Rico – not in costume but quite scary. Beecham took immense trouble over this recording and exceeded the number of sessions EMI had agreed. He decided to ask the orchestra to do four more sessions on the understanding that we would be paid when the royalties came in. Of course the orchestra agreed, though I can't recall whether we ever received any further payment.

Best of all was the 1949 film *The Tales of Hoffmann,* over which Beecham again took an immense amount of time and trouble. Michael Powell and Emeric Pressburger, the film directors and producers worked very closely with Beecham on every aspect of the film. All the music was recorded before the film was shot and the roles on screen were danced by a team of celebrated ballet dancers. Most of the female roles were danced by Moira Shearer and Robert Helpmann took the part of Lindorf, Coppelius, Dapertutto and Dr Miracle. Robert Rounseville both sang and acted the part of Hoffman.

In the past there were more performances of oratorios and other religious music at concerts, in churches and the concert halls than there are now. In the 1940s and 50s Handel's *Messiah* and Elgar's *Dream of Gerontius* were regular items each year and provided opportunities for some of the best British singers. Two regulars were Elsie Suddaby, known as 'The Girl with the Delicate Air', who was a fine soprano, and Heddle Nash, a tenor with a lovely Italianate voice. He was a most wonderful Gerontius, thought of then as the best interpreter of the part, and for me he remains the best. Years later, long after I had left the LPO, when we were recording *The Dream of Gerontius* with Sir Adrian Boult with the New Philharmonia Orchestra in 1975, Nicolai Gedda another outstanding tenor whose recording of Lensky's aria from *Eugene Onegin* made with the Philharmonia in 1953 is very beautiful, was the Gerontius. Although he was someone whose singing gave me very great pleasure he was unable to bring the heart-stopping fervour Heddle Nash brought to the part of Gerontius.

It was only when in 1957 we were rehearsing the opera *A Tale of Two Cities* by Arthur Benjamin for a BBC broadcast that it became apparent that Nash could not read music. Each aria was played to him on the piano several times and because of his acute ear and ability to memorise quickly that was all that he needed. He was not alone in not being able to read music. One of the most important roles the répétiteur had in the past was to teach the singers their part. Not being able to read music is not a bar to being a great artist.

Another great tenor, Beniamino Gigli, only a few years older than Nash, had been a star for forty years and was thought by many to have inherited the mantle of Caruso. On one occasion when I went to play at a commercial recording session with the George Melachrino orchestra, I found to my surprise – and delight – that instead of the light music arrangements for which Melachrino was famous we were to record several Neapolitan songs with Gigli. It was an especial treat to hear these songs sung idiomatically and though he was then in his sixties and his voice had lost a little of its bloom it still retained the bel canto for which he was famed.

The three outstanding tenors, Jon Vickers, Peter Pears and Placido Domingo could not have been more different to each other in voice and style. Vickers, powerful and virile was one of the finest heroic tenors of our time. He still remained very impressive when he sang some Wagner extracts at a concert with us at a Philharmonia concert not long before he retired.

I first heard Peter Pears in 1943. It was on a broadcast of the then recently composed *Serenade* by Benjamin Britten for tenor, horn and strings, a wonderful performance with Dennis Brain playing the solo horn part. More than thirty years later in 1977 or '78 Pears came to sing it with the Philharmonia at a Memorial Concert for Benjamin Britten, his long-time friend and companion. This was another wonderful performance and because of the occasion particularly moving. It fell to my lot as Chairman of the Council to go and thank Pears after the concert. I had been so overwhelmed emotionally as I listened to this beautiful music that I found that I was quite unable to do more than mumble an incoherent 'Thank you' before I hastened away.

For the past forty years no one has had a more remarkable career than the Spanish tenor Placido Domingo. He has performed over a hundred complete operas ranging from Mozart to Puccini, Verdi to Wagner, and including Berlioz, Ginastera and Zarzuela, the idiomatic Spanish form of operetta. No tenor has managed his voice and career more intelligently. But he has not been satisfied with being solely a great operatic tenor, he has also been a successful administrator. As well as continuing to sing new roles well into his sixties he increasingly conducts as well. I remember recording *Tosca* and *Aida* with him when he sang the roles of Cavaradossi and Radames. He was always charming, urbane and sang beautifully. He was also magisterial in an unobtrusive way. On the recording of *Aida*, with Riccardo Muti conducting, Domingo was joined by another Spanish artist, the soprano Montserrat Caballe, who had a beautiful creamy voice and superb *legato*.

The baritone Dietrich Fischer-Dieskau has had a long and prestigious career in opera and was one of the finest lieder singers of our time. The first time I saw Fischer-Dieskau was when he was only about twenty-four or twenty-five. We were rehearsing at the Abbey Road studios and as the tall young Fischer-Dieskau and the short elderly Sir Thomas Beecham came in through the door of studio they presented a surprising and amusing sight. They looked liked father and son, but with the father fifty years younger than his son.

My earliest recollection of taking part in performances with very fine singers was with the two sopranos, Joan Hammond and Maggie Teyte. This was when they sang with the LPO in the first half of the 1940s. By then Joan Hammond had been struck down by polio and was obliged to sing whilst in a wheelchair. This was particularly cruel for someone who had been an outstanding athlete and had had a distinguished career on the operatic stage. Nonetheless her voice remained full and strong when she sang *Tatiana's Letter Song* from Tchaikovsky's *Eugene Onegin*. One of my all-time favourites remains Maggie Teyte. This beautiful and sensitive artist was renowned for her singing of French music, though born in Wolverhampton. She studied with Debussy and was famous for her performance as Mélisande in his opera *Pelléas et Mélisande*. On several occasions she sang Ravel's *Scheherazade,* three songs with orchestra, with the LPO. Not only did she have a lovely voice but she was also enchanting and I think the most refined and delicate artist I can recall. It is so seldom that one hears French sung with a true French accent, other than by French singers.

Elisabeth Schwarzkopf was married to Walter Legge who founded and owned the Philharmonia Orchestra from 1945 until 1964, and she sang with us quite a number of times. She was a very fine artist and I recall a number of her performances, in particular when she sang *The Four Last Songs* by Richard Strauss, which I found extremely moving. There is one occasion I recall not only for her beautiful singing. We were at the Royal Festival Hall for a rehearsal in the morning for a concert that evening. Lucia Popp, then in her twenties and an extremely attractive young woman, looked very elegant when she came on the platform. She was followed by Schwarzkopf who was wearing an old raincoat and looked like a sack tied up in the middle. In the evening when Schwarzkopf came on she was wearing a beautiful white wig and a silver/blue dress, absolutely right for the arias from Strauss's last opera *Capriccio*. When she came onto the platform it was with such dignity and grandeur that she made everyone else on the platform look quite dowdy. The applause for her performance was so great that she agreed to sing an encore. The item she chose was a song from the operetta *Der Opernball, Im chambre séparée,* by the little known composer Richard Heuberger. Her performance showed that like most very fine artists she could sing a charming and lovely trifle as beautifully as *The Four Last Songs* or the *Missa Solemnis* by Beethoven.

Several years later I was sitting in one of the cafes on the Ring in Vienna having a quiet cup of coffee. One of the other customers, seeing my clarinet case with a Philharmonia label pasted on it, came over and started talking to me. He told me that the great violinist Fritz Kreisler had been a regular customer and that one evening Heuberger had arrived, extremely distraught, and told Kreisler that he was at his wits end. The first rehearsals for his new operetta were to start the following week and he had still been unable to write a really good tune for it. Apparently, after a few minutes thought Kreisler had scribbled some music on the back of a menu. It is said that it is this music that became *Im chambre séparée*.

There were so many superb artists who were singing during my time in the profession that there is only room to write about those that remain most vivid in my memory. To give some idea of just how many there were I will list some of the most distinguished that I remember I actually heard 'live' (as we say now) when taking part in performances with them: Joan Sutherland, Isobel Baillie, Eva Turner, Anna Moffo, Ileana Cotrubas, Mirella Freni, Irmgard Seefried, Janet Baker, Fiorenza Cossotto, George London, Peter Glossop, John Tomlinson. There were many more I was not fortunate enough to work with.

It is generally agreed that the overall standard of singing is not as high now as it has been in the past, at the same time as the standard of instrumental skill on all instruments has increased to the point where virtuosity has become relatively commonplace. It would seem that for some years a good many talented young singers have been prevailed upon to undertake roles for which their voices have not yet developed sufficiently and to sing far too frequently. One now hears so many artists who as long as they sing piano and mezzo forte sound fine. But when they have to sing forte and project over a large orchestra they develop an uncontrolled and intrusive vibrato.

Perhaps, in a world dominated by commercial interests, agents and others may allow an ambitious young singer to exploit their voice too quickly rather than letting it mature more slowly so that it can develop at its own pace. Rapid air travel, rather than the much slower and relaxed journeys by sea that singers were obliged to take in the past, has made it tempting to sing in San Francisco one day and in London a couple of days later. But there is no instrument so easily damaged nor as precious and vulnerable as the human voice. More valuable than any Stradivarius. Once lost it is irreplaceable.

But there are still singers who have been granted a fine instrument by nature and yet fail to excite listeners as in the past. Artists of an older generation – Jon Vickers, Joan Sutherland and others – make the point that they owed much to what they learned from the great conductors they worked with. Toscanini, Furtwängler, de Sabata, Walter, Beecham, Barbirolli and von Karajan and other very good conductors worked extensively in the opera house and had the same effect on singers that they had on orchestras.

It is the ability to express such a wide range of emotions with a beautiful and exciting voice that all the great vocal artists had, and some still have, that inspired audiences to such outbursts of enthusiasm. They can convey tenderness and rage, love and hate, charm and resolution, resignation, forgiveness and despair in a way that no instrument can hope to match.

Basil Tschaikov

20 Gentlemen and Players
(From Rogue and Vagabond to Professional Musician)

Music not accepted as a profession in the 19th century. Seeking professional identity – various associations – the London Orchestral Association, Archer Street, the ISM and MU. The effect of broadcasting and recording. Pirate, commercial and local radio. BBC radio since 1922.

By the middle of the 19th century it was generally accepted that a professional was someone who had a vocation and followed an occupation as his or her means of livelihood that required advanced learning and the passing of a test or examination whereby a qualification was achieved. If one was a professional it was assumed that one had the ability to choose whom one provided services to, rather than being employed.

The problem for performers was then, and continues to be, that though it requires long and hard study to acquire the necessary skill and understanding in the first place, and continual study and application thereafter, the judgement of whether a performance is 'good', 'very good' or 'not good enough' remains subjective. It is possible to test the level of technical proficiency a player has achieved and whether they can play in time and with good intonation, but no one has ever been engaged to play in an orchestra or group of any kind on the strength of having received an ARCM, LRAM, or any other qualification from a college of music or exam board. Teachers of music or any other subject can become qualified by passing the required examination. The performer never can.

All performers have had this problem: traditionally musicians, actors and dancers were never considered members of a profession. By the middle of the 19th century musicians had not yet established an association or union to distinguish themselves from amateurs. Indeed they were more often than not referred to as 'rogues and vagabonds'. Ladies and Gentlemen played music for pleasure, they were amateurs: musicians played for money. It was also the case that a number of Ladies and Gentlemen were better players and more musical than many of those earning their living as musicians. Only the outstanding touring international instrumentalists were held in awe, though even they were not often accorded equality of status by those they played to. On one occasion the great violinist Fritz Kreisler had been invited to play for the guests of a very wealthy music lover at a rather grand soirée. When Kreisler arrived the butler directed him to a side room where he could change and prepare himself. 'You will not be required to dine with the guests', the butler told him, 'your meal will be served to you here.' 'That is fortunate', Kreisler replied, 'otherwise my fee would have been much higher.'

Naturally the best musicians desired more than anything else to be considered members of a profession and attain the respectability and status then accorded to teachers, though many teachers were, in fact, very indifferent performers. In chapter 15 I recounted how a colleague still had a problem in 1947 when trying to convince his prospective father-in-law that as the principal trumpet in the Royal Opera House Orchestra (then a full-time well paid engagement) he did not require a 'day-time' job. The lack of any full-time engagements for even the very finest musicians in Britain during the second half of the 19th century and well into the 20th played a decisive role in musicians playing in orchestras of any kind being granted only a humble position in the social pecking order. In this respect the situation for British musicians was much less satisfactory than in many other countries where there had been opera houses employing musicians all the year round, in some cases from the middle of the 19th century. It was this more than anything that led to the 'deputy system' that played the major part in making the creation of a first-class symphony orchestra such a difficult task for Sir Henry Wood and others until the BBC Symphony Orchestra was formed in 1930.

Seeking Professional Identity

The attempts musicians made from about 1880 to attain respectability and a secure financial position increased and led to the formation of several associations and unions. It is interesting that by then composers, writers and painters had overcome the problem of respectability and, if they were successful had attained some financial stability. It seems that if one could produce an artefact, something that could be bought and sold and for which a price could be agreed, one was likely to be held in higher esteem than even the greatest degree of skill and artistry could achieve.

Whenever I have written about the 'music profession' and the 'professional musician' I have used the terms that are normal today to describe the profession and those who earn their living as instrumental performers. However, in the 19th century it was only those who taught music or were organists who were considered professional musicians. In 1880, in his book *The Musical Profession,* Dr Henry Fisher makes it quite clear that when he writes about 'professional musicians' he is referring to music teachers.

In 1882 the Society of Professional Musicians was formed, which in 1892 became the Incorporated Society of Musicians (ISM). The ISM claimed to be 'the only body of composing, teaching and performing musicians', though from the start its members were mainly teachers and have continued to be so until now. Only a few performing musicians, singers and instrumental soloists, very often those for whom teaching is their principal activity, joined this organisation. The source of the ISM membership has remained pretty much the same throughout the years and its aim has consistently been to obtain the best fees for their members. Respectability and opposition to the ideas of trade unionism were and have remained extremely important. By the middle of the 19th century the growth of the manufacturing industries led more and more of the population to leave the countryside for the towns and cities, with the consequence that the need for popular public entertainment grew enormously.

The increasing number of music halls and theatres in particular and the greater number of dances and other forms of entertainment required many more musicians. In the same way that the coming of the silent cinema in the early years of the following century was to bring a great influx of musicians, a good many of modest accomplishment, the need for musicians from the 1850s onwards provided employment for a similar number of those who were relatively unskilled. The general standard of performance that was tolerated at that time was extremely low. It was not hard to find musicians who would accept the indifferent working conditions and poor rates of pay that prevailed in the music halls. Employment for the highly skilled musicians who played in the orchestras for concerts, operas and oratorios was always unpredictable. They were paid much better than their colleagues in the music halls, but the concert season only lasted from September until April. With the coming of the railways and much easier and quicker transport seaside resorts began to prosper. The need for entertainment led to additional employment for these musicians in the summer months on bandstands, on the sea front and in parks.

How were musicians of such a diverse standard, ranging from outstanding artists, highly skilled musicians and many of quite a poor standard, as well as some who were only part-time musicians, to become a profession? They were engaged to play so many different kinds of music in such dissimilar venues – in music halls providing the music needed by clowns, acrobats, singers and every type of entertainer one can imagine; on bandstands playing everything and anything from music hall songs to concert overtures; in theatres where they might be called on to play musical comedies, operetta, grand opera or only incidental music; and in the concert halls playing marches, polkas, to accompany cornet and bassoon solos as well as symphonies and concertos.

In 1893, a year after the Society of Musicians had become the ISM, two groups of musicians each formed an organisation with similar intentions to each other but with a very different orientation: the London Orchestral Association (LOA), and the Amalgamated Musicians Union (AMU).

The LOA, like the ISM was strongly anti-union. It sought gentility and status and was keen to establish that its members were in a profession, not a trade. Its headquarters was in Archer Street in the West End of London and was generally referred to as 'the Club', because this is where musicians would go between a matinee and an evening performance in the many theatres nearby, or to find a deputy, or just to meet friends and colleagues. In the main meeting room there was a bar where tea, coffee and snacks could be bought. It also had a licence to sell alcohol which attracted a good deal more custom in the first decades of the 20th century when many musicians, particularly woodwind, brass and percussion players, were quite heavy drinkers. Downstairs there were washing facilities and changing rooms. On the walls there were racks where members requiring a deputy could leave a request, perhaps, 'Joe Bloggs needs 2nd clarinet for evening performance, Tuesday 23rd, 7.30 Her Majesties (Bb and A)'.

From the beginning of the 20th century and well into the 1920s and 30s most musicians who worked in the London theatres, restaurants and the orchestras had been members of the LOA but by the time I joined in 1942 it had become rather seedy. In the ordinary way, if my father had not suggested that I should, a young musician like myself would no longer have joined the LOA – it was just before I joined the LPO and I was by then already a member of the MU, as were all other musicians (including members of the LOA). In 1942 it was virtually only 'theatre musicians' who still went to the LOA. Very few of them ever played in either the symphony orchestras or the many small orchestras and ensembles that broadcast. Nor did they get the opportunity to play on recording and film sessions, which were the best-paid engagements. On the few occasions I went there I sensed a general atmosphere of envy and an undercurrent of discontent. The following year I did not renew my membership.

When the new 'jazz' music began to arrive from America, from about 1910 onwards, those musicians in London who started to play this music tried to join the LOA. Their applications were rejected because they were regarded as upstarts, not 'proper' musicians and were held in contempt by the members who felt that they would tarnish their own 'professional' aspirations, historically so important to them. Even in 1920 when everyone was dancing to the new dance music and dance bands were everywhere they continued to refuse membership to them. Undeterred by rejection the new jazz and dance musicians decided to meet outside in Archer Street itself. If you went to Archer Street on any day, especially on a Monday afternoon until the mid-1950s, you would find the whole street full of musicians. But then another group of 'upstarts' appeared on the scene – this time it was the pop groups.

I remember that in the 1940s whenever I had occasion to go to an instrument repair shop that was in Archer Street it would always be full of saxophone/clarinet, trumpet, trombone and double bass players, guitarists and drummers. There were also some string players, mainly violinists. They had taken up the saxophone and found lucrative employment in the restaurants and night clubs. When the patrons were having supper there would be quiet music, played by a quintet in which they would play the violin and then, when the dancing started, they would join the band, probably as second alto sax. Archer Street is where anyone would go if they wanted to book musicians for a 'gig', or to play on the big liners, which all employed musicians to play at meal times and for dancing, or for the summer seasons in the Holiday Camps. It was also where musicians would congregate to exchange gossip and find out what was going on.

In contrast to the LOA the Amalgamated Musicians Union's attitude was similar to other trade unions. Its primary objective was to obtain the best possible working conditions and pay for whatever employment its members undertook wherever that might be. When necessary it would use the same tactics and methods of persuasion as other trade unions: strikes, picketing and protest marches. The LOA did attempt to improve working conditions and rates of pay for its members but was unwilling to consider that they were 'workers'. As a result they never squared up to their employers forcefully enough to be really effective.

The AMU sought to set minimum rates for musicians playing in symphony orchestras, in theatres and music halls and when playing for dances. Later it negotiated with employers to include every area in which musicians were engaged. It accepted anyone without regard to their ability as long as they agreed not to work with non-AMU members and never to accept an engagement below the AMU minimum rate. It made no distinction between professional and amateur on the basis that anyone receiving payment for their employment as a musician was by definition a professional in contrast to amateurs who played for their own pleasure.

In 1894 and 1907 the AMU initiated negotiations with the LOA in an attempt to join forces but without success. By 1921 the AMU's membership had outgrown that of the LOA (which for a time assumed the title National Orchestral Union of Professional Musicians) to such an extent that at last the LOA agreed to join forces with the AMU, thereby creating the Musicians' Union (MU), the organisation that thereafter all professional musicians were obliged to join until Mrs Thatcher's government made the 'closed shop', which had been the union's power base, illegal.

When the LOA was absorbed into the MU it retained its premises in Archer Street for another 40 years. At first a good many of its members who were working in the West End theatres remained members, finding its club facilities very convenient. Gradually the LOA membership began to decline, though it continued to be very self-protective and exerted considerable influence within the London Branch of the Musicians Union where they dominated the Branch Committee well into the 1950s.

When I was taken to the MU offices in 1942 I was completely unaware of the Union's existence and at no time while I was in the Wessex Orchestra did anyone ask me if I was a member. In fact the fees that the orchestra were paid, I was to learn later, were all well below the MU minimum. During the following 38 years I can only recall having been asked to show my MU card once. If you were playing in any of the symphony orchestras or the many light orchestras that broadcast, it was taken for granted that you were a union member and it was the same in the West End theatres and for those playing for recording, films or TV, whether for the BBC or for one of the commercial stations. None of these musicians would have considered playing for under the MU minimum rate. However, there were other areas of employment where musicians who were finding it difficult to make a living would at times be prepared to do so. As might be expected, some unscrupulous employers took advantage of this to save money.

On one occasion in the 1960s I was asked to be an expert witness when the MU had taken one of these employers to Court for the way he had treated one of their members. This case concerned a drummer who had been contracted for six weeks by a suburban theatre, a former music hall in one of the less up-market areas of London, to play for a Christmas pantomime. As was quite normal at that time it was an exclusive contract, which meant that one could not be absent from any performance: no deputies were allowed. In addition he was required to agree that in the period preceding the first performance he would be available for rehearsal at any time.

Because six weeks' continuous work at that time of year was much sought after, some employers would save money by insisting that during the week or so of rehearsals preceding the first performance the musicians must make themselves available at any time throughout the day. Normally there would only be a limited number of three-hour rehearsals during a week, usually eight, for which the appropriate fees would be paid. Unfortunately at that time those engaged on stage still 'sailed before the mast' and unlimited rehearsals, sometimes going on for perhaps four or five hours, were not unusual. For many years, for musicians, a three-hour rehearsal meant three hours. This was understood and adhered to by all respectable managements.

When this particular musician accepted the pantomime season he told his employers that on one of the rehearsal days he had already taken an engagement starting at seven o'clock in the evening and would be unable to be available after six o'clock. They told him they were sure there would be no problem. But when the day came and they were half way through the afternoon rehearsal it became clear to him that it was likely to continue beyond six o'clock. In a break in the rehearsal he phoned several other drummers to see if he could find someone to cover for him after six. No one was free or could get there in time, so at six o'clock, making his apologies he left. The next morning when he arrived for rehearsal he found that his drum kit had been put out on the street, outside the stage door, and that someone else had been engaged in his place.

In Court the employer's solicitor argued that it was normal practice in the theatre for rehearsals to go on as long as necessary and that this musician had accepted the job knowing what the conditions were and had broken his contract and let his employers down. When I was called I explained to the magistrate that I had been in the profession for over twenty years and that this had never been the case for musicians. Wherever a musician was engaged for a rehearsal in any kind of orchestra it was understood that it was for three hours. If more time was required it was the employer's obligation to ask the orchestra if they could continue beyond three hours, and if they all agreed, to pay for the extra time. However, what was even more important was the principle that no one was obliged to remain. There were agreements in every area of musical employment between employers and the Musicians' Union. They all stated that the fee was for a certain length of time – whether for recording and film sessions, broadcasts, theatrical performances and dances. I suggested that this employer had broken this agreement and had taken advantage of musicians so in need of work that they too had been willing to break the agreement and betray their colleagues. It was judged that the employer had to pay the aggrieved drummer for the whole six weeks and pay the MU's costs.

In the past it was commonplace for all sorts of malpractice to take place in the employment of musicians and over the years when I was elected to various committees I was involved on numerous occasions in pursuing cases where musicians had been defrauded of moneys to which they were entitled. Quite frequently it was musicians, themselves members of the union, who were the worst offenders. Very often freelance musicians – only those in the contract orchestras – the BBC orchestras, the Regional orchestras and opera house orchestras were not – are engaged by 'fixers', themselves musicians. Now, in these politically correct times they are called contractors – though still within the profession referred to by their traditional name. Because they understand their colleagues better than those who are not musicians themselves they know what they are more likely to get away with; non-payment of repeat fees (the additional fee paid when a radio or TV programme is broadcast again), payment for 'doubling' (when more than one instrument is played, clarinet and saxophone or flute and piccolo, for example), and numerous other arcane additional payments.

The MU when it was first established was seen by members of the ISM and the LOA as an organisation concerned with 'workers' and because it was a trade union they were wholly opposed to it. However, by outlawing many of the practices that had contributed to their lowly status, in time the MU enabled musicians to achieve the conditions that led to them gaining professional status.

The Effect of Broadcasting and Recording

Before broadcasting and recording whenever there was a greater need for music, for example when there was an increase in the number of music halls and dances and later with the arrival of the 'silent' films, more musicians would be required. During my lifetime the opposite has been the case. As more people have listened to music the number of musicians has declined. The loss of employment for musicians has come from the increased use of records wherever employers have found it cheaper: mainly in broadcasting but also in restaurants, at dances and, whenever possible, to accompany theatrical entertainment. The invention of the tape recorder and subsequent developments have made it even easier for everyone to record 'off-air', from commercial tapes and CDs. More recently downloading music from the Internet in various ways is again reducing the need for 'live' musicians.

The use of electronic instruments has been another method of reducing the number of musicians required. The Lyons chain of cafes which in 1939 was employing 500 full-time musicians when the BBC was still only employing 400 (though to be accurate they were employing many more for occasional broadcasts), was one of the first to make use of the electric organ to replace the orchestras in one of their Corner Houses. When I interviewed Ena Baga, a very famous organist for more than fifty years, she told me how she had been invited by one of the directors of Lyons to replace the orchestra at their Tottenham Court Road Corner House restaurant by playing the Hammond Organ. This was an electronic organ that could simulate the sound of most of the instruments of the orchestra. She told me how she had been an MU member all her life but had no problem in accepting the job. Each time she arrived at the stage door she had to run the gauntlet of the members of the displaced orchestras (also MU members) but suffered nothing worse than some fairly friendly banter. Later, and much more effectively, the synthesiser has replaced musicians in every field of music.

The use of recorded music in broadcasting began the erosion of employment opportunities for musicians that continued throughout the second half of the 20th century. From the 1960s the BBC was constantly seeking to increase 'needle-time' and reduce the number of musicians they were required to employ. The use of the phrase 'needle-time' shows how long ago this agreement was made and was in operation, until 1967 the Phonographic Performance Ltd. (PPL) only allowed the BBC to play commercial gramophone records on air for 5 hours a day. This old fashioned term refers to the days, now almost forgotten, when we played '78' gramophone records and were forever changing the little steel needles that ran in the grooves of the record and later with LPs using stylus needles. The 'needle-time' agreement the BBC had come to with PPL, and as a result the MU, limited the number of hours during which records could be broadcast and guaranteed that an agreed number of musicians would be employed full-time in the BBC orchestras. It also guaranteed that a declared number of freelance musicians would be employed each year, those musicians employed in the numerous freelance groups to broadcast, and for solo and chamber music engagements.

There are now many more radio stations broadcasting music in Britain than there were in 1960, but virtually always from commercial recordings. The exception is Radio 3, which, though it too plays many commercial recordings, does broadcast studio recordings of its own orchestras and relays of their public performances and those of other orchestras.

Pirate, Commercial and Local Radio

The use of radio, or telephones as they were called in the very earliest days goes back much further than is generally known. In 1881 a Telephone Listening Room was set up at the Paris Electrical Exhibition. By holding a telephone receiver to each ear one could hear a performance from the Paris Opera. There were a number of listening points and listeners were only allowed a few minutes each before making way for those queuing up for an opportunity to hear what was going on at the opera. The microphones had been set up right across the stage in the footlights and linked in pairs. Because each listener held a receiver to each ear it was possible at a very early date for the listeners to hear the music in stereo.

In America in 1890 the concern was already that music would become available 'on tap' and that before long it would 'make incipient deafness bliss'. From 1900 onwards more and more enthusiasts, amateur and professional were experimenting with broadcasting in Britain and America. It was not too long before the commercial possibilities became apparent and though at first this was at a local level, the explosion of commercial radio stations in the USA, which began in 1922, depended on the stations being supported by the major advertisers and the use of the old 78 rpm black shellac gramophone records. Broadcasting in the USA has remained essentially commercial ever since.

In Britain broadcasting took a different route. In 1922 the British Broadcasting Company was formed by a group of wireless manufacturers including Marconi, with John Reith as general manager. The government decided in 1927 to establish the British

Broadcasting Corporation (BBC) as a broadcasting monopoly to be operated by a board of governors with John Reith (later Sir John) as the Director General. The BBC was funded by a licence fee to be paid by all owners of radio sets, the amount to be decided by Parliament. In this way the BBC became the first public service broadcasting organisation. In contrast to the USA advertising on radio was forbidden. Reith set himself a mission – to educate and improve the public through the programmes the BBC transmitted. His influence on broadcasting in Britain was to be profound and remained long after he left the BBC in 1938. Indeed until the present his dictum to 'inform, educate and entertain' remains a part of the BBC's brief.

His influence was to have a considerable effect on how the BBC responded to the sounds of rhythm and blues and rock'n'roll in the mid and late 1950s. It continued to broadcast programmes that ignored this new music, the music most young people wanted the chance to hear. In 1958 responding to this need, in Britain and on mainland Europe, pirate stations broadcasting recordings of this new music were set up on ships moored off the coasts of Denmark and Sweden. In 1960 a station off the Dutch coast claimed 5 million listeners. These stations catered for the new 'beat' generation that the national radio stations continued to ignore. The opportunity for most young people to hear the music they really enjoyed was on jukeboxes and Radio Luxembourg.

For some time there had been demands that commercial radio, stations similar to those that had been in America for more than 30 years, should be allowed in Britain. By 1960 the pressure on the government to issue licences for commercial radio increased. The main recording companies – Decca, EMI and Philips and others – were paying a large amount to Radio Luxembourg for broadcasting short extracts from the recordings they were issuing.

A number of small off-shore pirate radio stations had already been set up when in March 1964 Radio Caroline started broadcasting from a ship moored 5 miles off Harwich. Three weeks later they claimed an audience of over 7 million. They were followed by Radio Atlanta, Invicta, and Radio London which was largely financed by a consortium of Texan oil moguls. These stations were all financed by extensive advertising.

One of the biggest advertisers on Radio London was Recketts one of whose products was Beechams Powders. The Beecham Company was continuing its enthusiasm for advertising of every kind started by Sir Thomas's grandfather. I have one of the series of 12 Music Portfolios published at least a hundred years ago. It is beautifully bound in red leatherette with gold lettering on the cover and contains 120 well-known songs and piano pieces, including Rubinstein's *Melody in F, The Dead March in Saul* by Handel as well as *Little Brown Jug, Peggy Malloy* and *Down Among the Dead Men*. Scattered amongst the works of Chopin, Haydn, Johann Strauss, Beethoven, Mozart are pithy statements such as 'Health is wealth and BEECHAM'S PILLS are the Key to it!' '*CHEER UP!* BEECHAM'S PILLS are still worth a Guinea a Box and make life worth living!', 'Guard Yourself, and save the constitution by taking BEECHAM'S PILLS – The National Medicine.' My favourites are when an extra verse has been added as in '*Where are you going my Pretty Maid?*'

'Then take BEECHAM'S PILLS, my pretty maid,'
'Then take BEECHAM'S PILLS, my pretty maid,'
'I take them already, Sir,' she said,
'I take them already, Sir,' she said,

and in *Oft, in the Stilly Night* with the addition,

'Oft in the Stilly Night'
'I awake, and take some BEECHAM'S PILLS'

Even rarer and a treasured possession is a single sheet of toilet paper, in pristine condition, with the legend:

FOR PERFECT HEALTH
THE NATURAL WAY
TAKE BEECHAM'S PILLS
WORTH A GUINEA A BOX

Although in 1965 the Council of Europe had banned broadcasting from the pirate stations as well as any supplies to them of materials and equipment, in 1966 a National Opinion poll showed that Radio Luxembourg and Radio Caroline were each attracting audiences of nearly 9 million and Radio London over 8 million. Several others had audiences of more than 2 million each. All the stations played commercial recordings, which itself was illegal, supplied by all the major record companies, and were funded by the considerable revenue from the advertisers. Apart from any questions of legality the beaming of broadcasts to the mainland was interfering with the legitimate signalling of marine traffic. In the same year the UK government made it illegal to broadcast from ships or marine structures. Contravening the law could lead to two years imprisonment, a fine or both. The pirates responded by asking their listeners to write to their MPs demanding that they be allowed to hear the music the BBC were not broadcasting. In the discussions I later took part in as a representative of the MU, with the Postmaster General and some of his colleagues in the Conservative government, I learned that this was the largest post-bag MPs had ever received on any issue.

It was decided that the MU should meet the representatives of the BBC to see if it could be agreed that the air-time during which the BBC would be allowed to broadcast commercial recordings could be substantially increased. The meeting we had with the Board of the BBC went on for a very long time during which we were wined and dined. I was amused by the fact that now, as someone involved in demanding something in return for allowing the BBC to comply with the government's wishes, I was being treated to a first-class meal accompanied by excellent wines. I was also being treated with a civility I had never experienced in their canteen at Maida Vale whenever over many years I had played in their studios (and as I was still doing), whether in an orchestra, a chamber music ensemble or as a soloist. In return for agreeing increased air-time for a new channel, Radio 1, which would play commercial recordings similar to those broadcast by the pirates, the BBC agreed to guarantee additional employment for the musicians they employed other than in their contract orchestras. They also agreed to establish the BBC Training Orchestra, an orchestra for those who had finished their course at music college or university and wished to become orchestral musicians. Unbeknown to me at the time, the Training Orchestra was to be the precursor of something that would be very important for me some years later.

In December 1966 the BBC announced its new plans and the following September the Home Service became Radio 4, the Third Programme, established in 1946, became Radio 3 and the Light Programme was renamed Radio 2. The new programme Radio 1 was to be devoted to the music for which there was such a demand. Of the 33 disc jockeys employed by the BBC more than half were ex-pirates. I remember meeting Pete Murray, one of the 'big 4' DJs at the time. We had been at St. Paul's School together many years previously and he had been to concerts and seen me. Being a 'square' who never listened to Radio 1 I was quite unaware of the fact that he was a well-known figure and asked him innocently 'And what are you doing now?' With extreme modesty he said that the was doing a bit of broadcasting'. My young daughter who was with me later shamed me. 'Oh. Dear! You are old. Don't you know that was the famous Pete Murray who broadcasts all the time?'

As well as Radio 1 the BBC set up several low powered local radio stations and in 1969 the government licensed a further 12 local radio stations. In 1973 the government finally allowed a replacement of the service the pirates had provided and what those who for so long had wanted – commercial radio in Britain. Now, what the pirate stations had been doing had become legal. To some extent this is what the pirate stations had really been all about. They provided the means by which the advertisers and record companies who long before the new music had arrived wanted: to establish commercial radio in Britain. They had achieved their objective and could from then on benefit from the enormous financial advantage commercial broadcasting secured.

The battle against commercial TV had been lost in 1954 when the Independent Television Authority had been set up and a year later the ITV service began. By 1965 when regional franchises had been granted the whole country could receive commercial TV. When, in 1973 the government allowed commercial radio, as well as TV, the BBC was faced with competition that has had a significant effect on public service broadcasting. The gain, for a small number of musicians, was the very well paid work involved in recording the 'jingles', the music especially written to accompany the advertisements.

Was the long and hard-fought battle against commercial radio that the MU and its members waged, in part by their support of the BBC and public service broadcasting, worthwhile? There can be no doubt that for musicians such as myself it put off the evil day for a good many years. Since 1973 the amount of work for musicians in broadcasting on radio and TV has substantially reduced. I regret that musicians could earn very much more by providing the music for an advert for washing powder, for either radio or TV, than by playing Beethoven or Boulez in the Royal Festival Hall.

21 Learning and Teaching

*Opportunities for learning an instrument – in Brass and Military bands.
Music colleges and Teacher Training colleges.
The Calouste Gulbenkian Foundation – Making Music(1965) – Enquiry
into Training Musicians (1975). The BBC Training Orchestra.
The National Centre for Orchestral Studies (NCOS).*

Perhaps, because orchestral musicians had not passed any examination or test to prove they could do what they were actually doing (though some of them were doing it extremely well) and therefore had not received any diploma or credentials their skills were unrecognised. Since becoming a performing musician was not considered a suitable occupation for a gentleman it was nearly always the children of relatively poor families and immigrants who became professional musicians. To do so they had to learn how to play their instruments and it was to be a long time before an adequate music education was available to everyone.

In the 18th and 19th century learning to play the piano to a reasonable standard had become an accomplishment that every young lady from a 'good family' was expected to be able to demonstrate. Many a young man who fancied himself as a tenor or baritone was lured into marriage by an attractive young lady's prowess at the keyboard, which in the homes of the well-to-do would normally have been a grand piano. By 1900 the very much less expensive 'upright' piano had become very popular and because of its size could be accommodated in quite a small room. When bought second-hand or third-hand they had become affordable to most families. For the first half of the 20th century one could expect to find a piano in the homes of both the well-to-do and those of quite modest means and find that quite a considerable number of children were having piano lessons – some teachers charging as little as one or two shillings (5/10p) a lesson.

The piano has the advantage of being an instrument on which one can make 'pleasing sounds' immediately, in contrast to most other instruments on which the beginner may have difficulty in making any sound at all or produces noise rather than music. In the 1950s the guitar emerged as another instrument on which one could quite quickly play simple chords, again with a pleasant tone. It is sad that although so many children start to learn an instrument not very many have ever progressed beyond a quite elementary stage. In the past I often met people who when they learned that I was a musician told me that they had had piano lessons as a child and now wished that they had not given it up so early.

A keyboard instrument also gave players the opportunity to make music satisfactorily on their own; not only music written for the piano, but arrangements of popular songs of the day, selections from operettas and musical comedies (now called musicals) and light and symphonic orchestral music. Arrangements for two players, four hands at one piano, of overtures, symphonies, oratorios and even operas were for very many years extremely popular. In the first half of the 20th century if there were a member of the family who could play the piano they would provide the accompaniment for a 'sing-song'. It wasn't necessary to be able to play all the notes: a friend of mine used to say it was enough, if you could 'put up a framework'. Sometimes there would be other members of the family or friends who had some skill on other instruments – perhaps the violin, flute, clarinet or cornet, so that with the pianist 'filling in' the missing parts or the basic harmony it was possible to have a most enjoyable time. The old 'joanna', often beer-stained and in need of tuning, was to be heard in many pubs and of course a piano was essential from around 1910 in every silent film cinema.

More often than not it will be the parents rather than their children who will suggest that it might be a good idea to start having lessons on an instrument. A few children, once having heard a particular instrument, will give their parents no peace until they have been bought the instrument that has caught their ear. As a rule they will usually prove to be exceptionally talented – Yehudi Menuhin is a good example. If there is no one in the family or a friend who can start them off a teacher will have to be found. As well as there being plenty of piano teachers, because the stringed instruments had been acceptable instruments for well-bred people to play, there were also a good many teachers of the stringed instruments. A great deal of chamber music – the string quartets, trios, piano quartets and quintets by Haydn, Mozart, Beethoven, Brahms and many other composers had been written for and played in their homes by amateurs. There were therefore a number of really excellent violin teachers as well as many giving lessons of varying quality, some for as little as two shillings (10p) a lesson. During the 1920s a few secondary schools began to provide group tuition on the violin for sixpence (2½p) a lesson. Perhaps it is not surprising that in general the standard of this tuition was not very high. At the same time one could buy a perfectly adequate 'violin set' – that is a violin and bow – for £1.50, much cheaper than the cost of a piano. Those violins, without a bow, now sell for £300 to £400. Emanuel Hurwitz, leader of the English Chamber Orchestra for 20 years, told me that in about 1927 his father bought him a violin for which he paid £8. Fifty years later when he was a professor at the Royal Academy of Music some of his pupils had similar violins for which they had paid £4000.

Between 1880 and 1914 as a result of the Pogroms a considerable number of poor immigrant Jewish families had come to Britain from all over Europe, in particular from the Pale of Settlement, the area between the Baltic and the Black Sea. They had lived in *shtetls*, small towns and villages in Russia and Poland, where there had been a long tradition of violin playing within the Jewish communities. The majority settled in the large cities, Glasgow, Leeds, Manchester with the largest number in London. Many families took the opportunity to buy an inexpensive instrument for their sons and daughters and paid for them to have lessons. This led to a number of the most talented going into the music profession where from 1909 until 1928 there was so much employment for musicians playing in the small orchestras accompanying the silent films. They were then able to earn much more than their parents ever had. In 1943 there were still a great many Jewish string players in all the symphony, chamber and light orchestras.

It will probably have been less easy during the first decades of the 20th century to find a teacher if one wanted to learn a wind instrument. Unless you lived in one of the few towns that had an orchestra for part of the year the only person available will probably have been a player in one of the theatre orchestras who would not as a rule have been a player of a very high standard. Anywhere else it is likely it would be someone who themselves would probably be an amateur of limited ability who would be able to show you the very basic elements.

I was surprised to find that even in the 1950s when I was asked to give clarinet lessons at the Central School of Dance Music, where I was the only teacher who was an orchestral musician – all the others were jazz or dance band musicians – how many of my pupils had been self-taught until they came to me. They had taught themselves by listening to and watching others, perhaps finding information in an instrumental tutor or books and listening to broadcast and recorded performances. Later, when I interviewed a number of full and part-time musicians in the 1980s and 90s as part of Music Preserved's Oral History of Musicians in Britain, I found that quite a few had only had perhaps two or three lessons, usually after they had already acquired sufficient skill by themselves and had undertaken some professional or semi-professional work.

This was true not only for musicians in the field of popular music. I have known several outstanding orchestral musicians who either had had very few or no lessons at all. Jack Brymer was one who never had any lessons. Another very fine player, a timpanist, a principal in the BBC Symphony Orchestra, told me that he taught himself while he was in his teens and living in Nottingham. As there was no one in Nottingham to give him timpani lessons he decided that he would have to find a way to get into the concert hall whenever any orchestra was rehearsing so that by using his father's binoculars he would be able to see the timpanist's hands and find out how he tuned his instrument and used the drum sticks.

However, because of the brass band tradition that had started in Britain in the 19th century, in 1900 there were brass bands all over the country. There were also Town, Military and Salvation Army bands. All these bands were able to provide boys with an opportunity to learn a wind instrument. Boys would usually join a band when they were between ten and fourteen years old – depending on the size of their hands or the length of their arms. It is unusual to start any of the wind instruments much younger. They would receive basic instruction from the bandmaster or one of the older players in the band. Girls were also welcomed in the Salvation Army bands.

On joining a band the young musician would usually be provided with an instrument – not always of their choice as it would depend on what instrument was available. Arthur Wilson, the very fine principal trombone in the Philharmonia for many years, told me that when he first joined a band he had wanted to play the cornet, but as they were short of trombones, had a spare instrument and he was tall for his age with quite long arms, he was given a trombone and told to get on with it.

The bandmaster will frequently have been a retired bandmaster from one of the many Army Line Regimental bands. He will probably have studied at Kneller Hall, the Military School of Music, where as well as receiving tuition on his principal instrument and conducting he will have gained a limited working knowledge of all the instruments to be found in a military band. I have heard horror stories from a number of musicians of how they had been taught by someone whose own main instrument was the clarinet or the flute but who was teaching them the trumpet or trombone. They often had no real understanding of the difference between the embouchure (the subtle formation of the lips and muscles) required to play a brass instrument and that required for the clarinet or flute.

Whatever the instrument, the main reason why so few continue beyond a fairly elementary stage is the need for regular practice. Learning a musical instrument is very similar to becoming an accomplished athlete. As one progresses an increasing amount of work and commitment is required. On some instruments even to get to the stage of making an acceptable sound takes some time. Only the most naturally gifted child will from the start make an agreeable sound on the violin or oboe. Until sufficient skill has been acquired patience on the part of the beginner is required when learning nearly all instruments (those sharing the home with them will also need patience, sometimes a lot more). It can be some time before something that sounds like music can be heard. After a few months even gifted children find the need for regular practice every day becomes tedious. Without parental support and encouragement (often rather more than 'encouragement' is required) excuses and reasons for not practising become increasingly frequent.

The majority who continue to play their instrument beyond their school or university years are very often those who had the opportunity to play in a band, in an amateur orchestra or to make music at home with friends and family. The few who go on to become professional musicians very often come from a background where a member of the family is or was a musician or a keen amateur.

At the time I joined the profession in 1942 quite a number of the brass and woodwind players I played alongside in the London orchestras and on sessions, men then aged over 40, had come from working and lower middle-class families. They had left school at fourteen or at the latest sixteen. Some of the best brass players in the orchestras had been in one of the brass bands. The best of these bands such as the Grimethorpe Colliery, Black Dyke Mills, Fodens and Morris Motors were all 'works' bands. The first was the Black Dyke Mills Band, under another name, and the Besses o' th' Barn Band formed two years later. Some factories would employ a man because he was known to be an outstanding musician. Most often he would play the cornet and become the solo cornet in the band, the equivalent of the leader in a symphony orchestra. His contract would include playing in the company's band and he would frequently be given a job in the office rather than having to work in the mine or the factory. Some of the first bands had woodwind as well as brass instruments, and like the old New Orleans marching bands, in which many of the early jazz musicians first played, were often led by a clarinettist, playing the small, high pitched Eb clarinet.

In the past some of the finest principal trumpets in the symphony orchestras came from these bands: George Eskdale, for many years principal in the London Symphony Orchestra whose recording of the second and third movements of the Haydn *Trumpet* Concerto was a constant request on radio programmes such as *Family Favourites*. Harold Jackson, principal in the Philharmonia was a wonderful trumpet virtuoso. During the interval of one of the sessions when the Philharmonia were recording Wagner's *Tristan* with Wilhelm Furtwängler conducting, while the orchestra were having a well-earned cup of tea, my colleague Wilfred Hambleton (he was using the interval to try to find a better reed for his bass clarinet) told me that Walter Legge came into the studio to tell Furtwängler that he thought that Jackson sounded much too loud in one passage. 'Yes', said Furtwängler, 'but he is so good – he plays so well – I do not want to tell him.' Harry Mortimer, Jack Mackintosh and Maurice

Murphy were amongst other fine players from the brass bands. There had also been many local Village and Town bands (known as 'subscription bands') in the early 1800s; the Police and Temperance bands came later, (it is recorded that some of the bandsmen were not always as 'temperate' as might have been desired).

Another route that led into the profession for percussion, brass and woodwind players was via the Army bands. As well as the Guard's bands, which had a long tradition of producing fine instrumentalists, many of the line regiments also had their own bands. Boys from poor families, and a number from orphanages, would join the army at fourteen as band-boys and graduate to the band usually receiving tuition at Kneller Hall. When I came into the profession I remember there were some excellent flautists and clarinettists who had been in one of the Guard's bands. Oboists and bassoonists with an army background though technically good as rule tended to have a thin reedy tone.

Ambitious mothers have much to answer for but a few must be given credit for recognising that they have a musically talented child and 'encouraging' and managing a potential soloist towards a very successful career. In the same way parents who want their children to do well and teachers who want to please their pupils' parents may feel that by taking the Associated Board grade exams the children will maintain more regular practice in attempting to obtain a higher grade and this quite often does have the desired effect. On the other hand it not infrequently produces resistance. A large number drop out after Grade 5 when it starts to get more difficult and demands more daily practice if further progress is to be made. Parents and teachers often seem to forget that one learns an instrument to play and enjoy music. Too frequently, instead of playing for pleasure learning an instrument becomes just another subject to be examined. Those youngsters that have formed themselves into pop or rock groups, at school or later, have never needed to be encouraged to meet together to 'practise' because what they were doing was fun and what they wanted to be doing.

By the 1920s many more of those hoping to become musicians were going to the colleges of music. Many of the young string players Sir Adrian Boult recruited when the BBC Symphony Orchestra was formed in 1930 had only recently left music colleges. You could then start at college when you were as young as twelve, if you were sufficiently advanced – I was sixteen when I was accepted at the Royal College of Music in 1941. That is no longer possible. One must be eighteen and have at least two 'A' levels.

In 1942, the McNair Committee was set up to consider the 'supply, recruitment and training of teachers' and then in 1945 the Music Panel decided that the training of music teachers in schools was 'already seriously inadequate in every type of school' and that it was 'steadily worsening in quantity and quality'. They were, of course, commenting on classroom teachers: there was still very little opportunity for children to have lessons on an instrument. By 1948 it had been decided that only having the Graduate Diploma from the Royal College or Academy of Music or a Teachers ARCM or LRAM was an insufficient preparation for someone to be qualified to teach music in a school.

The first Teacher Training College to provide a two-year course for teachers of music, art and drama was Bretton Hall in Yorkshire, in 1949. In 1950 Trent Park on the outskirts of London established courses in the same subjects. Eight years later, while I was in the Philharmonia and also playing for *West Side Story,* I received an enquiry from Trent Park as to whether I would take on teaching all the woodwind instruments – flute, oboe, clarinet and bassoon. It would be for three hours on Wednesday afternoons. I accepted their offer with some trepidation because my knowledge of the flute, oboe and bassoon was limited, to put it euphemistically. On top of that, at that time there was an MU rule that if you were playing for a West End show you had to pay your deputy 25% in addition to what you were receiving. As there was a matinee on Wednesday afternoon and I was being paid rather well for doing *West Side Story* and the fee for teaching was going to be less I would be out of pocket. Some of my friends thought I was crazy.

When I went to Trent Park for the first time I found I was faced with nine students. They ranged in standard from near beginners to a couple who had already received their LRAM – they had been at Music College for three years and had come to do the one year post-graduate course that would give them Qualified Teacher Status (QTS). The others were either doing the normal three-year course with music as their main subject or in a few cases taking subjects other than music – English, History, Maths, etc. – and just wanted to learn to play better. I managed to keep just a page ahead of the non-clarinet students as the general principles of playing all the wind instruments is very similar: breathing, articulation, moving the fingers in the correct way and so on. I knew the tone they should produce by virtue of having played with very fine players for so many years. This was a very steep learning curve for me and, I am sure, resulted in slower progress for my pupils. My task was not made any easier by the fact that three hours for nine pupils allowed me only twenty minutes for each one.

Happily, for me and my pupils, a splendid man, Philip Pfaff, had just been appointed as the head of the music department (it was he who invited me to teach there) and there was also a far-seeing Principal of the college. Within a year or two we had appointed excellent teachers for each instrument. I continued to be a visiting lecturer at Trent Park for twenty years and I arranged a very fine colleague Gordon Lewin to take my place when I had to be elsewhere. Not only was he a very good clarinettist and saxophone player but also a very good composer and outstanding arranger, especially of music for wind ensembles. In fact, he wrote all the exercises and arranged the tunes I used in my clarinet tutor *Play the Clarinet* published in 1969 by Chappell and Co., and still in print after more than thirty years. It survived the takeover of Chappell, when all compositions that did not sell well enough to pay for the space the music took up on the shelves were pulped and, finally, after subsequent takeovers by other ever larger conglomerates, it was rescued and reprinted by Peters Edition in the late 1980s.

The gamble I took in agreeing to teach at Trent Park turned out to be a fortunate decision. It led to a wonderful opportunity for me to learn a great deal about teaching in general and meet some interesting lecturers in a number of other disciplines, as well as to writing *First Tunes and Studies,* a tutor published in 1960 by Schott and Co.. It also prepared me for my future position as Director of the National Centre for Orchestral Studies.

In time it became necessary for anyone wanting to teach in a state school, primary or secondary, to have Qualified Teacher

Status. It was not and still is not necessary for those teaching in an Independent (Public) School. The normal route to QTS is by taking the three-year course that leads to a B.Ed. or, for those who have completed three years at a music college, the one-year course that leads to the Postgraduate Certificate of Education (PGCE). I had a number of students who were taking the PGCE course, who were going on to be Peripatetic Instrumental Teachers and rather more who were taking their B.Ed. which would allow them to teach anything within the state school system including music, in class or as a peripatetic instrumental teacher. I did not have QTS, and was therefore not considered 'qualified' nor could I teach in a state school. However, I could teach and examine those who were going to do so. Like myself virtually all my colleagues in the profession including my fellow professors at the Royal College of Music, were debarred in the same way. Many highly qualified musicians who could have been extremely valuable part-time instrumental teachers were therefore unable to impart their skill and musical understanding, gained from their experience of working with fine conductors and soloists; they in their turn were denied the opportunity for self-examination that teaching others can provide. A teacher will often become a better teacher if able to perform, and a performer a better performer when challenged by teaching others.

At Trent Park I had a class for all those on the PGCE course who were considered 'Professionals', those who had been to music college for three years, flautists, oboists, clarinettists and bassoonists. I decided to get the clarinettists to teach the others the clarinet. My idea was that the clarinet students, supposed to be advanced players, would learn more about their instrument while trying to help beginners learn something about the fundamental techniques required to play the clarinet well. As soon as they could play in the bottom register, the easiest, they would play duets and trios (wonderfully and insightfully arranged by my friend Gordon Lewin), with a leading part that was interesting and the others with relatively simple parts suited to their ability. I insisted that no one went on to the next page of their studies until they had mastered the current page. This was especially important in regard to breathing and clean, clear articulation. At the end of about six months I always had some of the so-called 'Professionals' coming to me crying because the beginners, though they did not have their technique, could play the simple parts with better articulation than they could. As far as learning the absolute essentials on any instrument it is the first lessons that are the most important. Sadly, these vital lessons were at that time too often given by those insufficiently qualified.

The Calouste Gulbenkian Foundation, concerned with the examination and educational system in schools and music colleges and at advanced level, set up a committee under the chairmanship of Sir Gilmour Jenkins. Their report *Making Music* published in 1965 recommended that there should be earlier identification of talent and an increased number of specialist schools at primary and secondary level leading on to the Junior Departments at the music colleges. In 1971 the Inner London Education Authority did establish a specialist music course at Pimlico School, the only one of its kind in the maintained sector. It was extremely good and provided first-class tuition for gifted children. A number of specialist schools were also established in the years following the Report – the Purcell, Chetham, Menuhin, Wells Cathedral and St. Mary's (in Scotland) schools.

The report also recommended that the Royal College of Music, the Royal Academy of Music and Trinity College of Music should be amalgamated to form a National Conservatoire with four to six year courses that would lead to a Diploma in Performance. Not surprisingly there was no enthusiasm on the part of any of the conservatories to give up their individual autonomy. As usual the majority of the problems the Report highlighted were not solved.

By 1975 it had become apparent that the situation had deteriorated rather than improved. The Foundation decided that it was time to re-examine the problems that remained unsolved. This committee, The Committee of Enquiry into the Training of Musicians with John Vaizey as Chairman – he became Lord Vaizey in 1977 not long before the report was issued – was much more broadly based. It included representatives from the music colleges, education establishment, professional organisations, the BBC and the Musicians' Union. I was chosen to represent the MU because I was a professor at the Royal College of Music (I had been since 1964), was a member of the Executive Committee and Chairman of the Philharmonia Orchestra Council of Management.

The Enquiry's report *Training Musicians* published in 1978 considered every aspect of teaching and performing but paid particular attention to the standard of instrumental teaching with considerable emphasis on the preparation of musicians for the orchestral profession. In the committee's opinion there were still not enough top class soloists being produced and an extension of training was needed for those wishing to join an orchestra. In fact one of the prime movers urging the enquiry was the ABO, the Association of British Orchestras. The Association was particularly concerned that its members were unable to obtain 'sufficient recruits of the required standard – particularly string players – and that the training of those they did take was, in their view, incomplete'. They felt there was too much concentration on playing the solo and chamber music repertoire. In fact many students, particularly the string players were given the impression that playing in an orchestra was something to be avoided.

It was also reported to the Enquiry that many professional musicians, in particular the members of the regional orchestras, felt that their status, income and working conditions did not compare with those of their contemporaries abroad. The situation was much better for the freelance musicians, mainly based in London. One reason why the members of the four London Orchestras earned considerably more than their colleagues in the regional orchestras, who were on full-time contracts, was because they were paid separately for each engagement and were therefore considered to be 'freelance', which brought the benefits of being on Schedule D for tax purposes.

I had been a member of the MU negotiating group involved for some years in negotiations with the ABO on behalf of the musicians in the regional orchestras and knew how poorly paid and hard working the musicians in those orchestras were. At that time the salaries for the rank and file string players in the regional orchestras were under £4000 a year (a pint of beer then cost 20p) for a thirty-hour week, plus a good deal of travelling. It was clear to me that this was a significant cause of the orchestras' recruiting difficulties. As a professor at the Royal College of Music I was also aware that criticism of the extent to which students were prepared for the orchestral profession provided by the music colleges was justified.

Having taken part in discussions with the managements of the regional orchestras for some years I also understood the financial constraints under which they were forced to operate and that it was unlikely that the salaries of the musicians in those orchestras would be likely to improve to any extent. In fact, more than twenty-five years later nothing had changed and once again, in 2004, the low remuneration received by all orchestral musicians, in particular those in the orchestras outside London, was again being aired in the press. Their salaries had increased six-fold to just under £24,000 – but beer was nine times more expensive at £1.80 a pint.

The committee recognised that since the previous Enquiry in 1965 the opportunity for most children in primary and secondary schools to learn an instrument was very much better. Nearly all Local Education Authorities had Music Centres and peripatetic and part-time teachers. There were youth orchestras, brass bands and even jazz bands in which they could play. Some of the County Youth Orchestras were becoming increasingly good, and the National Youth Orchestra, in which the most talented played, was really excellent. The annual concerts they gave under very good conductors were outstanding.

The standard of those applying for entrance to the music colleges kept rising and I was aware from my teaching at the Royal College that the standard of instrumental performance by the best students was now extremely high. In fact over the years I had a number of pupils who when they finished at College were better players technically than I had been when I started in the profession. By 1980 I was auditioning entrants to the Royal College of Music who when still seventeen were offering the Carl Nielsen *Clarinet* Concerto, an extremely difficult virtuoso work that only a few of the best clarinettists of my generation would tackle. We were in a situation now that was the opposite to that I have described as being prevalent eighty and ninety years ago when there were only a handful of very good players. Now virtuosity, especially on the wind instruments was becoming relatively commonplace.

But still preparation for the orchestra was less than satisfactory. The BBC Training Orchestra, at first called the New BBC Orchestra, was established in 1966 as part of the deal that allowed the creation of BBC Radios 1 and 2. It was never really satisfactory for several reasons. The orchestra's status was always ambiguous: the members of the orchestra were no longer students and though employed on contract by the BBC to give a broadcast each week and a public concert once a month, they were supposed to be there to learn how to play in an orchestra. In fact, they received no 'training', only more rehearsal time for what were clearly professional engagements. Many freelance musicians felt that this 'student orchestra' was being used to reduce employment for them; some members of the BBC orchestras were concerned that these young musicians would be brought in to replace them. It was seen by the students who applied to join as a stopgap before they got a 'proper job'. They had no real commitment to the orchestra and could leave at any time if they were offered a place in an orchestra. Conductors were uncertain how to treat them – were they professional musicians or students? By 1972 the BBC decided it could no longer afford to maintain an orchestra of 65/70 and decided to reduce the orchestra to 35 and rename it the Academy of the BBC and then in 1976, before the Enquiry started considering how the preparation of musicians wanting to play in orchestras might be improved, the Academy of the BBC was disbanded.

Whilst we were discussing how the situation could be improved it was clear to me that the orchestras were not going to receive sufficient additional funding in the foreseeable future that would allow them to pay their musicians substantially higher salaries. However, I could see no reason why something should not be done to create a post-conservatoire or university course that would provide the opportunities for orchestral preparation everyone agreed was required.

I therefore decided to prepare an outline for a course for post-graduate students to include the way it should be organised, the staff required, the financial support it would require and where it might come from and give a copy to Robert Ponsonby, Controller, Music, BBC, and John Morton, General Secretary of the Musicians' Union, for their comments. Now that the BBC scheme had been abandoned the BBC and the MU were both ready to support another initiative. For the BBC it would be very much cheaper and the MU hoped to ward off suggestions from its members that it had allowed the BBC to break its agreement. Ponsonby and Morton responded well to my ideas.

I felt that this scheme needed to be attached to an organisation that could provide a Diploma that would provide those students who completed the course satisfactorily with some credential to show their future employers.

I went to the House of Lords and told Lord Vaizey of the plan and the approval it had received from the BBC and the MU. I asked him if he was able to suggest an organisation to which the proposed post-graduate course might be attached, somewhere the education authorities would approve and that could award a diploma of worth. He immediately said he would contact his friend Richard Hoggart, Warden of Goldsmiths' College, University of London. Two weeks later I met Dr Hoggart. His enthusiasm for the project resulted in it being agreed within a few weeks that the course should be established at Goldsmiths' College.

This gave me sufficient confidence to propose that the scheme be recommended in the Gulbenkian Enquiry Committee report. As might be expected there was considerable opposition from some members of the committee, especially representatives of the music colleges who saw any scheme as a rebuke to what they were offering. There were also those who held the view that the Youth Orchestras provided sufficient experience for those who would later go into the orchestral profession. They did not understand that in a professional orchestra the conductor/orchestra relationship and the inter-personal relationships between members is very different from the short-term 'holiday' atmosphere of a youth orchestra. Often, with minimum rehearsal time or under pressure to learn new repertoire, extremely blunt and sometimes wounding criticism can be experienced. It was preparation for this that the proposed intensive year-long course would seek to provide. This was not in any way to diminish the value of youth orchestras in giving so many young musicians the joy of making music together and sometimes taking part in wonderful performances.

After a considerable amount of discussion, in the end there was sufficient support for the Report to include the statement:

We also understand that there is a possibility that a post-diploma training scheme for orchestral players may be established in London at Goldsmiths' College as a result of talks now taking place between representatives of the BBC, the Musicians' Union, the ABO, the Arts Council and certain educational interests. We think a proposal along these lines is worthy of support.

In July 1977, before the Report *Training Musicians* had been published, the Advanced Orchestral Training Working Party was set up and while I was still playing in the Philharmonia and Chairman of its Council I was invited to be its Secretary. The Working Party held its first meeting on the 1ˢᵗ August 1977 with 3 representatives from Goldsmiths' College and two each from the BBC, ABO, MU and the Arts Council. A year later in August 1978 the Working Party was able to agree the Terms of Reference and Membership for the Executive Committee of the National Centre for Orchestral Studies (NCOS) and in September an advertisement for the post of Director of the NCOS was inserted in the usual national Daily and Sunday newspapers and periodicals. By November the many applicants for the post had been reduced to twelve and finally to four. When the decision as to who should be appointed had been decided a Press Conference was held at the Royal Festival Hall.

My appointment as the Director of the National Centre for Orchestral Studies in December 1978 was exciting, but frightening. I had been a professional clarinettist since I was 17 – for 36 years – and now I was taking a leap into the unknown. Once I stopped playing there would be no way back. I have often been asked over the last 25 years by acquaintances when they learn I was a musician, 'Don't you still play for your own pleasure?' When I tell them that I don't they are surprised. I explain that a musician is like an athlete. One has to be in training – that is why however good one is one has to keep practising. The better one has been the less pleasant it is to do it so much less well.

I hoped that my experience on the MU committees and as Chairman of the Philharmonia would be of some use. Now I would have to manage staff, be responsible for the administration and budgeting and make decisions about which conductors, coaches and examiners to engage and what programmes we should play. As Director of the NCOS I would meet people and become involved with music organisations beyond my experience as a performer.

After a month's holiday with friends in San Francisco I returned ready to embark with enthusiasm on this wonderful opportunity I had been given.

22 *No Longer a Performer*

The National Centre – Conservatoires around the world. Hong Kong – orchestral problems. The Chinese Orchestra. Financial difficulties at the NCOS. Competitions – opposing views.

When I became a member of The Committee of Enquiry into the Training of Musicians while I was still in the Philharmonia it had not crossed my mind that I might quite soon be ceasing to be a professional musician. Nor that I would have the opportunity to be involved in so many and diverse areas of the music world.

The National Centre for Orchestral Studies

The first news that a plan to create a training orchestra was being considered appeared in *Classical Music* in January 1978. Under the headline 'Training orchestral musicians for the 1980s' it stated that 'Following the publication of the Gulbenkian Report on *Training Musicians*, exciting moves are afoot to establish a major new training orchestra in London. The plan is the brainchild of Basil Tschaikov, Philharmonia clarinettist (and chairman of the orchestra's board) and professor at the Royal College of Music. He has prepared a paper on the establishment of a National Centre for Orchestral Studies at Goldsmiths' College, New Cross in south London. This has been presented to and approved by a working party (the Advanced Orchestral Training Working Party) comprising representatives of the BBC – the demise of whose own Academy training orchestra was a direct spur to the new scheme – the Musicians' Union, The Arts Council, the Association of British Orchestras and Goldsmiths'.

Then in August the *Times* reported 'A national centre to bring young musicians up to the standards of the leading orchestras will open in September next year at Goldsmiths' College, University of London. The National Centre for Orchestra Studies (NCOS) will provide a year-long diploma course for about seventy-five student musicians at a time. They are likely to have graduated from music colleges and universities. There is little organised training for young musicians who aspire to join leading orchestras but need to improve their skills. A similar organisation, the Academy of the BBC, closed last year because of a lack of funds. Students, who will be coached by leading conductors and performers, will be eligible for local authority grants but the cost of running the course is to be met for the first five years by such organisations as the BBC, the Independent Broadcasting Authority, the Arts Council, the Musicians' Union and the Performing Rights Society.'

At about the same time Goldsmiths' issued a Press Notice in which the representatives of the three organisations that provided support throughout the life of the NCOS stated their belief in this new enterprise. Dr Richard Hoggart, Warden of Goldsmiths' College and Chairman of the NCOS Executive Committee, is quoted as saying: 'We think a Centre of this kind is essential if we are not going to waste the talents of many of these young musicians and if the standard of British orchestral playing is to be maintained and improved to the highest international level.' John Morton, General Secretary of the Musicians' Union claimed it as: 'A valuable step, which will improve the status and recognition of the music profession. I hope this initiative will give greater impetus to music in the state education system.' The BBC's Controller of Music, Robert Ponsonby, welcomed the scheme: 'This proposal for the creation of a centre for orchestral training in Britain is very exciting indeed and the BBC is very glad to be involved as a sponsor of it. The centre deserves enthusiastic support from every sector of the profession.'

During 1978 and 1979 the Advanced Orchestral Training Working Party made great progress and before long evolved into the NCOS Executive Committee. Once the National Centre was established with The Lord Perry of Walton as Chairman of the Board of Trustees – he was also the Chairman of the University of London Goldsmiths' College Delegacy, its governing body – the Executive Committee became the Management Committee. One of the remarkable aspects of the NCOS was the way representatives of organisations that normally confronted each other across the negotiating table worked happily together on the Management Committee, made up of representatives of Goldsmiths' College, the Independent Television Companies Association (ITCA), the Independent Broadcasting Authority (IBA), the BBC, the Musicians' Union (MU) and the Association of British Orchestras (ABO), with the Warden of Goldsmiths' College as Chairman.

National Centre for Orchestral Studies Director: Basil Tschaikov

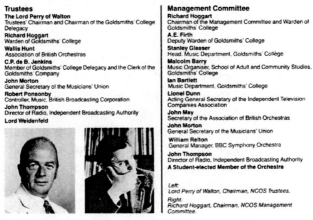

Left:
Lord Perry of Walton, Chairman, NCOS Trustees.

Right:
Richard Hoggart, Chairman, NCOS Management Committee.

The 1979 Board of Trustees and Management Committee.

The launch and press conference at the Royal Festival Hall in December 1978 attracted a good deal of favourable coverage in the newspapers and by February 1979 it was possible to insert advertisements inviting applications for the first course starting in September 1979. There were a great many applicants and the auditions in April lasted for several weeks until an orchestra of 70 was finally selected.

In order to prepare these young players for the profession the course provided the opportunity for them to study and perform the symphonic and chamber orchestra repertoire from the baroque, classical, romantic and contemporary periods, opera, light and session music, and to do so not only on the concert platform but also in the opera pit and in the broadcasting and recording studio. In a normal week they would be involved in about 25 hours of rehearsals, coaching sessions and concerts. In addition to their normal daily practice they usually found they needed to spend time preparing the new music they were faced with each week before the first rehearsal. This was especially the case for the strings. The NCOS paid for them to have a certain number of lessons with a teacher of their own choice. The number of lessons was determined by how much their teacher charged.

To take advantage of the outstanding international conductors that were attracted to London by the four London orchestras, the BBC Symphony Orchestra and two opera houses, the timetable was kept flexible so as to accommodate their availability. In this way the NCOS was able to persuade a considerable number of them to work with the orchestra. The orchestra would prepare the repertoire they were going to conduct by having sectional rehearsals with coaches and some full rehearsals, usually with a talented young conductor. It was fortunate that George Hurst who conducted the orchestra several times each year was not only an excellent orchestral trainer but had also taught many of those who later would go on to have successful conducting careers. Through him the NCOS were introduced to some of his ex-pupils. Adrian Leaper, Martyn Brabbins, Peter Stark and Mark Shanahan all gained valuable experience at the start of their careers both by conducting the orchestra and then attending the rehearsals and concert given by the conductor for whom they had prepared the orchestra.

Over ten years we were fortunate that Richard Armstrong, Vladimir Ashkenazy, Rudolf Barshai, Paavo Berglund, Rafael Fruhbeck de Burgos, Harry Christophers, Nicholas Cleobury, Colin Davis, Edward Downes, Mark Ermler, Robert Farnon, John Eliot Gardiner, Roy Goodman, Charles Groves, Vernon Handley, Richard Hickox, Lorin Maazel, Diego Masson, Charles Mackerras, Norman Del Mar, Yehudi Menuhin, Roger Norrington, Harry Rabinowitz, Simon Rattle, Gennadi Rozhdestvensky, Kurt Sanderling, Vilem Tausky and Barry Wordsworth all agreed to conduct the NCOS orchestras. Some of them came back a number of times. Because of the insight into the performance of the music that they had gained through years of conducting great orchestras all over the world, with so many of the best instrumentalists, they did far more than just rehearse and conduct performances. They gave the young musicians the benefit of their knowledge and understanding that turned their visits into wonderful master-classes in the art of orchestral playing.

We were usually able to prevail upon them to conduct repertoire that from my own experience I knew they did particularly well, though on one or two occasions I had to dissuade, in as diplomatic a way as possible, a conductor who wanted to conduct something he would not usually get the opportunity of conducting or to try out a work he might like to add to his repertoire. From time to time I was approached by conductors who wanted to conduct the NCOS orchestra who, again from my own experience, I felt were unsuitable. Dealing with them could be very difficult. But it had to be done because it was essential that the young musicians' time should not be wasted. It would be bad enough when they were in the profession and being paid for their trouble.

Whilst the young musicians were on the NCOS course they were given the opportunity to play as wide a range of music as possible. I always encouraged conductors to conduct music they had a particular interest in, be it contemporary music or the music of British composers, opera, light music, or those dedicated to the 'authenticity' movement and performance on period instruments.

Throughout each year there were sectional coaching sessions and, after the first year when we were fortunate to have an American student who was already quite experienced, we increasingly had a professional violinist to lead the orchestra whenever possible. From 1983 that was virtually all the time. For several years it was Peter Thomas, who was later captured by Simon Rattle to lead the City of Birmingham Symphony Orchestra and then James Coles, who had led several orchestras. They both took enormous pains to help the string players learn how to play in an orchestra. Learning to play in an orchestra is more difficult for string players, especially violinists. The concentration on the solo and chamber music repertoire they will have experienced at music college and at private lessons, where individual expressiveness is so important, does not prepare them for the discipline required within a violin section of perhaps anything from 16 to 20 players. It can sometimes be even more difficult for a very good violinist to come to terms with the restraints imposed within a section.

Bearing in mind the concern expressed in the Gulbenkian report and by the ABO about the standard of the string instrumentalists applying for positions, especially in the regional orchestras, the NCOS arranged for regular visits by the leaders of the London orchestras: Hugh Bean, Iona Brown, Rodney Friend, Barry Griffiths, Emmanuel Hurwitz, John Ludlow, Manoug Parikian, Carl Pini. In addition we were fortunate that Michel

Schwalbé, leader Emeritus of the Berlin Philharmonic Orchestra and Herbert von Karajan's leader for 30 years, agreed to work with the orchestra every year coaching and conducting the whole orchestra, concentrating on the string sections. Another particularly inspirational coach was the outstanding orchestral, chamber music and solo violist Frederick Riddle. Many of the most distinguished string, woodwind, brass and percussion principals in the London orchestras were also regular coaches and examiners.

The orchestra worked very hard, preparing the young musicians for life in the profession. The schedule for the very first week, in September 1979, is typical of how intensive the course was:

Monday
2.00 – 5.00   Full orchestra rehearsal, conductor John Forster: Brahms: Symphony No.2 and the Symphony in 3 movements by Stravinsky

6.00 – 9.00   Woodwind, brass and percussion, piano and harp (cond. Forster)

Tuesday
10.00 – 1.00   Strings only with John Forster
2.00 – 5.00   Full orchestra with Simon Rattle

Wednesday free

Thursday
10.00 – 1.00   Strings only and 2.00 – 5.00 woodwind and brass, both with Simon Rattle

Friday
6.30 – 9.30   Full orchestra Simon Rattle

Saturday
2.30   Full orchestra with Simon Rattle preceding a concert at 4.00 in the Great Hall, Goldsmiths' College.

As well as covering the standard classical and romantic repertoire it was felt that the orchestra should become acquainted with and play a good deal of contemporary music. Edwin

Roxburgh, himself a composer, rehearsed and conducted an extremely demanding and difficult programme:

Goehr	Metamorphosis
Varèse	Integrales
Stravinsky	Symphonies of wind instruments
Schoenberg	Kammersymphonie, op.9b

Throughout the following week the orchestra worked with Vernon Handley, who was a regular visitor and particularly helpful to the orchestra on every occasion. His programme this time consisted of Leonora Overture No.3 by Beethoven, Moeran's Symphony in G minor and Dvorak's Symphony No.7. The concert at the end of the week was in Greenwich Borough Hall, an excellent hall seating about 1000. This is the hall where the orchestra rehearsed and gave the majority of their concerts.

A week or so later, because on this occasion Colin Davis could only come for two days, the orchestra had several preparatory rehearsals before he arrived to conduct Sibelius Symphony No.1 and the Symphonic Variations by Dvorak.

The orchestra's first Concert in the Goldsmiths' Great Hall was given before an invited audience at the end of the seventh week. There had been three days of full orchestra and sectional rehearsals with John Forster, and two days when the strings worked with Manoug Parikian and the wind with Jack Brymer, before Charles Mackerras arrived. He then had three more rehearsals with the full orchestra followed by the concert:

Walton	Overture Portsmouth Point
Elgar	Enigma Variations
Brahms	Symphony No.1

During that first year the orchestra played a repertoire ranging from Handel to Lutoslawski and Messiaen, including opera in collaboration with the National Opera Studio and the Guildhall School of Music and light music. It recorded for broadcasting in the BBC studios at Maida Vale with Gennadi Rozhdestvensky, and a concert in the Greenwich Festival conducted by Sir Charles Groves was recorded for Capital Radio. An exciting element in the final term was when the orchestra went to France to take part in the Saintes Music Festival, where they gave two performances and recorded the Brahms German Requiem. They then went to

Angoulême to give another performance of the Requiem in the Cathedral and to Royan to play an orchestral programme.

Every year, in the second half of the last term we held the Diploma exams. There were four elements: the performance of a piece of one's own choice – a movement from a sonata or concerto, or some other suitable piece; the performance of any of the passages for their instrument from a number of extracts from the orchestral repertoire performed during the year, received a few weeks before the exam, as selected by the examiners, and some sight reading. This was a demanding experience for the students. They had to face two of the very best players of their instrument, just as they would when auditioning for one of the orchestras, as well as myself.

The fourth element was a 5000 word essay on any topic concerned with music, or a five-minute composition or arrangement. The 5000 word essay was the cause of a good deal of unhappiness to the students and a good deal of trouble to me. Many of the students who had been to music college objected to what they felt was an imposition and quite unnecessary for someone taking a course preparing them for the orchestral profession. The students who had been to university (always a minority) had no difficulty in writing an essay, but the majority of the students at the NCOS had been to a music college where the curriculum does not as a rule require any written work and had not done any for the past four years since they had left school. They were therefore quite unprepared for this element of the diploma. Even at school they had never had to write a self-motivated piece of this length. However, the University of London Delegacy insisted on this academic element if they were to award the Diploma. Assistance from lecturers in the large and excellent Goldsmiths' College music department was available, but the difference between their much more academic approach to music and the usually wholly practical performance orientated attitude of the members of the orchestra did not often lead to a very collaborative relationship.

Despite my warnings, every year one or two students, finding they had nothing original to say themselves, resorted, often in desperation, to copying fairly lengthy passages from books on their chosen topic. Of course, the well-read lecturers quickly recognised the source of their plagiarism. In academia this was considered a capital offence and could well lead to the dismissal of the guilty student. Within a culture in which to speak and write well is considered far more valuable than any manual skill, however much artistry is involved, the status of musicians has suffered. A good many of the most outstanding artists, used to expressing themselves through music, often have considerable difficulty in expressing their feelings in words. This has been more of a problem in Britain than in some other countries where there are courses within the universities for those wanting to become performing musicians.

It was generally recognised that it would have been absurd for a student who had done extremely well in all the practical elements to fail the Diploma because of failure in the written element. Equally, it would be ridiculous if a student whose practical work had been poor, but whose written work had been excellent, received a Diploma. In the end I was able to persuade the University that neither failure nor success in the written element should be a deciding factor in obtaining the Diploma.

During the first term of year two, on the 4th and 5th December 1980, the NCOS faced its most severe test. Her Majesty's Inspectors from the Department of Education and Science (DES) arrived. If the University of London was to continue to validate the Diploma it was essential that the Inspectors gave the NCOS a satisfactory report. Fortunately they did. Their conclusion was:

It is gratifying to be able to record the successful launching of this enterprise, brought into being in the face of considerable odds. In these early days, the main emphasis has been upon securing adequate recruitment, establishing vocational credibility and maintaining financial solvency. No doubt, as the Centre develops, and as the profession learns to accept better trained entrants into orchestral work, it will prove possible to extend some more of the educational aspects of the course without changing its essentially vocational nature. Meanwhile, the formation of the Centre is seen as an ambitious and imaginative initiative which deserves continuing support; even in the fourth term of its life, the results already achieved must be particularly encouraging to those whose faith and vision have followed this venture through to fruition.

Naturally, everyone was delighted. Coupled with the enthusiasm of the conductors who came to work with the orchestra everyone was happy. Simon Rattle in a video interview made for Goldsmiths' said, 'At the colleges playing in the orchestra seems to be something to be avoided …. Here, for the first time people leaving college will get a proper orchestral background instead of having to make mistakes … the people they've got working here and the schedule is absolutely marvellous. Any orchestra that has any sense would take a good deal of notice that students have been here. It is very exciting. There's no other training anywhere else in the world like this.' Colin Davis said 'To give these kids this kind of opportunity seems to me to be invaluable. The opportunity to find out about themselves – whether they really want to do this. The good ones will get tremendous confidence from doing this kind of thing.' Speaking about string players in particular he said, 'It will help them accommodate themselves not only musically but humanly.'

However, as Director I was already grappling with insufficient financial resources and a lack of co-operation from the managements of the orchestras and the organisation to which they belonged. These problems were to plague the NCOS throughout its existence.

Another problem was finding somewhere for the orchestra to rehearse and give concerts as Goldsmiths' Great Hall was in constant use. The orchestra gave about three or four concerts a year there. Fortunately Lewisham Council came to our rescue by making Greenwich Borough Hall, always referred to as GBH, available. This provided the NCOS with a 'home' where the orchestra could rehearse and give concerts and where it also had a room that doubled as the office for the personnel manager and librarian. However, it had the disadvantage that there were no other rooms in which sectional rehearsals could take place. The rooms really needed to be in the same building as the hall so that after each section – the violins, violas, cellos and basses – had been with their individual coach they could come together to rehearse in the hall. The same applied to the woodwind and brass sections. Accommodation in other places was found, but it was never entirely satisfactory.

The NCOS thought that it had solved the problem when I learned about the Blackheath Halls, only a mile or two away, in a much more salubrious neighbourhood. From 1939, throughout the war and until 1960, it had served as offices for various government departments and then for a further 16 years it did no more than house thousands of National Insurance cards. In fact it had not been used as a concert hall for more than 40 years. When I first saw the Hall it was empty and in a state of serious neglect. Vandals had taken the lead off the roof and removed, with some violence, the central heating radiators. Evidence of pigeons was thick throughout the building.

The Hall, a fine 19th century building, had been opened in 1895 by Lord Hugh Cecil. It had a main concert hall seating about 850, a recital room seating 300, a music room, excellent for lectures and a number of smaller rooms in which small groups could rehearse. From 1895 until the outbreak of the First World War, many major artists had appeared there; Sir Edward Elgar, Mark Hambourg, Clara Butt, Mischa Elman, Vladimir de Pachmann, Fritz Kreisler, Wilhelm Backhaus, Coleridge-Taylor and many others.

It was clear this building would provide all the accommodation the NCOS needed for rehearsal and performance and there would also be enough suitable rooms for the occasions when the orchestra divided into a number of groups for sectional rehearsals. Additionally, the offices, library and storage of instruments, as well as some social facilities for the orchestra could be in the same building. By 1985 the NCOS had reclaimed the Hall from the derelict condition in which they had found it, and it was widely reported that they would be taking up residence in 1987. However it was not to be. There were too many objections from local residents that it would not be sufficiently available to them for a wide variety of activities to take place, such as art exhibitions, workshops, film shows and several other activities, because of the amount of use the NCOS required. This severely restricted fund raising and the whole project collapsed.

Some years later the money was found to open the halls to the public. Though for a time chamber concerts were given there and sometimes the main hall was used for recording sessions by the London orchestras, it was never available to the local residents as they had wished and the venture proved to be uneconomic. The hall again became empty. It has now been acquired by Trinity College of Music, which after leaving London is resident in the truly splendid Old Royal Naval College in nearby Greenwich.

So, the NCOS remained in GBH, rehearsing and giving concerts. But, in order to give those on the course an overall experience of the life of a professional orchestral musician, they were also given the opportunity of playing in the opera pit, in the broadcasting studio and of experiencing the tension felt when the red light goes on in the recording studio and having to play the same difficult passage over and over again.

Playing in the orchestra did not yet usually require an orchestral musician to have to stand up and play as a soloist – since then educational work has played an increasingly important part in maintaining many orchestra's finances and so this has become very much more common. Now the musicians in a symphony orchestra, and not only the principals, frequently go into schools in small groups and are often required also to play a solo role. Back in the 1980s it was only the principals who would be asked to demonstrate the sound and range of their instrument and perhaps play a short solo passage in a work to be performed in the programme. The need to assume a soloist's stance, if only for a very short time, only really occurred at children's concerts when introducing the instruments of the orchestra. The NCOS established a relationship with several schools in the neighbourhood and gave regular concerts especially devised for them. For part of the concert some of the children were encouraged to come and sit in the orchestra next to the musicians. At the end of the concert the children had the opportunity of meeting members of the orchestra and have a closer look at the instruments and be shown how they worked. Sometimes a few of the braver musicians allowed the children to handle and even try to play a few notes on their instruments.

To play in the orchestra pit is quite a different experience from playing on the concert platform, both musically and psychologically. I never came to enjoy it as much as playing on the concert platform or in the studio. Some musicians prefer it. For the first few years the NCOS could only give the student the impression of playing in the opera pit. The orchestra would be joined by students at the National Opera Studio to perform a concert version of extracts from the operatic repertoire – arias, duets, trios, etc. on stage – while the orchestra was assembled on the floor below the level of the stage.

From 1983 onwards the orchestra was invited each year to take part in the Brighton Festival to play for a production put on by the New Sussex Opera Company. There were always four performances during the Festival which were performed in the Dome, a large hall where I had played many times in the past with the Brighton Philharmonic Orchestra. Over the years the NCOS took part in productions of two Verdi operas, *Aida* and *The Masked Ball*, *The Flying Dutchman* by Wagner, Gounod's *Faust*, *Andrea Chenier* by Giordano and *Benvenuto Cellini* by Berlioz.

The orchestra stayed in Brighton for a week taking part in other events in addition to playing for the opera. As well as the experience of being away from 'home' for a week and so as to prepare the young musicians for the joys of touring, the orchestra went on a short tour in England or abroad each year and did several 'one night stands' giving concerts some distance from London. This meant leaving quite early in the morning travelling by coach, a short rehearsal, a concert and then returning home at midnight or later. This gave rise to some complaining. During their professional life they were likely to find they would do perhaps three or four or more of these 'out of town' engagements on succeeding days, often much less enjoyable.

The most demanding performances the orchestra gave were those that were broadcast either in the BBC studios or relayed from one of their concerts. These were fully professional in the sense that they had to stand comparison with the BBC orchestras and relays of concerts by the major orchestras. As a rule the BBC chose unusual repertoire so as not to clash with or create too great a comparison with other orchestras. The broadcasts were usually with very good conductors. There were a number with Gennadi Rozhdestvensky, Sir Charles Groves and George Hurst, but probably the most exciting was the broadcast of Sir Michael Tippett's 4th Symphony, conducted by Sir Colin Davis.

With financial assistance from the Holst Foundation it was possible to instigate a composer-in-residence scheme. Each year from 1983 onwards a composer had the opportunity of working with the orchestra. Their compositions were included in NCOS concerts and at least one was always broadcast. Mark-Anthony Turnage related particularly well with the orchestra, perhaps because he was not much older than the players at that time. He dedicated his *Ekaya* to Adrian Leaper and 'my friends at NCOS'. He said, 'I think this course has changed a lot of my attitudes and prejudices towards players, and vice versa.' This was part of the intention of the scheme though it was not always as successful as it was with Turnage. A few of the young composers behaved as if the members of the orchestra were keys on a piano and could be treated as unfortunate necessities. For their part the orchestra did not always show sufficient understanding of the compositions that were still immature and perhaps contained impractical or impossible passages. Another composer who did have a good relationship with the orchestra was John Woolrich. Both Turnage and Woolrich have gone on to have very successful composing careers.

I was very keen that the young musicians at the NCOS should have the opportunity to experience the music of other cultures – Chinese, Indian, Asian, and African – at first hand. I especially remember an outstanding Chinese musician from Hong Kong who came to play to us. She was a virtuoso on the *pipa,* a beautiful Chinese pear-shaped fretted lute that sounds like a very delicate guitar. On another occasion two fine Indian musicians came to play to the members of the orchestra. For me the best of all was when we were allowed to play and receive instruction on the Gamelan at the Royal Festival Hall. This was a wonderful experience and an insight into a quite different kind of orchestra. It is made up of gongs, metallophones, xylophones, cymbals and drums and involves a different way of making music collectively.

It was a great disappointment to me that on every occasion when there was an event of this kind or when I had invited someone to give a talk on various aspects of music – jazz, changes in performance style, the music of other cultures and times – a number of those on the course were so disinterested that they did not attend. Between 1979 and 1990 their number increased. When I asked them why they had not taken advantage of learning more about other kinds of music they replied that they did not think these events furthered their future professional prospects and that they could spend their time more profitably by practising their instrument. I was sad to see a less vocational and a more commercial approach to being a musician develop as we progressed through the 1980s. On one occasion, when I was complaining to Philip Jones, the very distinguished trumpet player and Head of the Wind department at the Guildhall School of Music, that only about sixty per cent of the students attended these events, he said that I was very fortunate and that he was lucky if twenty per cent of his students attended similar events. Friends in other professions told me they were experiencing the same thing.

By 1986 I realised that the fees to conductors and coaches were continuing to rise as were staff salaries. Unless the income the NCOS was receiving could be increased it would be impossible to maintain the course at an acceptable standard for more than a couple of years. I knew that the colleges of music had already found that students from overseas were keen to come to Britain to study and that the fees they could be charged could be higher than those for British students.

When I expressed my fears for the future to the NCOS management committee and suggested that perhaps we should follow the colleges' lead I met with considerable opposition from the BBC, the MU and the ABO representatives. They had always been opposed to the NCOS accepting more than one or two overseas students each year, and then only if there was not a suitable British student. I felt I had to persist, as unless they could propose another method by which our income could be increased, the future looked very bleak. Perhaps the BBC, MU and the TV companies could increase their financial support for the Centre? Or the committee knew of some other source of funding that might be available. Otherwise the only solution seemed to be to try to attract more students from other countries. In the end it was reluctantly agreed that I should visit a number of conservatoires to find out what orchestral training was being provided elsewhere and what demand there might be for the course we were offering and if possible to encourage that demand.

Visiting conservatoires

I already knew about the situation in many of the European countries but little about the Scandinavian countries. I therefore decided I should begin by visiting four, Denmark, Sweden, Finland and Norway, and then return to base for two weeks to see that everything was going well with the course before setting off for the next four and a half weeks to visit the USA, Canada, New Zealand, Australia, Hong Kong, China, Japan and Taiwan. Unlike the many years I was in an orchestra and at the mercy of orchestral managements, this time I made all the travel and hotel arrangements myself. Though my schedule included visiting as many conservatoires and meeting as many people as possible in a short time (the NCOS Management Committee were naturally anxious that I should not turn these trips into an extended holiday), it was the most enjoyable and stress-free foreign travel I have ever undertaken. This was partly because I had decided to take my wife with me, at my own expense. Not only would this be a wonderful opportunity for her but I would be spared the loneliness so often experienced by soloists and conductors when travelling and having to stay in many hotels on their own.

In 1987, in mid-January, we set off for Denmark. I had not been to Scandinavia before and though I knew it would be cold at this time of year I was unprepared for just how cold it proved to be. I was surprised when I looked out of the hotel bedroom window in Copenhagen to see a ferryboat stranded, stuck in the ice on a canal near the hotel. In fact, a couple of days later it was my intention to take the hydrofoil to Malmö in Sweden, a short sea journey. But when we arrived at the hydrofoil we found that because it was so cold the sea was completely frozen over and we had instead to go on a ferryboat with two ice-breaking tugs dragging us through the ice. It was a wonderful, magical journey. During the two weeks in Scandinavia we experienced snowstorms and blizzards – on the train journey from Stockholm to Gavle the wind was so strong that it brought the overhead wires down and we were stuck there for several hours. Norway and Finland proved to be just as cold – not the dreadful damp cold we experience in Britain, generally accompanied by grey overcast skies, but bracing and with blue sky and the bright sunlight making the snow sparkle.

While I was making the arrangements for the tour I had been to the British Council Office in London to discuss the possibility of receiving assistance from their officers in the countries I was about to visit. Until then I had not had any dealings with the British Council and was delighted to find that I was met by charming, well-informed and extremely helpful members of the Council wherever I went. The first time I experienced this was in Copenhagen. I had had a meeting with the vice-principal of the conservatoire and been disappointed to find that there did not appear to be much enthusiasm for sending any of their students to the NCOS. However, James Moore the British Council Officer in Copenhagen raised my spirits. He was keen that the NCOS orchestra should visit Denmark and said he would help if our programmes included some music by younger British composers. He introduced me to an agent who was also keen the orchestra should visit and thought that some funding for an NCOS tour could be achieved. It would be wonderful if this could be arranged and this might well lead to the orchestra's performances inspiring some of the best students in Denmark deciding to come to the NCOS.

I found the conditions in the concert halls and conservatoires in the Scandinavia countries I visited to be excellent, especially so in Sweden. The Music School in Malmö, where I met the Assistant Director Martin Mastinson, was new and purpose built. The very fine concert hall, seating about 450, had a sound/vision control-room and was fully 'miked' as well as being extremely comfortable. But for me, used to the less than satisfactory teaching accommodation in the conservatoires in Britain, it was the teaching rooms that were most impressive. Each room had been built to acoustic principles with a sloping ceiling and non-symmetrical walls. The acoustics could be easily adjusted electronically; the floating ceiling panels could be moved to suit whichever instrument was being taught – making it less resonant for a trumpet lesson than one for the guitar. Each room had state of the art recording facilities. Equally valuable was the complete sound separation between the rooms and the corridors. In addition there were many practice rooms for the 450 students who also had the use of a good library, canteen and storage for the larger instruments.

The beautiful concert hall in Malmö seating 1300 was only a year old in 1988 when we were there. The conditions for the orchestra on the platform and back stage are quite remarkable. On the stage the height, angle of the back and seat of each player's chair was adjustable and there were Perspex, transparent baffles for those sitting in front of the brass and percussion players, at that time only used at rehearsals. Backstage the members of the orchestra had ample room for changing and resting.

In Gothenburg, a four-hour train journey from Malmö, we were met at the station and whisked off to the University for lunch. The teachers in Gothenburg already knew about the NCOS as several of their students had gained entry to the NCOS course in previous years and they were keen for us to hear some more of their pupils. I auditioned several who would come the following year to audition again in England for a place on the course.

The co-principal clarinet in the Gothenburg Orchestra, Urban Claesson, who had been at the NCOS only a couple of years before invited us to the orchestra's rehearsal the following morning. After the rehearsal he and another ex-NCOS student Roger Carlssen, now the principal percussionist in the orchestra took us out for a splendid lunch. It was most rewarding for me to meet these two young men again, now established and well regarded, so soon after I had known them only as students.

In Stockholm I auditioned a number of potential students who later gained places at the NCOS. Several are now working in one or other of the orchestras – one is now the principal clarinet in the very good radio orchestra that also regularly gives concerts in Stockholm. The next day to Gavle a town several hours by train from Stockholm to meet an ex-pupil of mine who was now principal clarinet in the Gavle Orchestra. That evening we went to one of their concerts. Again, a delightful concert hall, and a good, though small orchestra. After the concert we had to return to Stockholm. It was well after midnight by the time we arrived back; the streets were deserted and there was a blizzard that made being able to see where you were going extremely difficult. As we did not know Stockholm and neither of us has any sense of direction, we wondered if we would ever find our hotel. By chance we did, which was fortunate as the next morning I had arranged to listen to some more student auditions before we left in the afternoon for Helsinki.

In a country with a population of only 5 million Finland has a remarkable number of orchestras: twelve are professional and about the same number are semi-professional. I had hoped that we might be able to recruit a number of students, but it seemed that at that time some of those who did not go to the Sibelius Academy probably went to Russia to study. The standard of the players in the Academy Orchestra, which the Rector Ellen Urho, in charge at the Sibelius Academy, took me to listen to, was good. (Recently Finland has produced an astonishing number of very talented young conductors).

That same evening we left Helsinki to fly to Oslo. The next morning, before meeting the Dean of Studies Einer Solbu at the conservatoire there was time to explore this charming city. I already knew Solbu from my involvement in ISME, the International Society for Music in Education. In 1986 the NCOS orchestra gave two concerts at their Biennial Conference held that year in Innsbruck. During the two days I spent in Oslo I heard a number of the students. Again the standard of performance was generally very good. My last day in Norway was in Bergen where it proved impossible to arrange to hear any students in the short time I was able to stay there. As a consolation the Principal of the conservatoire Rolf Davidson took us to lunch at a wonderful fish restaurant in the Old City before we caught a plane back to London.

It had been a hectic but enjoyable two weeks during which as well as going to the conservatoires and concert halls I had also visited a number of the Music Information Centres. These were all very well appointed with informed and helpful staff and had a wealth of sheet music and scores as well as many recordings of solo, chamber and orchestral music, jazz and popular music, particularly by contemporary Scandinavian composers. I felt I had made some very useful contacts that could lead to an increasing number of young musicians applying to the NCOS after they had completed their conservatoire courses, but who still needed to hone their orchestral skills.

On the second leg of my travels I was looking forward to learning more about the conditions in conservatoires and finding out what degree of preparation for the orchestra was available around the world. Equally important, perhaps even more so, I wanted to learn to what extent it might be possible to interest those who might influence suitable students to apply to spend a year at the NCOS.

In New York I met the members of the National Orchestra Association who expressed interest in the NCOS. It seemed that the opportunities for gaining some experience was greater in the music faculties within the universities than in some of the conservatoires. This was confirmed when I met the President of the San Francisco Conservatory of Music. His views on preparing musicians for an orchestral career was very similar to that held in

Britain at that time: though not expressed openly, in fact, the orchestra was really seen as the last refuge for those not good enough to be soloists, chamber music players or teachers.

My visit to the wonderful Banff Centre for Continuing Education was delightful and inspiring. An arts, cultural and education institution, usually just referred to as the Banff Centre is situated in the Banff National Park in the Canadian Rockies. Here, in beautiful, peaceful surroundings (the first morning we were there I opened the bedroom curtains to find two moose quietly browsing just outside) there are facilities for writers and composers to stay for a while, away from the stress of city life. There were also courses for classical and jazz musicians, orchestral and ensemble courses under the direction of outstanding musicians. Tom Ralston and his wife, in charge of all the music activities introduced me to a number of performers and teachers that enabled me to make contacts that would be valuable in the future.

We then flew down to Los Angeles, before flying to Auckland, New Zealand, a twenty-hour flight, the longest I have ever undertaken. We spent four days in New Zealand meeting musicians and administrators in Auckland, Wellington and Christchurch in the universities and music colleges. I found that they were making an effort to provide some orchestral training and had a small post-conservatoire orchestra in Wellington supported by the radio authorities. Unfortunately, a lack of sufficient funds only allowed for a small orchestra that could really only tackle the chamber orchestra repertoire satisfactorily, and not long after my visit this brave attempt was obliged to close.

My next stop was Sydney, Australia. At that time there were ABC (Australian Broadcasting Company) symphony orchestras in the main cities – Sydney, Melbourne, Adelaide, Perth, Queensland – and smaller orchestras elsewhere. A few British musicians had gone out to join some of these orchestras and quite a number of Australian musicians had come to Britain, either to study or join the profession. As a result I already had contacts with teachers in the university, conservatoire and within the profession. It seemed that there might be a good chance that some young musicians wanting to become orchestral musicians would be interested in coming to the NCOS.

We had some free time in Sydney and as the weather was very warm we took the opportunity to take the ferry across to Manley, about a half-hour journey. In the evening we went to the Sydney Opera House to see *Eugene Onegin* for which the principal of the conservatoire had booked us the best seats in the house – his. But the very fine building that is called the Sydney Opera House turned out, in fact, to contain an excellent, large concert hall and a small theatre where the opera performances took place. The performance was rather a disappointment (*Eugene Onegin* is one of my favourite operas). The acoustic was not good and some of the singing was not of a very high standard.

Hong Kong

From Sydney we flew to Hong Kong where we stayed for just one night on the way to China. I had been to Hong Kong on two previous occasions. The first time in April 1981 was when I was invited by the Royal Hong Kong Jockey Club Music Fund to audition some young musicians with a view to them coming to the NCOS. The Jockey Club was incredibly rich and supported many charities. One was to pay for young Chinese musicians to go on to advanced music education not available in Hong Kong at that time. Several students did come to the NCOS. I realised that unlike the conservatoires that could accept a student on the recommendation of a distinguished teacher in another country, the NCOS had to take much greater care in selecting which students it could accept. A student accepted by a music college may prove to be less talented than expected or even not satisfactory in other ways. Accepting someone into an orchestra is very different. It only needs one player to wreck a whole string section; two or three can have a profound effect on the standard of the whole orchestra.

The day after I had returned to the National Centre, after the auditions at the Jockey Club, I received a telegram from the Hong Kong Philharmonic Orchestra (HKPO) asking me to return as soon as possible as they were experiencing some major problems in the orchestra. The most serious was that the orchestra were refusing to play for their principal conductor. He was Ling Tung, a Chinese-American who had been a violinist in the Philadelphia Orchestra. He later decided to be a conductor and for many years from 1968 until 1996 was the conductor of the Grand Teton Music Festival, held each summer in Wyoming. As about a third of the Hong Kong Philharmonic were Americans and another third Hong Kong Chinese he must have seemed to those making the appointment a good choice of conductor.

I already knew Ling Tung because it was with his co-operation that the New Philharmonia was able to regain the use of its original name, Philharmonia. When in 1964 Walter Legge decided to disband the Philharmonia and take the orchestra's name as well, for reasons that remain obscure the name was acquired by Mr Tung. Many years later when the orchestra learned about this it negotiated with him and in 1977, in return for being engaged by the orchestra to do a Royal Festival Hall concert and make two recordings, the Rakhmaninov Second Symphony and *Don Juan* by Richard Strauss, it was agreed that we could have our old name back. As a conductor he was competent enough but uninspiring.

In 1980 he was appointed the principal conductor of the HKPO. However by the following year it seems he had upset both the Chinese and the American musicians to such an extent that they were refusing to play for him and demanding his immediate dismissal. None of the members of the General Committee of the Hong Kong Philharmonic Society Committee had either the experience or the understanding needed to manage an orchestra, particularly in a crisis of this kind and did not feel sufficiently confident in their General Manager. In desperation they invited me to Hong Kong to try to sort things out.

The members of the Committee, which unusually combined both administrative and executive powers, were mainly appointed by the Hong Kong Government, (at that time Hong Kong was still a British Crown Colony) and the Hong Kong Urban Council, plus several wealthy British and Chinese directors of large companies. Nearly all the funding for the orchestra was provided by the Urban Council and the Government.

It was not until July that I was able to respond to their request and return to Hong Kong. The brief they sent me was, to say the least, somewhat daunting.

1. To review the day-to-day operation of the orchestra.
2. To assess the problems which have arisen at the player's level and to put forward proposals for solutions.

3. To review the management structure and responsibilities in respect of the operation of the orchestra.
4. To review the salary structure within the orchestra and put forward proposals for simplifying the structure and eliminating the anomalies.
5. To advise on the inter-relationship between the General Committee, General Manager and Music Director, and on the role that a new Music Director should be expected to play.
6. To advise on the terms of reference for the International Music Advisory Panel.
7. To give an assessment of the present standard of the orchestra in international terms and its strengths and weaknesses.
8. To examine: a) the role and contribution of the Philharmonic in the development of music in Hong Kong at all levels; b) the orchestra's declared policy of encouraging local players and to discuss with the Music Office and the Conservatory how this policy can best be achieved.

I soon found that John Duffus, their General Manager, was both charming and extremely capable but not strong enough to deal with the high-powered members of the Committee. They were all used to exercising authority. and wanted to make the decisions as to how the orchestra should be run. They were unwilling to let their manager do his job without interfering, believing that their ability to be successful in their particular field of administration gave them the skills required to run an orchestra. This attitude has at times created similar problems for orchestras and opera houses elsewhere over the years.

It was only going to be a year after my visit that talks were to begin between the British Government and the People's Republic of China that would lead to Hong Kong ceasing to be a British Crown Colony and those on the Committee representing the Urban Council were already keen to start exercising increased control of everything in Hong Kong. In the past, when I had been in discussion with politicians, both Conservative and Labour, such as Edward Heath (later Sir Edward), Sebastian Coe (now Lord Coe), Edward Short and Tony Banks, I had sheltered to some extent within a group. Now, in Hong Kong I was in a much trickier political situation and having to deal with conflicting cultures and the political aspirations of the Chinese and British government representatives on my own. My meetings with Sir Murray MacLehose the Governor (now Lord MacLehose), and the other civil servants were relatively straightforward, but when I met members of the Legislative Council and especially the Urban Council I needed to take much more care.

As usual, the discontent in the orchestra was not only their feelings about the conductor, though I have always found that if members of an orchestra are happy in their music making – and that most often depends on the conductor – other problems can be dealt with fairly easily. This was a classic case, containing all the problems I had seen in other orchestras (but never all together in one orchestra), in a tiny country with two cultures.

The orchestra complained that the principal conductor had far too many rehearsals during which he kept repeating the same passages over and over for no apparent purpose and without improving the performance. Also that the guest conductors were not of a standard the orchestra felt was suitable. Though the orchestra was capable of giving satisfactory performances with a good conductor who understood the standard he could get from a smallish regional orchestra where some players were of modest accomplishment, Ling Tung seemed to have arrived with expectations far beyond what was possible and without the skill to make the best of what was available.

They also complained that player/management communication was poor, which was not surprising as the librarian and the orchestral/personnel manager were both also playing members of the orchestra.

The musicians who had recently joined the orchestra, from the US, Britain and the Philippines were finding that the cost of housing was so high that they suffered financial hardship and this had led to various 'deals' having been arranged creating conflict within the orchestra itself, some musicians feeling that they were not being treated as well as others.

Coming from outside Hong Kong and with some reputation as a trouble-shooter the Committee allowed me to give them rather a hard time. The first thing they had to do was to recognise that they could not manage the orchestra themselves. Their task was to appoint the right people within the management structure, try out a number of guest conductors before appointing a principal conductor, or if the right person could be found – they are very rare – a musical director. He should not be involved in the management of the orchestra, as at present, and should only be concerned with musical matters. I persuaded the Committee that for the next nine months they should give John Duffus the chance to do his job without interference (I was confident that he could), engage a librarian and an orchestral manager and regularise the pay structure on a much fairer basis.

In most countries the members of orchestras belong to a Union or Association of some kind that conducts negotiations on fees, conditions and complaints on their behalf. This was impractical in Hong Kong as virtually all the professional musicians were either already in the HKPO or were those being used to supplement the orchestra. I suggested that a proper orchestral committee be formed. There had been a committee of sorts but no defined pathway between it and the management. This had led as always to the situation getting out of hand and turning into a public wrangle. A small committee should be elected by the members of the orchestra to meet the General Committee on a regular basis, at least three times a year and these meetings should not be seen only as an opportunity for expressing discontent. Rather, they should be the way in which players and management could learn more about each other's problems, aspirations and intentions. The orchestra should be encouraged to make recommendations and feel that they and their employers were engaged in a joint enterprise to make the orchestra and its performances as good as possible.

Finally, and essential for the future, better opportunities for local players must be created. Much improved instrumental teaching was needed – they should use the best players in the orchestra (mainly American) – and they should encourage as many Hong Kong musicians as possible to join the orchestra. Because the salaries for Chinese players was so low the best local players were leaving for better-paid employment elsewhere.

For the next few years I was retained in a rather informal way as a consultant. I was surprised (and delighted because it is so infrequent) that nearly all the recommendations I made in my report were implemented.

The Chinese Orchestra

The Hong Kong Philharmonic Orchestra was not the only orchestra in Hong Kong. For the Urban Council the Hong Kong Chinese Orchestra was probably more important. The first large folk instrument ensemble, The Broadcasting Company of China Chinese Folk Orchestra (now the China Broadcasting Chinese Orchestra), was created in China in 1935 and emulated the Western symphony orchestra.

By the time the Hong Kong Chinese Orchestra was established in 1977 the instruments included both traditional and modernised Chinese instruments that could now play a chromatic scale, as well as a few suitable western instruments. In addition to the arrangements of folk melodies the repertoire consisted of many new compositions, overtures, symphonies and concertos, often based on traditional melodies but increasingly using western harmonic and rhythmic techniques.

The orchestra is extremely popular and an important part of the musical life of Hong Kong. Some idea of the interest in traditional Chinese instruments is illustrated by two remarkable events. In 2001 there was a mass performance by one thousand *erhu* players of *Music for a Thousand Strings* and then in 2003 three thousand Hong Kong citizens came together to play a drum piece *The Earth shall Move.*

The instruments in a Chinese orchestra are divided into four sections: bowed strings, plucked strings, wind and percussion. Until the Chinese orchestra was created music in China was normally played by small groups or by solo instrumentalists following an oral tradition and using the pentatonic scale. Unlike the usual folk groups the members of a Chinese orchestra sit in a semi-circle and follow a conductor and play from written music. Whereas the normal ensembles would have only one of each instrument, these orchestras have a number of the bowed and plucked string instruments.

In China with its many regional music traditions, thousands of years old, there are hundreds of different instruments made from a great variety of materials: metal, stone, clay, skin, silk, wood, gourd and bamboo. The instruments mainly used in the Chinese orchestra include several two-stringed bowed instruments of various sizes: the *erhu* and *banhu* (both roughly violin pitch), *zhonghu* (viola pitch), *gehu and digehu* (cello and bass); the plucked strings are the beautiful *pipa (or piba)*, a lute and the *ruan*, another lute, round like a banjo, but beautifully crafted and with a delicate tone; there are also two dulcimers, the *yangqin* played with two bamboo sticks, and the *zheng*.

The wind instruments are the *suona*, made of wood with a metal bell and a double-reed, a loud instrument, and two kinds of bamboo flute, the transverse *dizi*, and the end-blown *xiao*. Both these instruments come in several sizes. The *sheng*, in the West often called the Chinese mouth organ, has been known for more than 3000 years and is one of the oldest Chinese musical instruments. It usually has between 13-17 bamboo pipes of different lengths, each with a free reed made of brass, all mounted on a base which is traditionally a gourd-shaped, wooden wind-chest. Music is produced by blowing and sucking the air through a metal tube connected to the base. By virtue of its construction, this instrument is capable of playing up to six notes simultaneously. From the base the air is blown through the pipes and the player decides the notes to be played by pressing keys near the base. By covering two or more holes on various pipes, chords can be played, a technique used in most Chinese folk orchestras.

The traditional Chinese percussion instruments include gongs of many sizes, cymbals, bells and chimes made of clay, stone or metal; clappers and temple blocks and many kinds and sizes of drums. The modern Chinese orchestra can now also include as many of the percussion instruments used in a symphony orchestra as the composer wishes.

There are now similar orchestras to those in Hong Kong and China in Singapore, Taiwan, Australia, the USA and Canada; sometimes two orchestras will join together as the Symphonisches Orchester Zürich and the China Broadcasting Orchestra did to perform the *East West Symphony*. The modernisation of traditional Chinese instruments required by the China Broadcasting Orchestra in 1935 started the process by which Chinese music and Chinese instruments are now used in pop music and are a popular part of World Music. The instruments and style of performance have been westernised and commercialised in the same way as so much folk music has been.

Continuing my visits to conservatoires

It is only a two-hour flight from Hong Kong to Shanghai, but whereas in Hong Kong the shops were full and the roads frequently traffic-jammed with buses and cars, in Shanghai and Beijing in 1987 there were far fewer shops and very few cars. I remember only a few big Mercedes taxis and when we were in one it was hair-raising. The taxi-drivers threaded their way with astonishing skill within inches of the thousands of bicycles, sometimes with more than one rider. Frequently a small trailer will have been attached, often rather dilapidated, filled with vegetables, or second-hand furniture, pots and pans and other household bits and pieces, and even an elderly relative with their legs hanging over the tailgate.

Though we had booked our flights to and within China and made our own hotel arrangements in Beijing and Shanghai, contrary to what we had been told to expect we were never asked any questions and were able to roam freely in both cities. As soon as the young people serving in the shops and hotels realised we were English they were anxious to practise the English they had studied and, to our surprise, were quite open in their criticism of the current regime. The increasing criticism of the regime we heard in 1987 escalated and finally resulted in the tragic and terrible events in 1989 when the students demonstrated in Tiananmen Square.

On the Sunday we were in Beijing I had no meetings and so we took the opportunity to do some sightseeing. We hired a taxi at the hotel – it was not possible to hail one on the street. If one was visiting several places it was necessary to keep the taxi waiting at each place, perhaps for some time. We first went to an enormous market, even bigger than the Flea market in Paris. There were stalls selling everything – we bought a large tablecloth and twelve napkins all covered in beautifully embroidered strawberries for a fraction of what it would have cost in Britain. We then visited Tiananmen Square, where our very obliging taxi-driver took some photographs of us, one of me standing in front of a large portrait of Chairman Mao Tse-Tung and the Forbidden City (now called the Palace Museum). The Forbidden City, where an extraordinary collection of many thousands of wonderful works of art, paintings, ceramics and porcelain of the utmost delicacy, begun in the 10th century, had been housed for five hundred years until the Japanese invaded China in 1931, was now open to the public, though nearly entirely empty. To preserve it the entire collection had first been moved to Nanjing, then to Shanghai and then on to a remote village in the south. In 1949 when it was captured by the army of Chang Kai Shek, all but 700 items out of this enormous collection were packed into ten thousand crates and as Chang's army was forced to retreat from mainland China it was finally shipped to Taipei in Taiwan.

In the evening we went to a concert of Chinese music to which we had been invited by the Director of the British Council in Beijing. This was the real thing; not a Chinese orchestra, but a number of groups of four or five musicians and individual soloists and singers playing and singing traditional folk music as it had been played for hundreds of years. A delightful end to a wonderful day.

My visits to the conservatoires and orchestras in Shanghai and Beijing were extremely interesting and, again, surprising. I was told by the Director of the Shanghai Conservatory of Music and several professors that during the Mao regime it was forbidden for them to teach western instruments or play western music. They were not dismissed, nor did they cease to receive their salaries. But they were obliged to come to the conservatory every day to be lectured on the iniquity of their former ways and to be instructed in the basics of the communist philosophy. When I met them they were again teaching their instruments as they had done before Mao's injunction. The general standard of the students in both conservatoires was technically good, but their performances often seemed to lack any real understanding of the music. In Shanghai I was invited by Chen Xie-Yang, conductor and Music Director of the Shanghai Symphony Orchestra, to a rehearsal and then to a recording session the orchestra was doing that afternoon. The orchestra was not yet up to the standard of professional orchestras in the West. There were some good players, especially in the strings, but too many of the members of the woodwind and brass sections were not really quite good enough. Xie-Yang, who also conducted in Beijing, arranged for me to meet the conductor of the symphony orchestra of the Central Philharmonic Society, Han Zhong-jie, and to attend one of his rehearsals when I was in

Beijing. This was a better orchestra, probably comparable with one of the BBC's less good regional orchestras in the 1950s.

We would have liked to have been able to stay in China for longer. We found the people extremely friendly and though we knew only one word in Chinese, 'Kne-howe' (that is how we pronounced it), meaning 'Hello' or 'Good day', we managed by gesture and in one way or another to communicate with people in what felt like a very relaxed atmosphere in both Shanghai and Beijing. I was invited to listen to some young musicians in their homes and found that the living conditions were, by our standards, quite appalling. A typical flat consisted of two small rooms and a tiny kitchen. The communal bathroom and toilet facilities were shared with perhaps five or six other flats. Each of these very small apartments with such limited space might be shared by three generations; the husband and wife, their children and their own parents.

When we arrived in Japan we were to find that everything was very different. As our taxi hurtled towards Tokyo from the airport, surrounded by large cars – no bicycles here – the meter recording the cost of our journey also hurtled forward. I wondered how long our money would last out. In Beijing the cost of a taxi for a whole morning had been about £1.50. In Tokyo that amount of money took us less than a mile. I had been to Japan with the Philharmonia in 1970 when the orchestra took part in Expo '70 in Osaka and then went on to Tokyo to do two more concerts. Even then the Japanese were vying with America to be at the cutting-edge of technology; by 1987 it seemed to me that they had achieved their objective, and yet at the same time retained much of the old-world values that had so impressed me when I was there in 1970.

Without doubt the three conservatoires I visited while I was in Tokyo presented the greatest contrast with those in Britain or any I had seen anywhere else. All three, Kunitachi College of Music, the Toho Gakuen School of Music and the Musashino Academia Musicae were privately owned and appeared to be extremely wealthy. Each had its own beautiful concert hall, recording rooms and equipment and excellent facilities for students. The Kunitachi College of Music Library has a remarkable collection of Beethoven scores that includes more than a hundred original editions and a number of manuscripts. A framed copy of a manuscript letter in

Beethoven's hand, which I was given, has a prominent place in my music room. The Musashino Academia has a very large museum of 3000 musical instruments from all over the world. As well as a separate piano museum and collection of European instruments there are collections from Africa, Asia, the Middle East, Latin-America and Japan. The Toho Gakuen School concentrated on inviting outstanding composers and performers such as Aaron Copland, Henri Dutilleux and Heinz Holliger. More recently in 2001 the Maazel/Vilar conducting competition was held at the School, using the college orchestra.

At all three I was treated as a visiting celebrity, fetched from my hotel and returned in the biggest and most luxurious fitted cars I have ever been in, wined and dined and shown the glories of each institution. This was very enjoyable, but it was soon very clear that there was little chance that we would attract any of their students to the NCOS. They sent most of their best students, those destined to become soloists, to the USA and a few to Germany. Those students who would become orchestral musicians received considerable opportunities within their own college orchestras.

My visit to Taipei, in Taiwan was disappointing as far as recruiting students was concerned. When I met Dr Chang, the Director of the Theatre and Concert Hall and President of the National Taiwan Academy of Arts, it did not take me long to realise that there were not yet any young musicians ready to benefit from anything the NCOS had to offer. But while we were in Taipei we had the opportunity to visit the National Palace Museum where the treasures captured by Chang Kai Shek's army in 1949 were housed. The National Palace Museum had been built as an exact replica of the Forbidden City in Beijing, where the treasures had been captured. There we saw a wonderful display of part of the collection – only a small part because it is so large that there is not sufficient room to display it all at once. It is quite incredible that the delicate Ming porcelain and other beautiful china ornaments, cups, jugs and plates survived undamaged as they were transported so far over land and sea by the retreating army.

Before returning to England we went back to Hong Kong so that I could see how things had developed since I was there in 1981 and cement the relationships I had made previously. My first call was to the Music Office to meet the new secretary of the Jockey

Club, Mrs Ngai. She told me that the Hong Kong Academy for the Performing Arts, which had only been at the discussion stage in 1981, was now starting to accept students and that she had arranged for me to meet Basil Deane and Angus Watson, the recently appointed Principal, who would show me over the new building that was now nearly finished. The following day I had the opportunity to inspect what looked as if it would soon be ready. It was a fine building and I looked forward in the coming years to a number of their students applying to the NCOS and being supported by Jockey Club scholarships.

The manager of the Hong Kong Philharmonic was now Stephen Crabtree who had been principal Double Bass in the LPO and an old colleague of mine. The orchestra was now well established and its former troubles were forgotten. John Duffus the previous manager with whom I had remained in contact since I had played a part in helping him through a difficult time, was now a successful agent managing concerts and theatrical tours throughout the region.

To celebrate the end of our travels John Duffus took us for a fabulous Chinese meal on a Junk moored in the bay where not only did we eat and drink well but saw a virtuoso display of hand thrown noodles. The next day we set off on the long flight home.

Back at the National Centre again

Three days after my return in March it was time for the entrance auditions for the 1987/88 NCOS orchestra. We were still unaware that events beyond our control would mean that my travels had been too late to be of any lasting value and that at the end of the 1988/89 course the NCOS would be obliged to cease operating.

From the start it had been very difficult for students who had been at a music college to obtain a grant for a further year's study at the NCOS. The courses at the music colleges, which had formerly been for three years, had recently been extended to four so that throughout the 1980s, as Local Authorities experienced increasing financial restraint, it became even more difficult. After five or six years the way in which the commercial television companies had been organised changed and they were obliged to substantially reduce the financial assistance they had been providing. A year or so later it stopped altogether. The final blow was the BBC's decision that they could no longer afford to continue funding the NCOS. In relation to the size of their overall budget the amount they had been providing was minuscule, but its withdrawal was the death of the NCOS. With only the money it was receiving from the Musicians' Union, some fees from a minority of students and one or two private donations, it was impossible to continue.

There was also the problem that though those musicians in the orchestras, who were also professors at the music colleges, were happy to come and coach and constantly told me how valuable they thought the course was, they were reluctant to recommend their very best students to apply to join the course. I understood their reluctance. After all, some 36 years previously in 1942 aged 17, I had left the Royal College of Music to join the Wessex Orchestra. Now I was myself a professor at the RCM and I was suggesting to my pupils that it would, in 1979, be a good idea to have this 'one year in protected accommodation'. The standard and conditions that prevailed in 1942 had given me the opportunity to prepare myself so that in 1943 I was capable of holding down the job in the LPO. Before about 1960 this is how most young musicians gained experience in advance of joining one of the major orchestras: by playing in small light orchestras, theatres and by providing the 'stiffening' that most amateur orchestras required when they gave a concert.

The reluctance a good many teachers had was caused by their concern that if their pupils were not always available to apply for an orchestral post as soon as it appeared another opening might not come along. Unfortunately it was impossible for students to obtain a grant, or even a partial grant unless the NCOS made it a condition of the course that students must commit themselves for the whole year. Nor would it have been possible to run the orchestra if players were to be leaving – we did not have any funds to replace them.

Between 1980 and 1990 the amount of employment outside the pop industry continued to decline, and has continued to do so since then. Nonetheless, most of those who came to the NCOS did go on into the profession. I rarely go to a concert, to the theatre or anywhere there is music – opera, ballet or a musical – when I do not see a former NCOS student. Some of my own RCM students came to the NCOS and are in various orchestras. Now, in 2006, one is principal in the Bournemouth Symphony Orchestra, and one who was co-principal clarinet in the LSO is now principal in the Royal Opera House Orchestra. Other clarinettists who came to the NCOS are now principals in the Stockholm Radio Orchestra, the Malmö Philharmonic and the Royal Liverpool Philharmonic.

This attempt to establish advanced preparation for the orchestra probably failed because many of those who could have made it possible believed that the Youth Orchestras provided sufficient opportunities to gain orchestral experience. Funds were found to enable the Youth Orchestras to go on overseas tours and the National Youth Orchestra and European Youth Orchestra were allowed to take part in the Proms, but the MU would not allow the NCOS Orchestra to do so.

Naturally, everyone found the sight and sound of the very young musicians exciting and felt that those who had been at music college for four years should be ready to take their place in the profession. Though the orchestra managements did not think that the young musicians leaving music college were ready, they wanted the best of both worlds – further preparation for their orchestras, while at the same time being able to take anyone they wanted from the course whenever they wanted to. In the first year a few of the orchestra managements unwilling to wait until their chosen player had completed the course tried to induce them to leave. The young musicians, of course, wanted to start earning as soon as they could. It may be that the existence and subsequent demise of the NCOS did lead to the music colleges providing rather more and better orchestral experience than they had previously.

The NCOS would probably be providing the advanced education that many musicians still believe would be valuable for the very best students leaving music colleges if the grants for a further year's study had been made available and there had been sufficient money to replace students leaving the course. In 1989 there was another attempt to create preparation for the profession, not only in Britain but for young musicians throughout Europe.

The considerable reduction in the amount of freelance work in broadcasting, recording and casual concerts for orchestral musicians means that there is intense competition for the few openings in the orchestras as well as in the freelance sector and only the most outstanding instrumentalists can gain a foothold in the profession. Those that do are extremely gifted instrumentalists. They have to learn very quickly how to respond to the demands and pressures of life for an orchestral musician.

Competitions

As well as their concern for improved preparation for orchestral musicians the 1977 Calouste Gulbenkian Committee spent a great deal of time considering music education throughout the education system, in particularly the standard of instrumental teaching at all levels. In their opinion there were still not enough top class soloists being produced, even though the 1965 Calouste Gulbenkian report *Making Music* had resulted in a number of specialist schools being established in the years following the Report – the Purcell, Chetham's, Menuhin, Wells Cathedral and St. Mary's (in Scotland) schools. They felt that there should be earlier identification of talent and an increased number of specialist schools at primary and secondary level leading on to the Junior Departments at the music colleges.

Through my involvement in these discussions I became much more informed about music education in general even though I had learned quite a lot as a visiting lecturer at Middlesex University. While at the NCOS I was invited to take part in several forums on music education and to be a visiting speaker at several universities and colleges of education. I was also asked to be a member of the jury of a number of music festivals and competitions. Two of the most important were the BBC Young Musician of the Year and the Royal Overseas League.

The BBC hold preliminary auditions for the Young Musician of the Year all over the country where a great many young musicians are heard. I have only been involved in the final two rounds for both these competitions. For the earlier rounds there are juries for each category, keyboard, strings, woodwind, brass, and in the BBC competition also for percussion. The winners of each category then go on to the final, where they are pitted against each other to produce an outright winner. At the final the contestants must play a concerto with the orchestra before an audience as well as the judges.

By the mid-1980s the number and variety of competitions had increased and has continued to do so. There were competitions for composers, conductors, quartets and for ensembles of all kinds – some for young performers, sometimes very young, others for already established, or those hoping to become established performers. The rewards varied considerably from relatively small money prizes and trophies to awards that not only offered much larger financial inducements but opportunities to perform in major national and international venues. Whenever the question of the value of competitions arose, as it increasingly did, it could generate a good deal of heated discussion. As competitions continued to proliferate an increasing rumble of discontent became apparent. Not, as might have been expected, from the unsuccessful or disappointed, but from distinguished performers and composers of national and international renown.

The competition that attracted the most critical attention at that time was the BBC Young Musician of the Year. The finals of this competition were shown on TV, and continue to be. As a music programme they were undoubtedly popular with the public, as they still are. For some years they attracted a viewing audience second only to the Last Night of the Proms. It was the size of the audience and the extent of the exposure to which these very young musicians were (and still are) subjected that worried many concerned musicians and teachers. The degree of publicity experienced in the final rounds is greater than that to which even celebrated artists at the peak of their careers are generally exposed. The pressure to accept engagements subsequently is irresistible. The effect this might have on young artists at a pre-conservatoire stage and the unfortunate consequences this could cause was of most concern.

One of the first groups to complain was the European String Teachers Association (ESTA). In its published report the argument against competitions is put very strongly: *The notion of 'winning and losing' implies the possibility of measuring achievement in its most important essentials. To allow the choice of a winner among many losers, it is necessary to set a standard against which they can be judged. Such a standard can only exist for simple, concrete attributes. There is no problem about finding an acceptable standard for comparing and making a judgement on the height of an object. If, however, instead of height, we wish to judge relative grandeur, no form of measurement is conceivable since too many intangible qualities are involved.*

In musical performance, the only measurable attributes are aesthetically insignificant. In the unlikely event of two listeners agreeing on the accuracy of a performance in respect of pitch, rhythm and dynamic variation, this would still leave out of account all the most important aspects of individual interpretation, and so, in performance (as in music examinations) the greater the accomplishment of the performer the less valid are attempts at 'grading'. The variety of performance in music is as important as the variety of appearance and character in human beings. Fashion, which plays such a deadening part in standardising appearance, also attempts to lay down laws of the same kind for music, to standardise interpretation. But art, like humanity, is individual and immeasurable and the conclusion must be drawn that, in the sense of 'winning and losing', artists cannot compete artistically.

The composer Alexander Goehr put the anti-competition view even more forcefully. When asked what he considered the essential characteristics of an ideal competition he replied, 'There are only un-ideal competitions. I cannot answer as I am totally opposed to the competitive spirit in performance.'

Lady Evelyn Barbirolli, the conductor Sir John Barbirolli's widow, formerly an outstanding oboist and then an adjudicator of a wide variety of events, expressed a very different point of view. Though she did express some concern for the effect over-exposure can have on performers of a tender age as a result of winning some prestigious events, she said 'I am in favour of competitions. They are necessary, and like it or not, they have become part of our musical life.'

Music in Time, published by the Jerusalem Ruben Academy of Music and Dance asked several famous international artists whether they thought there was a need for competitions as a method of introducing artists to the public. The composer and conductor Lucas Foss wrote: *In former days the teacher launched the young artist – then the manager. Now a manager only takes you on if you have won a competition.* And the cellist Janos Starker, *They are commercially important to accelerate the careers of really exceptional talents.* Isaac Stern, the virtuoso violinist, felt that, *In recent years* (he was responding during the 1980s), *unlike three or four decades ago, music competitions have, regrettably, become something of a necessity in presenting young talents to the international market. There has been such an explosion of performing possibilities, longer seasons, and general information available through radio and television that it has become much more difficult to capture the attention of the potential public and impresarios necessary to the young performer.* He was then asked, 'Can young artists really convey their abilities during competitions?' *'The answer depends on comparison with their performances outside the competitions. I personally could hardly have performed in the tense atmosphere of a competition. Certain performers do play well under these circumstances and yet fail to develop later when they are on their own. Perhaps it is because of the enormous concentration that they have given to the specific work demanded by the competition to the exclusion of all else, and what may seem like outstanding ability in general becomes particularised only for a certain series of works that have been carefully prepared.'* The pianist Tamas Vasary was more certain *'Competitions suit the athletic types, less the more introverted, sensitive types. Not all are able to show their best in competition conditions.'*

In an article in *Classical Music* the production team responsible for the BBC competition responded to the criticism levelled at that competition with considerable vigour accusing their critics of a *muddled attitude and having consulted very few people either inside or outside the profession and having consulted nobody who had participated recently in any of the competitions they criticised.* (though one of their production team was on the ESTA group that published the report *Music Competitions*). The BBC production team accused ESTA of having *a fundamental flaw – they started with their conclusions already formed and wrote the report to justify them.*

As a member of the National Music Council throughout the 1980s I was involved in several seminars the Council organised. The debate about the value or otherwise of competitions was still raging and in 1987 the Council decided that it should organise a seminar on this topic; a sub-committee was formed and I was elected chairman. My own feelings about competitions have always been somewhat ambivalent. On the one hand I feel very like Tamas Vasary, perhaps because whenever I have been put under that kind of pressure I have been conscious of my father listening and finding my performance inadequate. On the other hand, the force of the practical responses from Lady Barbirolli and Isaac Stern seemed to make good sense.

In my opinion competitions for young musicians, up to the age of 18, all playing the same instrument, with the minimum amount of media attention, or competitions for those who have already embarked on a professional career, such as the BBC Cardiff Singer of the World Competition, when publicity for those taking part will be valuable, should be encouraged. There are a number of competitions where musicians, still at school, playing a variety of instruments, at times even including singers, are pitted against each other. How does one judge the virtues of a violinist playing a wonderful work such as the Brahms' Concerto against those of a trombonist playing the attractive, but light-weight, Larssen Concerto, or between the qualities of a pianist offering the Beethoven 'Emperor' Concerto and a flautist playing the Ibert Flute Concerto?

Should judges assess candidates only on how they perform on the day or is potential more important? When Ginette Neveu was 16 and David Oistrakh 27 they both took part in the Wieniawski Competition; Oistrakh came 1st and Neveu 2nd. Does it make sense to grade artists of this calibre? Imagine if one had to decide between artists of this standard on different instruments.

By May 1988 a National Music Council seminar titled *Good Practice in Competitions* had been arranged with a panel of speakers from a wide variety of backgrounds: performers, competition winners, adjudicators, teachers, competition organisers and sponsors. The flyer for the event stated: *In the afternoon those attending the seminar will also have the chance to express their views on a subject upon which most musicians and those concerned with music have very determined opinions.* Neither the opportunity to hear what Peter Donohoe, John Carol Case, Lady Barbirolli, the organisers of some of the major competitions – including those organised by the BBC and the Royal Overseas League, nor the opportunity for everyone attending to air their own views, proved to be an inducement. Though the event had been widely publicised and was to take place on a Saturday in a central London venue, it had to be cancelled. Only three tickets had been purchased!

Why had there been no response from all those who had been expressing either their hostility or support for competitions so vociferously? I decided to write a letter for publication in the Incorporated Society of Musicians (ISM) journal of a kind that I hoped would stir up some controversy. This time there was absolutely no response at all. Perhaps there are too many vested interests for anything to change very much?

Had the seminar taken place the Council had intended to issue a report that it hoped might become a useful guide to all those interested in this important aspect of contemporary musical life. In 1990 Rhinegold, the publishers of the journal *Classical Music* decided to enclose a copy of a lecture originally given the previous year by Peter Renshaw, then Gresham Professor of Music, who had previously been the Principal of the Yehudi Menuhin School for nine years. He called his lecture *Competitions and Young Musicians; the place of competitions in the personal and musical development of young people.* He was strongly opposed to the way competitions were organised and presented two views of these events – a 'Marketing/Commercial' model and an 'Artistic/Educational' model. The latter as expressed in his lecture is idealistic and full of very good suggestions as to how it might be done, but, sadly, quite unrealistic.

'The utilitarian marketing model', he said, 'reflects the values of a tough entrepreneurial world which sees competitions as a sporting contest in which a potential star wins. The form of life which underpins this model contains many of the features associated more with the world of marketing: for example, corporate sponsorship wanting a readily identifiable return on its investment, through which a company can promote a winner and raise its public profile by being seen to promote the arts. In its strongest form this model is amenable to media hype and as such it can distort the nature and content of a competition.' He goes on, 'It could be argued, perhaps rather cynically, that by mirroring the tough realities of the market place, in which the survival of the fittest becomes the central guiding principal, this marketing model performs an invaluable service to the public, the sponsor and the performer alike.'

Renshaw suggested, and my own experience leads me to believe he was correct, that the conservatoires were over-producing professional musicians, so that competitions could be seen as a useful social mechanism controlling entry into the upper echelons of the profession. He said 'This might appear harsh, but there is no doubt in my mind that some teachers in some institutions are driven by a kind of killer instinct which is then caught by the more ruthlessly determined student.'

Now, fifteen years later, in the *Classical Music Guide to Music Competitions 2005*, there are over 250 music competitions listed. In an environment even more commercially driven than when Renshaw gave his lecture, it is only the ruthless student, soloist, chamber music player or orchestral musician, that will survive. The pressure that so many are now experiencing is also felt as keenly by musicians. There are those, and I include myself in their number, who, while recognising that competition can play an important part in increasing technical skills, regret the loss of sensitivity and individuality it so often causes.

23 An Astonishing Period of Growth

Pre-1939 – war-time and post-war increase in audiences for concerts and opera. Insufficient financial support. New repertoire – contemporary music. The Institut de Recherche et Coordination Acoustique et Musique. The future for symphony orchestras. The Wheatland Foundation. The Orchestra for Europe.

Before 1939 and the outbreak of the Second World War there were only two full-time symphony orchestras in Britain, the BBC Symphony Orchestra and the London Philharmonic. Though the Bournemouth Municipal Orchestra, unlike any of the other seaside resort orchestras, gave performances throughout the year and a few of its programmes were of entirely symphonic music it was not really a 'symphony orchestra'. The City of Birmingham Symphony Orchestra, the Hallé in Manchester, the Liverpool Philharmonic Orchestra and the Scottish Orchestra in Glasgow all had concert seasons that only ran from September until the end of April or early May. There was still no opera house open throughout the year – the seasons of opera and ballet at the Royal Opera House, Covent Garden, were also from September until May. If you did not live in or near one of the towns with a symphony orchestra there were from 1930 the regular broadcasts by the BBC orchestras and an increasing number of gramophone records, albeit in four-minute chunks, in the old 78 rpm format. The audience for opera, ballet and symphonic music remained, as it had always been, predominantly middle and upper-middle-class.

The majority of people listened to 'light' music and 'dance' music, broadcast by the BBC and Radio Luxembourg – it would be some years before improvised jazz would be broadcast by the BBC. Until 1940 when the twice-daily broadcasts of *Music While You Work* started there were broadcasts from a number of the larger seaside resort orchestras such as Eastbourne, Hastings and Blackpool, during the summer months, and from the larger Variety theatres and cinemas that employed a stage orchestra. The best was probably the one at the Commodore cinema in Hammersmith, London, which had an orchestra of about 35 conducted by Joseph

Muscant and later by Harry Davidson, who became very well-known for his Olde Time Dance Orchestra which broadcast for about twenty five years. I'm told it was Queen Mary's favourite programme. There were also many small ensembles that broadcast regularly – some of the best known were Fred Hartley's Novelty Quintet, the JH Squire Celeste Octet, the Cedric Sharpe Sextet, Albert Sandler and the Palm Court Orchestra. A good deal of the music played by the dance bands such as Henry Hall, Jack Hylton, Roy Fox and Jack Payne, though syncopated, would now be thought of as light music. Other opportunities to hear this kind of music were on the bandstands in parks and at the seaside, in restaurants and in the theatre. Some of the orchestras at holiday resorts were paid for by the local municipality and were quite large with as many as forty or fifty musicians. As well as playing on the bandstand they gave concerts in the local hall and were quite able to tackle some of the symphonic repertoire.

The programmes for the Southport Municipal Orchestra in 1940 were similar to those of most seaside resort orchestras in the 1930s, which usually gave three performances a day. At Southport they were at 11.00 a.m. and at 3.00 and 7.30 p.m., except on Sundays when, in deference to the prevalence of regular church going, the morning performance was omitted. Their afternoon and evening performances nearly always included an overture from one of the popular operas or a short work from the symphony orchestra repertoire. In one week as well as such novelties as *Dainty Doll* by Barnes, *Al Fresco* by Herbert, the Serenade *Portrait of a Toy Soldier* by Ewing and *The Teddy Bears Picnic* by Bratton, they included the overtures *Coriolan* by Beethoven, *Rienzi* by Wagner, *The Thieving Magpie* by Rossini and *Ruy Blas* by Mendelssohn. Their wide-ranging repertoire also included *The Dance of the Comedians* from *The Bartered Bride* by Smetana, the march *Pomp and Circumstance* (No.1) by Elgar, *Marche Slave* by Tchaikovsky alongside movements from Schubert's Symphony No.1, Hamilton Harty's *Irish* Symphony, and a movement from the *Symphonie Fantastique* by Berlioz. Though hardly ever played now, the overtures *Mignon* by Ambroise Thomas, *Zampa* by Louis Herold and *The Light Cavalry* and *Poet and Peasant,* both by Franz von Suppé, were all extremely popular and frequently played by symphony orchestras, on bandstands and, in reduced Tavan arrangements, in cafes and restaurants.

From 1930 when the BBC started broadcasting a wide range of symphonic music there can be no doubt that the performances by the BBC Symphony Orchestra in London and the other much smaller BBC regional orchestras, the relays from public concerts and the records played by Christopher Stone, the first DJ in Britain, all played a very important part in creating the audience that during WW2 (1939-1946) led to the dramatic increase in the audience for 'serious' music. Concerts by symphony orchestras began attracting large audiences.

But, perhaps more than anything else it was the creation in 1940 of the Council for the Encouragement of Music and the Arts (CEMA) that had the most effect. It enabled the orchestras to do lunch-time concerts in factory canteens and guaranteed a subsidy for concerts in smaller halls. These canteen concerts, held in an environment where people felt at ease, were very successful. It brought serious music to a very great number of people who would otherwise never have considered going to a symphony concert. CEMA funded by the Treasury and set up in the first place to provide funding for the arts with the intention of raising wartime morale was, in fact, to be the first time a state subsidy had been provided for the arts.

Until the Third Programme was created in 1946 there had been only two BBC programmes, both with a policy of mixed programming as favoured by Sir John Reith, Director General until 1938. A comedy show might be followed by a talk, a programme of light music or one of orchestral music played by one of the BBC orchestras. This was probably the only time that, by chance, most people might find they were listening to music of a kind they would otherwise never otherwise have heard.

The concerts the London Philharmonic Orchestra and the London Symphony Orchestra gave all over Britain throughout the war were another important element in creating an audience for serious music. I have already written about the concerts the LPO gave in theatres organised by Jack Hylton. Very few working-class people would at that time venture into an opera house or concert hall (or be able to afford to do so). But everyone was used to going to the theatre for variety shows, plays and musical comedies so that when the Carl Rosa Opera Company, which toured all over the country played in those theatres, it too attracted an audience from all classes. It was the same when the LPO started playing in the theatres, often in towns that did not have a hall large enough for a symphony orchestra. When I joined the LPO in 1943 and did those weeks in theatres every one of the eight concerts, each with a different programme, was sold out. The Wessex Philharmonic Orchestra, which gave concerts all over Britain from 1942 until near the end of the war, also played a part in bringing music to many places that had never seen a symphony orchestra before. It was much smaller and cheaper than the LPO and could be booked to give concerts in halls that were too small to accommodate or afford an orchestra the size of the LPO.

Then in 1942 the Liverpool Philharmonic became independent from the BBC Northern Orchestra in Manchester with whom it had shared a good many players. They became a full-time orchestra with financial assistance from the local council and engaged Dr Malcolm Sargent as their principal conductor. At the same time, by coincidence, the BBC decided to disband the Salon Orchestra it had formed at the beginning of the war from a number of the finest players in the country and some of them, (Anthony Pini, Arthur Gleghorn and Reginald Kell) joined the Liverpool orchestra as principals of the cello, flute and clarinet sections. They and a few other players from the Salon Orchestra proved to be invaluable in raising the standard of an otherwise provincial orchestra.

In 1943 John Barbirolli returned to Britain after being the conductor of the New York Philharmonic for seven years. I was then in the LPO and when we learned he was coming back we wanted him to become our principal conductor, but he had already accepted an invitation from the Hallé Orchestra in Manchester which like the Liverpool Philharmonic now had the funds to become independent and full-time. Within a few weeks of hectic auditioning he assembled an orchestra starting with the small nucleus of players who had not wanted to remain in the BBC Northern Orchestra when it went full-time. The following year in May 1944 the City of Birmingham Council authorised an annual grant of £7000 to the City of Birmingham Symphony Orchestra (CBSO) for the following five years plus another £7500 from the Education Committee if the Orchestra would guarantee to undertake education work 50 days a year. Their first concert as a full-time orchestra was in October of that year conducted by the newly appointed young English conductor George Weldon.

During the war the Bournemouth Municipal Orchestra struggled on as a skeleton orchestra, reduced to only 24 players but by 1947 it was back to 60 musicians and had appointed Rudolf Schwarz as its conductor. After a number of financially bumpy years the orchestra's management was taken on by the Western Orchestral Society and it became the Bournemouth Symphony Orchestra. The first concert under its new name was conducted by Sir Thomas Beecham, and Charles Groves who continued as its principal conductor until 1961 when he left to become the conductor of the Liverpool Philharmonic. By 1958, under his direction, the management were able to enlarge the orchestra to 75 players and it started to establish a considerable reputation.

By 1946 with the formation of the Philharmonia in 1945 and the Royal Philharmonic in 1946 as well as the orchestras in Manchester, Liverpool, Birmingham and Bournemouth, the number of full-time symphony orchestras, not counting the BBC orchestras had grown to six. The Scottish Orchestra, which had had such successful seasons pre-war with John Barbirolli and then Georg Szell as principal conductors had to wait until 1950, when its name was changed to the Scottish National Orchestra (SNO), before becoming full-time.

When the Royal Opera House, Covent Garden, reopened it was as a fully-fledged Opera House, even though there was still no opera company. On 20 February 1946 the House opened with a performance of *The Sleeping Beauty* danced by Ninette de Valois's Sadler's Wells Ballet, which became the resident ballet company. David Webster, the General Administrator and the Music Director Karl Rankl built an opera company – a remarkable achievement in such a short time – and in December 1946 the opera and ballet companies shared their first production, *The Fairy Queen*. The first performance, on 14 January 1947, given by the Covent Garden Opera Company, which in 1968 became The Royal Opera, was Bizet's *Carmen*. The ballet company had already become The Royal Ballet in 1956.

The establishment of the Third Programme in 1946 was another boost for serious music. Unfortunately it was also the start of ghettoised radio. From then on the Home Service and the Light and the Third programmes each had their separate identities. Then in 1967 the BBC was obliged to replace the banned pirate radio stations – in fact, illegal commercial radio stations. They had been broadcasting the current pop hit records and commercial advertising – 'jingles'. The new station, Radio 1 was born and the separation of the radio programmes became even greater. It was now extremely unlikely that anyone would inadvertently stray from Radio 1 into the hallowed realms of Radio 3.

I remember the discussions we had with the Government at that time. The Government were asking the BBC to establish a programme to replace the pirates. Of course this would involve a considerable increase in the number of records the BBC would need to broadcast. The Musicians' Union still had the 'needle-time' agreement with the BBC that restricted the number of hours they were permitted to broadcast commercial recordings. The MU was unwilling to discuss an increase in needle-time until it was convinced by the Government that it was really necessary. The Postmaster General, who led for the Government was a rather dour and humourless man, Edward Short. He assured us that it was absolutely necessary as MPs had all received thousands of requests – indeed demands – from listeners to the pirate broadcasts and he said that the Government were obliged to respond. When I asked him if the Government would now respond in the same way if the many viewers of the pornographic films that were being beamed from overseas were encouraged to write to their MPs he responded rather gloomily 'that I was being unfair'.

It was a foregone conclusion that the MU would have to agree to an increase in the number of hours that commercial recordings could be broadcast and, as I have written earlier, it did a deal with the BBC that resulted in more employment for freelance musicians in broadcasting and the creation of the Training Orchestra. The Home Service, the predominantly spoken word programme became Radio 4, with Radio 1 broadcasting pop music, Radio 2 'middle of the road', or light music (nearly everything not contemporary pop or classical music), and Radio 3 mainly for serious music and drama. Until 1993, when the target age range changed from 13 – 40 to 13 – 25, Radio 1 had been known as *Britain's Favourite Radio*. As a result of this change of age range it lost nearly a third of its audience and Radio 2 replaced it as the most listened to station.

The twenty years or so after the end of WW2 were probably the best years musically and financially there have ever been in Britain for a large number of orchestral musicians, whether they were freelancing or playing in one of the London orchestras. In addition to the four major London orchestras and the BBC orchestras resident in London there were orchestras at the Royal Opera House and Sadler's Wells Theatre, which had reopened in 1945 with the first performance of Benjamin Britten's *Peter Grimes*. It was decided in 1968 that the Sadler's Wells company should move to the London Coliseum, a very much larger House and provide the full opera repertoire in English. Six years later in 1974 it became the English National Opera (ENO).

There were also a number of other orchestras. One, never a full-time orchestra, was the short-lived National Symphony Orchestra, formed in 1942 by Sidney Beer, a wealthy amateur conductor. During the war he was able to engage the services of the finest young wind players who were then serving in the RAF Central Band, stationed at Uxbridge, or in one of the Guards Bands.

Before the orchestra was disbanded in 1946 it gave a series of concerts in the Royal Albert Hall and made several recordings for Decca as well as going on a European tour. Some of the recordings were well reviewed – not surprisingly since the orchestra comprised the very best musicians then working in London. While it lasted Sidney Beer was able to attract a remarkable number of the most outstanding players. Nearly all of them went on to be principals in either the Royal Philharmonic or the Philharmonia. Two became leaders of the RPO, David McCallum and Oscar Lampe and many as principals in the Philharmonia: Leonard Hirsch as leader, the violist Leonard Rubens, the cellists Douglas Cameron and Cedric Sharpe, and the wind principals, Alec Whittaker (oboe), Reginald Kell (clarinet), John Alexandra (bassoon), Dennis Brain (horn) and Harold Jackson (trumpet).

Another short-lived music enterprise, that while it lasted provided a very high standard, was the New London Opera, which the entrepreneur Jay Pomeroy started in 1942 at the Cambridge Theatre. With Alberto Erede as Musical Director he was able to attract international stars of the calibre of Margharita Grandi, Giuseppe di Stefano and Mariano Stabile. But by 1949 with the

Royal Opera House and Glyndebourne able to mount much better productions he decided to leave the stage.

Sir John Barbirolli.

As well as the symphony orchestras there were an increasing number of chamber orchestras and chamber music ensembles. The Boyd Neel Orchestra formed in 1932 was already well established and particularly famed for premiering a new work especially written for the Salzburg Festival, Benjamin Britten's *Variations on a Theme of Frank Bridge*, which did a good deal to establish Britten's reputation and also made the orchestra well-known internationally. The orchestra was disbanded during the war but restarted again soon after. Some years later it was renamed the Philomusica of London with Thurston Dart, who played a leading part in arousing a renewed interest in Baroque and early Classical music, conducting and leading from the keyboard. When, in 1959 the Academy of St. Martin in the Fields (ASMF) was formed by a group of eleven musicians it had no conductor. It was led by Neville Marriner (later Sir Neville), who until then had for some years been leader of the second violin section of the LSO. Very soon the Academy outgrew its original eleven players and its baroque repertoire and it became necessary for Neville Marriner to take on the responsibility of conducting the orchestra in an ever-expanding repertoire. It is now one of the most recorded groups in the world.

Even earlier than the Philomusica, Karl Haas, a refugee from Germany, had in 1943 started the London Baroque Ensemble, which he continued to conduct until 1966. Though now largely forgotten Haas was an early enthusiast and performer of baroque music and made a number of recordings of music by Handel, Bach and Boyce. At that time performances of baroque music were not always historically accurate in style or instrumentation. I remember taking part in a performance in the late 1940s under Karl Haas's direction of the *Overture* by Handel for two D clarinets and horn with Jack Brymer and Dennis Brain. In those days no one had D clarinets and so the parts had been transposed so we could play it on our Bb instruments.

Later, in the 1960s Karl Haas and the London Baroque Ensemble recorded and broadcast quite a lot of wind music. He was a lovely man and a fine musician: unfortunately he was an appalling conductor. I particularly recall taking part in the Baroque Ensemble recording of the Dvorak Serenade and in two BBC broadcast performances of the Richard Strauss Sonatina No.2 *'from a Happy Workshop'*, or *Wind* Symphony. We recorded the Dvorak without too many problems. However, the broadcasts of the *Wind* Symphony – 'live', as was still normal in the 1950s, were not without incident. The first performance went extremely well until we came to the last movement. Haas managed to conduct a considerable part of this quick movement giving the down beat on the second beat of each bar when we were playing on the first. Fortunately he had as always engaged a very good and experienced group of musicians and though the performance was not perfect it did not 'come off the rails'. Between the two performances, which were a few days apart, poor Karl had a nasty fall and injured both his arms. He arrived for the second broadcast with both his arms in slings. With a few nods of his head to start off each movement and without any further involvement on his part we were able to give a faultless performance.

Two more orchestras were started in the second half of the 1940s, both of them still active today, though one is now famous under another name. The Goldsbrough Orchestra was created by Lawrence Leonard and Arnold Goldsbrough in 1948 and was the orchestra with which the very young Colin Davis gained his early experience as a conductor. Until the orchestra changed its name to the English Chamber Orchestra (ECO) in 1960 it concentrated mainly on the baroque repertoire. As the ECO it gave its first concert in the Royal Festival Hall with a programme of Monteverdi opera extracts. Within a short while it made its first recordings and toured Britain with Colin Davis conducting and in 1961 became the resident orchestra for Benjamin Britten at Aldeburgh and has gone on to become one of the most successful chamber orchestras.

At just about the same time Harry Blech, a very well-known violinist, formed the London Mozart Players concentrating on performances of Haydn, Mozart and Beethoven. This orchestra, too, has survived to the present day though it no longer has the reputation it gained under Blech, who though extremely musical and able to produce excellent results with his own orchestra was a disaster when he came to conduct the Philharmonia. He just could not control a large symphony orchestra.

As important for London musicians as the increased number of established orchestras was the enormous amount of freelance work available: in broadcasting, both radio and TV. There were also a lot of sessions recording the background music for the films made in Britain as well as the music for many Hollywood films. Not only were session rates lower in Britain than in America, but because of their famed sight-reading skills British musicians recorded the music much more quickly, requiring fewer sessions and thereby reducing the cost to American producers even more. The many light music orchestras such as Mantovani's and George Melachrino's were still making recordings and there were a lot of sessions backing popular singers and some of the pop groups, when freelance orchestral musicians (and a few of the best players from the London orchestras) and the best of the dance band and jazz musicians would be engaged.

Although the future for professional orchestral musicians in Britain in the late 1940s and into the 1950s looked much better than at any time in the past, especially for the musicians working in London, the effect of insufficient state and municipal funding, a lack of contemporary orchestral repertoire capable of attracting audiences, and the new communication technologies, were in the following fifty years to bring about a gradual decline in interest and support for serious music that by 2000 had become extremely worrying,

Not enough Money

Ever since the contract symphony orchestras in Britain became full-time, the managements and the musicians playing in them have complained that the funds provided by the state and their local municipality have been insufficient for their needs and the cause of the problems they have always experienced. By 1950 the musicians were already beginning to have financial problems. As the years have gone by, because the increases in subvention have never matched the rising cost of living and mortgages, the situation has continued to get worse. The Musicians' Union's attempts to respond to the demands of their members for better salaries and conditions when negotiating with the Association of British Orchestras have never satisfied the players.

For nearly twenty years from 1960, I was one of those involved in negotiations on behalf of the contract orchestras and had to face the fact that the managements just did not have the money required to pay their musicians a more appropriate salary. After one set of negotiations, when we were obliged to agree an increase in their salaries that was very much less than we had been asked to settle for, the members of the orchestras were extremely dissatisfied and accused the MU of not really trying hard enough. One orchestra in particular was extremely vociferous. We arranged a meeting with the members of this orchestra and as one of the negotiators who was an orchestral musician, it fell to my unhappy lot to try to explain why we had not been able to obtain a result more to their liking. I told them that we were convinced there just was not the money available and that in the end the choice we had been forced to take was whether to accept less than a satisfactory increase or put the orchestra out of business. If any of them felt they could do better than we had I would be happy to let them take my place. Accompanied by a good deal of muttering and grim faces this orchestra reluctantly agreed, as the other orchestras had, to accept the increase offered by the management.

The managements were in a similar position in relation to their paymasters as the musicians were with them. Understandably, local authorities, battling with demands for improved services and lower rates, did not put requests for more money for the orchestras high on their list of priorities. In Britain there had never been a tradition of supporting orchestras, as there had been for so long in a number of other European countries, and though shortly after the war it was agreed that up to sixpence (2½p) in the pound could be raised for the arts from the rates, never more than one penny (less than a ½p) was ever raised.

The situation for musicians in the London orchestras was for many years very much better. The managements of each of the orchestras and the players in them were both able to benefit from the great deal of commercial recording and the film sessions for which the whole orchestra would be engaged. The rates for recording and film sessions were higher than for concerts and therefore welcomed by the musicians. The advantage for the management was that instead of incurring the cost involved in putting on a concert they received a booking fee for supplying the orchestra. But all good things must come to an end and as time went by the amount of recording and film work declined.

Because London audiences demanded nothing but the best as far as conductors and soloists were concerned and the fees for engaging these artists were generally greater than the total cost of the whole orchestra, even if the concert was sold out it was not possible to break even let alone make a profit. Without additional funds it would not be possible for any of the orchestras to continue to provide concerts with the international conductors and soloists needed to bring in the audience and with sufficient rehearsals for the orchestras to match the orchestras elsewhere with which they were being compared.

Each of the orchestras, with varying degrees of success, sought sponsorship from corporations or other commercial organisations. As audiences tended to be largely middle-class it was usually organisations and companies with a well-heeled clientele that were willing to enter into schemes of this kind. The advantage to the sponsors was that they received considerable exposure in the press and from advertising in the programmes where they were seen to be supporting cultural events. They also usually received a number of seats for each concert they supported.

The expression 'there are no free lunches' has never been truer than where sponsorship is concerned. Sponsors nearly always wanted to have some influence on the programmes of concerts they were sponsoring. The senior members of their management and their most favoured clients who attended the concerts were as a rule not enthusiastic about 20th century and contemporary music. This also played its part in making it more difficult to programme new music. Perhaps because orchestras were in receipt of some financial assistance from the Arts Council and municipalities, post-war music lovers did not continue the patronage from which the LPO and other concert giving bodies had benefited and which had enabled new music to be programmed in the past. The situation in this respect has remained much better in the USA to the benefit of their national composers.

New Repertoire – Contemporary Music

In the early 1950s there were already those, mainly critics, academics and other commentators on the state of the arts and music in particular, complaining that there was insufficient performance of 20th century music. However, when the orchestras attempted to programme works written thirty years earlier by the atonal and serial composers, Arnold Schoenberg, Anton Webern and Alban Berg, they played to very reduced audiences. Although Alban Berg's two operas, *Wozzeck* and *Lulu* have become part of the operatic repertoire, fifty years later the general concert-going public still cannot be persuaded to attend concerts that include this 'new' music, not even when most of the rest of the programme is made up of established popular favourites.

When music by the next generation of composers, Pierre Boulez, Luciano Berio, Luigi Nono, Karlheinz Stockhausen and Hans Werner Henze and others started to appear from 1950 onwards, to begin with for small or unusual groups of instruments and later for orchestra, though quite often not for the standard symphony orchestra layout, the demand that they should be given a hearing increased. Again, when music of this kind was programmed only very small audiences attended. The orchestras were unable to afford to play to less than half-full houses so that few orchestral concerts included contemporary music.

Only the BBC in Britain was in a position to perform music for which there was a relatively small audience. In 1959 they appointed William Glock (later Sir William) as Controller of Music. It is probably fair to say that no one tried to educate the public to understand and enjoy the music of their own time more than he did during his tenure as Controller between 1959 and 1972. Before going to the BBC he had been a critic for the *Daily Telegraph*, and then at the *Observer* until 1945. In 1947 he went to the first Edinburgh Festival to hear Artur Schnabel, with whom he had studied for several years, give a piano recital. Schnabel suggested to him that there should be a summer school in England where audiences and young musicians could have classes and listen to performances by outstanding artists, and said he thought that Glock should direct it.

Glock managed to raise the necessary finance and the following year a Summer School was established at Bryanston in Dorset. Later, in 1953 it moved to Dartington where it is still held each year. Many wonderful musicians have taught and given lectures there: including the composers Boris Blacher, Georges Enesco, Paul Hindemith, Benjamin Britten (who also came as a performer with Peter Pears) and even Igor Stravinsky. In the first year, the Amadeus Quartet was formed there and in the 1950s Elisabeth Schumann came to give recitals on several occasions as did Artur Rubinstein and Clifford Curzon. This tradition, started by Glock, has been carried on to the present day with the best composers, instrumentalists and quartets continuing to inspire generations of musicians and music lovers.

Glock's thirteen years as Controller of Music at the BBC were far more controversial. When asked what he thought as Controller he should offer listeners, he famously replied 'What they would like tomorrow.' Though he transformed the annual Prom seasons and the regular broadcasts by the BBC Orchestras by introducing music by contemporary composers who were writing atonal music and using 'progressive techniques' and infrequently broadcasting music by composers writing more 'conventional' music, his efforts in this direction do not seem to have had much effect on the general music public's willingness to listen to the music he felt they should like.

By 1953 the then young Pierre Boulez was already establishing himself as the most radical and fiercely polemical of all the young *avant garde* composers born in Europe during the mid nineteen-twenties. As a young man Boulez was extremely outspoken. In the 1960s his impatience at what he saw as the conservatism and inflexibility of music organisations, symphony orchestras in particular, led to two of his best-known quotes from that period: 'It is not devilry, but only the most ordinary common sense which makes me say that, since the discoveries made by the Viennese, all composition other than twelve-tone is useless.' He claimed that the simplest solution to the opera problem would be 'to blow up the opera houses.' He must have been glad his advice was not taken before he agreed to conduct in the opera houses in Bayreuth, Paris and the UK.

As part of his campaign to influence what audiences 'would like tomorrow' Glock decided in 1963 to appoint Boulez as the Guest Conductor of the BBC Symphony Orchestra and then, in 1972, as their Chief Conductor. This appointment was welcomed in the music press but met with a very mixed reception from the orchestra. A few players, including my old friend Jack Brymer who went to the LSO, left the orchestra to find employment in a less austere environment.

The Institut de Recherche et Coordination Acoustique et Musique (IRCAM)

In Paris in the 1970s President George Pompidou invited Boulez to create and direct IRCAM and provided the funds and suitable accommodation for it within the newly built Pompidou Centre. Boulez's objective was to bring science and art together in order to widen instrumentation and rejuvenate musical language. He made certain that one of the organisation's major objectives would be the interface of computer technology and acoustic performance and he therefore encouraged composer/performer collaboration at various stages of the creative process. The software IRCAM has developed for sound modelling, transformation, and synthesis has been designed for use with instrumentalists and singers as the sound input for music compositions.

Because of his own compositional methods and those of a number of his contemporaries Boulez was the first, as early as the mid nineteen-fifties, to propose that orchestras should be reorganised. The normal layout of the 'romantic' 19th century orchestra was no longer suited to the very different assembly of instruments composers now required. For example: a score might not require any violins and violas, but call for considerably more brass or woodwind instruments than are found in the normal symphony orchestra. Or the score might require only one flute but call for six clarinets (including an Eb, a bass and a contra-bass clarinet), two cor anglais and a contra bassoon. At times a composition would require no more than about 25 or 30 of the players in a normal symphony orchestra and at others a far larger number divided into two or three separate ensembles.

In 1968, in a lecture, Boulez was already putting forward the notion that 'the orchestra should be replaced by a kind of consortium of performers drawn on for ad hoc purposes. All that is very easy to say; and it is true that solutions of this kind can well be imagined … (and of course) there is an economic factor in music, and this factor always tells in favour of conservatism. By this I mean that in any organisation qualified for an activity of this kind it is very difficult to persuade people – simply from the point of view of intrinsic organisation – that things can be organised differently without creating major problems in any well-regulated economy.'

IRCAM has three primary missions: to promote both the creation and the development of contemporary repertoire by commissioning new works and performing them regularly; to increase the audience for the music of 20th and 21st centuries, through a diffusion policy which features a season of concerts in Paris, as well as international tours and audio-visual recordings; to contribute to training and professional placement for young musicians, instrumentalists, conductors and composers through workshops and score-reading sessions.

The instrumentation of IRCAM's *Ensemble Intercontemporaine* comprises thirty-one soloists (two flutes, two oboes, two clarinets, bass clarinet, two bassoons, two French horns, two trumpets, two trombones, tuba, three percussion, three keyboards, harp, three violins, two violas, two cellos, contrabass). Except that it has a very small string section it remains to the present day very much like many chamber ensembles that only play the classical, romantic and early 20th century repertoire.

The Future for Symphony Orchestras

The financial problems facing the costly, labour-intensive symphony orchestras everywhere, especially in Britain, the demands by the critics for the performance of more contemporary music and the increasing dominance of pop music on the airwaves and recordings, were by 1980 beginning to cause some concern. When, in 1985, the NCOS Orchestra was invited to play at the XVII International Society for Music in Education (ISME) Conference in Innsbruck I was asked to deliver a paper. I decided that the question of the symphony orchestra's future was important and was a topic on which I might be able to make a useful contribution.

Even though Boulez had tried while in charge of the BBC Symphony Orchestra and the New York Philharmonic Orchestra to effect some changes, he had – as he had predicted – been unsuccessful. As a former orchestral musician, and at that time Director of the NCOS preparing young musicians for a profession that was already recruiting far fewer musicians than the number of students who were at conservatoires all wanting to become orchestral musicians, I was naturally more concerned about their future than Boulez had been. He wanted to create the conditions that would make it possible for the performance of new compositions that the rigidity of a conventional symphony orchestra does not allow.

I chose as the subject for my talk 'The Symphony Orchestra: into the 21st century'. I thought that in this forum of educators it might be possible to bring my ideas to those who in their turn might influence younger musicians to consider how the symphony orchestra might be reorganised so as to become sufficiently flexible to respond to the demands of present-day composers.

The repertoire of the symphony orchestras was also being restricted by the 'baroque' orchestras playing the music of Haydn, Mozart and Beethoven in what they claimed to be the historically 'authentic' style of performance, on the kind of instruments that would have been available when their compositions were written. The idea that perhaps the music of later composers, Liszt, Brahms and Tchaikovsky should be played on instruments still in their time less perfected than those now available was being contemplated. The music of the period before the rise of the orchestra as we have known it from about the time of Haydn was also becoming more popular.

At the same time young musicians, especially the best of them, were increasingly preferring the freedom of expression that playing 'chamber music' provided. Not only in string quartets and the like, but in string, wood-wind, brass, percussion and mixed ensembles of various sizes, playing baroque, classical, romantic and contemporary music. Quite often they performed in venues other than those normally associated with concert giving: old people's homes, hospitals and prisons, as well as for music clubs.

At the Conference I put forward the idea that the orchestra should become a 'resource centre': a much larger group of musicians who would have the opportunity of playing a number of different kinds of music in various sized ensembles. It should no longer be necessary to decide to play in an orchestra and have little or no chance of playing chamber music: nor should those choosing to play chamber music be denied the delight of playing the great orchestral repertoire. This resource centre should also include composers; some might be composers-in-residence, as we had at the NCOS, others might also want to play in the orchestra or an ensemble. Their compositions could be tried out, with experiments and changes made in circumstances where there would be no risk to their reputation. Nor would there be the cost of rehearsals and mounting a public performance which might attract only a small audience. Within the area in which the 'centre' was resident those who wished to teach could provide advanced tuition in whatever branch of music they had expertise.

The Wheatland Foundation

The following year, 1986, I was invited to be a participant in another conference. This was to be organised by the Wheatland Foundation, which had been founded in the previous year by Ann Getty and Lord Weidenfeld to support programmes in the arts and the humanities. Ann Getty's husband, Gordon Getty, was then the head of Getty Oil, which he had just sold that year to Texaco for 10 billion dollars. He was also a classical music composer. This may be why the Foundation's first conference, held in Venice, had been about the future for opera. Jerusalem had been chosen to be the venue for this conference. It was to consider the future for the symphony orchestra.

Those of us from London flew to Jerusalem by El-Al, the Israeli air-line, in the kind of comfort I had not experienced before (nor have I since). My wife and I had three times as much space as is normally provided on Business class or that I have seen when walking through First class. We each had a large armchair and there was another one between us on which they placed the tray when they served us a splendid lunch. On arrival at Jerusalem airport we were whisked away by taxi to the King David Hotel. Our room, overlooking the Old City, was extremely large and luxurious and when we arrived we found a large bowl of strawberries and a bottle of champagne in an ice-bucket awaiting us. The next four days were spent in similar conditions and included a traditional Friday *Shabat* Dinner with the ebullient Mayor of Jerusalem Teddy Kollek, an Arab-style Dinner where we were seated on floor cushions and served by waiters in traditional costume, a splendid meal in the Dormition Abbey and finally a grand Farewell Dinner.

On one day our meetings were held in a hotel near the Dead Sea. While our sessions were in progress our spouses were taken on a guided tour of the Dead Sea and Masada Rock, where Herod's royal citadel had been. The citadel was the site of the most dramatic and symbolic act in Jewish history, when the rebels chose mass suicide rather than submit to Roman capture. The day after the conference ended we had a reception at the Knesset where we met President Chaim Herzog. To our surprise he addressed us in English with a pronounced Irish accent. Only later we learned that he had been born and lived in Belfast until he was seventeen.

The Foundation had invited a number of composers, conductors, performers, orchestra managers, producers of music programmes in radio and TV, agents and a critic. The conference Director was Peter Diamand who had been Director of the Holland and Edinburgh Festivals as well as General Manager of the RPO for a few years. At the time of the conference he was the artistic adviser to the Orchestre de Paris. Also present were Mr and Mrs Getty, Sir Isaiah Berlin and Lord Weidenfeld.

It was intended that the conference should examine and define the role of symphony orchestras in the changing environment for the performing arts; consider whether the contemporary orchestra was, as it had been called, 'an obsolescent instrument'; how it might evolve and change to meet the new needs of composers and performers and how it should come to terms with its dwindling audience and sometimes difficult relationship with the recording industry. How the education and training of orchestral musicians might be improved was also on the agenda.

The largest number of those taking part in the discussions were managers of the major orchestras in Europe and the USA. They included those from the New York Philharmonic, the Los Angeles Philharmonic, the San Francisco Symphony, the Israel Philharmonic, the Royal Concertgebouw, the Orchestre de Paris, the Zurich Tonhalle Orchestra, the Philharmonia Orchestra of London and two youth orchestras, the European Community Youth Orchestra and the German Philharmonic Youth Orchestra. There were four composers Pierre Boulez (also, of course, a conductor), Henri Dutilleux, Alexander Goehr and Joseph Tal. The conductors were Gary Bertini, Semyon Bychkov, Lawrence Foster and Catherine French; and the performers Isaac Stern, who also acted as chairman, Alfred Brendel, and three orchestral musicians.

There was general agreement that the present orchestra structure needed to change in some way if it was to satisfy the many composers who no longer found the standard classical/romantic orchestra met their needs. What so many composers now wanted was an assembly of instruments, very different for each piece, that they had decided their composition required. Unless the repertoire the orchestras now relied on to attract an audience was to be abandoned, how could the symphony orchestra satisfy those who were demanding that they play what composers were now writing? The fact that even those contemporary compositions that were written using the conventional orchestra did not attract an audience was never faced.

The conservatoires were blamed for not encouraging students to learn enough music composed after 1950: their education was too limited and composer/performer co-operation was not encouraged. The musicians in the orchestras needed to change their attitude to performing new music; the unions had to be persuaded to allow greater flexibility in contractual agreements; and finally, audiences needed to be more musically educated.

Anna Lindal, the assistant leader of the Stockholm Philharmonic, thought that the orchestra should become much more flexible, dividing into groups as required. Several managers pointed out that additional woodwind, brass and percussion players were nearly always called for and that these extras players would be very expensive. Also that quite often a number of those contracted full-time by the orchestra would be unemployed, but still have to be paid. Pierre Boulez made the same point as Anna Lindal and referred to his own attempts to do this with the BBC Symphony and the New York Philharmonic. Because of contractual difficulties and the resistance of some of the players when they were required to play in positions and with responsibilities they were not being paid for, it had not proved practical in either of the orchestras.

Pierre Vozlinsky, the General Administrator of the Orchestre de Paris, asked if the Foundation could take the initiative and launch an international campaign, so that information would reach professional circles 'to gradually move over to a system of individual service'. He pointed out that the discussions had clearly shown that there was no other way if the expense of performing contemporary music were not to be an insurmountable obstacle. This suggestion was not taken up by any of the other orchestra managers. No doubt the thought of having to engage an orchestra from a freelance pool for every concert was too daunting. Of course it is not in the power of composers or performers to initiate action that would change the structure of the orchestra. Only the Boards of management and their managers were in a position to do that.

Even though Peter Diamand, as Conference Director, several times drew our attention to the need to arrive at a recommendation for the Foundation to consider, and after a very great deal of discussion, the Conference remained unable to come to any positive conclusion on the all-important and central question regarding the future for the symphony orchestra: 'how it might evolve and change to meet the new needs of composers and performers'.

The Conference also devoted quite a lot of its time to considering the training that should be provided for those who wanted to become orchestral musicians. Several speakers said that there was evidence that many of the very best young players leaving conservatoires now no longer wanted to play in an orchestra all the time or for the whole of their career. Anna Lindal said that from her own experience, having only been in the profession for six years, she knew what it was like for a newcomer coming into an orchestra for the first time. After talking to many other young musicians she felt that the training of musicians for the orchestra was inadequate.

She went on to explain that despite the fact that one is already an expert on one's own instrument and comes with a great deal of enthusiasm, the training one has received gives little guidance as to how to play in an orchestra. Very little responsible orchestral work has been offered and students are seldom required to work to a deadline or a target and never have the opportunity of playing alongside a professional orchestral musician. 'It is usually the case that training takes place in the orchestra itself.' Lindal thought that it ought to be in the interest of orchestras themselves to found their own 'orchestra schools' so as to be certain of continuity and quality in their profession. 'But we need not only continuity in the profession but also change, dynamism and new ideas.' It should happen naturally that the young generation brings this with them. 'One must look far and wide to find training for a profession which is more conservative.' We are trained in a tradition, which at best belongs to the preceding generation.

My own experience, teaching at the Royal College of Music, bore out all that she had said. My pupils left college unprepared for life in the profession. I also remember that when I had been a member of the examining panel for the ARCM Diploma some members of the panel were unprepared to give a good mark to students who chose to present a contemporary work as their 'own choice' if it employed some of the new techniques, on the grounds that it did not give a proper basis for assessing their ability.

It was suggested that perhaps the Wheatland Foundation might explore the possibility of supporting projects specifically concerned with the education of orchestral musicians and assist, politically or economically any developments that might arise.

Having considered the preparation of young musicians for the orchestral profession the Conference turned its attention to the conditions then prevailing for those who were currently employed in the orchestras. What were the musicians themselves concerned about and were there ways the management believed things could be improved?

Isaac Stern thought that orchestral musicians were often required to work longer hours than was conducive to good performance while Pierre Boulez felt that what was destructive was playing 'fifty-two weeks, concert after concert, in exactly the same way, the kind of routine where one week cannot be distinguished from another, one day from the next'. Peter Pastreich, Executive Director of the San Francisco Symphony Orchestra, responded by saying that 'everyone knows that routine means playing with boring conductors and playing in a boring way. With the right conductor it doesn't matter how many concerts you have to play'.

A number of speakers were concerned, as Isaac Stern said, 'to ameliorate the tyranny of union rules, so often binding in freedom of work preparation and time and cost'. Peter Pastreich disagreed. 'No recording session would end prematurely if we just said beforehand that we're willing to pay overtime. It is a question of money rather than of union rules. The same is true for rehearsals. If we just said to the orchestra "keep on playing for as long as the conductor is conducting, we'll pay", the rehearsals would simply go into overtime'. I was surprised to hear this from a manager, but I'm sure most players would agree – as long as the conductor was not too boring!

The status of musicians in society, the degree of stress players experienced and the degree to which self-management could be acceptable, were all considered. Apart from the 'tyranny of the unions' nothing stirred so much emotion as the concept of self-management and far more time was spent on this subject than it probably warranted.

In reporting the views of the members of a select committee formed to discuss Education and Youth Orchestras, Joseph Polisi, the President of the Julliard School of Music in New York, told the Conference that 'one of the committee's major assumptions was that although proficiency must exist to ensure a successful professional life, technical ability must be viewed as only a means to an end: a conscious, creative process of music making. The concept of orchestral self-governance was agreed to be one way to achieve a sense of personal worth and responsibility as a musician and a member of society'.

Self-governance, the notion that the members of an orchestra should do more than express an opinion, that might or might not be followed up, was vigorously opposed by the majority of the orchestra managers. However, the most outspoken opposition came from Peter Heyworth, music critic of the *Observer,* who for a number of years had conducted a campaign against the London orchestras, mainly because of the lack of contemporary compositions in their programmes. He told the Conference, 'With regard to musicians taking over the decision-making process: some unflattering remarks have been made about the London orchestral scene, well justified, I think, since it is one of the scandals of the Western world and has been for a number of years. It was brought about by musicians taking over the decision-making process'. Hans Landesmann, the Artistic Director of the European Community Youth Orchestra, and a member of the select committee, pointed out that though Mr Heyworth believed the situation in London was so bad because the orchestras were self-governed, the Vienna Philharmonic had been self-governing from when it was established (as had the LSO) and had neither been managed badly nor done too badly.

As the only one taking part in this discussion with first-hand experience of playing in both a managed and self-governed orchestra, it was clear to me that whether an orchestra should be self-governing or not was usually beyond our control. Social and economic circumstances and a number of other factors affect what decision has to be taken. In the end the report from the select committee was accepted unanimously – though no conclusion had been reached.

Another committee dealt with 'The Orchestra as Workplace'. This committee perceived that 'there are major problems which make the orchestra a less than optimal workplace for musicians and administrators, resulting in interpersonal tension and inefficiency of operation, a lack of motivation and often of commitment to the institution. In addition, even when standards are high there is disaffection, emotional stress and increased evidence of illness associated with playing in a symphony orchestra.' They recommended a pilot scheme to identify what has an impact on morale and to what extent it affects performance; to study work-related medical problems; to look into possible changes in the organisational structure of the orchestra and methods of professional development. They assessed the cost would be about $400,000.

There was not a great deal of enthusiasm for attempting to raise what was at that time a considerable amount of money when orchestras were already experiencing the financial restraints referred to several times during the conference. Naturally, there was support for the idea that stress and medical problems should be examined, though Humphrey Burton, the BBC TV producer of many performing arts programmes, thought these recommendations were a very American problem where bringing in psychiatrists forms a part of everyday life. Christopher Bishop, Managing Director of the Philharmonia Orchestra in London, said that because the orchestras in London were self-governing and ran their own lives these problems did not apply. He thought that the members of the orchestras and their managers worked 'in an atmosphere of unity and willingness to work together'. The report of the Conference does not record whether the recommendations were agreed or not. However, it does record that the Conference Director, Peter Diamand, asked to be considered to have voted against.

Now, twenty years later on re-reading in the book *The Evolution of the Symphony Orchestra: History, Problems and Agendas* (Weidenfeld and Nicolson), a verbatim account of our discussions during the conference, I see that in welcoming us Isaac Stern remarked that our agenda was 'long and comprehensive' and that it would be 'something of a task to make order out of so many possibilities'. It will probably not come as a surprise to readers who have had any experience of conferences of this kind that such recommendations as were agreed have not been implemented. However, I have reported the proceedings rather fully because this was a unique occasion, the only time as far as I know when so many performers, managers of orchestras and a number of others with an interest and influence in the world of the symphony orchestra have met to discuss its problems and future prospects.

The Orchestra for Europe

My wife and I returned to Britain on the 2nd of January 1987, just a fortnight before we set off for Denmark and my visits to conservatoires around the world about which I have written in chapter 22.

When during 1988 the BBC told us that their own financial difficulties required them to make cuts in their expenditure and that they would not be able to continue funding the National Centre after the end of the 1988/89 course, I found that there were still a number of musicians and music educators in Britain and elsewhere who continued to believe that students having completed their studies at music college required further preparation before joining the orchestral profession. If we were going to have another attempt to provide orchestral preparation we should learn from our experience. I was also keen to see whether the ideas I had put forward a few years previously, at the ISME Conference in Innsbruck and in Jerusalem, were practical and could provide opportunities for composers and performers that did not exist in the inflexible symphony orchestra structure.

It had been clear to me for some time that to try to form an orchestra (or resource centre) each year, of the standard that would make the exercise valid, from young musicians in only one country and a few months after they leave their conservatoires and universities, had been a flaw in the NCOS plan from the start. Youth orchestras were able to draw on the most gifted from across five or six years and any other orchestra could select from thirty years or more. For ambitious students who had already done a few professional dates while still completing their course the image of the NCOS was unattractive. Why should they remain at college for an extra year? Later some of them did come to realise, too late, that they still required further preparation before entering the orchestral profession.

At the end of the section about the National Centre for Orchestral Studies in chapter 22, when I was lamenting the demise of the NCOS, I wrote that 'In 1989 there was another attempt to create preparation for the profession' or, as I have always preferred to call it, a first year in the profession in sheltered accommodation. As soon as we received the bad news from the BBC I put the ideas

I had expressed in Innsbruck and at the Conference in Jerusalem to the NCOS management committee. They realised that in any case the NCOS would have to be wound up at the end of the next year's course and that my ideas gave the possibility of continuing the kind of education they had worked so hard to provide for the past ten years. Goldsmiths' College and the University of London both agreed that I should go ahead to see what might be possible.

Before going any further I thought I should approach the Wheatland Foundation, which had suggested that it might support projects specifically concerned with the education of orchestral musicians and assist politically or economically any developments that might arise. I wrote to tell them that since the Conference the previous year I had visited conservatoires around the world and had meetings with directors, managers and administrators, both public and private. The problems everywhere were similar to those we had discussed in Jerusalem. Now we should obtain some hard facts in regard to the economics, structure, administration and the education we should provide for those wanting to become musicians then and into the following century. I was disappointed to receive a reply informing me that the Wheatland Foundation did not fund research projects. It now administered a translation fund, which gave grants to British and American publishers to assist them in translating works from a foreign language into English.

In the autumn of 1988, as the first term of the final NCOS course was beginning, I started the search for money and a suitable venue for this new venture. I was incredibly fortunate to meet Tony Goodchild, who had just come into a considerable bequest that allowed him to retire from being the head of a large school music department and concentrate on his first love, conducting amateur choirs. With his customary generosity, he assisted me in so many ways: paying for a number of trips around the country in his splendid new car, a very large and incredibly powerful green Jaguar, and on a few occasion the cost of going overseas. Without his financial help the NCOS would have had to draw on its rapidly dwindling bank account.

He also bought us a computer which in 1988 meant a very large piece of equipment that required those using it to learn a special language – this was quite a while before Windows, click and drag, the Internet, etc. had become something that children of five and six could operate with ease. The sight of it sent my otherwise expert secretary, who was a very fast typist and generally extremely resourceful, into a flat spin. Fortunately, a young lady we also employed in the office who until then had only undertaken very junior tasks came to our rescue. Quite soon she was managing this new technology with which we were now able to prepare the publicity material we needed for our new venture, The Orchestra for Europe (O for E).

After looking at several places we at last found what seemed could become the perfect home for the new orchestra – a beautiful redundant 18th century church, St. Thomas in Bristol, with a large hall attached. Both the church and the hall were large enough to accommodate a full symphony orchestra. There was also space for our offices, music library and to store the large instruments, the timpani, percussion and the double basses. For our purpose Bristol in the south-west of England would make an ideal base. It is one of the very few cities in Britain that has the characteristics of a mainland European city of the same size – about thirty-five to forty thousand inhabitants. It has a fine concert hall, the Colston Hall, where I had played many times, several theatres, including the lovely 18th century Theatre Royal, an excellent library and a University with a good music department. There was a fast and frequent 90 minute train service to London that would enable members of the orchestra to attend a wealth of concerts and if they wished, arrange lessons with many of the finest artists in Britain.

Bristol had other advantages as a base for a musical organisation as well as its concert hall. It had no resident orchestra of its own and there were several other towns within a radius of fifty miles where it could give concerts: Bath, Gloucester, Cheltenham, Swindon and Wells, all towns I had played in with one orchestra or another. The members of this music resource centre could make a real contribution to the cultural life of all these towns and cities.

Throughout 1989 discussions with the church authorities, the architects and our fund-raising efforts went well enough for the NCOS Management Committee and the Delegacy of the University of London to start taking the necessary steps to wind up the Trust. In October three months after the last concert by the NCOS orchestra at the Barbican in London, the NCOS Trustees and Management Committee was disbanded. It had been agreed that the money remaining in the NCOS Trust account, the music library, the musical instruments and the office equipment should all pass to the new Orchestra for Europe management structure and Charitable Trust, with Lady Evelyn Barbirolli OBE as Chair of the Management Committee, which would take on responsibility for the new orchestra. Lord Harewood (The Rt. Hon. The Earl of Harewood KBE) agreed to be the orchestra's President, bringing his invaluable experience gained at the Royal Opera House, English National Opera and the Philharmonia Orchestra; the Vice-Presidents Sir Yehudi Menuhin OM, KBE, Sir John Tooley, General Director of the Royal Opera House, and Richard Burke with his knowledge of the European Commission, each brought their wide experience of musical and political affairs. Sir Charles Groves CBE, agreed to be Chairman of the International Council of Consultants and Gennadi Rozhdestvensky, formerly Principal Conductor of the BBC Symphony Orchestra and the Bolshoi and then Chief Conductor of the USSR Ministry of Culture Orchestra was to be the Artistic Adviser. I was appointed as Artistic and Executive Director.

We thought there would be enough money in the new O for E Trust account for us to have time to raise the funds required for the new orchestral course, this time for young musicians from right across Europe, not only those in Britain. If a number of countries within the EC contributed to the funding of the enterprise we believed we this could achieve our goal.

Everything seemed to be going well, but ... I can do no better than to quote from the *Bristol Evening Post* of 1 November 1989:

The much-vaunted plans to move a European orchestra to Bristol (in 1990) have been put back for a year – a victim of Britain's medieval church laws. The Orchestra for Europe intended to move into St. Thomas' church, an elegant 18th century building near Bristol Bridge, in January. But the change of use of a church is a very complicated business. The city planners have to agree – so do the diocese, the Church Commissioners, the Redundant Church Advisory Board and the Privy Council. The St. Thomas' scheme is likely to be approved by the Privy Council, but only after it has been advertised for a period of up to Christmas. This means the builders can't get inside to start the alterations necessary to house a 90-strong orchestra of young musicians from all over the continent. The delay means that hundreds of applicants for places for next year's orchestra have had to be turned away and their money refunded.

In the end the Privy Council did agree, though first objections from the Georgian Society to anything in the church being changed had to be overcome. There was also a campaign against the hall adjoining the church being used by the orchestra. It had for some years been used as a night refuge for the homeless and a rather fierce correspondence against any change of use (though other plans for the homeless were being made) ran in the local newspapers for several weeks. With the help of the Church Authorities we also overcame this problem.

As well as approaches to companies and individuals I went to Brussels to speak to one of the EC committees, the Comite Jeunesse of the European Parliament, where I gained the impression that if we were to be based anywhere other than in England we might well have received funds. Unfortunately, at that time Mrs Thatcher had been busy wielding her handbag and the British were not very popular. Other visits included Madrid and Istanbul, where I attended the Conference of the Association of European Conservatoire and Academies and spoke to them about O for E.

Though we raised a good deal of money, 1990 was as bad a time as we could have selected – the BBC was not the only organisation to be making what Richard Hoggart called 'candle end' savings. Everyone was cutting back. The conductors and soloists we needed to book for the concerts we proposed to give in Europe had to be booked well ahead, at least one or two years ahead, often longer. We could have started but I was unwilling to risk having to cancel concerts at a later date because of lack of money or run into the kind of debt so many arts organisations had experienced. At the beginning of 1991 I felt I had to advise the management committee that we should call it a day. Extremely reluctantly they did so. The letters I received from artists, conductors and those who had hoped we could continue our work, are testimony to how disappointed many musicians and music-lovers were.

A few months after we had left, a tramp managed to get into the church and make a bed for himself on top of the organ and then in the morning he went on his way leaving behind him a smouldering cigarette butt. The very fine organ caught fire and was completely destroyed, as was nearly everything else in the church, leaving the whole of the roof and all the walls covered in thick black tar, the result of the smoke. It would have cost us a fortune to repair the whole building and in the meantime we would have had nowhere to work. So, as it turned out we were saved from what would have been a major financial disaster had we not decided to call a halt when we did.

24 Preserving Music Performances

*Music Preserved – a new archive. Performance Practice and Audience
Expectations – have they changed? Archive-videos.
The Oral History of Musicians in Britain.*

O nce it became possible to record in their own homes some
music lovers began making off-air recordings of broadcasts of
studio performances and relays of public concerts. The first
recordings were made on acetate discs, on which the sound quality
was rather poor and only about four minutes music could be
recorded. From the early 1950s open-reel tape machines were used
until the cassette tape recording machine arrived around 1965
which made it easy to make recordings lasting 30 or 45 minutes
with a very acceptable standard of reproduction. From then on
home off-air recording really took off and a great many tape
recordings were made of every kind of music. It is fortunate that
though until 1988 it was illegal to record off-air at all it does not
seem to have acted as a deterrent. Had it done so a great many jazz
and serious music performances that remain available for study
and enjoyment would have been lost for ever. Being illegal these
recordings remained hidden in people's homes, as have those made
since 1988 when the law was changed to allow home off-air
recording for one's own private use. In spite of it being illegal to
make off-air recordings, through one of those strange loopholes in
the law it was perfectly legal to sell equipment that combined a
radio and two tape decks. This not only provided the facility for
recording off-air but also for copying from one cassette tape to
another making it simple for tape collectors to make copies and
exchange tapes with each other.

I had never had an interest in collecting recordings of any kind
so I was unaware of this until 1980, when a few months after I had
been appointed Director of the NCOS I received a letter from a
member of the Royal Opera House Orchestra. Jon Tolansky had
been making and collecting tapes since he was a boy and had over
7000 acetate disks, open-reel and analogue tapes of public
performances dating back to 1933. His house had recently been

struck by lightning and though only a small number of his recordings had been damaged he was frightened by this event and was looking for somewhere safer to store his collection. He was enquiring whether the NCOS might have room. In fact the NCOS did not have any suitable accommodation for his collection, but nonetheless I was intrigued by his request and arranged to meet him.

When we met, Tolansky brought some of his treasured recordings with him. They were all recordings of public performances, some of which he knew I had taken part in: Mahler's Symphony No.1 with the LPO conducted by Bruno Walter in 1947; a performance of Berlioz's *Grande Messe des Morts* played by the BBC Symphony Orchestra conducted by Sir Thomas Beecham, also in 1947; Otto Klemperer conducting *Don Juan* and *Till Eulenspiegel,* both by Richard Strauss, with the Philharmonia at a concert in the Royal Festival Hall in 1958. He also brought the recording of the wonderful concert in 1965 when Stravinsky conducted the Philharmonia in a performance of his own suite (the 1945 version) from *Firebird*; and a recording of the occasion when in 1948 Kathleen Ferrier joined Sir Adrian Boult and the BBC Symphony Orchestra for a performance of Mahler's Third Symphony.

It seemed to me that here were outstanding performances, with all the immediacy and interpretative improvisationary elements heard at a 'live' performance. They should not only be saved to preserve our cultural and music heritage for future generations, but be available in an archive where the public, students and researchers could listen to them. If this was to become possible it would first be necessary to convince the Musicians' Union of their value and that they would not become a threat to their members.

The MU had never been really happy about recordings from the start. Recordings were always seen as a potential threat and though they represented a new and lucrative avenue of employment for a small number of its members, it feared that records could be used to replace many more. They were particularly opposed to any attempt to make on-site or off-air recordings unless their members received an additional payment for this service. With the advent of tape recordings and long-playing records that allowed long stretches of music to be recorded their fears were realised: over the years recorded music did substantially reduce the employment available to musicians in broadcasting – all commercial broadcasting stations rely virtually entirely on commercial recordings – and also for those who played for dancing.

Music Preserved

When Jon Tolansky and I met the Executive Committee of the MU we were able to persuade them of the extent and value of his collection, and eventually they agreed to allow him to retain it even though it was six years before the law was to be amended. The MU agreed to co-operate in seeking a way by which on-site recordings of concerts and opera could be made for an archive. They succeeded in convincing the Mechanical Copyright Protection Society (MCPS), representing the interests of composers and publishers, as well as Equity the actors' union, to which many singers were members, to join in this project. It took another five years of negotiations with performers, composers and their representatives, the broadcasters, performance venues and the recording industry before the Music Performance Research Centre (MPRC) was established as a company limited by guarantee with charitable status in June 1987. The MPRC was renamed Music Preserved in 2001.

The BBC very generously allowed the MPRC to use their control rooms and tie lines at the Royal Festival Hall and Royal Opera House so that with their own recording equipment and microphones, donated to them by Sony, they were ready to start making recordings. A few months later in October the MPRC made its first on-site archive-recording. It was of a rather unusual concert at the Royal Festival Hall, given by the London Philharmonic Orchestra conducted by Victor Borge, the unique Danish humorist and entertainer who was also a fine pianist and conductor. Sir Georg Solti joined him, but only to make a short speech. A week later the Centre made their first archive-recording at the Royal Opera House, a performance of Mozart's *Marriage of Figaro* conducted by Bernard Haitink.

Over the following years the MPRC continued to make on-site recordings of concerts and operas. During 1988 their recordings at the Royal Festival Hall included a Wagner programme conducted by Klaus Tennstedt, and a concert performance of Beethoven's *Fidelio* conducted by Kurt Masur, both with the London Philharmonic Orchestra and some concerts with the Philharmonia, among them a programme with Giuseppe Sinopoli conducting Mahler's Symphony No.1, the Maxwell Davies *Trumpet* Concerto, with John Wallace as soloist, and Elgar's *In the South*, and Esa-Pekka Salonen conducting *Lontanoi* by György Ligeti and Carl Nielsen's 5th Symphony. At the Royal Opera House as well as several other operas they recorded *Peter Grimes* by Benjamin Britten, Janácek's J*enufa*, and *Don Giovanni* by Mozart.

A notice always has to be put up back-stage a week or so in advance so that any member of the orchestra or chorus not wishing the recording to be made can post their objection. It required only one person to object and the recording could not take place. The same applies as far as conductors and soloists are concerned. Unfortunately, at the Coliseum some members of the English National Opera Orchestra did refuse permission and since then no recordings have been made there. A great pity, as most of the excellent productions of unusual operas, all in English, have not been recorded commercially. It would also have provided an opportunity to chart the rise of a number of very good British singers.

When in 1988 the law regarding off-air recording was changed the Department of Trade and Industry recognised the MPRC as a Designated Archive. This made it possible for them to realise their original intention and receive donations of previously unauthorised off-air recordings and also to start making off-air recordings themselves. For the first couple of years the only place the MPRC could find to house their recordings safely was in the basement of the MU offices – not a very satisfactory arrangement. Then, in 1989 the Corporation of London agreed to allow the MPRC to create a Listening Studio in the Barbican Library, within the Barbican Arts Centre in the City of London. This was an excellent venue where the recordings could be stored in ideal conditions and where the public could listen to them. Another generous donation from Sony provided all the play-back and listening equipment required for the two listening booths. An additional bonus was the willingness of the Barbican library staff to deal with those wishing to listen to any of the recordings.

Since then many thousands of recordings dating from 1933 have been donated to the archive. The donations have been in various formats: acetate discs, open-reel tapes and analogue cassette tapes. Their condition has varied considerably: a good many have been in excellent sound in relation to the recording techniques available at the time they were made and have been carefully preserved, but some of them have had faults of one kind or another. A great deal of technical work has been undertaken to repair and restore damaged recordings. Surface noise has been reduced as far as possible; drop-outs made more acceptable by fading in and out before and after the gap and if there is print-through – when a faint 'echo' of a passage can be heard before or after the actual music – it has been removed whenever possible. But the integrity of the original was and continues to be paramount. Changes to render a recording more acceptable to those who have become accustomed to the clinical standard of CDs and other forms of transmission have been resisted. The recordings were then transferred to DAT and later to CD, with funding from the Heritage Lottery Fund.

It soon became necessary to decide which recordings should go into the archive. A list of criteria was drawn up to guide those having to make the difficult decision as to what should be accepted. If a recording was to be kept in the archive it should be of an event of historic interest, an outstanding performance by an artist(s) or orchestra (necessarily a subjective judgement), performances by distinguished artists of music they had not previously recorded, or a public performance that differed to a marked extent from their commercial recording of the same music.

The legal agreements that now continue to protect Music Preserved's archive of recordings of public performances from exploitation and that have made it possible for them to create an archive where the public can listen, free of charge, do not allow anyone other than Music Preserved itself to copy its recordings under any circumstances. However, some years later it was agreed that in safe protected conditions, under the control of a member of the Music Preserved staff, extracts, and sometimes whole works, could be played at public and private events outside the Barbican.

Once it was free to take items from its collection outside the Listening Studio, Music Preserved initiated a National Access and Education Programme. Presentations of its holdings have been given all over the country sometimes at music societies, such as those in Torbay and Esher; at music colleges – Trinity College of Music, Birmingham Conservatoire – and most notably at the 1997 Edinburgh International Festival. The Festival was celebrating its 50th anniversary and invited Music Preserved to give a presentation every day throughout the three weeks of the Festival of some of its historic archive-recordings made at the Festival during the previous 49 years. Jon Tolansky introduced the recordings, which included some wonderful performances: the Brahms Double Concerto for Violin and Cello played by Joseph Szigeti and Pierre Fournier, Beecham conducting Sibelius 1 with the RPO, Guido Cantelli conducting *La Meri* and *Two Nocturnes* both by Debussy and Schumann's Fourth Symphony, the Shostakovich 1st Cello Concerto played by Rostropovich with Rozhdestvensky conducting the Leningrad Philharmonic, and the Stockholm Opera's performance of Janácek's opera *Jenufa* in 1974.

But it was the 1957 archive-recording of the complete opera *La sonnambula* by Bellini, with Maria Callas and Fiorenzai Cossotto, when the entire La Scala company had come to Edinburgh from Milan, that created the most excitement. Immediately after the end of the Festival they had made a commercial recording of the opera. Tolansky told me that the 1997 audience of over a thousand in the Edinburgh Queen's Hall had sat spell-bound throughout the performance of Music Preserved's recording of the opera with nothing to look at but the two loudspeakers on the stage. When the performance was over several members of the audience who had been at the actual performances forty years previously came to speak to him. They had bought the long-playing record issued shortly after the Edinburgh production, but they said that listening to the archive-recording was different – it was like being back again in the King's Theatre all those years ago.

Performance Practice and Audience Expectations 1900 - 2000

Since the 1970s an increasing interest and concern for 'authenticity' in performance had led to attempts to identify how the great masterpieces of the past had been performed, using contemporary reports and internal evidence from the music itself, but of course, a great deal still remained speculative. Now in the 1980s when the Music Performance Research Centre (MPRC) was being set up, musicians and music-lovers were listening to recordings made by orchestras from around the world and an increasing number were lamenting the decline in the individuality and spontaneity of orchestral performances – on record and in the concert hall – and the loss of clearly audible national characteristics of instrumental tone and musical style that had in the past distinguished one orchestra and performance from another.

Had performing in studios, rather than to an audience, and the advances in recording techniques that had and were continuing to take place had any effect on those frequently involved in studio broadcasting and recording? Did concert audiences have expectations derived from listening to many more commercial recordings than concert performances, since even the most ardent concert-goers spent far more time listening to broadcast and recorded music than attending 'live' music events?

The MPRC felt that the archive of historical and contemporary recordings of *live* performances it had created and the extensive collection of recorded interviews it possessed provided a research tool that could enquire into whether there was evidence that recording and broadcasting had influenced performances in the way that was being suggested. As Chairman of what was then still the Music Performance Research Centre, I applied to the Leverhume Trust for a Research Grant that would fund research into a number of questions regarding changes in performance practice.

The Trust responded favourably to this application for a grant and agreed to fund a two-year research programme. This enabled the MPRC to engage a part-time researcher. Leverhulme approved my directing the project, but as a member of the Council of a Company Limited by Guarantee I was not allowed to be paid for undertaking any work for it. They also approved Jon Tolansky as the part-time researcher.

The research programme included an examination of the differences between studio and public performances and a comparison of five orchestras between 1951 and 1975 and then in 1992. There was a questionnaire for audiences and questionnaires and recorded interviews with conductors, soloists, singers, recording engineers and orchestral musicians. Some of the performers had recorded on both 78 rpm and tape and others only on tape. The written accounts by artists about their relationship and attitudes to recording were collected.

The MPRC sought answers to these questions:

- Is there evidence that there has been a loss of individuality and spontaneity?
- Have national and local traditions of performance been affected or lost, as a result of the world-wide distribution of recordings and been replaced by a musical Esperanto?
- Has the intervention of recording producers and engineers, or the artificial balances created in the studio and by editing, had an effect on the artists involved?
- Do they perform differently in the studio than when in the concert hall or opera house?
- Is there evidence that audience expectations have been changed by listening to studio recordings on which the performers have concentrated on accuracy of instrumental technique, ensemble and intonation?
- Do public performances attempt to emulate the recordings?
- Is there any evidence that listeners are now more concerned with 'sounds' than content?

The MPRC started by comparing studio recordings and archive-recordings of public performances of five orchestras. The comparisons were always of the same music, played by the same orchestra and conductor within quite a short time of each other. On some occasions the two recordings had been made within a few weeks of each other.

Amongst the works selected were *The Walk to the Paradise Garden*, from *A Village Romeo and Juliet* by Delius, played by the RPO conducted by Sir Thomas Beecham; *Francesca da Rimini* by Tchaikovsky played by the Leningrad Philharmonic Orchestra conducted by Gennadi Rozhdestvensky; the Overture *Consecration of the House* by Beethoven, played by the Philharmonia and conducted by Otto Klemperer; *Roman Carnival Overture* by Berlioz played by the Cleveland Orchestra conducted by Lorin Maazel and *Moonlight*, one of the *Sea Interludes* from the opera *Peter Grimes* by

Benjamin Britten played by the Royal Opera House Orchestra conducted by the composer.

When the pairs of recordings were being analysed there was no difficulty in recognising which were the studio and which the public performances: there was a marked difference between them. On all the recordings that were compared there was far more rubato in the public performances and not only considerable differences of tempo – in general andante and adagio passages were taken more slowly and faster tempo markings played faster at concerts than in the studio – but variations within a given tempo were also quite frequent. It was much more difficult to be sure about differences of dynamics. Though there did appear to be a wider range of dynamics on the archive-recordings than those recorded in a studio, it was not possible to know whether this was inherent in the actual performance in the studio, or if they had been ironed out by the producer and his recording engineers in the course of editing. However, from the work that was undertaken on performances from the period 1975 to 1992, there is some evidence that the studio and concert performances were becoming more alike. The concert performances seemed by the mid-eighties to have become much less distinguishable from studio performances than had previously been the case.

Compilations were made of extracts from recordings made by orchestras in France, Germany, Russia, America and Britain between 1930 and 1992 and of ten orchestras from nine countries playing in the Royal Albert Hall within a period of six weeks during the 1992 Promenade concert series. The intention was to learn whether the distinct national characteristics of tone and the traditional elements in their performances in the 1930s had been retained. Another taped compilation of performances, this time of Ravel's *Bolero* made during the same period, show a quite remarkable change in the way the balance between the solo instruments and their accompaniment was considered appropriate. There is a marked increase in the prominence of the soloists in relation to their accompaniment from the 1970s onwards. This is particularly noticeable in the first very quiet solos for the flute and clarinet.

As well as this work a questionnaire addressed to members of the audience was left on each seat in the hall for concerts given at the Birmingham Symphony Hall, the Barbican Hall, the Royal Opera House and the Royal Festival Hall during 1993. It consisted of a single sheet of paper with the questionnaire on one side and a letter on the other explaining the reasons for it. The letter explained that the MPRC was engaged in an enquiry into what music lovers' expectations were when listening to 'live' and 'recorded' music, and the effect that performing at concerts and in the recording studio had on the artists themselves. The comparisons would be between recordings made in a studio and those made at concert performances. As well as the nearly 250 detailed replies to the questionnaires that were returned there were meetings with members of record societies where these questions were discussed.

The questions, which were quite far ranging were:

- Do you listen to music on the radio and on which stations?
- Do you own records and CDs?
- About how long do you listen to specific programmes or recordings each week and for how long when it is just background to some other activity?
- How often do you attend a concert or opera performance?
- What decides you to go – is it the music to be performed, the artists taking part or because you own or have heard a recording of the music or artist?
- What makes you buy a particular recording – the music, the artist or a critical review?
- Are you ever disappointed at a concert or at the opera after you have become familiar with the music from a recording?
- Are you disturbed by any blemishes or distractions that may occur at a concert or opera?
- Are you ever disappointed when listening to a recording after you have heard the music at a concert or opera?
- Is the sound quality of a recording of great importance to you?
- If the tone quality is thin or scratchy, as it can be on older recordings, does this make it unacceptable? Do you use the controls on your equipment to increase/decrease the volume, or only to listen to sections of the music you particularly enjoy?

Sadly it has not been possible for the extensive research that was undertaken to be completed as the necessary funding has not been available. The only part of the research to have been published so far is the comparison of the five orchestras. The chosen orchestras were the Cleveland Orchestra (US), the St. Petersburg Philharmonic (formerly the Leningrad Philharmonic), the Concertgebouw Orchestra (Holland), the Vienna Philharmonic (Austria) and the London Symphony Orchestra (UK). They were chosen because each orchestra had a strong tradition of performance, observable national characteristics and they had all taken part in the 1992 BBC Promenade season in the Royal Albert Hall. The archive-recordings of these performances in the Archive are not off-air recordings, but direct off-line checks provided to the Archive by the BBC. The result of this research was published by Harwood Academic Publishers in the 1997 edition of Musical Performance (Vol. 1, part 4). Copies of this publication and recordings of the extracts used to make the comparisons can be seen and heard at the Music Preserved Listening booths.

From its inception Music Preserved's intention was to chronicle the changes in performance style that had already taken place and would continue to do so in future. Equally, if not more important, is their aim to preserve performances of new music, very frequently not recorded commercially. It would be wonderful if in the future instead of having to rely on the often dubious written accounts, as we are obliged to do now when considering how the compositions of Mozart, Beethoven and many others were performed, we could actually hear how their music was played when they were alive.

Archive-Videos

BBC Libraries and Archives Division in 1994 donated a number of videos to Music Preserved. The videos made it possible for them to add another facility at its Listening Studio at the Barbican. These videos could no longer be broadcast by BBC, because of contractual agreements with the artists involved, nor could they be issued commercially at that time. Music Preserved has added to them by making a number of off-air television relays themselves including part of the BBC *Fairest Isle* Festival and have accepted donations of privately made off-air video performances.

Oral Histories

Music Preserved, not satisfied with only recording music performances decided to start recording interviews with musicians. Their intention was to trace how working conditions and standards had changed for them during the 20th century. Musicians from as many areas of the profession as possible were interviewed, including part-time musicians. In the series of interviews titled *The Oral History of Musicians in Britain,* musicians in their own words provide information about where they had been educated, where employed, what music they had played and with whom, and how they had been affected by the musical, technological and social changes that had occurred while they were in the profession.

In the relaxed environment, usually in their own homes where the interviews were recorded, it was possible for the interviews to be more like 'conversations'. The interviewees whether celebrated conductors, singers, soloists or members of orchestras and bands felt able to express their views and comments more freely than is often the case. In fact, on several occasions I had to ask whether they were sure they wanted what they had said to remain on a recording that would be in an archive where anyone who wished to could listen to them.

Two of those interviewed were more than a hundred years old when I recorded them. Bill Waller, who was a hundred, had been a horn player in Liverpool. He had known some of the great players who had played under Hans Richter in the Hallé at the end of the 19th century and himself played as an extra in the Hallé under Sir Hamilton Harty as well as for some of the successful musical comedies in the early 1920s. Sidonie Goossens, a member of the famous Goossens family, was the principal harpist in the BBC Symphony Orchestra when I first met her in 1932. My father had taken my mother and myself – I was then seven – to see the newly built Broadcasting House and attend one of the Orchestra's rehearsals. When I went to interview her 68 years later in 2000 she was 101. Her memory was still very sharp and she was able to recall her first professional engagements, chamber music and playing in theatres from 1916, during the first world war. Her orchestral debut was on June 7th 1921, in the orchestra which her brother Eugene had formed when he conducted the first British concert performance of Stravinsky's *Rite of Spring*. She remained the principal harpist in the BBC Symphony Orchestra from 1930 for over fifty years and was a favourite of composers from Stravinsky to Boulez and renowned for her ability to learn and play contemporary music right up to when she retired.

As well as interviews with distinguished orchestral musicians, including many I have already written about and a few less celebrated, there are interviews with jazz and dance band musicians, including band leaders and some who were only part-time musicians; there are also interviews with those who played in theatres, night clubs, on ships and bandstands. In fact anywhere that musicians are employed. In addition to the recordings that Music Preserved itself has made, there are sets of valuable interviews that have been donated to the Archive. Particularly important are the 50 that were made at the Royal Opera House as part of the Verdi Centenary with conductors, singers and members of the chorus and orchestra.

At a series of celebrity interviews, *Profile of the Artist,* mounted by Music Preserved and funded by Guardian Royal Exchange in a small hall within the Barbican Centre, the celebrated tenor Jon Vickers, the conductor Sir Edward Downes, and Gary Brooker from the group *Procol Harum,* and others, recalled their careers and listened with the audience to extracts from their own public performances preserved in the Archive. All the interviews can be listened to in the Music Preserved listening booths.

Perhaps these interviews – there are now nearly 200 – may prove to be as valuable for future generations in providing a picture of musical life in Britain in the 20th century as the recordings of the performances.

25 A Time of Change

Orchestras face increasing financial problems – reduction in recording work. Classic FM. Raymond Gubbay. 'Classical-crossover'. Jazz – dance bands – popular singers. The arrival of pop and rock music. World Music.

Gradually, towards the mid-1970s, those of us who had been playing in the London orchestras during the 1940s, 50s and 60s and seen the growth of audiences for symphony concerts and recordings became aware that all was not continuing as we would have wished. When I was chairman of the Philharmonia, during the second half of the 1970s, somewhat exaggerated reports of the poor audience attendance figures for the concerts given by the London orchestras began to appear in the press. They were accompanied from time to time by the recommendation that a new 'super orchestra' should be created by amalgamating at least two of the London orchestras. This was not a new idea. It had been around ever since the Goodman report in 1965 and came from those who wanted to save money. Others believed it might be possible by combining the best players from each orchestra to create one that would be better than any of those we already had. The financial problems with which the orchestras in Britain were grappling were not improved when in 1979 the Conservative Party was elected with a mandate to reduce taxation. It was not long before there was a reduction in arts funding in general. The Minister for the Arts thought that the reduction in personal taxation would leave more money for patronage. The natural scepticism of the members of the orchestras was in the event justified: there was no increase in patronage.

The orchestras in London, used to their schedule of concerts and tours being financially supported by the many recording sessions they had undertaken over the past thirty years, were by the early 1980s just starting to feel the impact of the reduction in the number of sessions on offer. It was not only in Britain that the audience for classical music was declining, though it was to take quite a while before it became as noticeable in those countries where there had been a tradition of permanent orchestras and regular concert attendance. By the beginning of the 21st century the programmes of the major orchestras in France, Germany, Italy and the Scandinavian countries had become very similar to those in Britain. The only orchestras that can afford to play new music fairly regularly – it is noticeable that more often than not it is music by one of their own national composers – remain the radio orchestras. A good deal of contemporary music for chamber ensemble and chamber orchestra is performed but, of course, the cost of the extra rehearsals required is very much less than for a large symphony orchestra and their concerts take place in smaller venues and to relatively small and rather specialist audiences.

In 1986 the lack of sufficient financial support nearly everywhere around the world, and the complaint by composers and critics that the performance of contemporary music was being neglected, led to the Wheatland Foundation conference, about which I have written in chapter 23. The conference was concerned with the decline in the audiences for symphony orchestra concerts and whether the contemporary orchestra was, as it had been called 'an obsolescent instrument'. How might it evolve and change to meet the new needs of composers, performers and audiences? The conference came to no conclusion because, in my view, it was unwilling to face two important facts: the symphony orchestra, able to play the symphonic repertoire from Haydn to Shostakovich, was no longer the instrument contemporary composers required; and that the mainstream audience for classical music continued to find (twenty years later it still does) most of the orchestral music written since 1960 not to its taste. Neither William Glock, when he was Controller of Music at the BBC, with his declared intention in 1959 to provide listeners with 'What they would like tomorrow' nor Pierre Boulez at IRCAM in Paris, nor the effort of others to bring about what Glock had tried so hard to achieve seem to have had any effect. Now nearly fifty years later nothing has changed. Nor did the Wheatland conference take into account the increase in other forms of entertainment that had become available or the changes in social behaviour.

Today's audiences for symphony concerts, opera and chamber music are very different from those when the music was written during the 18th and 19th centuries, who mainly came from the middle and upper-middle-classes. They had servants and the time to prepare themselves for an evening's entertainment and would have changed out of the clothes they had been wearing during the day. Those in the stalls and boxes will have been in formal evening dress, the dress imitated by the members of the orchestra at that time and which continues to be worn by the orchestras today, though the dress code for audiences now varies from smart casual to unsuitably informal.

Until the beginning of the 20th century and to some extent as late as 1939 and the start of the 2nd World War, a good deal of the music played at concerts and at the opera will have been by composers whose chamber music quite a number of the audience will have played themselves. It was not at all unusual for families and friends to play chamber music, trios, quartets and piano quartets for their own pleasure and sometimes to be joined by one or more wind instrumentalists. The chamber music of Haydn, Mozart, Beethoven and Schubert was already standard fare and as chamber music by Mendelssohn, Schumann, Brahms, Tchaikovsky and Dvorak and others was published throughout the 19th century it soon became part of the repertoire for many groups of amateur musicians. Some of them will have been very good players though no doubt some will only have been of a standard similar to that about which I have written in reporting my early experiences of playing the Mozart Clarinet Quintet. Until the early years of the 20th century a lot of orchestral music and opera was also published in piano arrangements for four hands.

The children of these families will have *heard* this music from an early age without even being aware of it. There was no need for them to attend children's concerts at which they would have to sit quietly and *listen* to music that was unfamiliar and have it explained to them. At the many children's concerts in which I have taken part I am sure there will have been some for whom this will have been a wonderful experience and the start of a lifetime's love of music. A rather larger number of the young people were quite obviously bored and often misbehaved. For them the concerts were not a natural occasion for enjoyment but part of the school curriculum. If children are to develop a love of classical music they need to have the opportunity of *hearing* it from as early an age as possible; not in a formal way, but as part of their environment. They should hear it from the radio and CDs while having breakfast and at other times when they will absorb it unconsciously. But since the beginning of the 20th century there has been very little chamber music suitable for the average amateur and gradually the opportunity for children to hear music played within the home environment virtually disappeared. In fact it is an entirely different kind of music that has for many years past been part of their aural background.

The decline in patronage and subsidy, essential if a symphony orchestra is to remain solvent, already a cause for concern in 1986, continued to decline until by 2000 it was causing many orchestras and opera houses to restrict their programmes and in some cases to cease altogether. It was not only in Britain that national and local authorities responding to increased demands on their funds and not wishing to increase taxation began to economise by making cuts where they felt it would cause the least unfavourable response. They recognised that symphony orchestra concerts and operas were of interest to only a minority of their taxpayers and that this would be the easiest place to start making economies. In some places there were even demands that support for something of interest to so few should not be borne by taxation from the many.

Why is it that very little classical music composed after the middle of the 20th century is still only able to attract a small audience? Though there had been far fewer concerts and no recordings or broadcasts during the one hundred and twenty-five years between 1780 and 1902, the innovative compositions by Haydn, Mozart, Beethoven, Berlioz, Wagner and all the major orchestral compositions by Richard Strauss had been accepted into the repertoire in their own lifetimes. In contrast, in the first decade of the 21st century symphony orchestra concert programmes in Europe still remain much as they have been for a hundred years or more. With the exception of Shostakovich, Messiaen and Britten, there are hardly any other composers who were born after 1905 whose works have entered the repertoire to any extent. A young musician joining an orchestra in 1892, fifty years before I did and having a career lasting forty years would by 1932 have played a very similar repertoire to that which I played and which the orchestras are still playing now. By 1950 the compositions by Richard Strauss, Bartók, Stravinsky, Prokofiev, Hindemith, Walton and even Alban Berg's atonal Violin Concerto had become accepted and regularly performed. Many of the compositions first performed between 1880 and 1930 that were new in style and content soon became part of the repertoire. Even *The Rite of Spring* by Stravinsky, which had been the cause of such an unprecedented uproar and scandal in 1913, could be played at the Queen's Hall in musically conservative Britain in 1931 without comment. During my own time as an orchestral musician I played in the first performances in Britain of a number of compositions that are now part of the repertoire, though there are hardly any new compositions I first played after about 1965 that have gained a place in the public's affection.

Though the major symphony orchestras have continued to have financial problems caused by falling audiences and insufficient patronage or subsidy, it is evident that there is still a considerable audience for the popular classical and romantic repertoire, including music composed in the first part of the 20th century. The Raymond Gubbay concerts and the Classic FM broadcasts still continue to attract very large audiences.

The concerts promoted by Raymond Gubbay year after year, with virtually the same programmes, fill the Royal Albert and Barbican Halls. His 'Classical Spectacular' concerts, which have attracted audiences for over 15 years – there have been about 200 performances – not only take place in London and other cities in Britain, but are now successful throughout Europe and in Australia. The programmes for these extremely popular concerts are much more like those we played when I was in the London Philharmonic Orchestra in the 1940s. They usually have between four and seven items, in contrast to the programmes of the major orchestras in more recent years which seldom consist of more than three compositions, two in the first half and one in the second, which is usually a work lasting between forty minutes to an hour – sometimes longer.

At a time when television and the computer dominate so many of our lives it seems that the eye has become more important than the ear. Gubbay has responded by making many of his presentations both visually and musically attractive. The 'Classical Spectacular' concerts, which nearly always include the 1812 Overture 'with Thundering Cannons and Muskets and Indoor Fireworks', or his 'Mozart Festival', 'Johann Strauss' Orchestra, Mozart by Candlelight and Johann Strauss Gala concerts, all have a visual element absent from the regular symphony concerts. Whilst the symphony orchestras agonised about whether men should continue to wear the traditional 'tails' and women wear 'long black', or if they should find some more contemporary dress, Gubbay did not hesitate to advertise that for his Mozart concerts the musicians would be dressed in 'authentic 18th century costumes' and for the Strauss and Viennese programmes the orchestra would be 'directed from the violin in the traditional Viennese manner'.

As well as his own orchestra, the London Concert Orchestra, made up of freelance musicians, Gubbay also regularly employs the London Philharmonic, Royal Philharmonic, Philharmonia and English Chamber Orchestras, often playing programmes that include Beethoven's *Eroica* or 9th symphonies and the well-known violin concertos, piano concertos and overtures.

Gubbay has also established a large audience for ballet and opera by staging spectacular arena productions of both genres at the Royal Albert Hall. Over the last decade his staged events together with his concert runs, mean that his company is now the hall's biggest annual tenant after the Proms. In 2005 over Christmas and the New Year he presented 150 Festive Classical Concerts around Britain, including 18 at the Albert Hall and 15 at the Barbican.. In all, the Gubbay organisation presents some 600 opera, ballet and concert performances at major concert venues each year.

His spectacular productions of opera or ballet, staged 'in the round' in the arena at the Royal Albert Hall are more visually exciting than is possible in an opera house. Though his concerts have rarely received any attention in the press, the operas have been given enthusiastic notices by the critics. And, in the same way that English National Opera bridged the gap between opera and musical theatre when it staged Bernstein's *On the Town,* Gubbay has presented a massive 'in-the-round' staging of Kern and Hammerstein's 1927 Broadway classic *Show Boat,* directed by Francesca Zambello, whose production for Gubbay of *La Bohéme* at the Royal Albert Hall was also so well received.

The symphony orchestras and opera houses everywhere, with various levels of subsidy, have experienced financial difficulties, frequently going into debt. But Raymond Gubbay who has always attracted large audiences, never employs expensive conductors or soloists and has the minimum of rehearsals – very rarely more than one for a concert – has actually made a profit. Clearly it is not whether there is a 'big name' conductor or soloist or which orchestra is playing that attracts so many people to attend these events: it is what music is on the programme, what music they will hear. Another important element is that a Gubbay concert has for many come to stand for an event that one can trust to provide an enjoyable night out, even if you don't know the names of the pieces on the programme. Simon Rattle, when he was at Birmingham, built up this degree of trust in his audience so that he was able to put on programmes, including contemporary compositions, that in London would have played to only a small audience.

When Classic FM, the commercial radio station playing recordings of classical music, first started in 1992 it was ridiculed because it was obvious that most of their presenters were not conversant with the classical music repertoire. Musical gaffes and mispronunciations abounded. But the informal, laid-back style of the presentation met with approval. Within quite a short time their presenters became more expert and the criticism disappeared. The station which claimed to play 'the world's most beautiful music' had realised that what most listeners wanted to hear was well-known and well-loved music. There is no doubt that BBC Radio 3, however much it denies that the changes in its programming have not been influenced by this new upstart classical music station, has introduced programmes that have become increasingly more like those of Classic FM in form, though the content has as a rule remained more serious and has been aimed at the more informed listener. Now BBC Radio 3 broadcasts much more 'light music' and jazz than it did in the past.

Classic FM has from its inception been the most listened to classical music station and has consistently attracted a larger audience than BBC Radio 3. I have been surprised that many of my friends and other members of the audience I meet at concerts at the Royal Festival Hall and elsewhere tell me that they prefer to listen to Classic FM, even with the interminable adverts, than Radio 3, which a number of them feel tends to treat its listeners as if they were music students and, in an effort to avoid playing too many 'favourites', seek out more recherché repertoire that sometimes might be of interest to a more specialist audience. At the end of 2005 Classic FM was reported as having 4.1% (5.3

million) of the national weekly share of the radio audience for classical music, as compared with 1.2% (2.1 million) for BBC Radio 3. But, during the same period the figures for BBC Radio 1, broadcasting pop recordings and BBC Radio 2 middle-of-the-road music, were very much larger, 9.4% (10.3 million) and 15.6% (12.9 million). The other stations broadcasting music (virtually all on recordings of pop music), the commercial radio stations and BBC Local Radio had over 50% of the listening audience.

The concerts promoted by Raymond Gubbay and the success of the commercial radio station Classic FM continue to prove that there is a very large audience for orchestral music composed before about 1960. But it seems that what the majority of listeners still want more than anything else are good tunes. As he so often did, Sir Thomas Beecham put it most succinctly. In an interview, printed in the *New York Times* when he was living in the USA in 1942, he is reported as saying 'The only music that lives does so because of its melodic beauty and significance, which makes it remembered.' Compositions that stir the emotions and are not too long tend to be most popular, as do extracts from longer works – one or two movements from a symphony or concerto. It seems that nothing has changed very much since Sir Henry Wood started conducting the Proms in 1895.

In September 1997 at the Klassik Komm Conference in Hamburg, Peter Gelb, then the President of Sony Classical, no doubt prompted by the problems his company was experiencing is reported as saying, 'For the classical record industry, the writing is already on the wall'. All the major record labels were suffering significant declines in sales of standard repertoire recordings, but were at first very reluctant to admit or even to try to understand the causes. By 1995 Sony had been obliged to shut down its headquarters in Hamburg, even though it had started two high profile projects, one with Giulini and another recording the Verdi operas at the New York Metropolitan Opera House. It had also acquired the video productions of Herbert von Karajan. They had been very expensive but found few sales. Gelb went on to say, 'had the record labels been cultivating and encouraging greater originality and creativity from performers and composers in recent decades, instead of passively and almost exclusively recording standard works without consideration of popular demand, but only at the whim of a handful of maestros eager to see their own performances permanently documented on disc, the collapse wouldn't have been so sudden or dramatic. But, unlike the pop sector of the record industry where creativity is encouraged, classical record executives long preferred solely to play the role of curators … nothing more. So, all they recorded were the same pieces over and over again.'

Gelb, not satisfied with lambasting his colleagues in the record industry, then attacked the critics who he said seemed to share a common goal, 'to confine all new classical music to an elite intellectual exercise with very limited audience appeal. By their rules, any new classical composition that enjoys commercial success is no good. To become successful new music must be heard in concert halls, on classical radio stations and television so that audiences have the opportunity to hear the music – and to respond.' He thought that the way forward lay in encouraging composers to write works for the widest possible audience, sometimes by connecting them to a prominent soloist or to a feature film, and by more artists performing and recording popular, less demanding music. If the classical record industry was to be revitalised it must develop its marketing and recording strategies. In recommending what by then was already being called 'classical crossover' he attracted some adverse criticism.

But when Peter Gelb suggested that classical artists should take part in recordings of more popular compositions he was only harking back to what had been commonplace in the early days of recording. The great operatic artists regularly recorded much lighter, more popular music as well as operas and the well-known operatic arias. Enrico Caruso, as well as recording arias from *Rigoletto, Tosca, Otello* and many other operas, recorded drawing-room ballads, Neapolitan songs, such as *O Sole Mio*, and even lighter fare, O'Hara's ,*'Your eyes have told me what I did not know'* and the patriotic first world war favourite *'Over There'*, by the American super-star George M Cohan, best known now for the song *Yankee Doodle Dandy*. Amelia (often called Amelita) Galli-Curci, the highest paid singer of her day (she was paid even more than Caruso), recorded *Abide with me, Mah Lindy Lou* and *Home Sweet Home,* as well as a wide-ranging operatic repertoire that included Rossini, Verdi, Puccini, Meyerbeer – *The Shadow Song,* from his opera *Dinorah,* was one of her favourites. The Irish tenor John McCormack, another very fine artist, was immensely popular with lovers of opera and popular music alike. He made recordings of Mozart, Donizetti, Bizet and Puccini arias alongside Victor Herbert's *I'm falling in love with someone,* many Irish songs – *Mother Machree, The Garden Where the Praties Grow, Trottin' to the Fair,* and his collaboration with the great violinist Fritz Kreisler in arrangements such as the *Berceuse* from the opera *Jocelyn* by Godard and *Serenata* by Moritz Moszkowski.

The music that the great artists in the first part of the 20th century were performing was still part of a much more integrated repertoire. But after the middle of the century very little classical music has been composed that has become popular enough to carry on this tradition. Until the beginning of the 1900s there had only been folk music and art or composed music. Composed music included music for the church, the concert hall and opera house, and chamber music, originally played in a domestic setting, as well as the music played in the theatres, restaurants and on bandstands and most importantly for dancing. Composers from the time of Haydn, Mozart and Beethoven to Sibelius, Elgar and Stravinsky composed music for many kinds of occasions – religious music, symphonies, sonatas and short pieces of a much lighter character. In the 18th century they were quite happy to compose marches and, in the time of the earlier composers, dances and what was in effect 'background' music. The waltzes of the Strauss family, Lanner and Waldteufel, the Savoy operettas by Arthur Sullivan and the at one time popular compositions by Albert Ketelbey – *In a Monastery Garden* and *In a Persian Market,* all inhabit the same milieu.

The Parting of the Ways

But then, from about 1910 onwards a new kind of music started to arrive from America – ragtime, blues and jazz. This was to be the beginning of an ever-increasing divide between popular and classical music that was to continue throughout the rest of the century. This new music originated in the southern states of America at the turn of the century, to a large extent in the mixed Negro and Creole community in New Orleans, where the many brass bands that led the parades and celebration marches would 'rag' or 'jazz-up' the music. When these bands accompanied a funeral cortege to the cemetery it was customary to play a dirge, very slowly and mournfully, or an old Negro spiritual such as

Nearer My God to Thee, but on returning home the band would break into a fast upbeat version of *When the Saints Go Marching In* or a ragtime song such as *Didn't He Ramble* and those following the procession, the famous 'second line' would strut, dance and sing. The 'first line' were the family members of the deceased, the hearse and the band. This tradition still continued in New Orleans even when the style of music changed with the brass bands continuing to improvise and 'funk-up' contemporary pop songs.

As well as the numerous society dances that required skilled musical ensembles at which waltzes and quadrilles were played – the music of the middle-class – there were also the many dance halls and brothels in the Storyville District, where the musicians played the new syncopated, jazz music similar to that which they played in the Parade bands.

New Orleans was the home of many of the early jazz musicians who can still be heard on the recordings they made: the trumpet players Joe 'King' Oliver and his pupil the great Louis Armstrong, the trombonist Kid Ory, the clarinettists – Johnny Dodds, Jimmy Noone and Sidney Bechet – and the bass player 'Pops' Foster, to name only a few. The Dixieland revival in the 1940s brought back some of the musicians who had been obliged to find other work during the long years of the depression. It was some of these musicians, now elderly, that I heard when I visited New Orleans in 1950 with the Royal Philharmonic. They were playing in the Bunk Johnson band (though Johnson had died just the previous year) and Papa Celestin's with Alphonse Picou, by then seventy-eight, and still going strong.

In 1919 Sidney Bechet had come to London with the Southern Syncopated Orchestra where he was heard by the Swiss conductor Ernest Ansermet. Ansermet was enormously enthusiastic about Bechet's playing and the music this group played. In one of the first serious reviews of this new style of music and playing he wrote in *Revue Romande*, published in Switzerland: *They are so entirely possessed by the music they play, that they can't stop themselves from dancing inwardly to it in such a way that their playing is a real show. When they indulge in one of their favourite effects, which is to take up the refrain of a dance in a tempo suddenly twice as slow and with redoubled intensity and figuration, a truly gripping thing takes place: it seems as if a great wind is passing over a forest or as if a door is suddenly opened on a wild orgy.*

Not only was the music new but it also required a new kind of musician. To play this new syncopated music the musicians needed to be more relaxed and respond to a rhythm and style for which their training and experience had not prepared them. To begin with the new dances were played by the same kind of bands as before except that the wind instruments, in particular the cornet or trumpet, were given the melody more frequently. At the same time as the arrival of this new music the development of the improved double-sided ten-inch record allowed a few early recordings of ragtime, dixieland, the blues and jazz, most often recorded by military bands, to become available in Britain. After 1918 as more recordings became available and some of the returning soldiers reported what they had heard the US bands playing, ballroom dancers wanted to have the new music played more authentically.

The Original Dixieland Jazz Band (ODJB) made what is reputed to be the first Jazz record in 1917. Two years later in 1919 as part of their tour in Europe they played at the London Hippodrome. Though British bands had made some recordings of ragtime music from 1912 it was not until after the ODJB's visit that jazz-styled dance bands really took off in Britain. From 1920 more and more small British bands were formed and by 1925 the bands led by Jack Hylton, Henry Hall, Jack Payne, Billy Cotton and Debroy Somers and his Savoy Orpheans Orchestra were playing in the best hotels in London and elsewhere. The visits of several American bands to Britain led to complaints by British musicians and in the mid-nineteen-twenties the Musicians' Union was able to get a ban imposed on visiting bands that remained in force for over thirty years. I remember how after the war ended in 1945 my non-orchestral colleagues had started complaining that they did not have the opportunity to hear and meet the outstanding American players. It was in fact the British jazz musicians' complaints that played a major part in the ban at last being rescinded in 1956.

Harry Gold with his bass saxophone.

However, this ban did not preclude individual American musicians from working in Britain. One of the most outstanding was Adrian Rollini, a wonderful player of the rarely heard bass saxophone. The only British player of renown who regularly played this very large instrument was Harry Gold, who had a group aptly called *Harry Gold and his Pieces of Eight.* He was a very small man, barely taller than his saxophone. When I interviewed him for Music Preserved's Oral History of Musicians in Britain he was already in his nineties. At the end of the interview he apologised for not being able to offer me a cup of tea as he had to hurry off to a session. When we left his flat together I offered him a lift in my car. He refused my offer saying it would be easier by train, and to my astonishment he hurried off to the nearby Underground station carrying his large heavy instrument. Rollini was noted for playing unusual instruments and invented two: one was the 'goofus', a sort of harmonica. Very few were made, but a development, the melodica can still occasionally be found. He also invented a tiny clarinet, about 10 or 12 inches long, which the famous music firm Keith Prowse offered for sale. It was made of ebonite and called 'The Hot Fountain Pen'. When I played the Eb clarinet I remember that some of the dance band musicians I worked with called my small clarinet a Red Hot Fountain Pen.

Adrian Rollini was one of several white American jazz musicians who came to Britain and played at the Savoy Hotel with Fred Elizalde, now largely forgotten but who influenced many jazz musicians and other band leaders. Other American musicians that came to Britain were the saxophone/clarinettist Danny Polo and Van Phillips. I met Van Phillips at meetings of the Musicians' Union in the 1940s when I was only eighteen or nineteen, when he played an important role in the Union's development, and to some extent mine, too. As well as being a fine musician, by then he had ceased playing and was a theatre conductor for musicals. The Starita brothers, Al and Ray, two more American musicians, had bands in which some of the best young British jazz musicians played and who were later to have bands themselves. At the same time as these musicians were coming to Britain some British bandleaders were visiting America: Ambrose, Spike Hughes (his book *Opening Bars* is worth reading by anyone interested in the early days of jazz) and Ray Noble.

Popular music, the music played for dancing, heard in musicals, listened to on records and later on the radio, continued to be 'dance music', really a form of commercialised jazz. The jazz big band/swing era is generally considered to have begun in 1935, when Benny Goodman's band played jazz in Los Angeles to a large enthusiastic crowd of dancers. (Goodman had been one of my heroes since I was at school. In 1981, when he came to Aldeburgh to play the Mozart Clarinet Quintet with the Amadeus Quartet I was able to sit in on one of his rehearsals and afterwards spend an hour with him playing and talking together. A wonderful experience.) The best of the big and swing bands in Britain and America dominated the record charts and air-waves and were also very successful on stage and when touring. Through the 1930s and 40s the Count Basie, Duke Ellington, Artie Shaw, Glen Miller, Stan Kenton, Tommy and Jimmy Dorsey bands and a number of others were all tremendously popular. In the 1940s, with the beginning of bebop and then free jazz and jazz-rock, jazz, which had been primarily music for dancing, started to be listened to by

A number of band leaders meeting with the General Secretary of the Musicians' Union, Hardie Ratcliff, in 1947. Standing Lew Stone, from his right, clockwise: Ratcliff then Billy Cotton, back view of Chappie D'Amato, Sid Phillips, Harry Gold, Eric Robinson, Buddy Featherstonehaugh, Miff Ferrie, Lou Preager, Victor Sylvester, Billy Ternent.

an increasing number of musicians and their audience as an art form, music for its own sake. 1947 saw the beginning of the end for the big bands. Though Harry James, Tommy Dorsey and others were unable to continue to be full-time bands, they did re-assemble from time to time. Big band/swing music continued to be popular in Britain much later with Ted Heath, Lew Stone and several other bands continuing well into the 1960s – John Dankworth has continued recording and at the end of 2005 he received a knighthood, the first time a jazz musician has received this honour.

As popular as the bands were their vocalists. Most of the singers, to begin with often called 'crooners', started in one or other of the successful bands. From Bing Crosby onwards the best of them tended to leave the bands and create a career for themselves as solo artists. Generally they continued to be successful for much longer than the bands did. The very best of them were outstanding artists to be compared, in my opinion, with the finest *lieder* singers. If one listens carefully to Billie Holiday, Ella Fitzgerald, Rosemary Clooney, Nat 'King' Cole and, nearer our own time Tony Bennett, one can hear subtlety of phrasing, articulation and colouring of the finest quality. Frank Sinatra and Peggy Lee seem to me particularly outstanding. Their interpretation of the words often disguises their banality and their use of dynamics, emphasis and artful changes of *crescendo, diminuendo* and *timbre* could serve as a lesson for singers and instrumentalists. I quite recently heard a very fine recording of a song by Hugo Wolf, one of the greatest of the *lieder* composers, without knowing who was singing: I was astounded to find it was Barbra Streisand.

I was born in 1925, three years after the Marconi Company had set up the British Broadcasting Company in May 1922, and so radio has played a very important part in my life. It has given me both the opportunity to learn from hearing performances by great artists in all fields of music and endless hours of pleasure. And by providing well-paid employment for my father it allowed me to have a comfortable middle-class childhood. The Marconi Company having recognised the commercial possibilities of broadcasting brought together a consortium of radio manufacturers with the aim of establishing radio stations around the country. In 1922 a new company, the British Broadcasting Company, was established with a radio station and studio in Marconi House in the Strand, London. Its calling signal was 2LO. From the start the government had been opposed to this scheme but later that year it decided to grant the company a licence to operate. Funding for the programmes was to be provided by a tax collected from the sale of wireless sets and an annual listener's licence fee of ten shillings (50p). The following year the number of licences had risen to 500,000 and the studio moved from Marconi House to Savoy Hill, also in the Strand. When at the end of 1926 the British Broadcasting Company licence expired a government committee decided that the Company should be replaced by a public authority and in 1927 the British Broadcasting Corporation, the BBC, was created.

Broadcasting, which had started in America in 1920, had already become extremely popular by 1922 when it commenced in Britain. To begin with there were crystal sets that relied on a 'cats whisker' to find the right spot on the crystal for the station one wanted, but it was not long before sets with valves and an accumulator (an acid-lead battery) became available. I remember going with my father, it was probably 1931 or 1932, to the radio shop or garage to get the battery recharged, and then a day or two later a boy from the shop would usually bring it back. By then my father was in the BBC Symphony Orchestra but he used to tell me about his experience of broadcasting in the old 2LO days. In 1923 the station formed an orchestra on a part-time basis in which a number of the players who were later to join the BBC Symphony Orchestra in 1930 as principals played – Sidonie Goossens (harp), Eugene Cruft (double bass) and Frederick Thurston (clarinet) for whom my father used to deputise. Then in 1927 the Wireless Military Band was created with B. Walton O'Donnell as conductor and my father as Solo Clarinet (the equivalent of leader of an orchestra), until he joined Thurston in the BBC Symphony Orchestra as co-principal in 1930. This was a remarkable band and had its own arranger, Gerrard Williams. The programme for their first broadcast gives some idea of the diversity of their repertoire: the March from the *Crown of India* suite by Elgar, the second and third movements from Mendelssohn's *'Italian'* Symphony, A Folk Song Suite by Vaughan Williams, a selection from the opera *Cinq Mars* by Gounod, Tchaikovsky's 1812 Overture and the Symphonic Poem *Le Rouet d'Omphale* by Saint-Saëns. A number of pieces were especially written for the band including those by Gustav Holst and Vaughan Williams.

Under Sir John Reith's direction the BBC music programmes were generally of a rather serious nature – perhaps rather too serious for a good many listeners. Until the end of 1925 the only dance bands that broadcast from outside the BBC studios were the bands at the Savoy Hotel which broadcast three times a week. From then onwards more and more of the bands in other hotels and clubs were broadcast – those at the Piccadilly and Carlton hotels, the Kit-Cat and Embassy clubs. Jack Payne's first broadcast was from the Hotel Cecil in 1925 and then in 1928 he was appointed BBC Director of Dance Music and his orchestra became the BBC Dance Orchestra with the signature tune *'Say it with Music'*. When he left the BBC his place was taken in 1932 by Henry Hall who had first broadcast in 1924 from the Gleneagles Hotel in Scotland. His signature tune was *'Here's to the Next Time'*. From then on until the 1950s all the best British bands broadcast regularly: Roy Fox, Harry Roy, Carroll Gibbons, Jack Hylton, Lew Stone, Billy Cotton, Geraldo and Ted Heath, either from the venue they were performing at or in the BBC's studios.

In the mid-1950s popular music underwent yet another major change of direction. The era of the immense popularity of the American and British dance and swing bands throughout the 1930s and 40s was starting to come to an end. However, for Bing Crosby, Frank Sinatra, Ella Fitzgerald, Connie Francis, Doris Day, and Pat Boone – in the late 1950s second in popularity only to Elvis Presley – Perry Como, Nat 'King' Cole and Tony Bennett and so many others, there continued to be a considerable following.

What was to become a full-blown cultural revolution that would affect audiences and musicians alike all over the world was the arrival of pop music. Pop aims to appeal to as many people as possible and is essentially conservative. It is commercial music professionally produced and packaged by the record companies, radio programmers and concert promoters and central to the 'music industry'. To be most profitable it is necessary for there to be a constant series of entries into the 'Top 10' creating million-selling hits. It is unusual for a singles hit to remain in the Top 10 for more than six weeks. But there have been exceptions: Cliff Richard and the Beatles have each sold at least 21 million and several others have sold over 10 million. Albums sell in even greater numbers: 5 are listed as having sold more than 40 million, many artists have sold 20 and 30 million and nearly sixty have sold 15 million. The record is held by the Beatles who are reputed to have sold over 500 million.

By the mid-1960s the ascent of rock, which had already begun some years earlier, was in full swing. In the 1940s there was already rhythm and blues and rockabilly to be followed in 1955 by Rock and Roll, now nearly always written rock 'n' roll. The recordings *Rock Around the Clock* and *Shake, Rattle and Roll* made in America in the 1950s by Bill Haley and the Comets, were massive hits which led to this group being the first to tour Britain. Chuck Berry (*Roll over Beethoven*), the pianist Fats Domino with *Whole Lotta Loving,* and Elvis Presley, the best-selling singer of them all with a string of successful records: *Blue Suede Shoes, Heartbreak Hotel* and *Hound Dog* and many more paved the way in Britain for Lonnie Donegan, Tommy Steele, Billy Fury and above all the Beatles. From then on pop and rock music and other genres of popular music – ska, reggae, disco, heavy metal, rap, hip hop, R&B, techno, dance, punk and many more, including 'underground' and electronic music of various kinds – became dominant, with new groups and artists each seeking to identify themselves with their individual style of music and performance.

Often the visual element at concerts and on videos seems to have become as important as the music itself. Those attending rock concerts do not have to sit or stand silent and undemonstrative. Nor do they risk censure from those around them if they move in response to the music or show visible emotion, hum along with a tune or tap their foot in time to the rhythm. In fact they are encouraged by the often exaggerated gestures and movements of the artists on stage to be active participants in the event. Swaying, waving their arms in the air, singing along, shouting and cheering. This is very different to the way those attending any kind of classical music concert behave. A silent, more reverential posture is normal and movement of any kind or a whispered word to one's companion quickly attracts frowns and 'shushing'.

Whilst I was in the profession from the mid-1940s I frequently took part in sessions alongside musicians who did not play in symphony orchestras and I even played with the Beatles on their *Sgt. Pepper's Lonely Hearts Club Band* album. To begin with, backing for the groups was supplied by freelance orchestral musicians and from the late 50s this provided very lucrative employment for a fair number. But by the 1980s the groups playing pop music infrequently used any orchestral musicians and this led to many of those session musicians who would not have considered playing in a theatre becoming only too glad to find some fairly regular employment playing for the increasing number of musicals that were now successful.

The opera singers and solo instrumentalists who wished to follow the famous artists of the past and perform popular music had found from the 1940s that they increasingly had to draw on compositions by jazz influenced composers such as Gershwin, Cole Porter, Jerome Kern and Richard Rodgers. The use of microphones by popular singers and the different vocal technique this required presented problems for an opera singer accustomed to singing in large opera houses and projecting their voice and emotions. Very few have been really successful: as a rule they have lacked the right vocal quality or diction and the correct feel for the rhythm. A notable recent exception is Bryn Terfel, a wonderful operatic baritone who miraculously seems to be able to combine singing the major Wagner roles in the principal opera houses around the world with recording popular melodies.

World Music

As early as 1898 the Gramophone Company, and a few years later Odeon, started sending engineers to almost every country in the world to record the local folk music. Their motivation was to sell as many gramophones as possible. Essentially they wanted to sell their machines into the domestic markets everywhere they could. For most of the early companies, the manufacture of records themselves was not the first consideration, but was found necessary in order to maximise the sale of the machines. A great many recordings were made in each country because it was thought that the availability of recordings of their own music – relatively cheap to produce – would create new markets and increase the sale of gramophones. These recordings were not made to preserve the local folk music and there was seldom any attempt to 'Europeanise' the performances or issue them outside the country of their origin. However, they did create an enormous volume of recordings of ethnic music of which most of us are entirely ignorant.

In 1966 David Lewiston, who had been a student at Trinity College of Music in London but was then living in New York, decided to take off and start recording the ethnic music of peoples in the then still more remote parts of the world. He was not an ethnomusicologist nor an academic and was, it seems, motivated solely by his interest and delight in all the new musics he discovered. The first of these recordings of the Nonesuch Explorer Series was released on vinyl in 1967. Over the next twenty years more of his recordings were issued. One of the records containing excerpts of Bulgarian songs, Javanese Court Gamelan and Japanese *shakuhachi*, was sent into space by NASA on a Voyager spacecraft in 1977 with a message attached from the then US President Jimmy Carter: *This is a present from a small distant world. This record represents our hope, our determination, and our good will in a vast and awesome universe.*

It was not until *The World of Music and Dance* (WOMAD) was conceived in 1980, inspired to begin with by pure enthusiasm for non-western music, that people in the West other than ethnomusicologists and those who had bought the records made by David Lewiston became aware that there were so many other very different musical languages. It was often said 'music is a universal language'. But to anyone accustomed only to what we in the West call music, the music of the Sámi people, the music of the Australian Aborigine or the *Noh* theatre music of Japan, *nohgaku* and many other musics will sound as strange and as incomprehensible as their spoken languages.

My own introduction to world music had by chance occurred long before 1980. While I was a member of the Musicians' Union Executive Committee one of the benefits of attending the often very boring meetings of the committee was that from 1967, when it was first published, I received at each meeting a copy of the International Music Council (UNESCO) quarterly journal *The World of Music*. Through reading the articles in *The World of Music* I became acquainted with music I knew very little about and a great deal I had never even heard of: the music of the Orient, Africa, Japan, Islam, Turkish classical music, the Gamelan music of Bali, to mention only a few. I found that I enjoyed the sound of Chinese, Indian and Gamelan music, though I understood nothing of the cultures of which they are a part.

When I first started reading about the music of other cultures I had the opportunity to attend a performance of the Japanese *Noh* theatre given by a visiting *Noh* company from Japan. This was my first experience of hearing music that was completely foreign to my ears: it was a unique experience. The *Noh* plays, mostly written six hundred years ago, still attract large audiences in Japan today. In fact there has been something of a revival in recent years and for the first time female actors have taken part in what has always been a wholly male preserve. The actors wear elaborate costumes and masks to identify whether the character they are portraying is male or female, a ghost or a demon, and all their movements are highly stylised. A remarkable element of the masks is that they are constructed so that as the actor tilts his head backward or forward the facial expression can change from fierce to smiling, happy or sad.

The performance is accompanied by music played usually by four musicians and a small chorus. The musicians, who are also elaborately costumed, sit on one side of the stage and remain very still except when they are playing. Their instruments are the *nohkan* – a flute which makes strange whistling sounds varied according to events and characters in the play, and three types of drums: the *Ko-tsuzumi*, a small drum held at the shoulder, the *O-tsuzumoi*, which is larger and held on the left hip, and the *Taiko*, a large drum placed on the floor and beaten with two thick sticks. The smaller drums are played with the finger tips. At various times the drummers shout out what are called *kakegoe*. These calls are signals from one drummer to another and also from the drummers to the actors.

The musicians sit motionless with their hands tucked into the wide sleeves of their costume and each time music is required, with one accord and without any obvious sign having been given, assume a playing position and start to play. The music is a combination of eerie whistles on the *nohkan*, different each time, and drumming, interspersed by the *kakegoe* calls from the drummers and a *hishigi,* which is a very sharp tone – the highest note the *nohkan* can produce. If these musicians had been giving a recital at the Wigmore Hall wearing traditional evening dress and had created a similar 'soundscape' even those who enjoy the most *avant-garde* music would find more than a few minutes of this music hard to take.

The first WOMAD festival, held in England in 1982, and subsequent festivals played a big part in increasing the demand for recordings of non-western music. WOMAD's aim was 'to excite, to inform, and to create awareness of the worth and potential of a multicultural society and to celebrate the many forms of music, arts and dance of countries and cultures all over the world.' A few years later those record companies that were issuing Indian, African, Latin American music and the music of many other countries decided that it would be much easier for customers at music and record shops to find all these recordings if they were put on one rack under the general heading 'World Music'. By 1994 these recordings and the world music festivals held around the world had become so popular that a *Rough Guide to World Music* was published. The *Guide* includes virtually every music culture, national, regional and local and provides details of commercial recordings (now available in various formats) of the traditional and contemporary music of the people living in places as remote as the Kathmandu Valley in Nepal, Bioko (formerly FernandoPo) a tiny island off the coast of Cameroon, and the nomadic horsemen of Outer Mongolia in central Asia.

The World of Music was published by UNESCO in association with the International Institute for Comparative Music Studies and Documentation and was in fact intended essentially for those concerned with ethnomusicology. Thomas Edison's invention in 1877 of the phonograph enabled ethnomusicologists to listen to repeated hearings of the on-site folk music recordings they had made. A few years later Alexander Ellis devised a way to divide the octave into 1200 equal parts, which he called *cents*. This allowed a proper recognition of the many non-western scales and an understanding of music that used other tonal systems than the diatonic scales. They came to realise that the Western system was not superior, only different.

At the beginning of the 20th century Cecil Sharp, Percy Grainger, Béla Bartók and Zoltan Kodály were all recording folk musicians in Europe and elsewhere. Many scholars were also busy recording folk music all over the world. The earliest recordings of the music of the many Native-American Indian tribes, had been made in the USA in the 1890s by Jesse Fewkes. None of these recordings nor the folk music recordings reviewed in *The World of Music* in the late 1960s and during the 1970s were intended for commercial distribution. It is clear from the reviews of the music being studied at that time that the sound quality of some of the early recordings was not very good.

But while the ethnomusicologists were concerned with understanding the music of cultures other than those of their own western tradition, those who have been attracted to World Music have enjoyed it for its own sake because, as Beecham put it in another context, 'they like the noise it makes'. The record companies quickly realised that here was another music for which there was an ever growing audience. The 1994 edition of the *Rough Guide to World Music* has 697 pages and is a treasure-trove of information with articles about hundreds of different musics and details of recordings that are now available for each of them. Because of the expanding reach of the recording machine it now has to be published in two volumes. If I were obliged to choose one book to have if I were left marooned on a desert island it would be the one volume *Rough Guide to World Music*.

The arrival of the pocket-sized transistor radio in the mid 1950s, and to an even greater extent since 1979 the availability of the *Walkman* portable transistor cassette tape player have, in the same way as Coco-Cola, McDonalds and Kentucky Fried Chicken, played their part in creating what is now a 'borderless' world. In effect the world's musics have become borderless – they have all been thrown into the melting pot. Of course, there are still groups of aficionados who continue to love and protect their own music and maintain it in as pristine a condition as possible. Lovers of western classical music are one of them, probably the largest. To say, as it frequently was little more than 25 years ago that 'music is a universal language', was not true; now, to a great extent, it is.

The phrase 'crossover' in relation to music performance seems to have come into use initially in the 1960s and 70s, in the first place mainly as a marketing tool. As music became increasingly commercialised – became an industry – the record companies were constantly seeking to extend and increase their sales. One way was by appealing to more than one audience. By combining country (or country and western) music with elements of pop, the multimillion-dollar music industry centred in Nashville created a music attractive to a much larger audience. Another early form of crossover in the 1960s was jazz-rock. Soon there were so many styles and types of crossover that the process became very difficult to follow. Before long the Top 40 charts were full of recordings by crossover artists, and albums – the aim being to get into the Top 10.

As a result of the crossover phenomenon there is scarcely any music that has not been affected by crossover or fusion. The classical music of India, China, Japan and Europe and other cultures, folk music and jazz, have all been increasingly influenced and in some cases virtually supplanted by rock and pop. Indigenous musics that had flourished for hundreds of years now only have a specialised audience of enthusiasts. The most recent to feel the effect of crossover has been western classical music. We now have classical crossover music, crossover artists, crossover albums.

On recordings of the music of three relatively small local communities one can listen to their music, unknown outside their own community until recently, as played and sung before and after the effect of crossover and fusion. Good examples of what has happened everywhere are the Celtic music of Ireland, the music of the Sámi people who live in 'Lapland', a region in the most northern parts of Norway, Sweden, Finland and Russia, and the Australian Aborigines, each with very different musics and each belonging to a minority community.

To hear how great a change has taken place in the performance of Celtic traditional music in little more than fifty years first listen to the classic recordings made by Johnny Doran, the great player of the *uillean* pipes and Michael Coleman the Sligo fiddler, both made in the first part of the 20th century. Then to the music of the Pogues, one of the most successful of the Irish folk rock bands of the 1980s and 90s, who combined Irish folk with Latin and Balkan rhythms, or the Moving Hearts, a band which included in its line-up such diverse instruments as guitar and *bodhran* (the large Irish frame drum), *bouzouki* (the long-necked lute from Greece), the Irish bellows-blown *uilleann* pipes, alto sax and bass.

The music of the Sámi people who are nomadic and number in all only about 45,000/50,000, is a good example of what can happen to a local music with an extremely long tradition. The most important element in Sámi music is the *joik* or *yoik*, an improvised style of singing, sometimes accompanied by a drum and *fadnu* (the Sámi flute). The *joik* songs often illustrate the close relationship the Sámi people have with their environment. There are very few recordings of the genuine Sámi *joik*. There are two or three commercial recordings, the British Library Sound Archive has seven field recordings made in 1997, but by far the easiest way to hear this rare music sung is by going to the Google website. Put in Sámi of far Northern Europe and then go to Sámi Culture – University of Texas. To hear a short clip of the Sámi flute, the *fadnu*, put in Sámi music and then go to Sámi etnam.

However, there are now a great many crossover and fusion recordings of this music. Most well-known and popular is Mari Boine who, like the Pogues and so many others has combined her own native music instruments and style with those of other cultures: jazz, rock, *joik* – the traditional Sámi chant. Her band will at times include bass, keyboards and guitars, Sámi and African drums, Indian flutes, the Peruvian *charango* (a small guitar) and the Arabic fiddle. In the past the Sámi, or Lapps, have been discriminated against and made to feel worthless. When Mari Boine, an ardent protester, was asked to perform at the opening ceremony of the Winter Olympics in Lillehammer she refused because she felt she was just being used as an exotic decoration. In fact, another Sámi artist, Nils-Aslak Valkiapää, from Finland did accept and his performance is included on an album on which he is accompanied by keyboards, saxophone and flutes.

The traditional music and culture of the Australian Aborigines is so different from our own that it is difficult to take in just how dramatic a change has taken place in the last thirty years. Ever since the European settlers arrived in the late 1800s the Aborigines have suffered dispossession of their land and the suppression of their language and culture, which is at least 40,000 years old and believed to be the oldest still extant. In the 1900s separation from the White man and from their own Aboriginal culture was official government policy, even to the extent in the 1930s of separating them from their children. To understand how great the change that has taken place has been it is necessary to know something of their past.

To the Australian aborigines ('the people who were here from the beginning'), music was an integral part of everyday life and a unifying force in their culture. Aboriginal mythology recalls a time in the remote past in the *Dreamtime*, when totemic spirits wandered all over the continent singing the names of birds, animals, plants and the things around them. These songs brought the world into existence and the totemic spirits left emblems across the continent. The paths between them are called *songline*. The music is very rhythmic with a lot of hand clapping, body slapping, stamping and clapping *bilma* (ironwood clapsticks) or boomerangs. The only 'instruments' were the digeridoo (digeridu) or *yadaki,* a hollowed out branch of a tree, blown at one end and unique to the Aborigines, a 'bull-roarer' (there is no translation for the Aboriginal instrument, a slat of wood whirled around on the end of a piece of cord) and the gum-leaf, which was blown in rather the same way as children blow a piece of grass held between the thumbs.

The effect of separating the Aborigines from their own culture allowed their music to be supplanted by western pop and rock. An important development for them was the establishment of the

Institute of Aboriginal Studies in 1964, where there is an extensive archive of recordings of indigenous Aboriginal music collected over the last hundred years. Some of these recordings and a few genuine performances of traditional music are available commercially.

From the end of the 1960s and increasingly in the 1970s the Aborigines increased their campaign for indigenous land rights. When some of them became aware of their music heritage it became a vehicle for social protest. By the mid-1980s very many Aboriginal rock bands had been formed and were playing all over the country with politics always a part of their music. There are now a considerable number of commercial recordings. Formed in 1986 Yothu Yindi's pop success came as a surprise and helped bring many Aboriginal issues into mainstream Australian affairs. Other popular Aboriginal music bands have been the Desert Oaks Band, the Warumpi Band, Blackstorm, and Archie Roach (voice and guitar). As well as traditional Aboriginal instruments bands now frequently include synthesiser, a number of western percussion and other instruments.

The folk music of other much larger communities have all become part of mainstream popular music, in particular reggae from Jamaica, the hillbilly music from the Appalachian mountains that became bluegrass and country and western, and the many offshoots and combinations of music from Cuba, Puerto Rico, Colombia and other south American countries that, mixed with big-band jazz, we call Latin American. All these musics had in the beginning helped primitive man alleviate the weariness and tedium of manual labour, prepare warriors to face their enemies in battle, placate the gods and give thanks for a good harvest. Most religions have always recognised the importance of communal participation and have given their congregations an opportunity to take part, with chanting and hymn-singing as an aid to escape from themselves and the real world and enter into another more spiritual state of mind.

Folk music, for many hundreds of years – in some cases thousands of years – remained the only *popular music* with characteristics that until recent times distinguished it from professional musical performance. It allowed ordinary people a form of self-expression that in some way involved their participation, singing or playing an instrument, hand clapping and dancing.

As a result of increasing industrialisation, first in Britain around 1850 and before long in the USA and Europe, large numbers of the rural population migrated to the towns and cities. During the first half of the 20th century this was to occur throughout the rest of the world. Urban life allowed more leisure time and provided new more sophisticated forms of entertainment. In a different environment and away from their former cultural roots it was in the Music Halls in particular that the recently created industrial working-class first heard a new kind of popular song. The artist would sing a couple of verses and choruses and then encourage the audience to join in singing the chorus with them. With their easily learned catchy melodies they soon became extremely popular and within a short time had replaced the old folk tunes in their affection. It was not long before increasing affluence enabled working-class families to acquire a cheap piano and purchase sheet music copies of the most popular of the songs they heard at the music hall and the bandstand. This was the first step towards an increasing commercialisation of music.

Earlier I described how the ability to record music has resulted in performers losing some control over their own performances, and how it has reduced employment opportunities for orchestral musicians; the effect it has had on audiences and their expectations, and on the actual style of musical performance itself. But above all recording made it possible for a performance to become a commercial object, something that could be bought and sold – and that could become an extremely valuable commodity. As well as the quality of both the recordings and playback equipment reaching a very high standard it has become easy to hold extremely large amounts of music on one artefact.

Wherever you go there is music of some kind. It is now difficult to avoid. It accompanies virtually every TV and radio advert and is very frequently played constantly in supermarkets, shops and restaurants. Mobile phones use a snatch of music – Beethoven, Tchaikovsky, the Beatles or the latest pop hit. Music is also increasingly being used in news bulletins to raise the tension (in a similar way to how it is used in films) as background when conflict of any kind is being reported. Even so it seems that many of us cannot get enough music. We choose to listen to it on our own a great deal of the time, at home, either on CDs, the radio, TV or on the Internet, and now frequently on mp3s and iPods when we are on the move – walking about, or on public transport, and even when at work. There is one major difference in that this vast amount of music is ingested without any participation on the listener's part – it is an entirely passive experience. Yet the many millions who have been listening to the pop and rock related music on CDs and radios, or, more recently, downloaded it from the Internet and other sources – legally or otherwise – still flock in their tens of thousands to concerts where they can see and hear their favourite performers and to a limited extent participate in the event. Perhaps this is also why the Proms continue to attract such large audiences each year, even to those concerts that include contemporary music that as a rule drives audiences away.

26 *Where Now?*

The influence of folk music – popular music on classical – classical music on popular. Acoustic and electronic instruments. Electronic Music.
The three Tenors – 'popular' classical music.
Increasing 'classical-crossover' – steep decline in symphonic recordings.
Updated opera productions. Hope for the future.

At neither the International Society for Music in Education conference in Innsbruck in 1985, when I chose as the subject for my talk 'The Symphony Orchestra: into the 21st century', nor a year later at the Wheatland Foundation conference, did any of us anticipate how soon so many people would have computers that would give them access to music programmes and radio stations world-wide. Or that they would be able to download and record music so easily. By the late 1990s and the start of the 21st century mobile phones and mp3 had become commonplace and a few years later so had the iPod.

Composers have always found inspiration from, or been influenced by, the *popular* music in their environment – their own folk music – from Haydn who drew on Croatian and Gypsy melodies to Bartók, Kodály, Vaughan Williams and Charles Ives, who made use of American folk tunes and ragtime dances. Once composed, commercial *popular* music began to replace folk music as 'the music of the people' and to some extent popular and classical music gained inspiration from each other.

Not long after the beginning of the 20th century some classical composers, though they did not borrow melodies, started to use the rhythms and stylistic effects of the new popular music – ragtime and jazz. Debussy in 1908 for the *Golliwog's Cakewalk*, Stravinsky for his *Ragtime for 11 Instruments* in 1918 and Milhaud in 1922 in *La création du monde* and a *Jazz Symphony* and a *Jazz Sonata* by George Antheil are early examples.

Examples of another form of crossover, that between the popular music of the first half of the 20th century, jazz, and western classical music, were two compositions premiered in the 1950s.

The Swiss composer Rolf Liebermann's *Concerto for Jazz Band and Symphony Orchestra*, written in 1954, not only combines jazz and symphonic music but makes use of serialism as well. It has had a number of performances and was still being played in 2003 when it was in the programme of the New York Pops at Carnegie Hall. Another serialist attracted to the hybrid jazz/orchestra was Matyás Seiber who came to England from Hungary in 1935, when he was already 30. He had always been interested in jazz and when he received a commission from the London Philharmonic in 1958 decided to collaborate with John Dankworth to compose *Improvisations for Jazz Band and Symphony Orchestra*. Richard Rodney Bennett, best known for his film and concert music, was asked by the great American tenor saxophonist Stan Getz if he would compose a concerto for him. Bennett's wide musical sympathies, which include both jazz and serialism – the latter no doubt as a result of his study in Paris with Pierre Boulez – made him an ideal choice. However, this was his first venture into crossover. Unfortunately, Getz died in 1990, before the concerto was completed. The first performance had to wait until 1992 when the very fine British saxophonist John Harle played it at the Proms.

In 1922, George Gershwin, then only 24, composed a short 25 minute jazz opera *Blue Monday,* which was orchestrated by Will Vodery. Paul Whiteman who had conducted the 1922 performance was so impressed that he asked Gershwin to compose a symphonic jazz piece for him to conduct at a concert he was planning. It was for this concert in 1924 that Gershwin composed his best known work, *The Rhapsody in Blue,* which was orchestrated by Ferde Grofé. The concert in New York's Aeolian Hall was a major event and attended by amongst many Stravinsky, Rakhmaninov, Kreisler, Heifetz, Stokowski and other notable musicians. When the following year *Blue Monday,* now renamed *135th Street,* was given a concert performance in Carnegie Hall, it was re-orchestrated by Ferde Grofé. After that Gershwin went on to compose (and orchestrate himself), the Concerto in F for piano and orchestra, *An American in Paris* and the opera *Porgy and Bess,* at the same time as he was composing popular songs – *Fascinating Rhythm, The Man I Love,* and countless other wonderful songs and musicals – *Oh Kay!, Funny Face, Strike up the Band* and the music for Fred Astaire and Ginger Rodgers films. All before his early death at 39.

Gershwin, though not a classically trained composer, was the first to compose what might be called symphonic jazz and has probably been the most successful in composing jazz orientated music for the symphony orchestra. However, he was not the first to compose a serious piece in the style that had originated in the southern states of America at the beginning of the century. In 1911 the Negro composer Scott Joplin, best known for his *Maple Leaf Rag* and *The Entertainer*, published at his own expense *Treemonisha,* his attempt to create an indigenous black opera. It received a single concert performance with piano accompaniment in 1915 but, to his great disappointment, failed to gain approval. However, a staged revival in 1975 by the Houston Grand Opera Company with a new orchestration by Gunther Schuller, who also conducted the performances, was a very considerable success. It is reported that the finale *A Real Slow Drag* had to be encored three times. After the performances in Houston the opera was taken on tour and recorded in 1976 by Deutsche Grammophon. I heard *A Real Slow Drag* when it was played at the Proms, sung by Jessye Norman with chorus and orchestra, in a very exciting performance which was enthusiastically received by the Prom audience.

While in the past it was classical composers finding inspiration in popular music, since the beginning of the 20th century the tide has turned and it has been popular music that has been raiding the classical repertoire. I remember *I'm Always Chasing Rainbows,* based on the *Fantasie Impromptu in C Sharp Minor* by Chopin, still being very popular when I was a child in the late 1920s and early 1930s. Amongst many classical compositions that were used in popular music in the 1930s, 40s, and 50s, were a Mozart piano sonata, which became *In an Eighteenth-Century Drawing Room, Song of India,* Tommy Dorsey's arrangement of one of the themes in *Scheherazade* by Rimsky-Korsakov and *Summer Moon,* based on the *Berceuse* from Stravinsky's ballet music for *The Firebird,* which Lauritz Melchior sang with considerable success. George Forrest and Robert Wright, who had had a big success, first in New York and then in 1946 in London with *Song of Norway,* a reworking of themes from the music of Grieg, then plundered the music by Borodin for *Kismet,* an even bigger success. During its London run in 1953 I played in the orchestra a number of times. Forrest and Wright had arranged the music tastefully, but could not escape trivialising Borodin's original. The best known song *Stranger in*

Paradise was based on a melody from the *Polovtsian Dances* in Borodin's opera *Prince Igor* and the *String Quartet in D* provided *Baubles, Bangles and Beads* and *And this is my Beloved*, the quartet's lovely second movement, originally in 3/4 time now changed to 4/4. Even that could not wholly spoil this wonderful music. I wonder if those who had not heard Borodin's music before (the large majority) will have enjoyed it any less, in its somewhat debased form, than those of us who had enjoyed the original?

Few contemporary composers seem to have drawn on rock music for inspiration to any extent so far, though from the late 1950s and until the present time a surprising number of pop and rock artists and groups have incorporated extracts from or allusions to classical music. Elvis Presley had two massive hits: the first *It's Now or Never* making use of *O Sole Mio,* which many years earlier had served Caruso very well. It had another outing as the backing for a long-running TV advert for a well-known ice-cream. The other, *I Can't Help Falling in Love With You* included an old favourite *Plaisir d'Amour,* by the 18th century composer Padre Giovanni Martini. An example of classic rock's borrowing from another genre was Procol Harum's number one hit in the UK charts in the 1960s *A Whiter Shade of Pale.* In this they made use of Bach's *Air on the G String* (often mistakenly written in Internet record advertisements as *Air on a G String* – a rather unfortunate error) and *Sleepers Awake,* from his *Cantata No.140. Annie's Song,* with a little help from the big tune in the second movement of Tchaikovsky's 5th Symphony provided both John Denver and the flautist James Galway with major hits and, more recently, Muse, a hard rock band, which has quite frequently blended classical music elements with their own, sampled some of Rakhmaninov's *Second Piano Concerto* for their song *Space Dementia* in their album *Origin of Symmetry.*

In 1967 the Moody Blues were asked to make a rock version of Dvorak's *New World* Symphony, but succeeded in persuading the record company to let them write their own composition instead. Probably the first example of crossover of pop group and symphony orchestra was when this group recorded *Days of Future Past,* which was orchestrated by the well-known composer and arranger Peter Knight, with the London Festival Orchestra. For their subsequent adventures into this kind of composition they used the mellotron (a synthesiser that contains samples of all the orchestral instruments), which was no doubt considerably cheaper than engaging an orchestra.

A more interesting example of pop and symphony crossover was when in 1969 Deep Purple, a hard rock group, joined the Royal Philharmonic Orchestra for a concert in the Royal Albert Hall to play Jon Lord's *Concerto for Group and Orchestra,* conducted by Malcolm Arnold (later Sir Malcolm). The rehearsals did not go well – the orchestra which had been rehearsing Arnold's 6th Symphony (the first piece in the concert) were not too happy to be working with a pop group and it seems not too co-operative either. It took all Malcolm's charm plus, at one point some extremely strong language, to pull things together. A recording of this concert (not including the symphony) was issued in 1970. Thirty years later, in 1999, Deep Purple did two performances (one now issued as a DVD) of *Concerto for Group and Orchestra,* this time with the London Symphony Orchestra. Malcolm Arnold was to have conducted but sadly by then he was not well enough and Paul Mann took his place.

In 1970, the year after their very successful concert, Malcolm Arnold again conducted the group, this time with the orchestra of the Light Music Society, in another piece by Jon Lord, his *Gemini Suite,* which had been commissioned by the BBC. It was recorded 'live' at the concert, but not issued until many years later as *Gemini Suite Live.* A year after the concert a studio recording of a revised version of the *Suite* was issued under its original title.

A number of composers have tried to combine western classical music with that of another culture. One of the first was John Mayer who from the 1950s was blending Indian and Western music. Born in India he came to Britain as a very young man to study violin and composition at the Royal Academy of Music. He joined the Royal Philharmonic Orchestra as a violinist whilst I was in the orchestra and we became friends. In fact, in 1960 he composed several short exercises for my tutor *First Tunes and Studies.* A few years earlier Sir Charles Groves, then conductor of the Liverpool Philharmonic Orchestra, commissioned Mayer to compose a piece for his orchestra and in 1958 they gave the first performance of Mayer's *Dance Suite,* for sitar, flute, tabla, tambura and orchestra – it would probably now be called 'crossover'.

In 1966 Mayer teamed up with the great Jamaican alto saxophonist Joe Harriott to form an ensemble Indo-Jazz Fusions: The Joe Harriott-John Mayer Double Quintet. The band combined elements of classical, jazz and Indian music, with on the Indo side John Mayer on violin and harpsichord, plus sitar, flute tabla and tambura, and on the jazz side Joe Harriott on alto plus trumpet, piano, bass, and drums. The band had considerable success and made some very good recordings. When Joe Harriott died in 1973 Mayer decided to close the band down and it was not until more than twenty years later in 1995 that he re-formed the band, this time as John Mayer's Indo-Jazz Fusions, with a group of much younger musicians. He said that he felt that this new group out-performed the Harriott-era ensemble because now they had far more familiarity and facility with Hindustani improvisational techniques. This group produced several CDs and continued until Mayer's death in 2004.

It is not possible to write about the effect that the cross-fertilisation of so many varied musics has brought about without mentioning Frank Zappa. He was one of the most remarkably gifted and eclectic performers and composers of our time. In his relatively short life – he was born in 1940 and died aged only 52 in 1993 – he played and composed in every style from blues to avant-garde, taking in jazz, many forms of rock, including rock-opera, and the most contemporary techniques of classical music of his era on the way. When he was a very young man his own orchestral compositions were to a considerable extent influenced by Stravinsky and Webern and in particular by Edgard Varèse. He also included *sprechstimme* (a kind of speaking/singing voice) in a similar way to Arnold Schoenberg and Alban Berg.

Zappa recorded a programme of his own music with the London Symphony Orchestra, conducted by Kent Nagano and in 1992, a year before his death, he had a tremendous success in Frankfurt at a concert of his own work with the Ensemble Modern. His recorded legacy of every kind of popular (and unpopular) music is immense. It includes recordings with his group *The Mothers of Invention,* jazz and, quite amazingly, a recording he made in collaboration with Pierre Boulez at IRCAM. On *Boulez Conducts Zappa: The Perfect Stranger* a number of the tracks are played by the Ensemble InterContemporain, conducted by Pierre Boulez and the rest are played by Zappa on the synclavier (a cross between a synthesiser and a computer, an instrument that became a favourite for Zappa), under the strange name the *Barking Pumpkin Digital Gratification Consort.*

Frank Zappa was, perhaps more than anyone else, a one-man melting pot of the world's music – the complete crossover man. This extraordinary and quite frequently outrageous and satirical man, as well as being a remarkably creative musician, was also a virtuoso guitarist, an accomplished commercial artist, a recording and mastering engineer and a skilled producer of his own work.

As long ago as 1907 there was an interest in how electricity could be harnessed to increase the vocabulary of sounds that could be used to compose music. In his book *Sketch for a New Aesthetic of Music* published that year Ferruccio Busoni discussed the use of electrical and other new sound sources in future music. He wrote of the future of music:

Music as art, our so-called occidental music, is hardly four hundred years old; its state is one of development, perhaps the very first stage of a development beyond present conception. And we talk of 'classics' and 'hallowed traditions'! And we have talked of them for a long time! We have formulated rules, stated principles, laid down laws — we apply laws made for maturity to a child that knows nothing of responsibility! This child-music – it floats on air! It touches not the earth with its feet. It knows no law of gravitation. It is well nigh incorporeal. Its material is transparent. It is sonorous air. It is almost Nature herself. It is free!

But freedom is something that mankind has never wholly comprehended, never realised to the full. Man can neither recognise nor acknowledge it. He disavows the mission of this child; he hangs weights upon it. This buoyant creature must walk decently, like anyone else. It may scarcely be allowed to leap — when it were its joy to follow the line of the rainbow, and to break sunbeams with the clouds!

Varèse, a pupil of Busoni, was influenced by him to a great extent. When he was still studying at the Paris Conservatoire he was already saying 'I refuse to submit to sounds that have already been heard. Rules do not make a work of art. You have the right to compose what you want to, in the way you want to. I long for instruments obedient to my thought and whim, with their contribution of a whole new world of unsuspected sounds, which will lend themselves to the exigencies of my inner rhythm'.

I recall that in the 1940s while I was still a student I had one of those small, six or seven inch, 78 rpm records with pieces by Varèse on it. They were both extremely avant garde – *Ionisation,* written for percussion instruments, and *Octandre* for woodwind and brass. Varèse felt constrained by the conventions of the orchestral palette and believed that composition could be freed by the use of electronic devices. He said, *'The raw material of music is sound'* and he became so frustrated that he was unable to continue composing with the sounds produced by the instruments available to him. He felt that composers were obsessed with tradition and were limited by the composers who had preceded them. He anticipated that a machine would be invented that would provide opportunities to explore a far greater range of pitch and volume and release us from the restrictions of the tempered scale.

Once the tape recorder had been perfected in the early 1940s it was not long before composers were splicing together a variety of sounds, musical, mechanical and natural, to produce what came to be called Musique Concrète, which has been used most effectively as background music for radio, TV and films. It has also been used with success by both classical and popular composers that include Pierre Boulez, the Beatles, Karlheinz Stockhausen, Pink Floyd and Iannis Xenakis.

For a long time Varèse ceased to compose until in the 1950s when composers had started using some of the new technologies that had become available – he was already in his seventies – he came to life again. Probably the first important composition to use taped sounds and acoustic instruments was his *Deserts,* composed between 1950 and 1954. His next composition *Poeme Electronique* was performed in the Philips pavilion, at the World Fair in 1958, largely through the efforts of the great architect Le Corbusier. The pavilion was designed under Le Corbusier's direction by another composer Iannis Xenakis (also an architect), one of whose works was also played at this concert.

Poeme Electronique includes a great variety of recorded sounds which were heard by visitors to the pavilion from the 425 loudspeakers positioned around the hall. It is hardly surprising that further performances have been limited – if, indeed, there have been any. In 2006 the Library of Congress issued a recording using the tapes that Varése had made for the original performance.

From the 1950s onwards more and more devices were invented that enabled music to be composed entirely without instrumentalists or with a combination of acoustic and electronic instruments. Compositions that combined acoustic and electronic instruments such as *Turangalîla-Symphonie* by Olivier Messiaen, first performed in 1949, which requires a very large orchestra and an Ondes Martenot (an electronic instrument invented by Maurice Martenot in 1928), still remain in the orchestral repertoire. By the 1960s synthesisers were becoming more manageable and in the 1970s both classical and rock musicians were making more use of them. In 1977 IRCAM opened at the Pompidou Centre in Paris, under Pierre Boulez's direction with Luciano Berio and Vinko Globokar also involved. By then a variety of synthesisers were being used by virtually all rock bands. It was already unusual to see an acoustic instrument being played in any of the bands and when they were they would be electronically enhanced. They needed to be if they were to be heard. To begin with the groups used analogue synthesisers but by the late 1970s a number of digital synthesisers would become available as well as synclaviers, samplers and other electronic devices.

Radio, TV and film were quick to make use of the effects that the electronic instruments could provide. In the 1950s the BBC Radiophonic Workshop started to use them to provide music and effects of all kinds and the ever popular TV series *Dr Who* has from 1963 to the present day always used these instruments to provide background music. A particularly effective use of the unearthly sounds these instruments can produce was in the 1971 film *A Clockwork Orange*.

I have never had any involvement in playing in a rock or pop group. My only personal contact with this field of music has been through Rick Wakeman. In the late 1960s when he was a student at the Royal College of Music – his principal study was the piano – he came to me for clarinet lessons, his second study. It was clear to me from the start that his interest in playing the clarinet was minimal, but he was an agreeable chap and I got him talking about what interested him. I don't think he learned much from me about playing the clarinet since I doubt that he made any attempt to play it from one lesson to the next. However, I did learn a good deal about pop and rock music from him. He did not remain at the Royal College for very long and it was only a year or two before I was seeing his name as a prominent keyboard player, first of all in 1971 with a very successful band at that time, *Yes.* His use of electronic keyboards became legendary, and on videos I have seen him surrounded by a vast array of keyboards, usually playing two at a time and going swiftly from one pair to another. He was something of a showman, as many pop and rock stars are, frequently appearing wearing a silver cape.

A few years later I received a phone call from the BBC asking me if I would take part in a programme they were making about Wakeman. His fame was such that they were making a documentary about his life and wanted to include something about his time at the College. As it seems he had told them I was the only one at the College that he had any time for, would I be willing to be interviewed whilst giving a lesson at the Royal College of Music? The BBC had to get permission from the College, which they gave, though I don't think it did anything to enhance my reputation there. On the other hand when the programme was broadcast I was able to bathe in reflected glory. I was amazed at the number of neighbours and acquaintances who saw the programme and were impressed at my being in it.

In a previous chapter I have written about light music, the music that a great many people enjoyed. They preferred Ketelbey, Eric Coates, selections from operas and ballets ('the tuneful bits') the music played in restaurants, and the BBC *Music While You Work* and similar broadcasts. I remember when I was a young man hearing them say, 'I like music – but not that heavy stuff'. Later light music orchestras like those of George Melachrino, Eric Robinson and Mantovani captured the same audience. In the 1960s two other groups that became very popular with this audience were the Play Bach Trio and the Swingle Singers.

The Play Bach Trio, also known as the Jacques Loussier Trio, consisted of Jacques Loussier on piano plus double bass and percussion. The trio used Bach's compositions as the basis for their tasteful jazz improvisations which, though some serious music lovers hated what they felt was sacrilege and the debasing of great music, continued to record and give concerts until they disbanded in 1980 having sold over six million records.

The Swingle Singers, an *a cappella* group of eight singers, with bass and drums to define the rhythm, began in 1962 when a group of freelance session singers working in Paris became tired of always singing background – *oo's* and *ah's* – behind people like Charles Aznavour and Edith Piaf. They decided that in their spare time they would try out Ward Swingle's suggestion and read through some of the preludes and fugues from Bach's *Well-Tempered Clavier* just to see if they were suitable for vocalising. They found that they were swinging Bach's music quite naturally and as there were no words they improvised a kind of 'scat' singing. By 1963 they felt confident enough to approach Philips with the idea that they might make a record. Philips agreed and when the recording, *Bach's Greatest Hits* came out in the US it quickly became a great success.

For the next 10 years between touring they recorded about a dozen albums covering an extraordinary range of music, from Bach to Berio and Mozart to the Beatles and all sung in the same style as their first Bach recording. The classical music critics' response ranged from enthusiastic to hostile. As with the Jacques Loussier *Play Bach Trio* there were some critics and music lovers who were appalled and one or two musicians I knew even believed that it was a sign of moral corruption.

In 1969 the Swingle Singers were asked by the New York Philharmonic Orchestra if they would premiere *Sinfonia,* a large work for orchestra and 8 voices composed by Luciano Berio. The premiere was conducted by Berio himself and recorded live by CBS. It was a couple of years after Ward Swingle had decided to disband the group in France and came to England in 1973 that Gavin Henderson, then manager of the Philharmonia, and I met Swingle and some other members of the group he had formed in Britain with the idea of them doing a performance of *Sinfonia* with the Philharmonia. At that time the Philharmonia did not have sufficient funds to risk putting on a concert that might not provide a large enough audience to cover the cost of mounting it. I think we were rather put off because we learned that they had tried a few times to combine works of Berio with their traditional repertoire and found that although the audience accepted arrangements of Bach, madrigals, folk songs and jazz standards, they drew the line at Berio. To quote Ward himself, 'People sometimes come to a *Sinfonia* performance expecting to hear something like our *doo-boo-doo* Bach – they generally look for the nearest exit after the first movement. Could they possibly have been expecting the Sinfonia from Bach's *Second Harpsichord Partita?*

In 1981 the group were asked to make another recording of Berio's *Sinfonia*, with Pierre Boulez. conducting. In his book *Swingle Singing* Ward Swingle recounts how Boulez, after a very loud and dissonant orchestral passage, stopped the orchestra and asked the 2nd bassoon player, 'In the 9th bar of letter I, shouldn't that be an F-sharp?' The

Pierre Boulez.

bassoon player realised his mistake but just couldn't believe that Boulez could have heard it. I remember similar incidents when Boulez was conducting the Philharmonia.

Both the Jacques Loussier Trio and the Swingle Singers showed yet again that the vast majority of people wanted music with a tune. It doesn't matter whether it is classical music, jazz, pop, rock or music from another culture, if it has a good tune, one that can be sung or hummed, even if somewhat inaccurately, they will be enjoyed. The multi-million sales of the Royal Philharmonic's recordings proved that once again. The first of the *Hooked on Classics* series was issued in 1981 and continued successfully for a number of years and is reputed to have sold over ten million albums. The arrangements were made and conducted by Louis Clark who had been the arranger for the Electric Light Orchestra. His arrangements consisted mainly of adding a rhythmic beat to extracts from well-known works by classical composers. The beat would be fast or slow depending on the item. This small selection gives some idea of the eclectic repertoire covered by the original records issued on LPs: excerpts from; *Also Sprach Zarathustra* by Richard Strauss, the march *Colonel Bogey* by Kenneth Alford, Haydn's Trumpet Concerto, the *Rhapsody in Blue* by George Gershwin, Bach's *Ave Maria*, *Capriccio Italien* by Tchaikovsky, Mozart's *Rondo Alla Turca*, a Violin Concerto by Vivaldi and the *Gymnopédie No 2* by Erik Satie.

Again, though these recordings sold in their millions, there were those who were unhappy about what was being done to classical music. A review in the *All Music Guide* is a good example of the strength of feeling these recordings evoked: *Devoid of any true musical worth, Hooked on Classics places many familiar classical themes to an oppressive synthetic drum track. These medleys are only of interest to those who always liked the tunes in classical music but wished there was a stronger backbeat.*

By the 1990s there were so many forms of 'popular music' – what should we call them – pop, rock? Even 'popular' is not accurate as some of them have a more limited audience for their concerts and recordings than classical music has. On the other hand some have vast audiences. As a musician I have always been interested in what new music was being composed whether it was in my own field of classical and light music, or rock and pop, but after the 1960s I found that it was only occasionally that I played or heard a new work with much pleasure. I listened if possible to the same piece several times to see if it would become more agreeable. But in the main it did not. It seemed to me that all music was becoming increasingly cerebral or aggressive.

Muzak was sometimes called elevator music, because of its omnipresence in America in their lifts. I remember hearing it first when I was in the USA in 1950 with the Royal Philharmonic Orchestra as we zoomed up and down twenty floors or more to our bedrooms – it was a kind of musical wallpaper, but not unpleasant. Nor was ska, which became reggae in the late 1960s, nor, as far as I was concerned was pop music into the 60s. But from the 1970s onwards I found the bewildering variety of genres and sub-genres of rock, with a few exceptions each louder and more aggressive than the last, less and less agreeable. Was this just because I was getting older – I was still only in my early fifties then – or because the environment had become more violent and produced a music that reflected the anger and resentment that seemed to be growing ever stronger? Punk rock and then hip hop and rap, were part of a culture that seemed to me to be becoming increasingly aggressive and that included graffiti, break-dancing and a particular attitude to dress.

Hip hop and many of the versions of rock that appeared from the late 1980s, various electric dance musics – techno, rave, trance, drum and bass and ambient music, to name but a few – used samplers which allowed sounds already recorded, whether music, mechanical or natural, to be re-recorded and made into a 'composition', sometimes by over-recording, over-lapping, adding new elements from an instrumentalist and a number of other techniques.

I had for some time wondered why quite a few young men wore their trousers hanging from their hips in a way that I found less than attractive. It was a long time before I learned the reason for this fashion favoured by devotees of breakdancing to hip hop music, that includes jazz-rap and gangsta-rap. Breakdancing requires a great deal of energy and freedom of movement calling for clothes that are loose fitting. Baggy trousers are important. But why did they have to be worn as if they were about to fall down? I found out later that this form of dancing originated in the Bronx, in the 1980s a derelict and violent area of New York where gang warfare was rife. Many of the young men and some young women had at one time or another served a prison sentence during which their belts had been removed for obvious reasons. No doubt a combination of old habits and the wish to be comfortable when dancing – it is suggested that gang wars developed into gang dancing contests – resulted in this style of dress.

The heading 'Music' in British newspapers and magazines now nearly always refers only to pop and rock music. The *New York Times* also lists its news items about music in this way. Jazz, which had been such an influence on the early rock musicians and has continued to be an influence, now has a long enough history to cohabit with classical music on BBC Radio 3 and is often reviewed on the same page as classical music in up-market newspapers. Every month The *Observer* includes a colour supplement of about seventy-five pages called the *Observer Music Monthly*. It covers most forms of popular music and sometimes the rock influenced world music, but very seldom mentions classical and jazz.

The BBC's magazine *Radio Times*, with sales of 1.1 million each week, has the second largest distribution of any magazine in

Britain and is therefore seen, if not read, by a very large number of people. In July, during the 2006 BBC Prom season, nowhere throughout its 138 pages was there a section, or even a paragraph, about what is now called Classical music, a genre that also includes so much else that is not rock or pop. On the page headed MUSIC, now solely concerned with rock music, there was a highlighted section 'This Week's Music Choices'. The six choices for one week were: programmes about a new pop artist and her group; the Queen of hip hop Soul; the Art of Pop; the Cambridge Folk Festival; the Queens of Heartache and a programme about a rock star whose behaviour as a result of his taking psychedelic drugs such as LSD led him to behave in such a disruptive and erratic way that his group had to engage another guitarist to back him up when he was hardly able to play.

To realise the extent that attitudes have changed one needs to recall that in 1927, when Chappell's withdrew its financial support for the Promenade Concerts, the newly established British Broadcasting Corporation – the BBC – with Sir John Reith's slogan 'to inform, educate and entertain', took over the promotion of the Proms. For the next three years the concerts were given by 'Sir Henry Wood and his Symphony Orchestra', until in 1930 the BBC established the BBC Symphony Orchestra, the first full-time symphony orchestra in Britain, and subsequently created a number of regional orchestras. The BBC has, to its very great credit, continued to promote the Proms for over seventy-five years. But, clearly the spirit of Sir John no longer inhabits the *Radio Times*.

Of course rock is now no longer an infant or an adolescent music, having been with us for over fifty years. Everyone under the age of sixty born into every economic class will have lived in an environment surrounded by this genre of music. Evidence for the effect this has had is provided by two excellent long-running programmes on BBC radio and TV.

The basis of the Radio 4 programme *Desert Island Discs,* which has been running for over sixty years, is that someone who has distinguished themselves in some way in politics, industry, business, sport, the arts or one of the professions is interviewed and chooses eight records they would wish to take if they were marooned on a desert island. In the past the choices were usually of classical and light music, some songs from musicals and jazz.

Now it is predominantly contemporary popular music of some kind.

University Challenge broadcast on BBC 2 pits two teams from different universities against each other to answer a number of wide-ranging difficult questions. These require considerable knowledge in many subjects that include the sciences, history, geography, politics, music and the arts. The average age of the teams of students is about twenty-one. These programmes have been so successful that they now do some programmes called *University Challenge: the Professionals.* Again two teams, average age forty-five to fifty-five, are pitted against each other to answer similar questions. When questions on music require answers it is clear that both age groups in general are poorly informed, but usually better informed about popular than classical music. Extracts that are selected from classical music that have been used as backing for TV advertisements are more likely to be correctly answered than others.

Can it be that, as well as being tuneful, compositions such as the *Verdi Requiem,* Copland's ballet music for *Rodeo, Carmina Burana* by Carl Orff, Dvorak's *New World* Symphony,and one of Mozart's piano concertos, which was used as background music for the film *Elvira Madigan* and which is now often called by the title of the film, rather than the boring *'No.21',* were all chosen because they are all out of copyright and incur no royalties?

The concert held the evening before the 1990 FIFA World Cup in Rome, held to raise money for José Carreras's International Leukaemia Foundation – he had recently recovered from leukaemia – also gave his friends Plácido Domingo and Luciano Pavarotti the opportunity to welcome him back after his successful treatment. It was a great success and was the start of The Three Tenors phenomenon. They repeated their success at subsequent Cup Finals in Los Angeles (1994), Paris (1998) and Yokohama (2002). They also gave concerts in other towns to enormous audiences, usually in large outdoor venues and did not restrict their repertoire to only operatic extracts. They included items as varied as *Torero Quiera* by Manuel Panella Miguel Roai, *You'll Never Walk Alone* by Rodgers and Hammerstein, *Granada* by Augustín Lara, *I'm Dreaming of a White Christmas* and *Amazing Grace.* These concerts shown on TV and available on recordings appealed to the world-wide audiences that enjoyed concerts put on by Raymond Gubbay and others, the Classic FM type broadcasts and the recordings and concerts by artists such as the Jacques Loussier Trio and the Swingle Singers.

As might be expected there were opera buffs who scorned the selection of bits out of the operas, torn from their proper settings and sometimes sung by all three tenors at the same time, while there were others who felt that these concerts brought opera to many who had previously had no contact with it before, though there is no evidence that the audiences at opera houses increased as a result of this exposure. Rather it proved, once again, that what the majority of people enjoy is 'a good tune'. Not long before he died Sir Thomas Beecham put it more succinctly: he is quoted as saying, *'The function of music is to release us from the tyranny of conscious thought.'* Recent enquiries into whether the sound of music can actually help those experiencing pain seem to suggest that it can. At the same time there is sufficient evidence that some forms of rock have very much the opposite effect. Perhaps neither of these phenomena should surprise us: mothers have been singing lullabies to their infants, lovers serenading and warriors singing, dancing and marching to victory or defeat, as far back in time as we have any information.

The vastly greater profits made by the record company, in spite of the tremendous fees paid to the three tenors and their conductors Zubin Mehta and James Levine, accelerated the classical record industry's decision to follow the path taken by popular music, which had shown for at least thirty years that the crossover of genres increased sales. It was around this time that I first became aware of the phrase Classical Crossover. The sale of classical recordings, however successful even in the halcyon times from the 1950s into the 1980s, had never matched in number and therefore profitability that of other more popular music recordings. The up-front cost of engaging a symphony orchestra, a famous conductor and perhaps a soloist is so much greater than for other music, and more sessions are required to produce a symphony lasting anything from thirty to fifty minutes or longer; furthermore, as a rule, because of its complexity, less music can be successfully recorded in each three-hour session. This has always been reflected in the recording fees the Musicians' Union has agreed for the members of symphony orchestras, which from the start of recording have always been lower than for the recording of all other forms of music, which require fewer musicians, take less time to record and sell in greater numbers.

The tradition of symphony orchestras playing non-symphonic music goes back a long way. Four years after the formation of the Boston Symphony Orchestra in 1881 the Boston Pops Orchestra was founded as an off-shoot of the symphony orchestra – in effect the symphony orchestra without its principal players, what in America they call their 'first chair men'. The major orchestras all had co-principals, as the BBC Symphony Orchestra had in 1930 when my father was the co-principal clarinet with Frederick Thurston. The Pops Orchestra's programmes consisted of light classical music, tunes from the current hit musicals, and sometimes a novelty piece. The Pops programmes are much the same now except that the items from musicals and the novelty pieces have changed. From 1930, when Arthur Fiedler became its principal conductor, the orchestra is reputed to have sold the most recordings of any orchestra – in total over 50 million, in a variety of formats. The most popular has been *Sleigh Ride* by Leroy Anderson, not a piece usually found in a symphony orchestra's repertoire. Since 1980 John Williams, famous for his film music that includes *Star Wars* and *Indiana Jones,* has been their principal conductor. Of a number of other Pops orchestras in America the Cincinnati Pops Orchestra, under its conductor Erich Kunzel, has since 1977 probably been the most successful and like the Boston Pops has made many recordings.

The continuing success of the Three Tenors throughout the 1990s led the record companies to search for other recordings that would sell in their millions – *The Three Tenors in Concert* sold ten million copies. In 1992 the recording of the contemporary Polish composer Henryk Górecki's Third Symphony, for soprano and orchestra, sold more than 1 million CDs and for a time was played regularly on Classic FM. Even more remarkable was the success of *Chant*, a record of Gregorian chant sung by Benedictine monks in northern Spain, which achieved sales of over four million copies.

Increasing numbers of easy listening albums of extracts from the most popular classical music and opera and recordings of lighter music played by outstanding artists like Itzhak Perlman and Joshua Bell began to appear in place of new recordings by the orchestras. In 1995 the young violinist Vanessa Mae released an album *The Violin Player* that featured her playing a fusion of classics, pop, rock and techno – compositions that ranged from Bach to rock. She was also featured emerging from the sea with her dress wet and clinging to her shapely body. Being young, attractive, and if possible sexy, became a feature of what was by then becoming known as Classical Crossover.

For many years the Grammy Awards for Classical Music had been the most prestigious prizes for classical music and musicians. In 1999 a new category was added – Best Classical Crossover Album. The first one was awarded to the cellist Yo-Yo Ma for his recording of *Soul of the Tango - The Music of Astor Piazzolla*. Some of the most recent winners have been the violinist Joshua Bell with the percussionist Evelyn Glennie and others for *Perpetual Motion*, André Previn with the London Symphony Orchestra for *Previn Conducts Korngold (the film music for Sea Hawk; Captain Blood, etc.)* and in 2006 *The Turtle Island String Quartet and the Ying Quartet* for *4+four*. This is one of the most interesting awards so far. Turtle Island String Quartet, an innovative string group, improvises and arranges an extraordinary range of music that includes jazz standards, classical, country, rock, New Age, swing, Latin and Middle Eastern music. On this particular album they have collaborated with the Ying Quartet and included their usual variety of sources plus a re-arranged version of Darius Milhaud's *La Création du Monde*.

A year later, in 2000, the British Phonographic Industry (BPI), the organisation of record companies, decided to start the Classical Brit awards. The Brit Awards, for the pop industry, had for many years been a very successful marketing device and it was hoped that the Classical Brits would do the same for the ailing classical market. Until then there had only been the Gramophone Awards for classical music. Voting for the awards was by a committee that included industry executives, representatives from the media, the British Association of Record Dealers, members of the Musicians Union, lawyers, promoters, and orchestra leaders. I have always been interested in who the 'orchestra leaders' have been as I have never come across anyone who admitted being involved in the voting. The categories in the first year were: British Artist of the Year, Female Artist of the Year, Album of the Year, Young British Classical Performer, and Outstanding Contribution to Music. The award for Best Album of the Year is voted for by listeners to Classic FM.

In the same year the British Artist of the Year Award was given to the fourteen-year-old Charlotte Church whose recording *Voice of an Angel,* on which she sang arias, sacred and traditional songs had been a big success. Three years later on *Dream a Dream* she sang mostly Christmas carols and pop songs. This was the start of her future career as a pop singer. The other awards were received by Martha Argerich, Bryn Terfel, Andrea Bocelli (for *Sacred Arias,* the Album of the Year), Daniel Harding and Nigel Kennedy. In the following years the categories changed and additional categories were added. In 2001 the Album of the Year was Russell Watson's *The Voice*; in 2002 the biggest-selling Classical Album was Russell Watson's *Encore* and the Outstanding Contribution to Music went to Andrea Bocelli who in 1993 won the Album of the Year with *Sentimento;* the 1994 Album of the Year was won by Bryn Terfel with *Bryn;* in 2005 and 2006 the Album of the Year went to Katherine Jenkins.

When Peter Gelb, then the President of Sony Classical, said in 1997 'For the classical record industry, the writing is already on the wall', I wonder if he foresaw the extent to which this would have come true by 2006? By then the major labels were only infrequently producing new recordings. The smaller companies, Harmonia Mundi, Hyperion, Chandos, Opera Rara and the low-cost phenomenon Naxos continued to be more successful.

By 2006 a number of major orchestras in Europe and the USA – the first in Britain had been the London Symphony Orchestra in 1999 – began issuing recordings on their own labels. The Musicians' Union was obliged to allow the orchestras to record their concert performances without any additional fee to the musicians on the understanding that when the sales provided sufficient profit the musicians would receive a share. This did away with the cost previously incurred of paying a large number of musicians for recording the music in the studio and, of course it reduced the income earned by the musicians. As the average sales for each recording has been in the 8000 to 12,000 range the profit required to pay an orchestra of eighty has yet to be reached. However, in the circumstances the musicians are glad if the recordings act as a spur to audiences attending their concerts. It is now even possible at the end of some concerts to buy a recording of the first part of the concert you have just attended.

There is not a lot that can be done to change the format of the symphony concert in order to make it more attractive to those who have been affected both by the popular music with which they have been surrounded all their lives and by the changed listening habits that the new means of communication have brought about. Various attempts have been made but nothing has made any real difference. Neither by the orchestra wearing a more contemporary style of dress nor by changing the time the concerts are held so as to make it easier for the audience to come straight from work. Nor has having shorter, one-hour concerts at lunch time nor creating a more friendly, intimate atmosphere by the conductor talking to the audience about the programme; nor by having a glass of wine before or after the concert with an opportunity for members of the audience to meet and talk to players from the orchestra.

It has been much easier in the opera house to bring productions more up to date. Among Jonathan Miller's many opera productions both his 1982 production of Verdi's *Rigoletto* for which the setting of the opera is changed from Mantua to Little Italy, with the Mafia replacing the Duke's court, and his version of Bizet's *Carmen* which he updated to Franco's Spain, were extremely successful. The American Peter Sellars' productions have been rather more radical (though some of Miller's later productions followed suit). Sellars set Mozart's *Così fan tutte* in a diner on Cape Cod, *The Marriage of Figaro* in a grand apartment in Trump Tower in New York and *Don Giovanni* in New York's Spanish Harlem. His production of *Don Giovanni* that I saw, with sub-titles in English, so changed not only the milieu but also the characters in such a way that it seemed to me the nature of the work became distorted.

But this was as nothing compared with what Glyndebourne decided to do as part of their education programme. For several years they have tried to stimulate an interest in opera in children, believing that if you catch them young enough a future audience will be created. *Misper,* for the under twelves, and *Zoei* intended for teenagers are both original works by John Lunn. They were written for and performed by the children themselves, in collaboration with professionals. They received praise from the critics but have not maintained a place in Glyndebourne's repertoire nor been put on elsewhere. *Zoe* was shown on Channel 4 but had poor viewing figures. Then in 2005 an 'operatic thriller' in three acts, *Tangier Tattoo*, again by John Lunn was mounted, this time aimed at an older audience, the eighteen to thirty-year-olds. The General Director David Pickard said 'It's quite racy – that's partly because we wanted to create a piece which that particular age group could relate to'. Like the previous two Lunn operas the story had similar ingredients to many TV series and plays – sex, violence, intrigue and mystery. Depending on the age range of the audience the degree of each element has varied. The music for *Tangier Tango* is very loud, making use of elements of pop music and electronic samples, so that the singers had to be 'miked'. Even though operas have sometimes failed because the story and libretto have been unsatisfactory, in the end if the music is really good even a stupid story will not wreck it. Lunn's music does not seem to have been strong enough to attract a young or an older audience.

I was saddened, remembering the wonderful performances I had been so fortunate to take part in at Glyndebourne, to read that the following year, in yet another endeavour to attract a younger audience, Glyndebourne had asked the rapper Paradise to create a hip hop opera from Mozart's *Così fan tutte*. When he was asked how he came to be involved in this project he said '...*they wanted to reach the youth, because they felt their target audience was too narrow, about 65 and over. They wanted to tap into the youth culture as well, and a guy in Germany actually came up with the idea of 'hip h'opera', fusing elements of hip hop and opera ...* '. In March 2006 the transformation of *Così fan tutte* into *School 4 Lovers* by rapper Paradise and the producer and saxophonist Charlie Parker changed the setting from Naples to an inner city estate. The role of Don Alfonso was played by Paradise, who said this fusion was '*neither culture shock, nor culture clash – this is cultural evolution!*'

The comments in the press, before the opera was actually produced, about the kind of 'street' language co-opted into the adaptation called *Hip Hop Così: 'School 4 Lovers'* were unfavourable. I have been unable to find out whether any of the three performances that the opera house told me were sold out were attended by the critics, as there seem to have been no reviews. However, it seems to me we do not need to be worried on Mozart's or his librettist Da Ponte's behalf. This masterpiece has survived several centuries and even though it had to wait until 1910 for Beecham to give its first unexpurgated performance in Britain it has lost none of its beauty and insight. What is so worrying is that because no work of our own time is attractive enough to entice an audience it was considered necessary to distort and even cannibalise one of the most beautiful operas in order to provide contemporary entertainment.

The Spanish director Calixto Bieito's staging, first for Barcelona and then for English National Opera, of *Un ballo in maschera* by Verdi, in which in the opening scene the conspirators are found sitting on the toilet with their trousers down was even more disagreeable than *School 4 Lovers*. Still, we must be grateful that so far we have been spared his violation of Mozart's *The Abduction from the Seraglio* for the Komische Oper in Berlin. He decided that this opera is about prostitution, drug abuse and sadistic violence. The details are too disgusting to describe and would certainly have received an X certificate if it had been a film.

The changes in lifestyle and listening habits referred to earlier have over the past twenty years or so had an increasing effect on the music profession. By the end of the 1990s the reduction in the amount of work available and the earning capacity of musicians in Britain had declined sufficiently for the Musicians' Union to commission a survey of musicians' employment in the period between 1978 and 1998. The report of the research carried out at Westminster University, *Nice Work if you can get it! A survey of Musicians' Employment*, was published in 2000. In comparing the situation with twenty years earlier the researchers found that less work was available in all sectors of the profession – less live performance, broadcasting, recording and teaching than previously and that fees in general were worth less in real terms. It was also noted that in a number of orchestras fewer musicians were now being employed.

The decline had been felt most keenly by orchestral musicians for whom broadcasting and recording had been an important source of income for both those in the London orchestras and freelance players. The report showed that not only had there been a reduction in employment but also that the number of players engaged full-time in the contract orchestras, in which average salaries remained pitifully low, had also declined over the previous twenty years. Since the end of the 1990s more young freelance classical musicians had been obliged to create their own small chamber groups and become far more entrepreneurial and self-promoting than had been necessary in the past. The number leaving the conservatoires has continued to be far greater than the profession can absorb so that many have had to find additional employment outside performing and teaching in order to survive financially.

I use the term orchestral musician to mean all those who are not jazz, pop or rock musicians of any kind. Because of the number of years of preparation required before entering the profession, orchestral and chamber musicians hope from the start to remain professional performers throughout their lives. This has rarely been the case for pop and rock musicians because the nature of their music is far more ephemeral. With the notable exception of a few groups such as the Rolling Stones and the Who and some individual artists who have been exceptionally successful the great majority of pop and rock musicians remain working for only a few years. For those who compose their own music and lyrics it is difficult to continue to be creative over many years and performers in this genre need to be able to reinvent themselves as fashion changes. Many who set out seeking fame and fortune abandon their quest within quite a short time when they find it eludes them. Even the Beatles, probably the most successful and influential group – they are credited with having sold over a billion records before 1990 – remained together for less than ten years.

While attendance at art galleries for exhibitions of masterpieces of the past are increasing and those for contemporary painting, sculpture, installations and light shows are attracting even larger crowds, why is it that concert attendance continues to decline and cause concern and programmes of contemporary music still appear to drive the average music lover away?

Not only is going to a concert so much more expensive than going to an art gallery, but going to a concert has become unnecessary. One can now listen to music whenever and wherever one is so much more conveniently and cheaply. Perhaps even more important is the freedom that a visit to any form of art provides in contrast to the need to commit oneself to two hours of passive concentration when attending a concert. At a concert one cannot go back and forth to a phrase or passage one has enjoyed as one can go back and look at a picture or a piece of sculpture – nor as one can when listening to a recording.

A piece of contemporary art in whatever form can be ignored or passed by quite quickly whereas if one is listening to a piece of music in a concert hall it requires considerable courage to get up in the middle of a performance, disturb one's neighbours and walk out. While new classical music composers have been addressing an ever decreasing audience, the music of the past has for the last fifty years been trying to reinvent itself. On the one hand there are those who play Mozart in a style that purports to be 'authentic' and on what pretend to be 'original instruments', though they are reproductions with improved intonation without which they would be unacceptable to a modern audience. On the other hand there are those willing to turn classical music into 'easy listening' and happy to change the story, the words and the culture of operas so as to imitate our own contemporary culture.

Having been involved in the music profession, the music business and now the music industry for over sixty years I am saddened that the profession I have known is being swept away and that the music I love and which in the first twenty years as a player seemed to be growing in popularity has fallen on such hard times. But I am not surprised. As Chairman of the Philharmonia, in the mid-1970s I suggested to my colleagues, who were already becoming concerned for the future, that as much as we all loved the music we played and the life we were lucky enough to enjoy, it would not go on for ever – nothing ever has or ever will. We had seen other thriving industries disappear; coal mines closed, the steel industry collapse, shipbuilding and fishing ...

The Musicians' Union, in the past, when I had been involved in negotiating with employers at every level from night club owners to representatives of the BBC, ITV and the major record companies, had then been able to be effective on behalf of its members and could rely on their support because it represented their wishes. With the changes in the law that made the 'closed-shop' illegal together with a reduction in employment opportunities and sufficient financial support for symphony orchestras and opera houses, the Musicians' Union's ability to bargain on behalf of its members has been substantially reduced.

A time when everything is valued in terms of how much money it can make is not one that is good for the performing arts and this is especially so for classical music, which is so labour intensive. While popular music, responding to the current mood throughout the world, becomes either more aggressive or maudlin, classical music and jazz have become increasingly more cerebral. And while the advances in communication technology have made the commercialisation of popular music one of the most profitable industries, classical music is attempting to fight a rearguard action.

In a world rife with conflict of every kind and when it seems we are bent on destroying our own environment it is difficult to be optimistic. But out of the old something new always grows. There is so much new technology young people are using in remarkably inventive ways that perhaps this is the way music will go. No doubt in the 17th century when musicians were playing recorders, natural trumpets and viols and before the well tempered scale which adjusted the notes within an octave so it became possible to modulate from one key to another, they would be astounded to see the instruments we play and the music we take for granted. However music is presented and whatever it will sound like, I hope it will provide as much pleasure and inspiration as the music I have known has given me. For thinking and feeling people, contemplating the future is not easy. But of one thing we can be absolutely certain: as long as there are men and women there will be music.

Bernstein, Leonard: 108, 150-1, 353

Berry, Chuck, (Charles Edward Anderson): 365

Bertini, Gary: 323

Besses o' th' Barn Band: 251

Bieito, Calixto: 399

Birmingham Conservatoire: 340

Birnbaum, Leo: 73

Bishop, Christopher: 328

Bismarck, Otto von: 162

Bizet, Georges: 15, 39, 77, 211, 308, 357, 397

Blacher, Boris: 317

Black Dyke Mills Band: 251

Black Sea: 3, 4, 33, 248

Blackheath Halls: 272-3

Blackstorm: 374

Blech, Harry: 313

Bliss, Sir Arthur: 17, 131

Bloch, Ernest: 198

Blumlein, Alan: 170

Bocelli, Andrea: 396

Böehm System: 24

Böhm, Karl: 95, 116

Boine, Mari: 372-3

Bolshoi Ballet Company: 114, 169, 332

Boone, Pat: 365

Borge, Victor: 337

Borodin, Alexander: 379-80

Borthwick Library: 117, 134

Boston Pops Orchestra: 394

Boston Symphony Orchestra: 198

Bottesini, Giovanni: 94

Boulez, Pierre: 26, 126-7, 195, 245, 316, 318-20, 323-4, 326, 347, 349, 378, 382, 384-5, 388

Boult, Sir Adrian: 9, 11, 13, 16-18, 44, 57-8, 110-1, 224, 252, 336

Bournemouth Municipal Orchestra: 32, 34-5, 137, 304, 308

Bournemouth Philharmonic Orchestra: 35

Bournemouth Symphony Orchestra: 296, 308

Bowman, Sidney: 173

Boyce, William: 25, 28, 312

Boyd Neel Orchestra: 311

Brabbins, Martyn: 266

Brahms, Johannes: 15-6, 32, 72, 78-9, 106, 127, 162-3, 186, 192, 196, 201, 211, 247, 268-9, 301, 320, 340, 350

Brain, Aubrey: 3, 11,

Brain, Dennis: 3, 11, 75, 140-1, 205, 207-8, 225, 310, 312

Brain, Leonard: 311

Braithwaite, Warwick: 58

Brangwyn Hall: 46

Brangwyn, Sir Frank: 46

Brannigan, Owen: 220

Bratton, John: 305

Brendel, Alfred: 195, 200, 323

Bretton Hall: 253

Brighton Festival: 275

Brighton Philharmonic Orchestra: 275

Bristol Evening Post: 332

British Artist of the Year: 396

British Association of Record Dealers: 395

British Broadcasting Company: 161, 240, 363

British Broadcasting Corporation: 9-12, 14, 16, 31, 38, 44, 46, 133-4, 138, 159, 161, 166, 171-4, 176, 180, 196, 202, 207, 225, 236, 238-41, 243-4, 256, 259-61, 263-4, 275, 277, 292, 295, 301, 304, 306, 308-9, 312, 317, 333, 337, 349, 401

British Council: 278-9, 291

British Library Sound Archive: 372

British Performing Arts Medicine Trust: 97

British Phonographic Industry (BPI): 395

Britten, Lord Benjamin: 15, 17, 126-7, 186, 199, 225, 310-1, 313, 317, 338, 343, 351

Broadcasting House: 12, 14, 346
   Maida Vale: 12, 172, 211, 224, 243, 269
      Portland Place: 12

Hurlstone, William: 36
Hurst, George: 266, 275
Hurwitz, Emanuel: 248, 267
Hylton, Jack: 10, 58-60, 159, 305-6, 359, 364

Ibert, Jacques: 301
Incorporated Society of Musicians (ISM): 232-3, 238, 301
Independent Broadcasting Authority (IBA): 264
Independent Television Companies Association (ITCA): 244, 264, 401
Indo-Jazz Fusions: 382
Inner London Education Authority: 256
Institut de Recherche (IRCAM): 304, 318-9, 349, 382, 385
Institute of Aboriginal Studies: 374
International Institute for Comparative Music Studies: 370
International Leukaemia Foundation: 392
International Music Council (IMC): 368
International Society for Music in Education (ISME): 281, 320, 329, 377
International Society for the Study of Tension in Performance (ISSTP): 97
Ireland, John: 17
Israel Philharmonic Orchestra (formerly The Palestine Orchestra): 19, 323
Ives, Charles: 377

Jackson, Gerald: 51
Jackson, Harold: 251, 310
Jaffa, Max: 30, 34
James, Dr Ian: 97
James, Harry: 362
Janáček, Leoš: 127, 338, 340
Jarred, Mary: 222
Jenkins, Katherine: 396
Jenkins, Sir Gilmour: 256

Jerusalem Ruben Academy of Music and Dance: 299
Jerwood Library: 117, 134
Joachim, Joseph: 161-2
Johnson, Bunk, (William Geary): 86, 358
Jones, Philip: 208, 276
Joplin, Scott: 197, 379
Joyce, Eileen: 53-4, 57-8
Juilliard School: 197, 326
Juler, Pauline: 180
Jurinac, Sena: 215-6, 218, 220

Karajan, Herbert von: 89, 94-5, 98, 102, 116-7, 193, 210, 229, 268, 355
Katchen, Julius: 200
Kaye, Danny (David Daniel): 107
Kell, Reginald: 71, 182, 205-6, 307, 310
Kempe, Rudolf: 141
Kennedy, John: 11, 211-2
Kennedy, Lauri: 11
Kennedy, Nigel: 11, 211, 396
Kentner, Louis: 200
Kenton, Stan (Stanley): 361
Kenyon, Nicholas: 15
Kern, Jerome: 353, 366
Kersey, Eda: 53
Ketelbey, Albert: 357, 386
Klassik Komm Conference: 355
Klemperer, Otto: 102, 118-9, 121, 126, 336, 342
Klezmer Bands: 3, 197
Klosé, Camille: 23, 24
Kneller Hall, Military School of Music: 250, 252
Knight, Peter: 380
Knussen, Oliver: 47, 94, 127
Knussen, Stuart: 47, 94, 127
Kodály, Zoltán: 17, 370, 377
Kollek, Teddy (Theodor): 322
Komische, Oper: 399
Korngold, Erich: 395
Koussevitsky, Serge: 18, 126
Kovacevich, Stephen: 200
Kreisler, Fritz: 34, 106, 112, 166, 190, 196, 227-8, 231, 273, 357, 378

Kubelik, Rafael: 216
Kunitachi College of Music: 292
Kunz, Erich: 215-6, 218
Kunzel, Erich: 394

La Scala, Milan: 103, 340
Lalo, Édouard: 190
Lambert, Constant: 17, 58, 127
Lampe, Oscar: 75, 210, 310
Lancaster, Osbert: 222
Landesmann, Hans: 327
Lanner, Joseph: 357
Lara, Augustin: 392
Larsson, Lars-Erik: 301
Lauder, Sir Harry (Henry): 147, 154
Le Corbusier (Charles-Édouard Jeanneret-Gris): 384
Leaper, Adrian: 266, 276
Lee, Jenny (Baroness Lee of Asheridge): 143
Lee, Peggy (Norma Deloris): 363
Legge, Walter: 12, 116, 119-20, 135, 140, 142, 167-8, 227, 251, 284
Lehár, Franz: 15
Lehmann, Lotte: 201
Leinsdorf, Erich: 110
Leipzig Gewandhaus Orchestra: 106
Leningrad Philharmonic Orchestra: 340, 342
Leonard, Lawrence: 312
Leoncavallo, Ruggero: 137, 163
Leverhulme Trust: 341
Levine, James: 393
Levintritt Competition: 197
Lewin, Gordon: 254-5
Lewis, Joseph: 15-16
Lewis, Richard: 216, 218, 220, 222
Lewiston, David: 367-8
Library of Congress: 384
Liebermann, Rolf: 378
Ligeti, György: 338
Light Music Society: 381
Lindal, Anna: 324-5
Ling Tung: 283-4, 286
Liszt, Franz: 189, 201, 320

Liter, Monia: 173
Liverpool Philharmonic Orchestra: 47, 137, 304, 307-8, 381
Lombardo, Alberto: 155
London Baroque Ensemble: 312
London Concert Orchestra: 353
London Festival Orchestra: 380
London Mozart Players: 313
London Music Festival: 18
London Orchestral Association (LOA): 230, 233-6, 238
London Orchestral Concert Board: 144
London Philharmonic Orchestra: 1, 2, 12-13, 31, 50-1, 53, 55-60, 64-71, 73, 81, 98, 102-3, 107-110, 112, 119, 128, 131, 135, 138-41, 164-6, 171, 177-8, 181-2, 189, 193, 206, 208, 210-11, 215, 226-7, 234, 294, 304, 306-7, 316, 336-8, 353, 378
London Philharmonic Post: 81
London Symphony Orchestra: 37, 47, 64, 81, 91-2, 94, 103, 109-10, 114, 121, 131, 135, 138, 171, 177, 188, 206, 208, 251, 306, 311, 318, 327, 345, 381-2, 396
London, George: 228
Lord, Jon: 381
Los Angeles Philharmonic: 322
Loussier, Jacques: 386-8, 393
Ludlow, John: 267
Lunn, John: 397-8
Lutoslawski, Witold: 269
Lympany, Moura: 54, 111
Lyons Corner House: 30, 32-3, 239
Lyons, Joseph: 32-3

Ma, Yo-Yo: 200, 395
Maazel, Lorin: 102, 120, 266, 342
Maazel/Vilar conducting competition: 293
MacDonagh, Terence: 73, 184, 218
Mackerras, Sir Charles: 266, 269
Mackintosh, Jack: 251
MacLehose, Lord Murray: 286

Thomas, Peter: 267
Thorpe, Tony, (Anthony): 93
Three Choirs Festival: 159
Three Tenors, The: 377, 392, 394
Thurston, Jack, (Frederick): 6, 9-11, 30, 35-6, 202, 205, 364, 394
Tippett, Sir Michael: 126, 128, 275
Toho Gakuen School of Music: 292-3
Tolansky, Jon: 335-7, 340-1
Tomlinson, Sir John: 228
Tooley, Sir John: 332
Tortelier, Paul: 188, 197-8, 203
Toscanini, Arturo: 9, 18-9, 98, 116, 120, 229
Trent Park: 253-5
Trier, Steven: 83
Trinity College of Music: 117, 134, 256, 273, 340, 367
Troise, Pasquale: 173
Tschaikov, Anissim: 3, 5-7, 11, 17, 21-2, 24, 36, 63-4, 70, 76, 147-8, 150, 153, 156, 172, 176, 180, 190, 211, 234, 346, 364, 394
Tschaikov, Anton: 3-6, 34
Tschaikov, grandfather: 3-5
Tschaikov, Jimmy (James): 3, 5, 33
Tuckwell, Barry: 208
Tung, Ling (see Ling Tung)
Turnage, Mark-Anthony: 275-6
Turner, Dame Eva: 228
Turtle Island String Quartet: 395

Uchida, Mitsuko: 200
Ulanova, Galina: 169
University Challenge: 392
University of London: 270-1, 330-1
Urho, Ellen: 280
USSR Ministry of Culture Orchestra: 332

Vaizey, Lord John: 256, 260
Valkiapää, Nils-Aslak: 373
Valois, Ninette de: 308
Van Phillips: 361
Varèse, Edgard: 269, 382-4

Vasary, Tamas, piano: 300
Vaughan Williams, Ralph (see under Williams):
Verdi, Giuseppe: 117, 163, 214, 216-7, 226, 275, 347, 355-6, 392, 396, 399
Vickers, Jon: 225, 228, 347
Vienna Court Orchestra: 91
Vienna Opera House: 117
Vienna Philharmonic Orchestra: 117, 122, 135, 178, 327, 345
Vinter, Gilbert: 180
Vishnevskaya, Galina: 199
Vivaldi, Antonio: 389
Vodery, Will: 378
Voss, Louis: 174
Vozlinsky, Pierre: 324

Wagner, Richard: 16, 35, 52-3, 72, 89, 91, 110, 126, 137, 168, 212, 225-6, 251, 275, 305, 337, 351, 367
Wakeman, Rick: 385-6
Waldteufel, Émile: 117, 137, 357
Wallace, Ian: 221
Wallace, John: 338
Wallenstein, Alfred: 221
Waller, Bill (William): 346
Walter, Bruno: 18, 65, 102, 105, 164, 229, 336
Walton, Bernard: 211
Walton, Richard (Bob): 73, 208
Walton, Sir William: 17, 126, 128, 269, 351
Warumpi Band: 374
Watson, Angus: 294
Watson, Russell: 396
Weber, Carl Maria von: 7, 29, 37, 126, 207
Webern, Anton: 17, 127-8, 316, 382
Webster, David: 308
Weidenfeld and Nicolson: 195, 328
Weidenfeld, Lord: 321-2
Weingartner, Felix: 91, 126, 189
Weizmann, Dr Chaim: 19
Welch, Elizabeth: 207

Weldon, George: 60, 308
Welitsch, Ljuba: 216-7, 224
Wells Cathedral School: 256, 297
Wessex Philharmonic Orchestra:
31, 35-41, 44, 46-8, 52-4, 60, 127,
189, 202, 236, 295, 307
Wheatland Foundation, The: 304,
321-8, 330, 349, 377
Whiteman, Paul: 378
Whittaker, Alec: 310
Who, The: 400
Wiedoeft, Rudy: 158
Wieniawski, Henryk: 34, 190, 197,
301
Willemson, H F: 72
Williams, Gerrard: 364
Williams, John: 394
Williams, Ralph Vaughan: 17, 25-
6, 28, 126, 128, 159, 162, 188, 364,
377
Wilson, Arthur: 250
Wilson, Marie: 98, 211
Wireless Military Band (later BBC
Military Band): 171, 364
Wolf, Hugo: 363
Wood, Dennis: 46
Wood, Haydn: 15
Wood, Sir Henry: 18, 63-4, 71,
110, 137-9, 175, 190, 231, 355, 391
Woolrich, John: 276
Wordsworth, Barry: 266
World of Music and Dance
(WOMAD): 368-70
Wright, Robert: 379

Xenakis, Iannis: 384
Xie-Yang, Chen: 291

Yindi, Yothu: 374
Ying Quartet: 395
Ysaye, Eugene: 163

Zadek, Hilde: 220
Zambello, Francesca: 353
Zappa, Frank: 382-3
Zareska, Eugenia: 215
Zarzuela: 226

Zhong-jie, Han: 291
Zurich Tonhalle Orchestra: 323